PREFACE

The extraordinary knowledge about the durg is the blessing endowed by God Jupiter (God of Healing) to the medical fraternity and to the profession of Pharmacy.

The first edition of "Text Book of Pharmaceutical Organic Chemistry" has been written to confirm the needs of students and teachers of Diploma in Pharmacy Part-II as per new syllabus prescribed by Pharmacy Council of India in Education Regulation, 1991.

Pharmaceutical organic (medicinal) chemistry is a very dynamic branch of pharmacy which deals with the basic structural chemistry of drugs. On going research mandates every student and teacher involved with pharmacy to update his/her knowledge about current practice and trends in this subject. Every effort has been made to include these recent trends and knowledge in this textbook.

The structure of this book is simple, self-explanatory and easy for the readers to grasp the subject. The book has been divided into 32 chapters based on classification of drugs. Further, every chapter starts with a brief introduction followed by an updated classification and discussion about the important drugs specified in the syllabus. The structure, IUPAC nomenclature, physical properties, storage actions, uses and official preparations of the drugs listed in Indian Pharmacopoeia have been dealt with in comprehensive but precise text. A detailed index at the end of the book will be of great help to the readers.

We have made every possible effort to make this textbook informative and useful to the teachers and students of Diploma in Pharmacy. We recognised that many areas of controversy still exist and therefore we shall be extremely grateful to our readers for their valuable suggestions and comments.

We sincerely appreciate the help rendered by the teachers, colleagues and students as well as the management of L.M. College of Science and Technology, Jodhpur for providing much needed assistance for preparing this text. We also thank Dr. Manish Parekh for his special assistance in co-editing and updating the text.

We are extremely grateful to Mr. S.K. Jain (CBS Publishers & Distributors) and his staff for preparing an excellent book which hopefully lives to the expectations of our readers.

We feel indebted to all the students of pharmacy who have provided an impetus to embark on this venture and to whom we dedicate this textbook.

Dr. ANIL BHANDARI
Dr. G.K. SINGH

Textbook of Pharmaceutical Organic Chemistry

As per Education Regulation 1991

Anil Bhandari M Pharm, PhD
Senior Lecturer, LM College of Science and Technology
Jodhpur 342003 (India)

GK Singh M Pharm, PhD
Senior Lecturer, LM College of Science and Technology
Jodhpur 342003 (India)

CBS

CBS Publishers & Distributors Pvt Ltd

New Delhi • Bengaluru • Chennai • Kochi • Kolkata • Mumbai
Hyderabad • Jharkhand • Nagpur • Patna • Pune • Uttarakhand

Textbook of Pharmaceutical Organic Chemistry

As per Education Regulation 1991

ISBN: 978-81-239-0680-5

First Edition: 1999
Reprint: 2003, 2004, 2005, 2006, 2007, 2008, 2010, 2013, 2015, 2016, 2017, 2018, 2019, 2021

Published by **Satish Kumar Jain** and produced by **Varun Jain** for

CBS Publishers & Distributors Pvt Ltd

4819/XI Prahlad Street, 24 Ansari Road, Daryaganj, New Delhi 110 002, India.
Ph: 011-23289259, 23266861, 23266867 Website: www.cbspd.com
Fax: 011-23243014 e-mail: delhi@cbspd.com; cbspubs@airtelmail.in.

Corporate Office: 204 FIE, Industrial Area, Patparganj, Delhi 110 092
Ph: 011-4934 4934 Fax: 011-4934 4935 e-mail: publishing@cbspd.com; publicity@cbspd.com

Branches

- **Bengaluru:** Seema House 2975, 17th Cross, K.R. Road, Banasankari 2nd Stage, Bengaluru 560 070, Karnataka
  Ph: +91-80-26771678/79 Fax: +91-80-26771680 e-mail: bangalore@cbspd.com
- **Chennai:** 7, Subbaraya Street, Shenoy Nagar, Chennai 600 030, Tamil Nadu
  Ph: +91-44-26680620, 26681266 Fax: +91-44-42032115 e-mail: chennai@cbspd.com
- **Kochi:** 42/1325, 1326, Power House Road, Opp KSEB, Ernakulum, Kochi 682 018, Kerala, India
  Ph: +91-484-4059061-65,67 Fax: +91-484-4059065 e-mail: kochi@cbspd.com
- **Kolkata:** 6/B, Ground Floor, Rameswar Shaw Road, Kolkata-700014 (West Bengal), India
  Ph: +91-33-2289-1126, 2289-1127, 2289-1128 e-mail: kolkata@cbspd.com
- **Mumbai:** PWD Shed, Gala no 25/26, Ramchandra Bhatt Marg, Next to JJ Hospital Gate no. 2, Opp. Union Bank of India, Noorbaug Mumbai-400009, Maharashtra
  Ph: +91-22-66661880/89 e-mail: mumbai@cbspd.com

Representatives

• Hyderabad	0-9885175004	• Jharkhand	0-9811541605	• Nagpur	0-9421945513
• Patna	0-9334159340	• Pune	0-9623451994	• Uttarakhand	0-9716462459

Printed at Rashtriya Printers, Dilshad Garden, Delhi, India

SYLLABUS

1. Introduction to the nomenclature of organic chemical systems with particular reference to hetero-cyclic system containing upto three rings.
2. The Chemistry of following Pharmaceutical organic compounds covering their nomenclature, chemical structure, uses and the important physical and chemical properties (Chemical structure of only those compounds marked with asterisk (*).
3. The stability, storage conditions and the different types of Pharmaceutical formulations of these drugs and their popular brand names.

Antiseptics and Disinfectants - Proflavine*, Benzalkonium chloride, Cetrimide, Chlorocersol*, Chloroxylene, Formaldehyde solution, Hexachlorophene, Liquified phenol, Nitro furanton.
Sulfonamides - Sulfadizine*, Sulfaguandine*, Phthalyl sulfathiazole, Succinyl sulfathiazole, Sulfadimenthoxine, Sulfamethoxy, pyridazine, Sulfamethoxazole, co-trimoxazole, Sulfacetamide*.
Antileprotic drugs- Clofazimine, Thiambutosine, Dapsone*, Solapsone.
Anti-tubercular drugs - Isoniazid*, PAS*, Streptomycin, Rifampicin, Ethambutol*, Thiacetazone, Ethionamide, Cycloserine., pyrazinamide*.
Antiamoebic and Anthelmintic Drugs - Emetine, Metronidazole*, Halogenated hydroxyquinolins, Diloxanide foate, Paromomycin, Piperazine*, Mebendazole, D.E.C.*
Antibiotics - Benzyl Penicillin*, Phenoxy methyl Penicillin*, Benzthine Penicillin, Ampicillin*, Cloxacillin, Carbenicillin, Gentamycin, Neomycin, Erythromycin, Tetracycline, Cephalexin, Cephaloridine, Cephalothin, Griseofulvin, Chloramphenicol.
Antifungal agents - Undecylenic acid, Tolnaftate, Nystatin, Amphoterecin, Hamycin.
Antimalarial Drugs- Choroquine*, Amodiaquine, Primaquine, Proguanil, Pyrimethamine*, Quinine, Trimethoprim.
Tranqillizers- Chlorpromazine*, Prochlor Perazine, Trifulo Perazine, Thiothixene, Haloperidol*, Triperodol Oxypertine. Chlordiazepoxide, Diazepam*, Lorazepam, Meprobamate.
Hypnotics- Phenobarbitone*, Butobarbitone, Cyclobarbitone, Nitrazepam, Glutethimide*, Methyprylon, paraldehyde, Triclofos - sodium.

General Anaesthtics- Halothane*, Cyclopropane*, Diethyl ether*, Metho-hexital sodium., Trichloroethylene.

Antidepressant Drugs- Amitriptyline, Nortryptyline, Imipramine*, Phenelzine, Tranyl cyromine.

Analeptics - Theophylline, Caffeine*, Coramine*, Dextroamphetamine.

Adrenergic Drugs- Adrenaline*, Noradrenaline, Isoprenaline*, Phenylephrine, Salbutamol, Terbutaline, Ephedrine*, Pseudo ephedrine.

Adrenergic antagonist- Tolazoline, Propranolol*, Practalol

Cholinergic Drugs- Neostigmine*. Pyridostigmine, Pralidoxine, Pilocarpine, Physostigmine*.

Cholinergic Antagonists- Atropine*, Hyoscine, Homatropine, Propantheline*, Benztropine, Tropicamide, Biperiden*.

Diuretic Drugs - Furosemide*, Chlorothiazide, Hydrochlorothiazide*, Benzthiazide, Urea*, Mannitol*, Ethacrynic acid.

Cardiovascular Drugs Ethyl nitrite*, Glyceryl trinitrate, Alpha methyldopa, Guanethidine, Clofibrate, Quinidine.

Hypoglycemic Agents - Insulin, Chlorpropamide*, Tolbutamide, Glibenclamide, Phenformin*, Metformin.

Coagulants and Anti-Coagulats - Heparin, Thrombin, Menadione*, Bishydroxycoumarin, Warfarin sodium.

Local Anaesthetics - Lignocaine*, Procaine*, Benzocaine.

Histamine and Anti Histaminic Agents - Histamine, Diphenhydramine*, Promethazine, Cyproheptadine, Mepyramine, Chlorphenitramine*.

Analgesics and anti-pyretics-Morphine,. Pethidine*, Codeine, Methadone, Aspirin*, Paracetamol*, Analgin, Dextropropoxyphene, Pentazocine.

Non-steroidal anti-inflammatory Agents- Indomethacin*, Phenylbutazone*, Oxyphen butazone, Ibuprofen.

Thyroxine and antithyroids- Thyroxine*, Methimazole, Methylthiouracil, Propylthiouracil.

Diagnostic Agents - Iopanoic Acid, Propyliodone, Sulfobromophthalein sodium, Indigotindisulfonate sodium (Indigo carmine), Evans blue, Congo red, Fluoresein sodium.

Anticonvulsants, Cardiac glycosides, Antiarrhythmic, Antihypertensives and Vitamins.

Steroidal Drugs - Betamethazone, Cortisone, Hydrocortisone, Prednisolone, Progesterone, Testosterone, Oestradiol, Nandrolone.

Anti-Neoplastic Drugs - Actinomycins, Azathioprine, Busulphan, Chlorambusil Cisplatin, Cyclophosphamide, Daunorbicin hydrochloride, Fluorouracil, Mercaptopurine, Methotrexate, Mitomycin.

CONTENTS

CHAPTER 1

INTRODUCTION

Pharmaceutical organic chemistry is the branch of chemistry dealing with drugs having an element carbon obtained from naturally or synthetically. The natural sources may be from plants, animals or minerals. These agents are classified as alkaloids, vitamins, glycoside, hormones, antibiotic, etc.

Most of the naturally occurring active compound is structurally modified to obtain semisynthetic and synthetic drugs. All these agents are classified according to their use. These drugs are generally nonionic and have readily absorbed by the body tissue and effected organisms. Biological action of these agents varies with their isomeric forms.

Medicinal chemistry is concern with techniques of isolation, purification, synthesis, preparation of synthetic analogs, metabolism and made of action. The various pharmacopoeias describe the standards of drugs, their common applications and various dosage forms.

The physical standards are discuss as form, colour, odour and solubility parameters. These solubility parameters are at average room temperature. The following terms used and their meanings are as under:

Insoluble	:	1 in more than 10,000
Very slightly soluble	:	1 in 1,000 to 1 in 10,000
Slightly soluble	:	1 in 100 to 1 in 1000
Sparingly soluble	:	1 in 30 to 1 in 100
Soluble	:	1 in 10 to 1 in 30
Freely soluble	:	1 in 1 to 1 in 10
Very soluble	:	1 in less than 1

Storage of drugs is also an important parameter. Sunlight, moisture, temperature, etc are certain factors that can promote the degradation of potent medicaments. The specific condition of storage, as well as information regarding incompatibility of drugs is also vital. All the drugs are covers in the subsequent chapter according to syllabus as per E.R. 1991 covering all the important aspects, necessary for the Diploma students.

A special chapter has included to stress the naming of these drugs under IUPAC nomenclature. This book incorporates only those drugs that have commonly used and prescribed in syllabus.

CHAPTER -2

NOMENCLATURE

Organic compounds are numerous. There are different names for a single compound. In Geneva a system for naming organic compounds was established and is called IUPAC system. This system is adopted by "International Union of Pure and Applied Chemistry" (IUPAC). This system of naming organic compounds is called IUPAC system of nomenclature.

The organic compounds are classified into two groups:

ORGANIC COMPOUNDS

- **Aliphatic**
  - **Open chain**: Butane, Pentane
  - **Alicyclic**: Cyclopropane, Cyclobutane
- **Cyclic compounds**
  - **Homocyclic** (Aromatic): Benzene, Naphthalene
  - **Heterocyclic**: Pyrrole, Thiophene

There are different IUPAC system for open chain, Aromatic and Heterocyclic compounds.

IUPAC System for open chain organic compounds

This system is a basic system for naming various organic compounds. It is applicable to aliphatic compounds. The following rules govern the nomenclature of aliphatic compounds.

1. **Selection of the longest carbon chain**

A longest unbranched carbon chain is selected, the compound is considered as the derivative of the alkane containing that chain.

```
CH3
|
CH-CH2-CH3
|
CH3
```

Butane derivative
(not a propane derivative)

```
        CH3
        |
        CH2
        |
CH3-CH2-CH-CH3
```

Pentane derivative
(not a butane derivative)

CH_4	-	Methane	C_6H_{14}	-	Hexane
C_2H_6	-	Ethane	C_7H_{16}	-	Heptane
C_3H_8	-	Propane	C_8H_{18}	-	Octane
C_4H_{10}	-	Butane	C_9H_{20}	-	Nonane
C_5H_{12}	-	Pentane	$C_{10}H_{22}$	-	Decane

2. **Selection of Carbon Chain**

If there are two or more possibilities of longest carbon chain, than the carbon chain having more alkyl substituents is preferred.

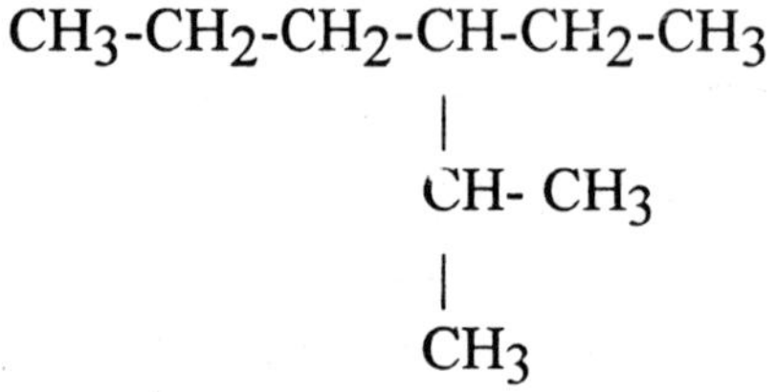

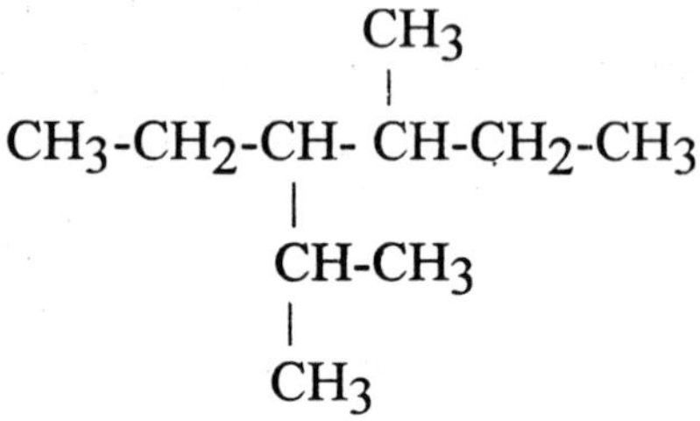

3. **Numbering of Carbon Atom in the Chain**

The numbering of carbon atoms in a carbon chain starts from that end which gives least number to substituent or substituents. If more than one substituents are present then sum of numbers of carbon from which the substituent are attached is least; will be the correct numbering system e.g.

1' 2' 3' 4' 5' ‘incorrect
5 4 3 2 1 correct

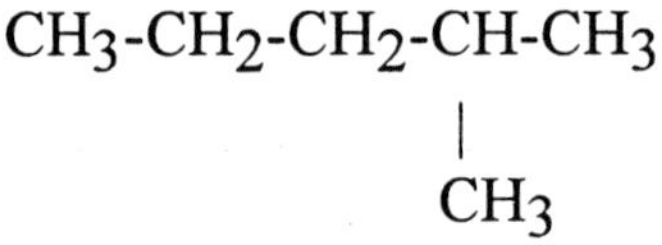

1' 2' 3' 4' 5' 6' ‘incorrect
6 5 4 3 2 1 correct

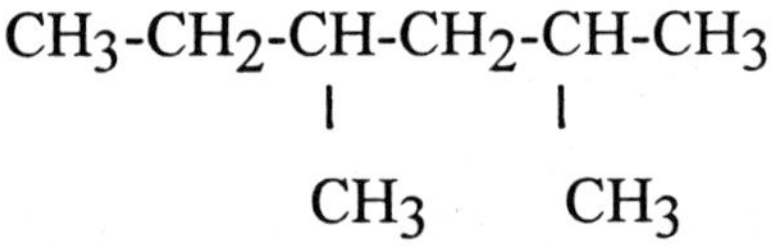

If two different alkyl groups are substituted in the same chain and sum of their numbers remain same using a different number system then numbering will start from that end at which a substituent comes first in alphabetical order. E.g :

1' 2' 3' 4‘ 5’ 6' ‘ incorrect
6 5 4 3 2 1 correct

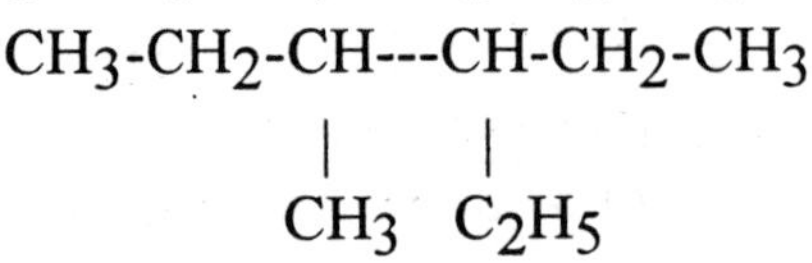

If two or more substituents are identical and attached at different positions than di, tri, tetra, penta and hexa prefix is attached before the substituent group with various numbers.

4. Functional group

If a compound contains any of the following group then it is called functicnal group. These functional groups should get priority over substituent or side chain in numbering the basic chain. While naming such compounds a particular suffix is added to the name of parent alkane chain. The following table shows the suffix for various functional groups. The carbon present in the functional group and is also a number of continuous chain then this carbon is included as the member of longest chain while carbon of substituent will not be included in the chain.

When more than one functional groups are present then the functional group coming first in the below table will act as functional group and rest are considered substituents. This series is called preferential series. When the compound contains Ist to VIII functional group of the table than numbering will start from the carbon of functional group.

5. **Alphabetical rule**

While writing the name of an organic compound substituents are written first followed by name of parent carbon chain as central part and finally suffix if the functional group. In this all the substituents are arranged in the alphabetical order.

IUPAC for Homocyclic (Aromatic) compounds

Aromatic compounds are divided into two groups

(1) Compounds having one cycle

(2) Compounds having more than one cycle (poly-nuclear).

The aromatic compounds have their own names for the purpose of IUPAC. These are :

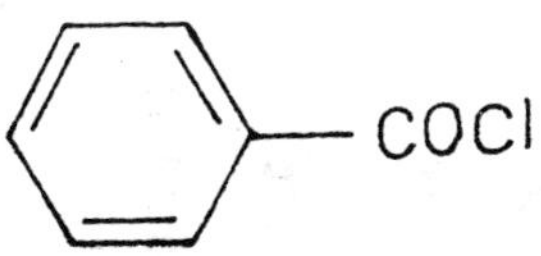

Benzoyl Chloride

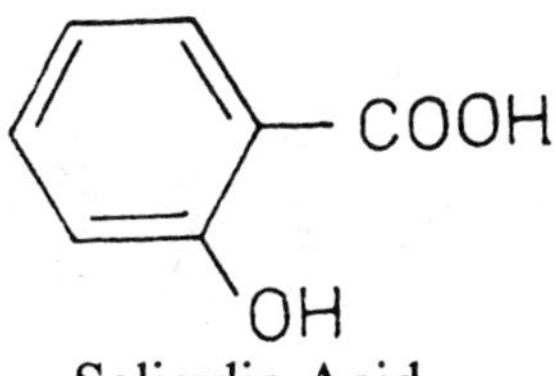

Salicylic Acid

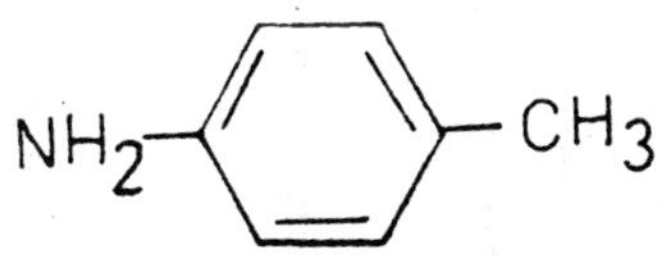

P- Toluidine

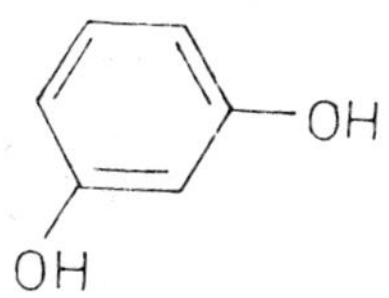

Resorcinol

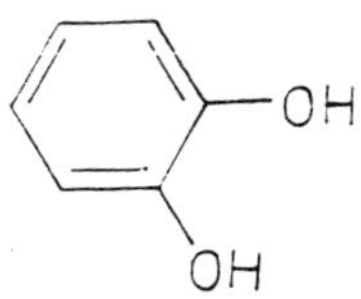

Catechol

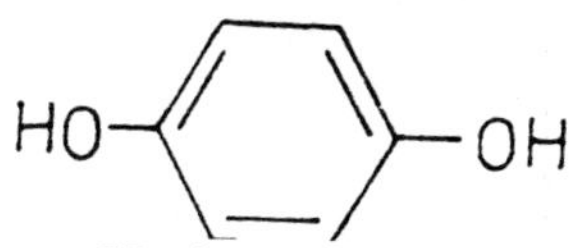

Hydroquinoline

Formula	Common name	suffix	IUPAC Name	Prfix
-C(=O)-OH	Carboxylic acid	Oic acid	Alknoic acid	Carboxy
$-SO_3H$	Sulphonic acid	Sulphonic acid	Sulphonic acid	Sulpho
- C(=O)-OR	Esters	alkyl...oate	alkylalkanoate	Alkoxy
-C(=O)-X	Acyl halide	Oyl halide	alkanoyl halide	Halformyl
$-CONH_2$	Amide	Amide	Alkanamide	Carbamoyl
-C≡N	Nitrile	Nitrile	Alkane nitrile	Cyano
-CHO	Aldehyde	Al	Alkanal	Oxo, formyl
>C=O	Ketone	- One	Alkanone	Oxo, keto
-OH	Alcohol	- Ol	Alkanol	Hydroxy
-SH	Thiol	- Thiol	Alkane thiol	Mercapto
$-NH_2$	Amine	Amine	Alkanamine	Amino
=	Alkene	-ene	Alkene	ene
≡	Alkyne	-yne	Alkyne	yne
$-NH-C(=NH)-NH-C(=NH)-NH_2$	Guanidine	-----	Guanidine	Guanidine

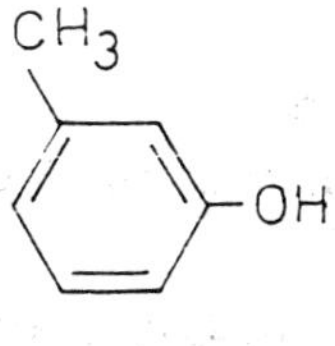

M- Cresol

Tosyl

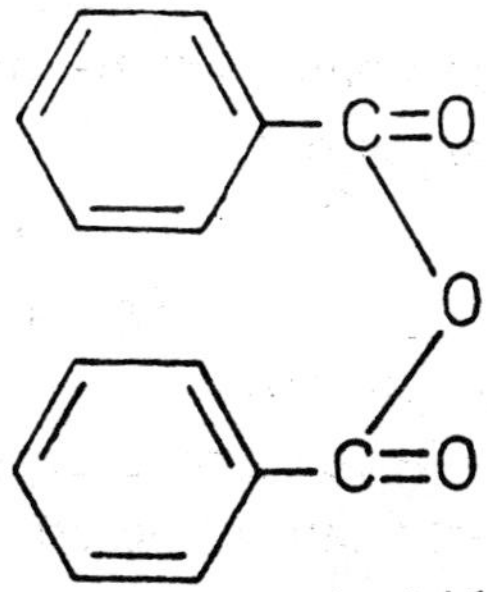

Benzoic Anhydride

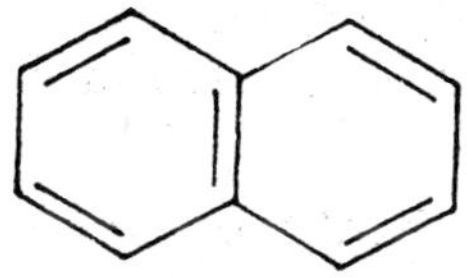

Naphthalene

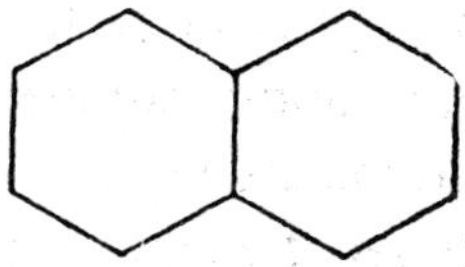

Decalin

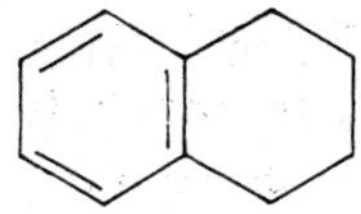

Tetralin

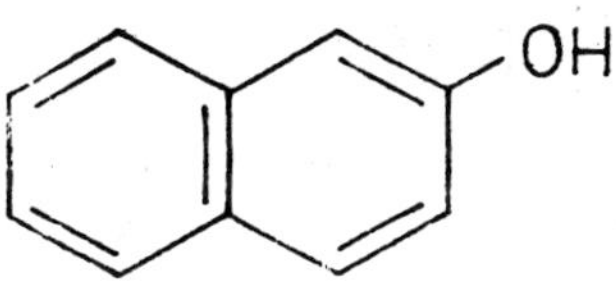

β Naphthol

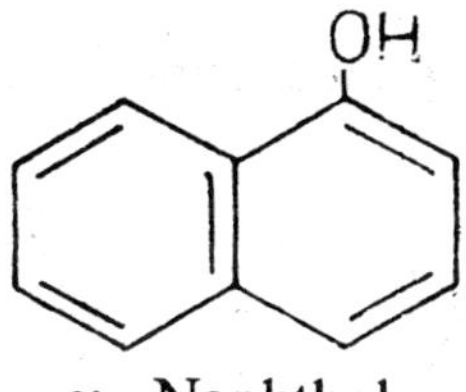

α Naphthol

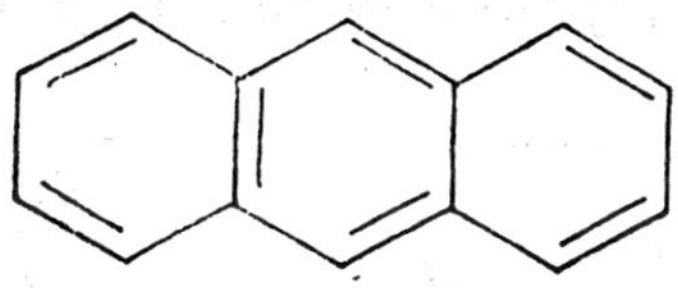

Anthracene

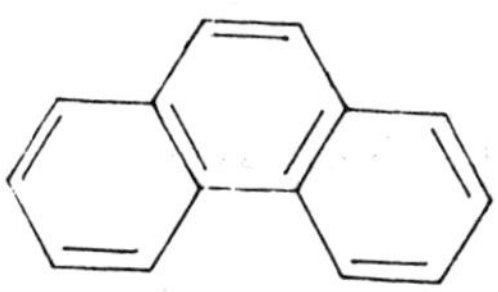

Phenenthrene

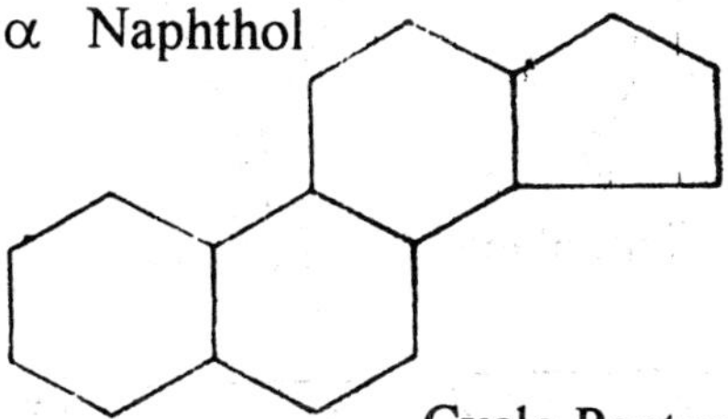

Cyclo Pentophenenthrene

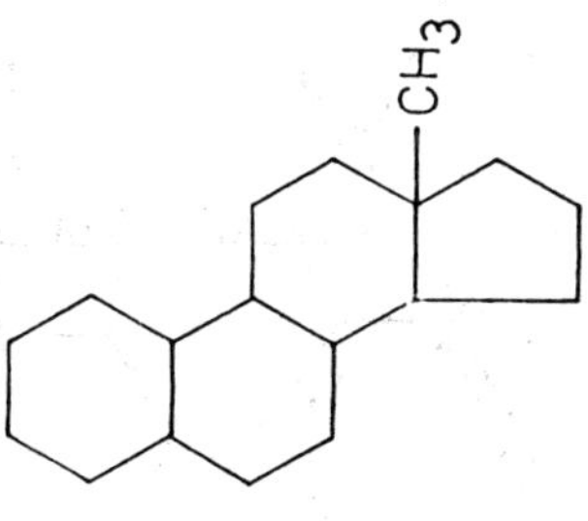

Estrane

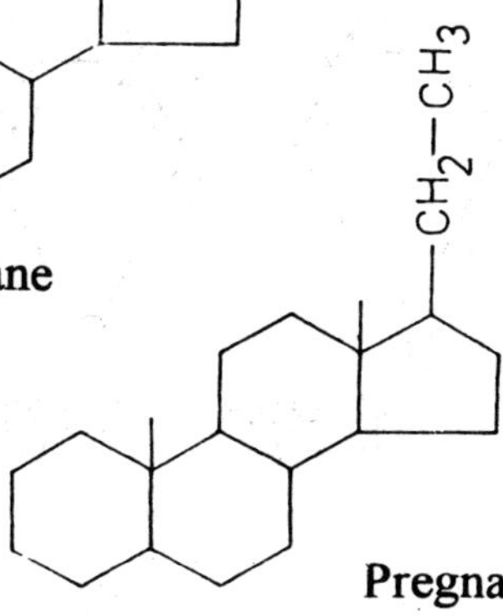

Pregnane

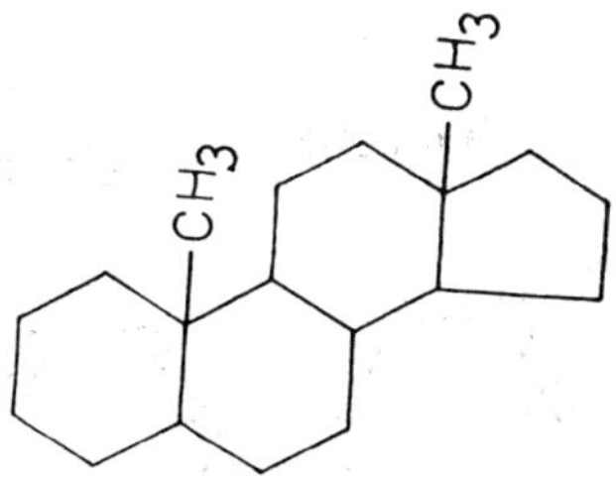

Andrane

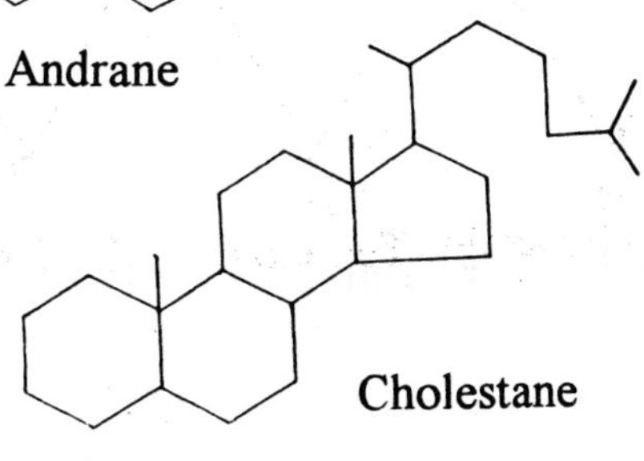

Cholestane

Apart from these nucleus if any side chain is attached then naming of side chain will be done separately and is added to the IUPAC name of aromatic compounds.

IUPAC for Heterocyclic compounds :

The following rules are followed for the naming of Heterocyclic compounds.

[1] When a heterocyclic compound contain only one hetero atom the numbering will start from the hetero atom. Exceptions are isoquinoline ring and isoindole ring.

[2] If more than one hetero atom is present in the ring then numbering will start as per preferential series (O, S, N, P etc.) and a numbering system is selected in which sum of the numbers given to hetero atoms are least.

[3] When two or more hetero atoms of a similar atom are present then a prefix like di, tri, tetra, etc. are used. The word oxo for oxygen, thio for sulphur, azo for nitrogen, etc.

[4] There are basic rings having fixed name for IUPAC. They are :-

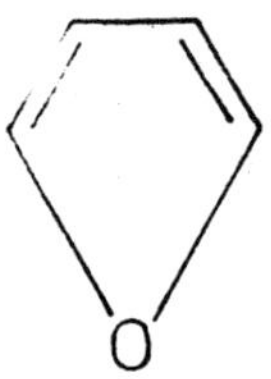

Furane

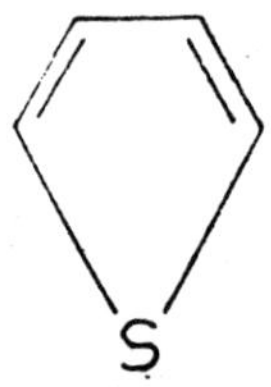

Thiophene

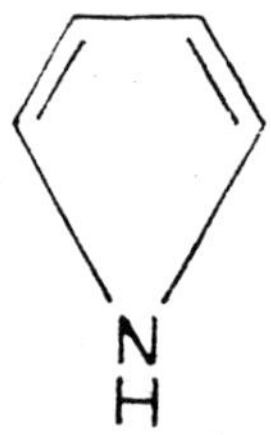

Pyrrole

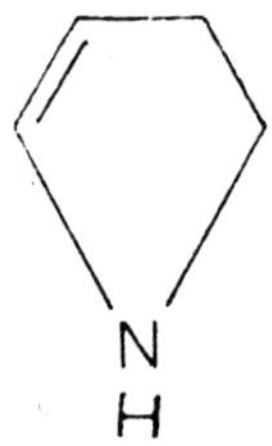

2-Pyrrole

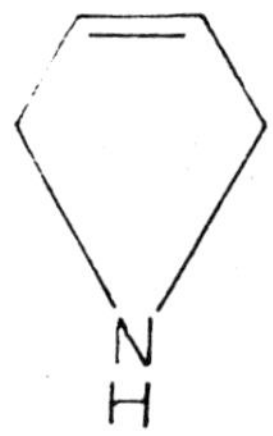

3-Pyrrole

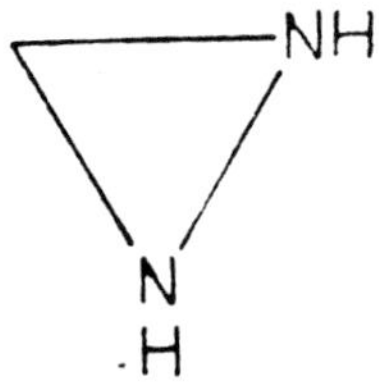

Diaziridine

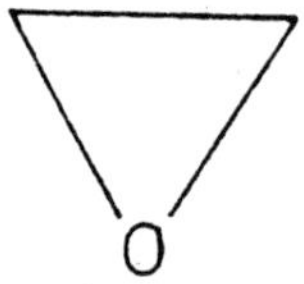

Oxirane

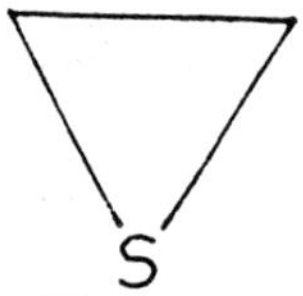

Thirone

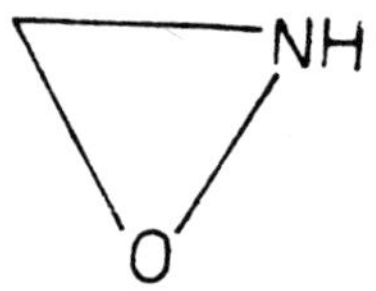

Oxaziridine

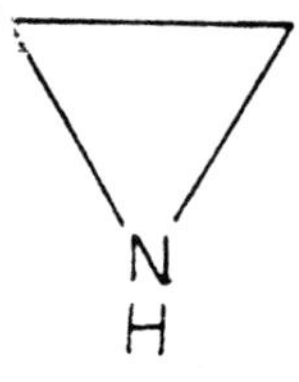

Aziridine

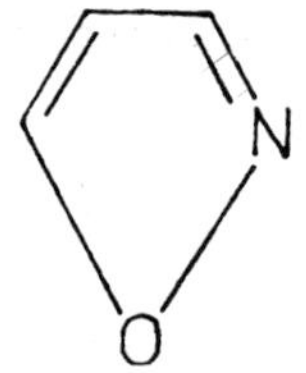

Iso Oxazole

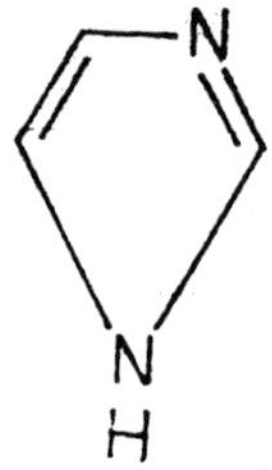

Imidazole

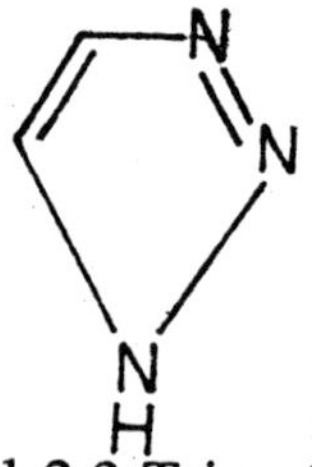

1,2,3 Triazole

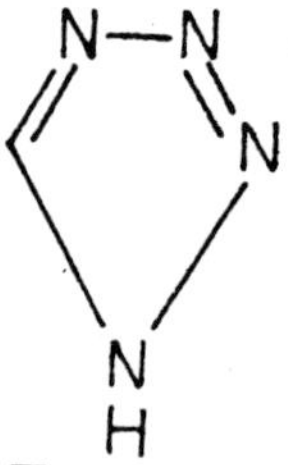

Tetrazole

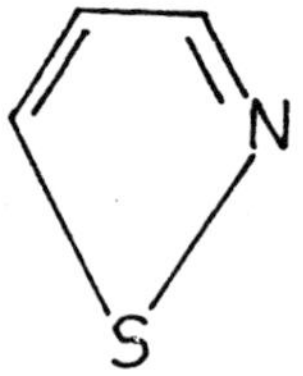

Iso Thiazole

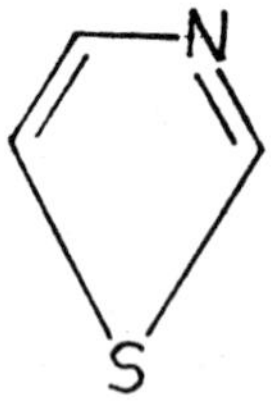

Thiazole

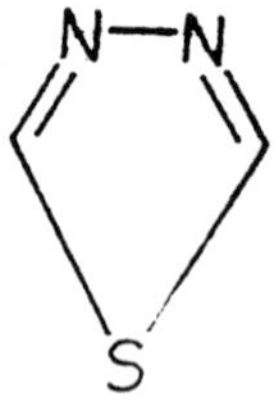

1,2,4 Thiadiazole

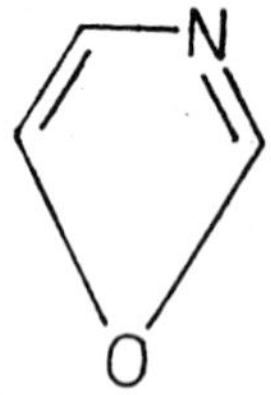

Oxazole

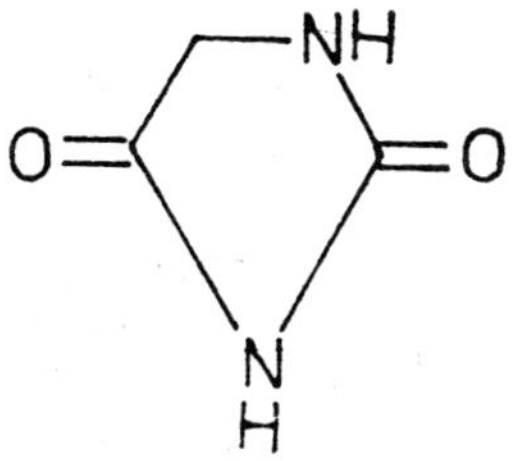

Hydantoin

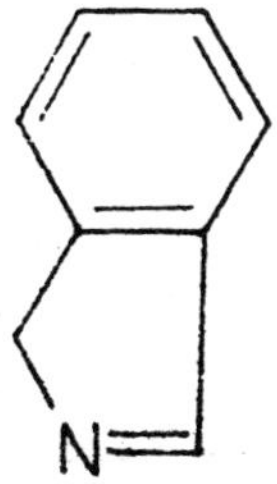

Iso Indole

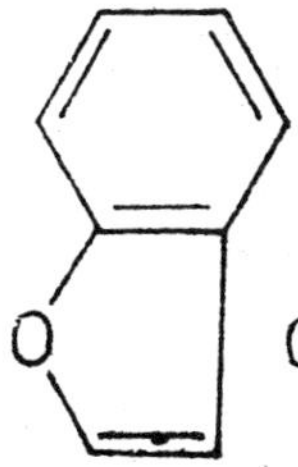

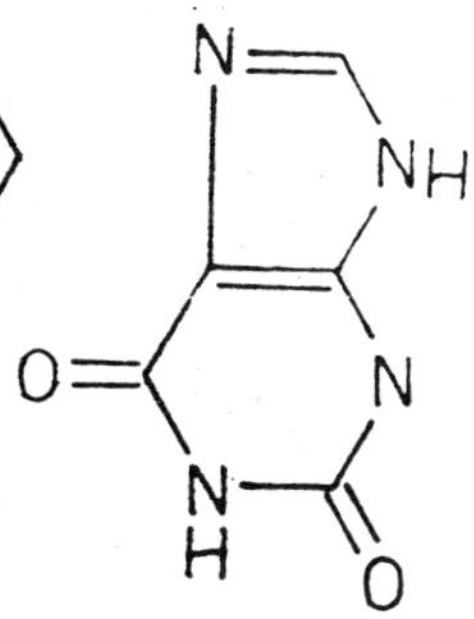

Xanthine

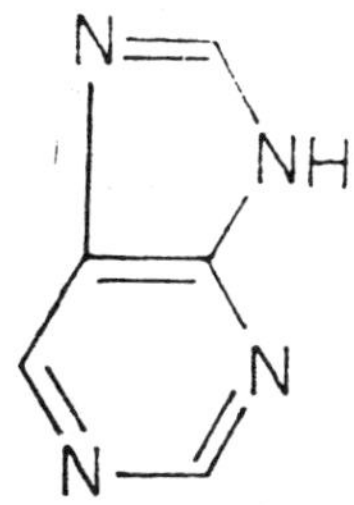

Purine

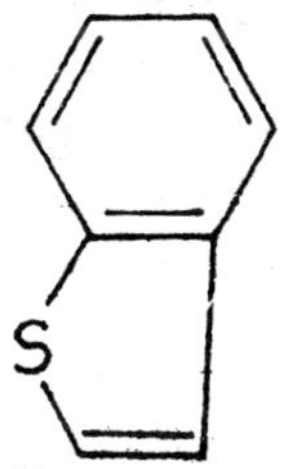

Thio-Napthene

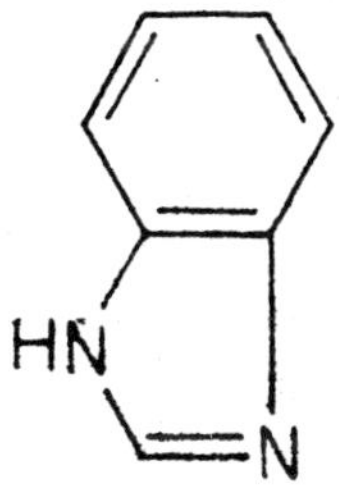

Benzimidazole

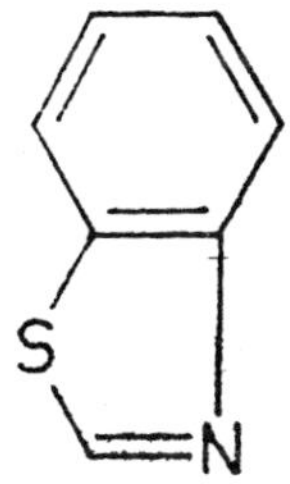

Benzthiazoie

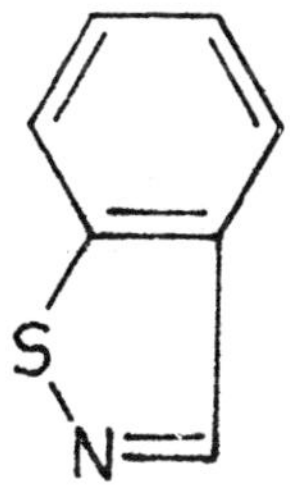

1,2 Benzisothiazole

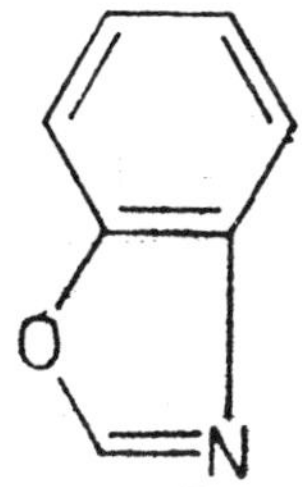

Benzoxazole

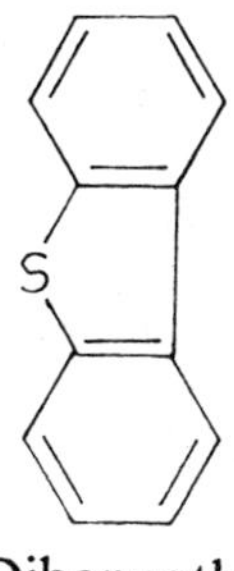

Dibenzothiophene

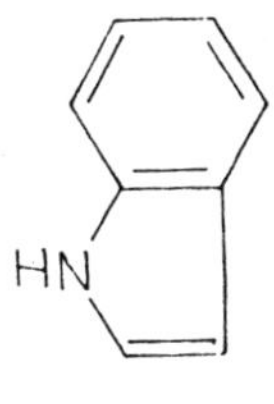

Indole

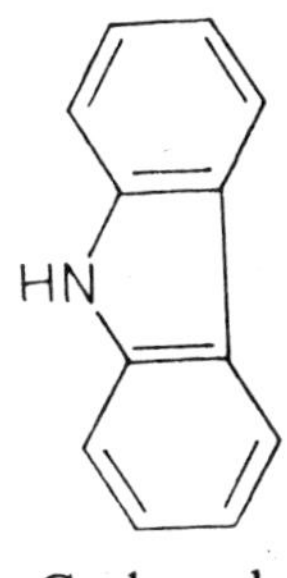

Carbazole

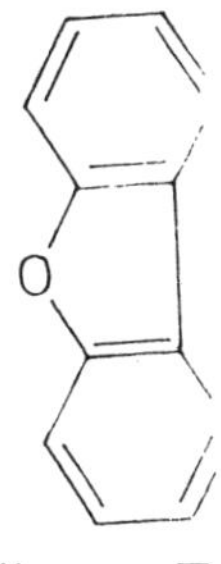

Dibenzo Furane

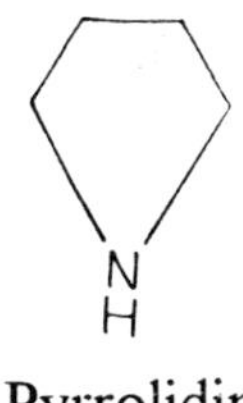

Pyrrolidine

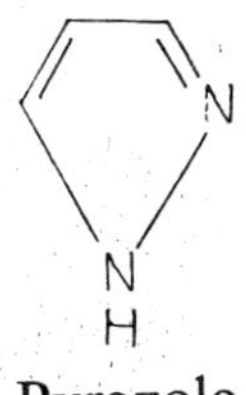

Pyrazole

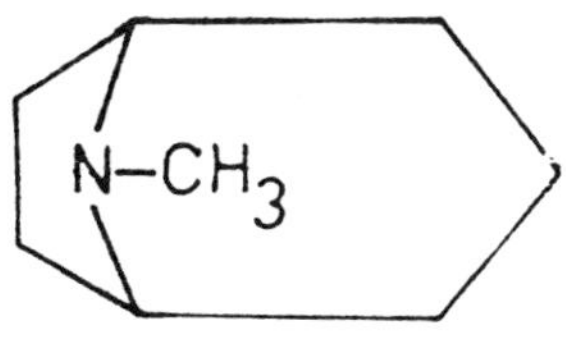

Tropane

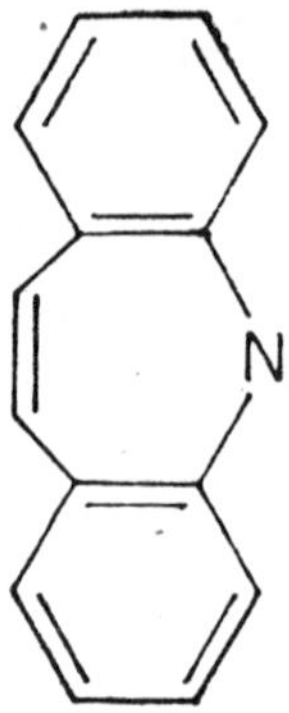
Dibenzapine

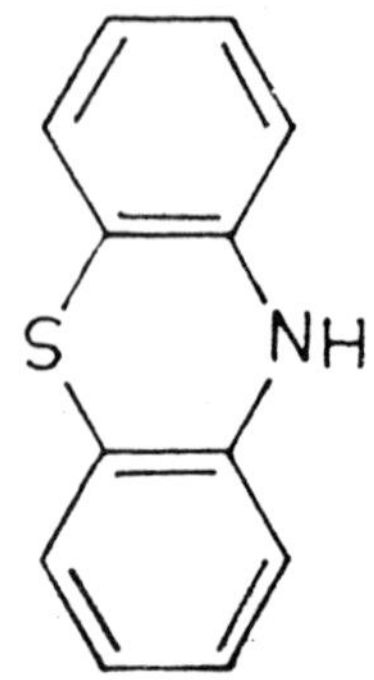
Phenothiazine

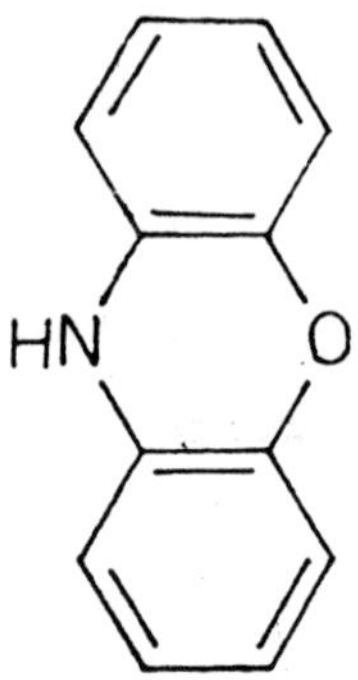
Phenoxozine

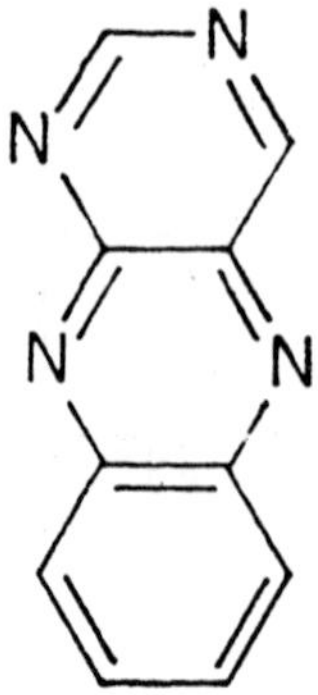
Alloxozine

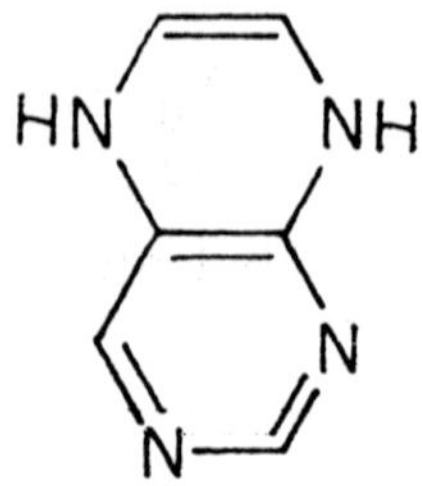
Pteridine

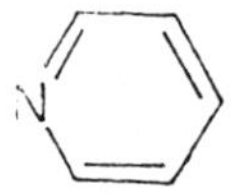
Pyridine

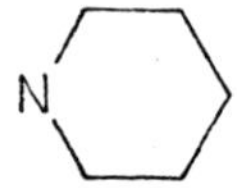
Piperidine

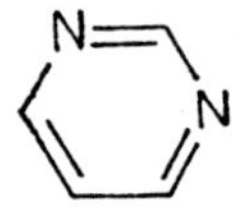
Pyrimidine

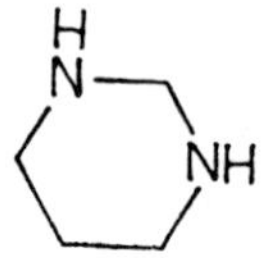

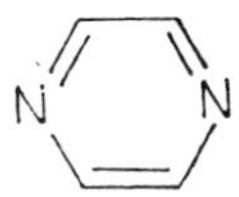
Pyrazine

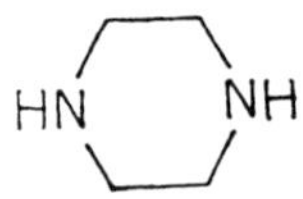
Piperazine

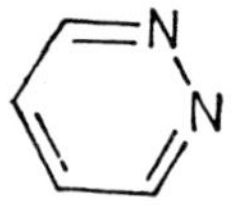
Pyridazine

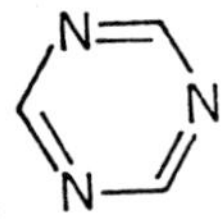
1,3,5 Triazine

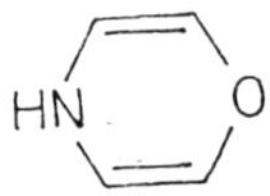
1,4 Oxazole

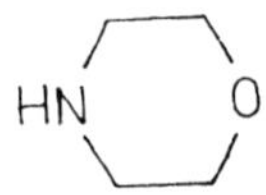
Morpholine

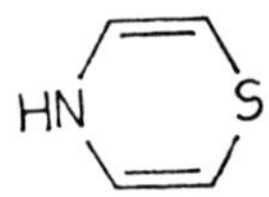
1,4 Thiazine

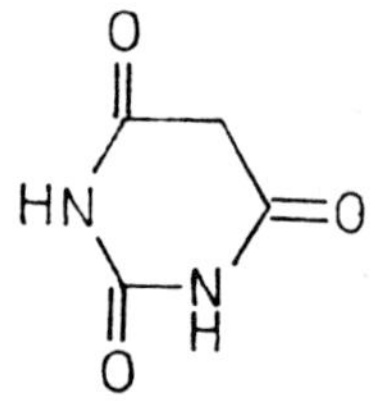
Barbituric Acid

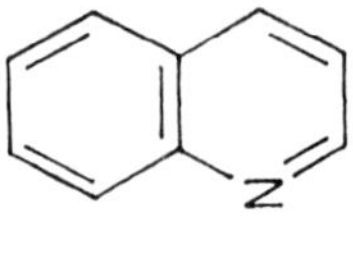
Quinoline

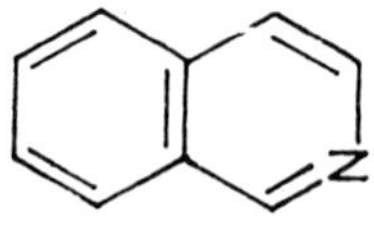
Isoquinoline

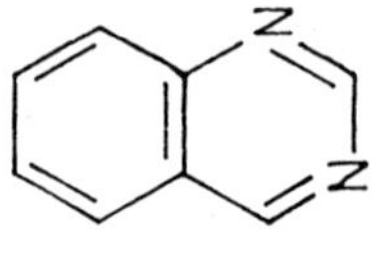
Quinazoline

Phthalazinen

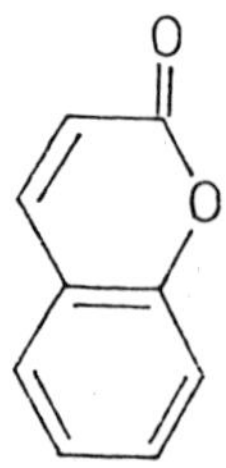
Coumarine

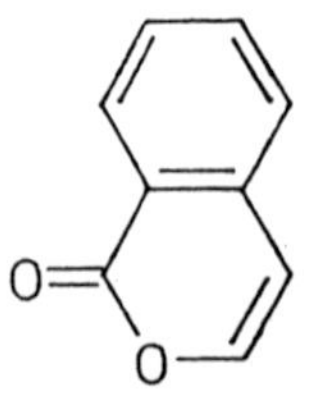
Isocoumarin

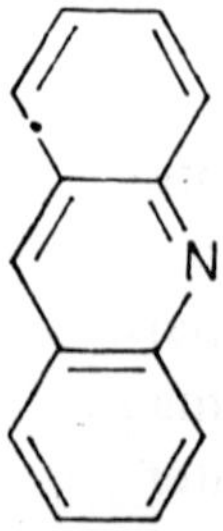
Acridine

CHAPTER -3

ANTISEPTICS AND DISINFECTANTS

Disinfectants and antiseptics are use to inhibit the growth or to kill pathogenic microorganisms in the vegetative or nonsporing state. There is often confusion between the term antiseptic and disinfectant. The term antiseptic is use to a chemical agent that destroys microorganism on living surface while disinfectant also destroys microorganism on inanimate surface or reduces the number of microorganisms to a safe level on an inanimate (non-living) object.

Sterilization is the total removal or destruction of living microorganisms and spores. Sterilization has done by filtration, dry heat, moist heat, radiation or by chemical agents.

Preservatives are use to prevent microbial spoilage of preparations; in pharmacy, preservatives should be capable of inhibiting the growth or killing of microorganisms and maintain the sterility of the preparation.

Antiseptic and disinfectants are use in hospitals, public buildings, sanitation, farms and in houses for cleaning purpose.

Classification : These are classified as follows -

Alcohols	:	Ethyl alcohol, Isopropyl alcohol
Aldehydes	:	Formaldehyde, Acetaldehyde
Cationic surfactant	:	Benzalkonium chloride, cetramide
Chlorhexidine	:	Chlorhexidine salts
Dyes	:	Acridine derivatives-proflavin, acriflavin
Mercurials	:	Thiomersal,Mercurochrome
Phenols	:	Phenol, chlorocresol, chloroxylenol, Hexachlorophane
Miscellaneous	:	Nitrofurantoin

Alcohol

Alcohols are bactericidal agents having little activity against bacterial spores, it is used as an anti-septic for skin and disinfectant for hard surfaces. It is also used for sclerotherapy. Alcohol is toxic when consumed internally in high dose. It impairs mental co-ordination causes gastric disturbance, respiratory depression, damages brain and liver and produces drug dependency. Ethanol is miscible with water and in organic solvents. It volatalises when exposed to air.

C_2H_5OH CH_3CH_2OH $CH_3CH(OH)CH_3$

Ethanol Isopropyl alcohol (propane 2-ol)

Action and Uses : Ethanol is mainly uses before surgery but some times Isopropyl alcohol can also be use. These are use as disinfectants for hypodermic syringes and needles. Isopropyl alcohol can not destroy spores of clostridium species. It also acts as substituents.

ALDEHYDES

Formaldehyde

A 40% solution of formaldehyde is called formaline. It is a clear colourless liquid, has a characteristic pungent irritating odour. It is miscible with water and alcohol and should be stored in air tight containers between 15-25°C

HCHO H-C(H)=O

Formaldehyde (methanal)

Action and Uses : It is a powerful disinfectant, active against bacteria, fungi, viruses and bacterial spores. It is also used for fumigation. It causes dermatitis and sensitivity reactions. Its injection may cause serious effects including pain, damage to mucous membrane, metabolic acidosis, convulsions, etc. When it is applied to skin, it hardens the epidermis and also causes diarrohea, pneumonia and intestinal bleeding while its vapour causes irritation to eyes, respiratory tract and nose, causing coughing, spasm and oedema of the larynx and asthma.

BENZALKONIUM CHLORIDE

Benzalkonium chloride is a quartarnary ammonium cationic surfactant. Chemically it is an alkyl, benzyl, dimethyl ammonium chloride. It is available as a white or yellowish white powder thick gel or gelatinous mass with aromatic odour which is hygroscopic . It is very soluble in alcohol, water and ether but insoluble in organic solvent. Its aqueous solution is alkaline which forms foams on shaking. It is incompatible with anionic surfactant, citrates, iodides, nitrates, permangnate, salicylates, silver salts and tartarate. It is also incompatible with aluminum, cotton dressings, H_2O_2, kaolin, flourescin sodium, hydrous wool fat etc. It should be stored in airtight containers protected from light but it should not be stored in rubber containers.

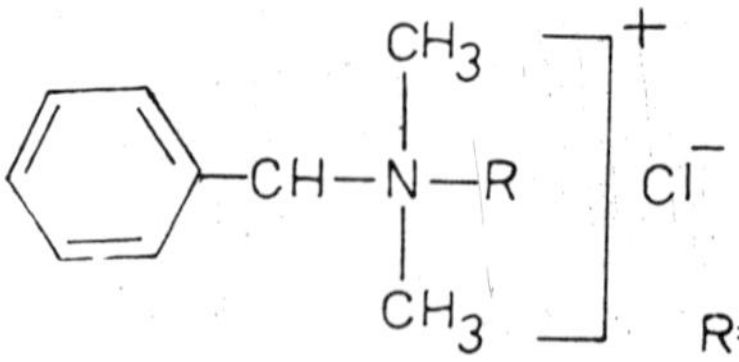

R=C_8H_{17} TO $C_{18}H_{37}$

Benzalkonium chloride

Action and Uses :It is used as a detergent for pre -operative painting of unbroken skin in a dilution of 1 in 500 or on mucous membrane burns, wounds and broken skin in a dilution of 1 in 1000 or more.

As a very dilute solution it is used for irrigation of bladder, urethra, vagina, throat, and as an eyes wash etc. Repeated use of this agent may cause hypersensitivity.

Official: Benzalkonium chloride I.P.

CETRIMIDE

Cetrimide is a quaternary ammonium cationic antiseptic. Chemically it is a tetradecayl trimethyl ammonium compound. It is a white to creamy voluminous free flowing powder with a faint characteristic odour and soapy bitter taste. It is soluble in water, alcohol and ether. It is incompatible with anionic soaps, Iodine and alkali hydroxides.

It should be stored in air tight containers. Its 4% solution when stored may be contaminated by pseudomonas species therefore 7% ethanol or 4% isopropyl alcohol should be added.

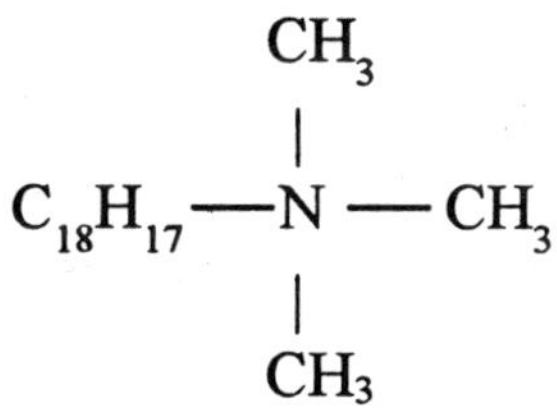

Cetrimide

Actions and uses : It has a similar action as that of benzalkonium chloride but is relatively nontoxic. It is active against gram positive organisms, less active against gram negative and is inactive against acid fast bacilli, and bacterial spores. A 1 to 3% solutions is used for seborrhoea of scalp. Cetrimide should not be applied repeatedly to the skin and a wet dressing should not be left in contact because of skin hypersensitivity.

CHLORHEXIDINE HYDROCHLORIDE

It is a white crystalline, odourless powder with a bitter taste. It is soluble in glycol, slightly soluble in alcohol and almost insoluble in water. It is incompatible with soaps and other anionic materials, alginates, tragacanth, etc. Its acetate salt is incompatible with potassium iodide, borates, bicarbonates, carbonates, chlorides, citrates, nitrates, Phosphates etc.

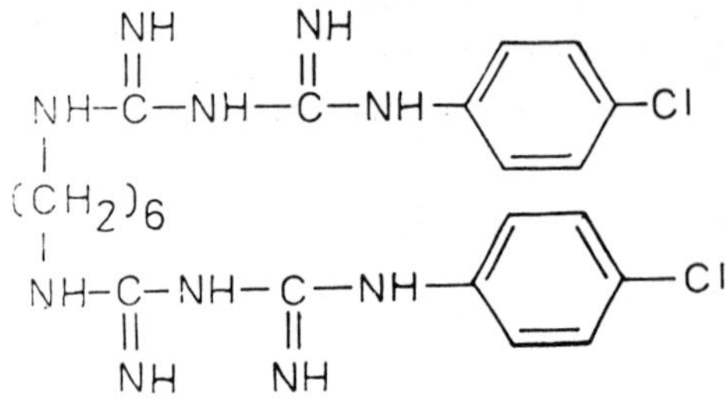

IUPAC Name :1,1'-Hexamethylene bis[5-(4-chlorophenyl) biguanide]

Actions and uses : It is a nontoxic antiseptic, active against gram positive and gram negative organisms but inactive against acid-fast bacilli, bacterial spores and fungi. It is used in the treatment of wounds, burns, irrigation of bladder, serious surfaces. It is also used for the disinfection of hands before surgical procedures, mouth wash to inhibit the formation of bacterial piaque on the teeth. It is used in dusting powders, creams, ointments, lozenges and as antiseptic in surgical dressings. Its strong solutions may cause irritation, in mouthwashes. It also causes burning sensation of tongue and haemolysis on accidental ingestion.

Official preparation : Chlorhexidine gluconate solution I.P.

ACRIFLAVINE

It is a deep orange, odourless granular powder. It is soluble in water, sparingly soluble in alcohol and nearly insoluble in ether, chloroform and ester. It is a reddish-orange dye when dissolved in water, shows fluorescence and is sensitive to light.

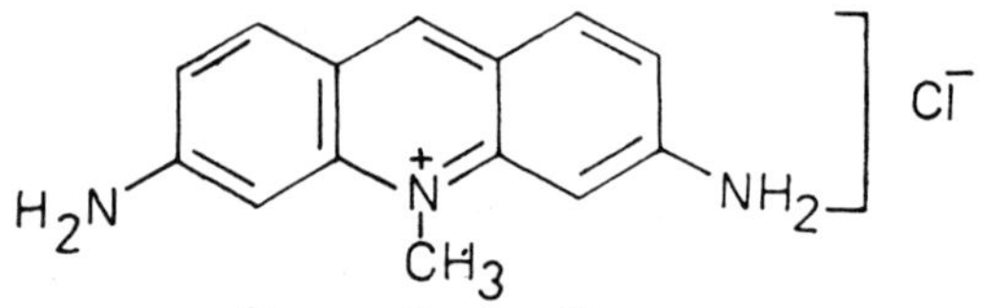

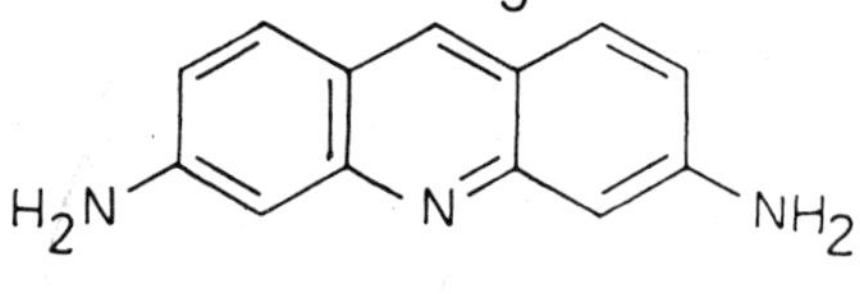

Actions and uses : It is an antiseptic and antiinfective used locally in wounds.

PROFLAVINE

It is an acridine derivative. It is an odourless hygroscopic orange to red crystalline powder. It is soluble in boiling water, glycerol, slightly soluble in alcohol; practically insoluble in ether and chloroform. It should be stored in air tight containers protected from light.

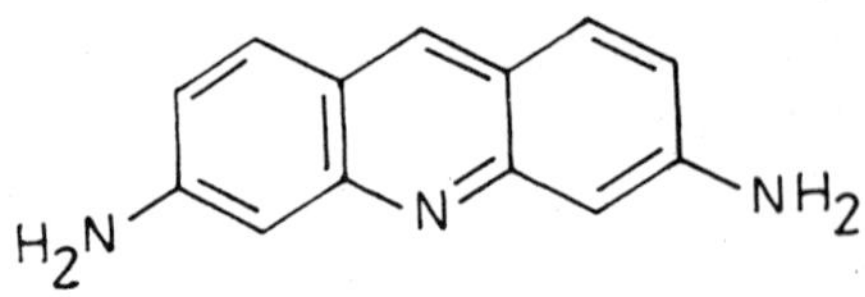

IUPAC Name :- 3,6- diamino acridine.

Actions and uses : Proflavine is a slow acting antiseptic used in the treatment of infected wounds or burns of external ear, mouth, throat and skin. Generally a 0.1% solution is used for wound or burn washing but if treatment is prolonged, a weak solution is used. It provides a stain on skin-which can be washed with very dilute acidic solution.

PHENOL [CARBOLIC ACID]

Phenol is available as deliquescent, colourless or faintly pink needle shaped crystals with a characteristic odour. It is soluble in alcohol, ether, chloroform, liquid paraffin glycerol, alkalis etc. It should be stored in airtight containers protected from light, in a cool place [below 15°C]. It is incompatible with salts of non-ionic surfactant.

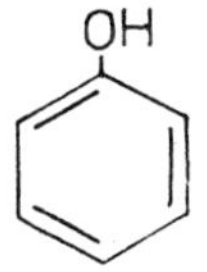

IUPAC Name : Phenol OR Hydroxybenzene.

Actions and uses : Phenol is a corrosive and its injection causes pain and gastrointestinal upset. It is an antiseptic and disinfectant against a wide range of micro-organisms and viruses. A concentrated solution causes destructive effect on tissues also and skin becomes white blue due to precipitation of proteins. When phenol penetrates into deeper tissues it causes paralysis of sensory nerves leading to painless gangrene. Liquid phenol is used in dentistry and as an analgesic in 5% solution to desensatatise the pulp of deciduous teeth.

CHLOROCRESOL

Chlorocresol is a phenol derivative. It is a colourless or faintly coloured crystalline solid powder with characteristic phenolic odour. It is slightly soluble in water, very soluble in alcohol and freely soluble in ether and in fatty oils. It should be stored in air tight containers protected from light. It's aqueous solution acquires yellowish colour when exposed to light and air. It is incompatible with codeine phosphate, dimorphine, quinine, methyl cellulose and non-ionic surfactants.

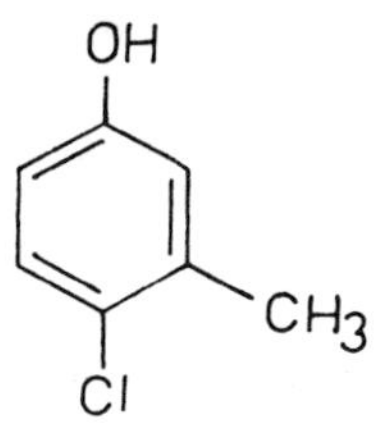

IUPAC Name : 4-chloro-3-methyl phenol.

Actions and Uses : It is a potent chlorinated phenolic disinfectant active against gram-positive and gram-negative organisms as well as against fungi but less active against bacterial spores. Its 0.1 % concentration in aqueous ingestion is used as preservative. It was also used as a bactericidal for sterilization. It is mainly used as disinfection and preservative for the preparation of external use.

Official: Chlorocresol I.P.

CHLOROXYLENOL

It is a white or cream coloured crystalline powder with a characteristic phenolic odour. It is very slightly soluble in water but soluble in alcohol, ether, terpenes and alkali hydroxides. It is incompatible with non-ionic surfactant and methyl cellulose.

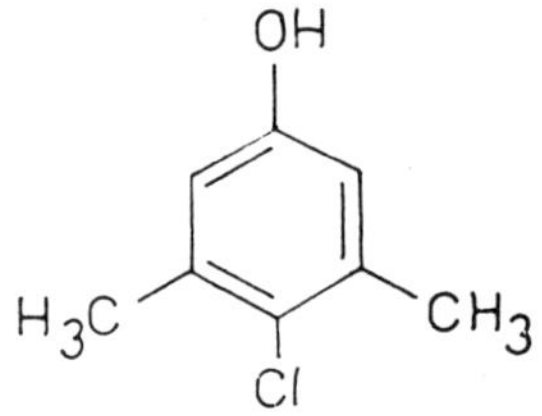

IUPAC Name : 4-chloro-3,5-dimethyl phenol;
OR 4-chloro-3,5-xylenol.

Actions and Uses : Chloroxylenol is a chlorinated phenolic antiseptic and highly active against gram-positive bacteria. Its solution is used for application on skin wounds and other topical preparations. Its activity increases by the addition of adapic acid.

HEXACHLORPHENE

It is a white or pale buff coloured crystalline powder having slightly phenolic odour. It is practically insoluble in water but soluble in alcohol, ether, acetone and solution of alkali hydroxides. It should be stored in air tight containers protected from light. It is incompatible with iron and decolourises solution and the sequestrant such as disodium edetate is added.

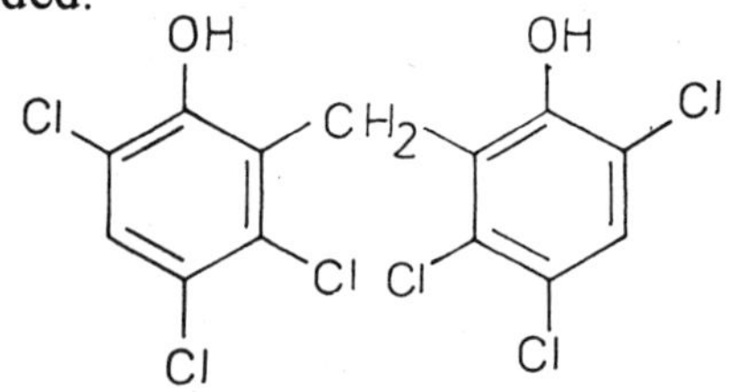

IUPAC Name : 2-2'-methylenebis (3,4,6-trichloro phenol)

Actions and Uses : Hexachlorophene is a chlorinated bisphenyl antiseptic, active against gram-positive and gram-negative bacteria. It is more active at pH 5 to 6. It is used in soaps and creams in a concentration of 0.23 to 3% for skin disorders. A 3% solution is used for disinfection of, hands before surgery and also to control staphylococcal infection in the new born baby.

NITROFURANTOIN

It is available as odourless yellow crystals or fine powder with a bitter taste. It is very slightly soluble in water, alcohol, glycerol and acetone but slightly soluble in dimethyl formamide and macrogol-300. It should be stored in air tight containers protected from light below 25°C.

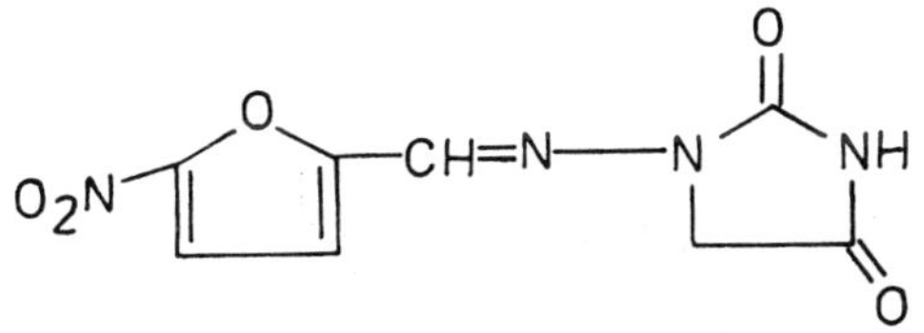

IUPAC Name : 1-(5-Nitro furfurylidene amino) imidazolidine -2,4-dione.

Actions and uses : It is a broad spectrum anti-bacterial agent and effective concentrations can be achieved in tissues without intolerable side-effects. It is used in long term chronic infections in the treatment of urinary tract infection . Some times it may produce nausea, abdominal discomfort, drowsiness, pulmonary-odema etc.

Official: Nitofurantoin I.P.

CHAPTER - 4

SULPHONAMIDES

Sulphanilamide was first synthesized in 1908 by '**Gelmo**'. The first clinically important derivative was prontosil, an azo dye that metabolized in vivo to sulphanilamide. The derivatives of sulphanilamide are called sulphonamides.

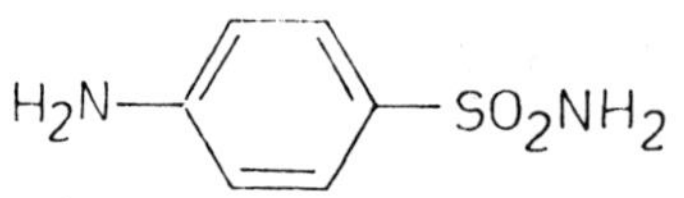

Sulphanilamide

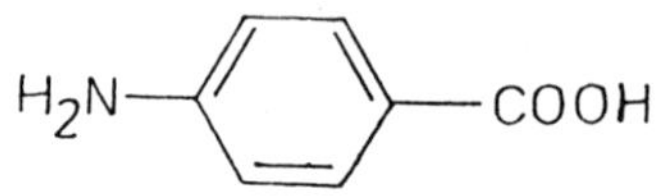

PABA

Sulphonamides are structural analogues of Para aminobenzoic acid (PABA). PABA is essential for the synthesis of folic acid in bacteria and sulphonamides acts as competitive antagonists of PABA. Sulphonamides are bacteriostatic agents and active against gram-negative, gram-positive bacteria and protozoa. These are cheap and safe antibacterial agents.

Classification : Sulphonamides are classified in following types. :

(A) **Therapeutic classification**

1. Sulphonamides used in eye infections - Sulphacetamide.
2. Sulphonamidesused for intestinal infection - Sulphadiazine
3. Sulphonamides used for systemic infection - Sulfadimethoxine.
4. Sulphonamides used for urinary tract infection - Sulphamethoxy pyridazine.
5. Sulphonamides used for topical infections - Silver Sulfadiazine

(B) **Classificaton as per duration of action**

1. Short acting (Half life less than 10 hours) - Sulphathiazde, Sulfisoxazole.
2. Intermediate acting (Half life between 10-24hrs) - Sulphasomizole, Sulphamethoxazole
3. Long acting (Half life about 24 hours) - Sulphadimethoxine, Sulphamethoxy - pyridazine.
4. Ultra long acting (Half life more than 36 hours) - Sulphadoxine, Sulphamethopyrazine.

SULFADIAZINE

It is available as an odourless, tasteless, white or yellowish-white crystal or powder. It is practically insoluble in water, chloroform and ether, very slightly soluble in alcohol and acetone, soluble in alkali hydroxides and carbonates, and dilute mineral acids.

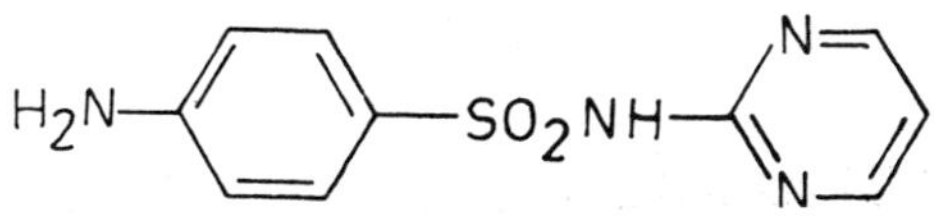

IUPAC Name : N'-(pyrimidin-2-yl) sulphanilamide

or

4- amino-N′-2-pyrimidinyl benzene sulfonamide.

Actions and uses : It is affective in the treatment of ß haemolytic strepto-cocci, pneumococci, meningococci, gonococci and E.coli. It is an important agent for acute phase of infection like gas gangrene. It is also recommended with pyrimethamine in the treatment of toxoplasmosis. It may produce nausea, vomiting and diarrhoea as undesirable side effects.

Officials : Sulfadiazine, B.P., I.P.

Sulfadiazine Injection/Tablets, B.P.,I.P., U.S.P.

SULFAGUANIDINE

It is available as odourless, white crystals or powder, which darken on exposure to light. It is soluble in dilute mineral acid and boiling water; slightly soluble in water and alcohol and very slightly soluble in acetone. It should be stored in light resistant and air tight containers.

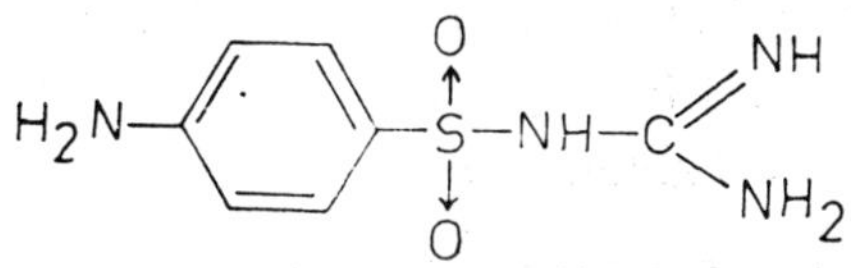

IUPAC Name : 2-(4-Amino benzene sulphonyl) guanidine.

Actions and uses : It is poorly absorbed in G.I.T.,therfore used in the treatment of local intestinal infections such as bacillary dysentery. It is also recommended in amoebic dysentery, ulcerative colitis and other intestinal bacterial infections.

Officials : Sulfaguanidine, I.P.

Sulfaguanidine, Tablets I.P., B.P.C.

PHTHALYLSULFATHIAZOLE

It is an odourless, white crystalline powder, slightly bitter in taste. It is insoluble in chloroform and water but, slightly soluble in ether and alcohol and readily dissolves in alkalis and acids. It should be stored in light resistant and well closed containers, because it slowly darkens on exposure to light.

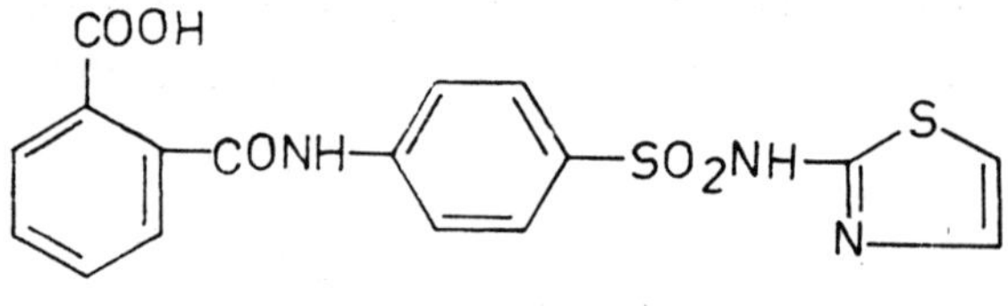

IUPAC Name : 2-[[[4-{(2-Thiazolyl amino)sulfonyl} Phenyl] amino] carbonyl] benzoic acid or

4'-[N -(Thiazol -2 yl) sulfamoyl] phthalanilic acid.

Actions and uses : It is poorly absorbed in G.I.T and used in the local G.I.T infections similar to sulfaguanidine.

Officials : Phthalylsulfathiazole, I.P.
Phthalylsulfathiazole, I.P.

SUCCINYL SULFATHIAZOLE

It is an odourless, white or yellowish white crystalline powder with a slightly bitter taste. It is soluble in alkali hydroxides and carbonates but practically insoluble in chloroform and ether. It should be stored in well closed light resistant containers.

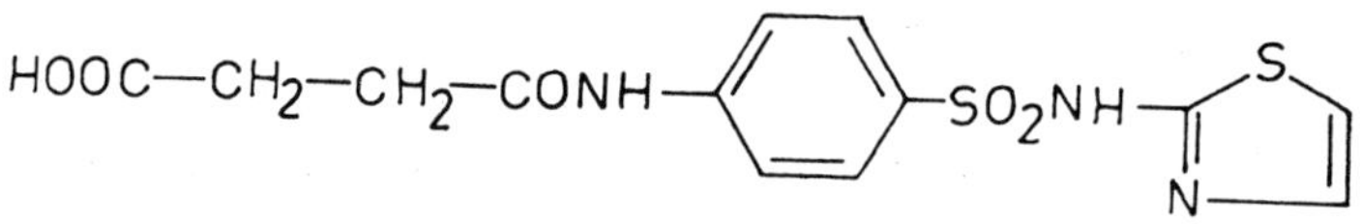

IUPAC Name : 4'-(Thiazol-2-yl sulphamoyl) succinanilic acid.

Actions and uses : Its action and uses are similar to phthalyl sulfathiazole.

Officials : Succinyl sulfathiazole, I.P.
Succinyl sulfathiazole Tablets, I.P.

SULFADIMETHOXINE

It is an odourless, tasteless, white or creamy white crystalline powder. It is soluble in dilute mineral acids, alkali hydroxides and carbonates. It should be stored in well closed light resistant containers.

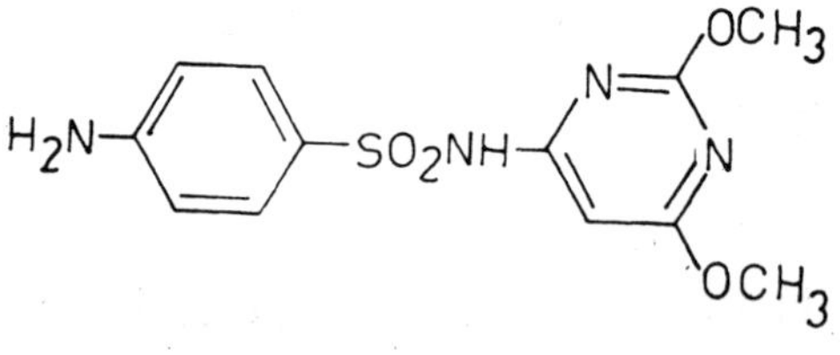

IUPAC NAME : N'-(2,6-Dimethoxy primidin-4-yl) sulphanilamide.

Actions and uses : It is rapidly absorbed in G.I.T. and blood concentrations are maintained for atleast 24 hours. It is highly protein bound which affects its rate of excretion and therefore has a half life of 20 to 40 hours. It is used for systemic-infections.

Officials :Sulfadimethoxine, I.P.
Sulfadimethoxine Tablets, I.P

SULFAMETHOXYPYRIDAZINE

It is an odourless, white or yellowish white crystalline powder, and has bitter taste towards the end. It is soluble in dilute acids and alkali, but very slightly soluble in water, alcohol and acetone. It should be stored in well closed light resistant containers.

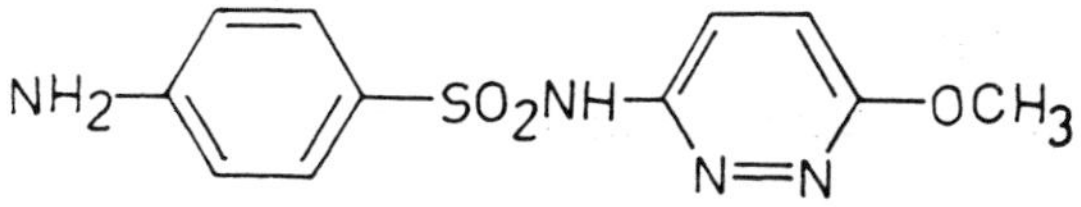

IUPAC Name : N'-[6-methoxypyridazin-3-yl] sulphanilamide.

Actions and uses : It has actions, uses and side effects similar to sulfadimethoxine and as with other long acting sulphonamides. If is very soluble in neutral or acidic urine, therefore can be used orally in the treatment of urinary tract infections.

SULFAMETHOXAZOLE

It is an odourless, white or yellowish white, crystalline powder with a bitter taste. It is soluble in alkali hydroxides; slightly soluble in alcohol, acetone and very slightly soluble in water. It should be stored in light resistant airtight containers.

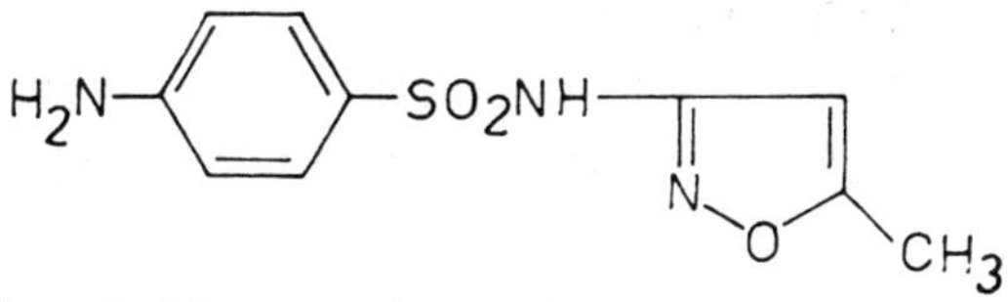

IUPAC Name : N′-5[methyl isoxazole-3-yl] sulphanilamide.

Actions and uses : It is an antibacterial agent similar to sulphadimidine. It's therapeutic blood concentration reaches within 2 hours and maintenance doses are given at an interval of 8 to 12 hours.

It is given in combination with trimethoprim under the name of co-trimethoprim. Trimethoprim acts on folic acid reductase and synergistic actions of combination drug are produced. Co-trimethoprim is very widely used in all type of infections.

Official : Sulfamethoxazole I.P.

CO-TRIMOXAZOLE

Co- trimoxazole is a combination of sulphamethaoxazole and trimethoprim in 5:1 ratio.

IUPAC Name : 5-(3,4,5-Trimethoxybenzyl) pyrimidine-2,4-diamine.

Actions and uses : It acts by PABA inhibition and as folic acid inhibitors by the action

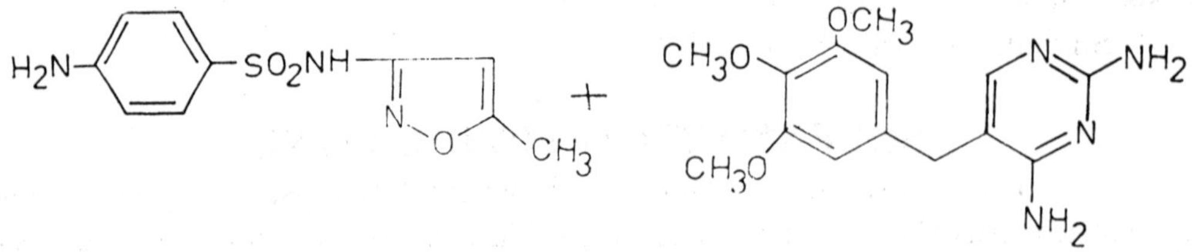

of trimethoprim on folate reductase. It is active against wide varieties of infections, i.e., Genito-urinary tract infections, bronchitis, pneumonia and other infections.

Officials : Co-trimoxazole I.P.
Trimethoprim and sulfamethoxazole tablets I.P.

SULPHACETAMIDE

It is an odourless, white or yellowish, white crystalline powder with slight bitter taste. It is very slightly soluble in alcohol and acetone but soluble in water. It should be stored in air tight containers protected from light.

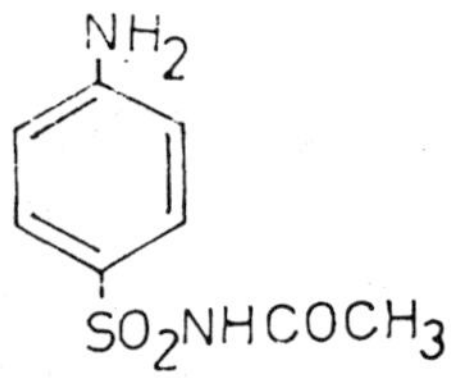

IUPAC Name : N'-acetyl sulphanilamide.

Actions and uses : It is commonly used as sodium salt in the treatment of prophylaxis of ocular infections and burns. It is also useful in urinary tract infections without any damage to kidney .

Officials : Sulfacetamide I.P.
Sulfacetamide sodium I.P.
Sulfacetamide Eye ointment I.P.

(1) Sufadimenthoxine : Rhone poulene : Madribon Tab.
ADULTS : initial-1gm. maint. 500 mg.
CHILD : 10 mg./kg body wt/kg.

(2) Sulfamethoxazole : Albert-David : Alcorim-F tab.

(3) Co-trimoxazole : Rhone-poulenc : Antrim tabs,
Dec Pharma : Cidal tabs,
Wellcome : Cotrimoxazole tabs, Sepmax, Septran
ADULTS : (160 mg. Trimethoprim+800 mg. Sulphamethaoxyozole) Cotrimoxazle 2 times daily for 7-14 days.
CHILDREN : (6-12 mg. tMP+30-60 mg 5 mg)/kg/24 hrs also inj are available.

(4) Sulfacetamide : Nicholas : Albucid Eye drop
East India : Locula

CHAPTER - 5

ANTIMYCOBACTERIAL AGENTS

Mycobacterium is a genus of acid-fast bacilli belonging to family Mycobacteriaceae. Tuberculosis is a disease caused by *M.tuberculosis*; which is characterised by the formation of tubercles or nodular bodies. *M.leprae* is responsible for human leprosy (Hansen's Disease).

ANTITUBERCULAR DRUGS

Tuberculosis is a chronic disease caused by acid-fast aerobic bacillus Mycobacterium tuberculosis [*M. tuberculosis*]. The bacterial cell wall is compose of high lipid content resulting in a high degree of hydrophobicity and resistance to alcohol, acids, alkali, etc. The organism is transmitted via respiratory route either as droplet form or as desiccated airborne bacilli. The organism appears in water droplets expelled during sneezing or coughing. This disease mainly effects the lungs but can also spread through the bloodstream and lymphatic system to brain, bones, eyes and skin (extra-pulmonary T.B.). Extrapulmonary T.B. is common in HIV infected patients.

Classification : Antitubercular drugs are classified as per choice of agents. The first line agents are used in the initial stage of T.B., but when bacteria become resistant to these agents then the second line agents are used.

(A) **First line agents** :

(I) **Chemotherapeutic agents** : Isoniazid, Pyrazinamide, Ethambutol.

(ii) **Antibiotic** : Streptomycin, Rifampicin.

(B) **Second line Agents** :

(I) **Chemotherapeutic agents** : Ethionamide, Para amino salicylic acid (P.A.S.).

(ii) **Antibiotics** : Cycloserine, Kanamycin.

ISONIAZID

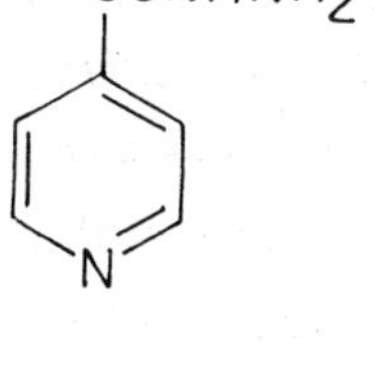

IUPAC Name : Iso nicotinoyl hydrazide

OR

Pyridine-4-carbohydrazide.

Actions and uses : It acts by affecting electron transport system and conversion of NAD^+ to NADH. It is mainly use in the treatment of pulmonary tuberculosis and is also effective in extra-pulmonary tuberculosis such as meningitis and genito-urinary tuberculosis infections. INH develops resistance within a few weeks therefore it should be combined with some other agents.

Generally it is given orally but in certain cases its intra-muscular injection is also recommended. It may produce constipation, difficulty in starting urination, dryness of mouth, peripheral neuropathy, alteration in liver function, etc.

Official compounds : Isoniazid I.P.
Isoniazid Tablets I.P.

PARA AMINO SALICYLIC ACID

It is an odourless, white to cream coloured crystalline powder, sweet and saline in taste. It should be stored in well closed containers in a dark place. Its solution decomposes slowly and darkens in colour.

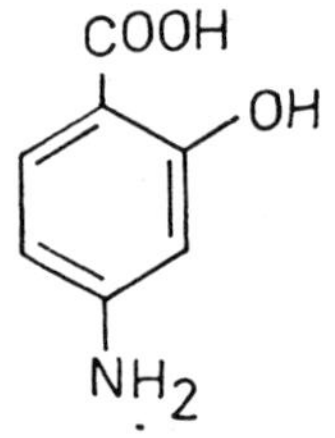

IUPAC Name : 4-amino-2-hydroxy-benzoic acid.

Actions and uses : It is bacteriostatic in nature and can arrest the growth of tubercle bascilli, but doses not eradicate them. Bacteria develop immediate resistance to this drug therefore it should be given in combination with other drugs. It may cause epigastric discomfort, anorexia, nausea, vomiting, etc.

STREPTOMYCIN

It is an almost odourless, hygroscopic white powder with a bitter taste. It is soluble in water but very slightly soluble in alcohol, ether and chloroform. It should be stored in airtight containers not exceeding a temperature of 30°C. If it is intended for parenteral use, it should be packed and sealed in sterile containers.

Streptomycin is an aminoglycoside. It is produced by the fungi *Streptomyces griseus*. It acts by inhibiting protein synthesis and also misreading of m-RNA template. The drug diffuses across the cell membrane of *Mycobacterium tuberculosis* and enters the cell. It binds 30s ribosomal sub unit that is its primary site of action.

IUPAC Name : O-2 deoxy-2-methyl amino α glucopyranosyl (1-->2)-O-5 deoxy-3-c formyl-α-lyxofuranosyl - (1→4)-N^3 N^3-diamino-D-streptamine.

Actions and uses : It is active against infections caused by *Mycobacterium tuberculosis*, E. coli, klebsiella pneumoniae and some species of *salmonella*. This drug produces more toxic effects and resistance develops rapidly. Generally it is given in combination with other chemotherapeutic agents to prevent drug resistance. It causes autotoxicity, nephrotoxicity and neuromuscular blockade on use for some time.

Official : Streptomycin sulphate I.P.
Streptomycin tablet I.P.
Dihydrostreptomycin sulphate I.P.
Dihydrostreptomycin sulphate injection I.P.

RIFAMPICIN

It is an odourless, brick-red to red-brown, crystalline powder. It is soluble in chloroform and methyl alcohol, very slightly soluble in alcohol, acetone and ether. It should be stored in light resistant, air tight containers in a atmosphere of nitrogen.

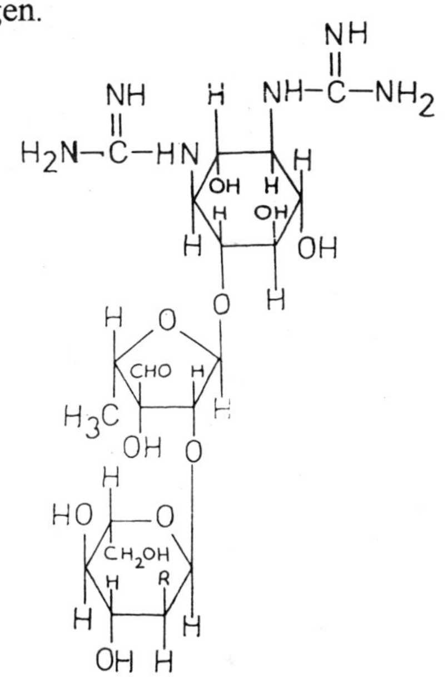

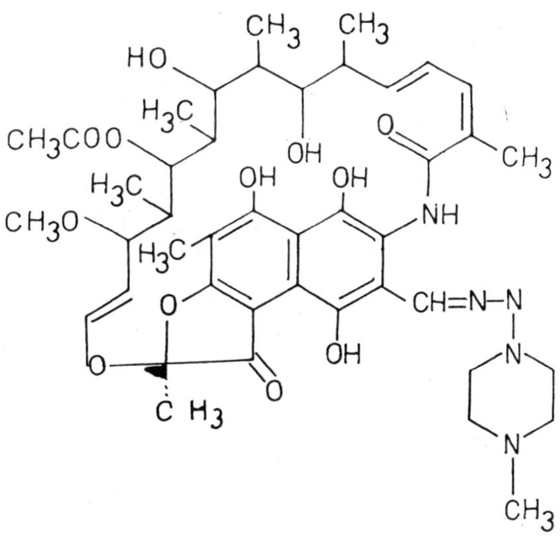

STREPTOMYCIN **RIFAMPICIN**

IUPAC Name : 3-(4-Methyl piperazin-1-yl iminomethyl) rifamycin SV

Actions and Uses : It is a semisynthetic antibiotic prepared from rifamycin B,which is an antibiotic isolated from *Streptomyces mediterranei*. It is used to treat biliary infections and tuberculosis. Generally it is reserved for T.B. and it is given with isoniazide, streptomycin or with ethambutol but not with para amino salicylic acid. Combination therapy prevents the drug resistance. It increases the metabolism of hypoglycemic drugs, anticonvulsants, corticosteroids and oral contraceptives. It causes red staining of secretions, altered liver functions, and a flu like illness on prolong use.

ETHAMBUTOL

It is an odourless, white crystalline powder, bitter in taste. It is freely soluble in water, soluble in alcohol; and slightly soluble in ether and chloroform. It is a hygroscopic compound, stored in well-closed containers.

$$
\begin{array}{c}
CH_2OH \\
| \\
CH_2\text{-}NH\text{-}CH\text{-}CH_2\text{-}CH_3 \\
| \\
CH_2\text{-}NH\text{-}CH\text{-}CH_2\text{-}CH_3 \\
| \\
CH_2OH
\end{array}
$$

IUPAC Name : N N^1-Bis (1-hydroxy methyl propyl) ethylenediamine

Actions and uses : It is a tuberculostatic drug, which acts by interfering with synthesis of RNA. When it is used alone it clears sputum of myobacteria within three months but relapses may occur. Prevention of relapses is achieve by combination therapy with isoniazide. Ethambutol is also recommend for the patients, who became resistant to other drugs. Ethambutol leads to retrobulbar neuritis and disturbance in colour vision on use for some time.

Officials : Ethambutol Tablet I.P.
Ethambutol Hydrochloride I.P.

PYRAZINAMIDE

It is an odourless, white, crystalline powder with a bitter taste. It is soluble in ether and chloroform, slightly soluble in water and alcohol. It should be stored in air tight containers.

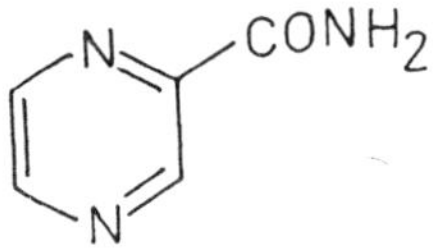

IUPAC Name : Pyrazine-2-carboxamide.

Actions and uses : Pyrazinamide is a tuberculostatic drug. Bacterial resistance to the drug may develop within 6-8 weeks and therefore it should also be given in combination with other drugs. It may cause of liver damage, anorexia, nausea and rashes, etc.

Officials : Pyrazinamide I.P.

THIACETAZONE

Thiacetazone is available as an odourless pale yellow crystals or a crystalline powder. It is slightly soluble in alcohol and very slightly soluble in water. It should be stored in airtight containers, protected from light.

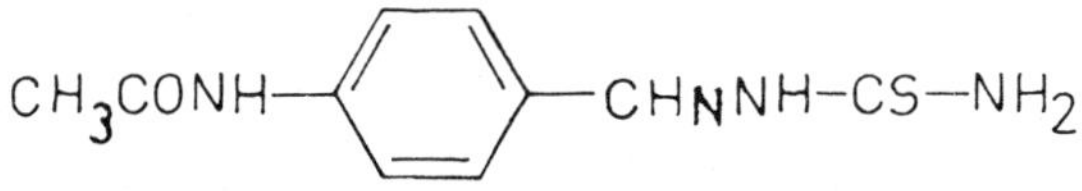

IUPAC Name : 4-Acetamido benzaldehyde thiosemicarbazone.

Actions and uses : It is a myobacteriostatic agent, used in tuberculosis as well as in leprosy. It is use in combination with streptomycin and isoniazide as first choice of treatment. The undesirable effects of this drug are allergy, skin rashes, nausea, hepatitis, etc.

Official : Thiacetazone I.P.
Thiacetazone and isoniazide I .P.

ETHIONAMIDE

Ethionamide is a bright yellow crystalline powder with a slight odour and an unpleasant sulphurous taste. It is sparingly soluble in alcohol, slightly soluble in chloroform but very slightly soluble in ether and water. It should be stored in well closed containers protected from light.

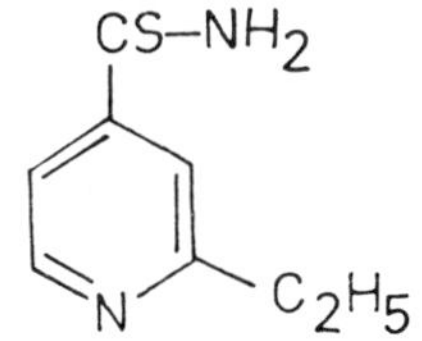

IUPAC Name : 2-Ethyl pyridine-4-carbothiamide.

Actions and uses : It is also tuberculostatic agent. It is used in combination with amino salicylate in the treatment of pulmonary and extra pulmonary tuberculosis but the organisms readily develop resistance. It should not be given in pregnancy. It also causes metallic taste, nausea, liver damage, etc.

CYCLOSERINE

It is an odourless, white or pale-yellow crystalline, powder with slightly bitter taste. It is soluble in water and alcohol but slightly soluble in ether and chloroform. It is a hygroscopic compound and should be stored in air tight containers below 25°C.

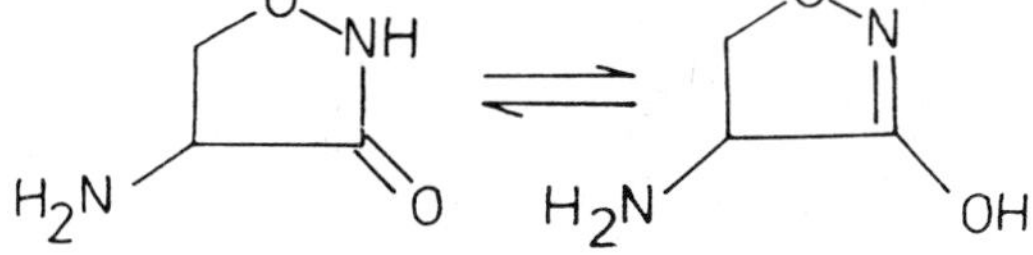

IUPAC Name : 4-amino iso-oxazolidin-3-one.

Actions and uses : It is a natural antibiotic obtained from a fungus, *Streptomycies* *orchidaceae*. It is active against both gram-positive and gram-negative bacteria, i.e., M. tuberculosis, Streptococci, E.coli, etc. It is mainly used in pulmonary tuberculosis where organism is resistant to streptomycin or the patient is hypersensitive to streptomycin. It should not be given to patients of epilepsy and other mental disturbances.

ANTILEPROTIC AGENTS

Leprosy is more common in tropical countries. The disease is caused by acid fast, aerobic bacillus *M. leprae*. This bacteria was first invented by Hansen in 1873, hence this disease is also called Hansens disease.

Leprosy is characterized by lesions in the skin and peripheral nerves. Human leprosy can not be transmitted to animals easily. Transmission to human, requires prolonged intimate contact for several years. Treatment of leprosy also requires prolonged drug therapy.

CLASSIFICATION

1. Sulfones	:	Dapsones, Solapsone.
2. Phenazines and other agents	:	Clofazimine, Rifampin.
3. Natural Agents	:	Chaulmoogra oil.

DAPSONE

Dapsone is a white or creamy white, colourles, crystalline powder with a slight bitter taste. It is soluble in dilute mineral acids and acetone but very slightly soluble in alcohol. It is hygroscopic and therefore it should be stored in well-closed containers.

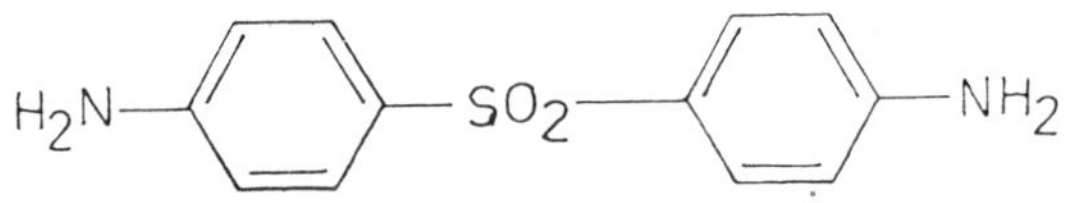

IUPAC Name : bis(4-aminophenyl) sulfone.

or

4,4'-Diamino diphenyl sulfone.

Actions and uses : Sulphone acts as a bacteriostatic agent, similar to sulphonamides. It competitively inhibits PABA, thus inhibiting the formation of bacterial folic acid. It is used for lepromatous and tuberculoid types of leprosy. It i also used in dermatitis herpetiformis, in mycetoma and suppresses malaria parasite (*P.falciferum*). It may produce side effects like nausea, vomiting, nervousness, anemia,etc.

Officials : Dapsone I.P.
Dapsone tablets I.P.

SOLAPSONE

Solapsone is a white powder. It is soluble in cold water and practically insoluble in cold alcohol. It is hydrolised in presence of acids into cinnamaldehyde, dapsone and sulphurous acid. Generally it is available as sodium sulphonic salt.

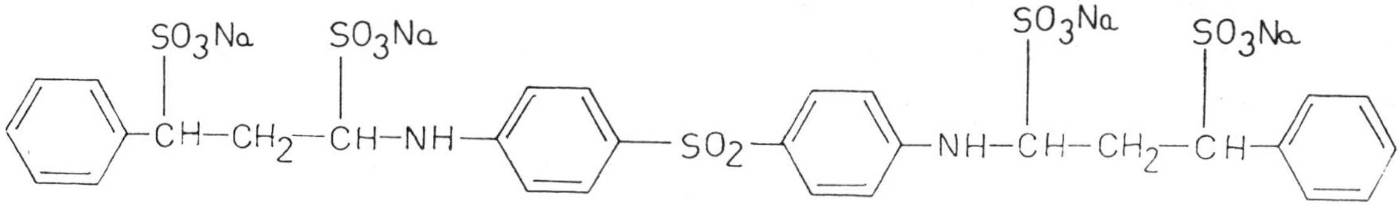

IUPAC Name : Tetrasodium 3,3'-diphenyl -4,4'-sulphonylbis (1-anilinopropane-1,3-disulphonate).

Actions and uses : Solapsone is an antileprotic drug used similar to dapsone. It is given orally, subcutaneously or as an intra-muscular injection which gets converted into dapsone salt.

CLOFAZIMINE

It is a phenazine derivative which is a water insoluble dye [Dark red to orange]. It is soluble in dimethyl formamide and macrogol-400, very slightly soluble in glycols and alcohols, and practically insoluble in water.

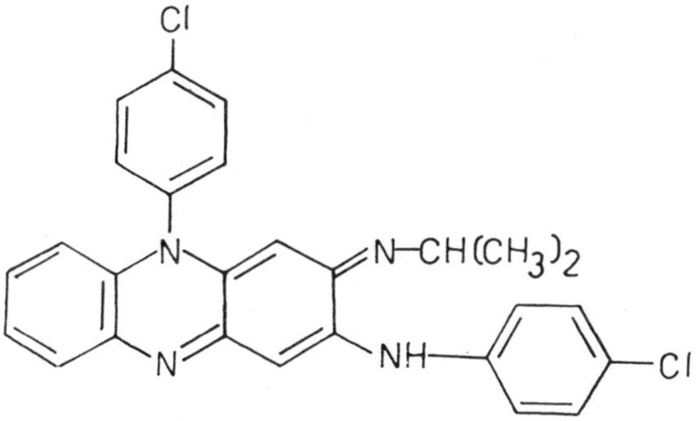

IUPAC Name : 3-(4-chloroanilino)-10-(4-chlorophenyl)-2,10-dihydro 2-phenazin-2-ylidene isopropylamine.

Actions and uses : It is active against mycobacterium, actinomyces, streptomyces, species, etc. It is specially used where bacteria become resistant to dapsone. It is contra-indicated in the first trimester of pregnancy.

Officials : Clofazimine I.P.
Clofazimine capsules I.P.

THIAMBUTOSINE

It is an odourless white or creamy white crystalline powder with a bitter taste. It is soluble in chloroform, acetone and very slightly soluble in water. It should be stored in air tight containers protected from light.

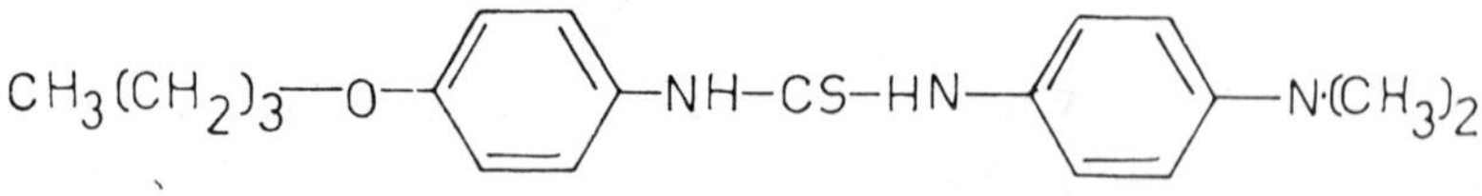

IUPAC Name : 1-(4-butoxy phenyl)-3(4-dimethyl aminophenyl) thiourea.

Actions and uses : It is a thio-urea derivative. It is used in the treatment of leprosy but develops bacterial resistance and its applications are limited. It is generally given with isoniazid. It is also used in the treatment of dermatitis herpetiformis.

ANTILEPROTIC DRUGS

(1)Clfazimine : Astra-IDL : Clopodap, Clofozine Cap.
SG Pharma : Hensepran Cap. 100 mg
200 mg daily for 3 weeks, in child 1-2 mg/kg daily one almost and as directed by the physician.

(2) Dapsone : B. Wellcome : Tab. Dapsone 25,50,100 mg
ADULTS : 100 mg./day depending upon body wt.
CHILDREN : 1-2 mg/kg/body wt.

ANTITUBERCULAR DRUGS

(1) Isoniazid : Pfizer : Isonex Tab. 100 mg, 300 mg
Adults : 3-5 mg/kg body wt. to 300 mg daily once a day.

(2) PAS : MAC : Erbazide tab. 400 mg

(3) Streptomycin : IPCA : Icpazide (liq. 100 ml) and Tab.
Warner : Isokin tabs. 100 mg, 300 mg
CHILDREN : 10-20 mg/kg of body wt. once a day.

(4) Rifampicin : Sarabhai : Ambistryn Inj., Siticox Cap.
Ranbaxy : Tibirim Cap.

(5) Ethambutol : Plethico : Koxi tab.
Lupin : Combutol
ADULTS : 15 mg./kg body wt. daily as single dose, Retreatment 25 mg/kg body wt. as a single dose for 60 days then 15 mg/kg body wt.
CHILDREN : Same dose according to wt. Avoid below 3 Yrs.

(6) Thiacetazone : Parke Davis : Isokin T Forte

CHAPTER - 6

ANTIAMOEBIC AND ANTHELMINTIC DRUGS

Amoebiasis occurs mainly in tropical regions. Amoebiasis is caused by a protozoan *Entamoeba histolytica*. It is transmitted by ingestion of water and foods contaminated by fecal matter from infected persons or flies. Common manifestations of amoebiasis are dysentery, fever, intestinal bleeding, etc. The protozoa affects normal bacterial flora of the large intestine but some times it may spread to other organs (e.g.- liver) of the body. Acute amoebiasis leads to amoebic dysentery associated with mucoid stool and abdominal pain. The drugs used as antiamoebics are classified as :

(I) **Natural drugs** : Emetine and dehydroemetine.

(II) **Synthetic drugs** :

(1) **Quinoline derivatives** : Chloroquine, Iodoquinol.

(2) **Miscellaneous** : Diloxanide, Metronidazole, Tinidazole, Secnidazole.

Helminthiasis is a disease caused by parasitic worms, living in the alimentary canal of secondary host (human). three categories of worms normally infect man. They are :

(1) **Nematodes** : *Ascaris lumbricoides* (round worm); *Enterbious vermiculis* (thread worm); *Strongyloides stercoralis* ; *Ancylostoma duodenale* (hook worm).

(2) **Cestodes** : *Taenia species* (tapeworm).

(3) **Trematodes** : Flukes or Blood flukes.

Infecting Helminth	**Drugs used**
(1) **Nematodes** :	
Ascaris lumbricoides (round worm)	Piperazine Thiabendazole Mebendazole.
Strongyloides stercoralis	Mebendazole, Thabendazole
Ancylostoma duodenale (hook worm)	Mebendazole, Thiabendazole
(2) **Cestodes** :	
Taenia species (tapeworm)	Mebendazole, Dichlorophen quinacrine, Niclosamide
(3) **Trematodes** :	
Flukes or blood flukes	Antimony potassium tartrate

EMETINE

Emetine is an alkaloid obtained from the plant *Cephaelis ipecacunha* (Ipecacuanha). It is available as a hydrochloride salt. It is an odourless, white crystalline powder with a bitter taste. It should be stored in air-tight containers protected from light because, on exposure to light it turns faint yellow. It is soluble in water and alcohol.

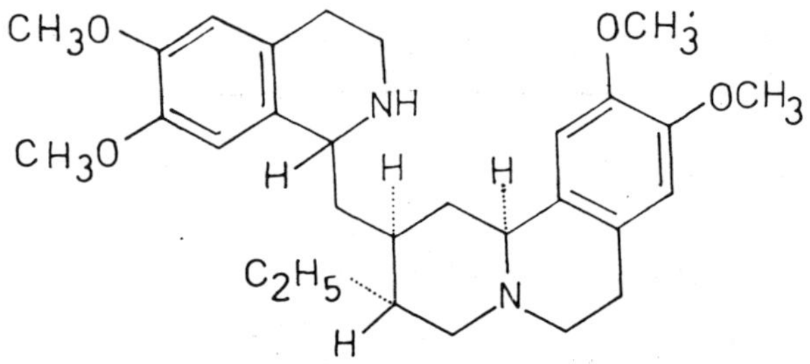

IUPAC Name : Emetan, 6',7',10,11-tetra methoxy.

Actions and uses : Emetine hydrochloride is an amoebicidal agent. It eradicates amoeba from both intestinal and extra-intestinal sites. It has been replaced by less toxic drugs like metronidazole. In hepatic amobisis it is given alongwith chloroquine. Its other analogs are also in practice.

Officials : Dehydroemetine Hydrochloride I.P.
Dehydroemetine Injection I.P.
Dehydroemetine Tablets I.P.
Emetine Hydrochloride I.P.
Emetine Injection I.P.

METRONIDAZOLE

It is a white or creamy white crystalline powder with a slight odour and a bitter saline taste. It is soluble in water, slightly soluble in alcohol and chloroform but very slightly soluble in ether. It should be stored in well closed, light resistant containers.

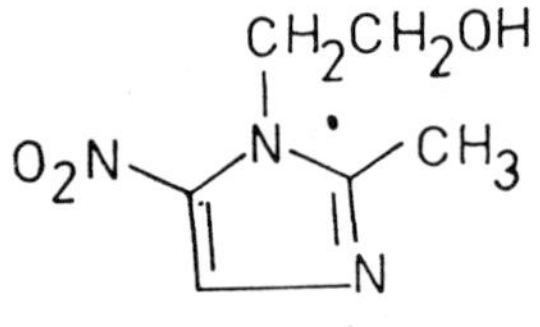

IUPAC Name : 2-(2-Methyl-5-nitro imidazole-1-yl) ethanol.

Actions and uses : Metronidazole is active against Trichomonas vaginalis, Entamoeba histolytica (amoebisis), Giardia lamblia (Giardiasis) and acute ulcerative gingivitis. It is inactive against aerobic and facultatively anaerobic bacteria. It is used in the treatment of both hepatic and intestinal amoebiasis. It is available as metronidazole benzoate. The salt is almost tasteless and acceptable.

Officials : Metronidazole I.P.
Metronidazole Injection I.P.
Metronidazole Tablets I.P.
Metronidazole Benzoate I.P.
Metronidazole Benzoate oral suspension I.P.

IODOCHLORHYDROXYQUIN

It is a spongy brownish yellow coloured salt with a characteristic odour. It is soluble in hot ethyl acetate and boiling acetic acid but practically insoluble in water and alcohol. The drug darkens on exposure to light, therefore it should be stored in light resistant and air tight containers.

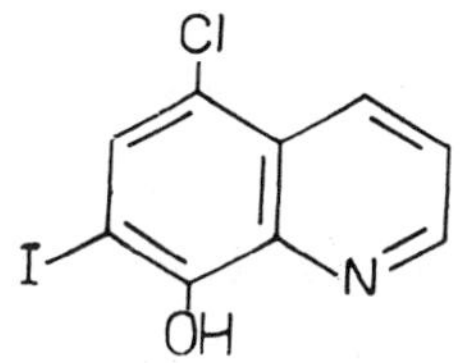

IUPAC Name : 5-chloro-7-iodo-8-quinoline.

Actions and uses : It is a halogenated derivative of 8-Hydroxyquinoline. It is used as topical intestinal anti-infective agent. It is given orally in amoebiasis, but causes neurotoxicity therefore it is not recommended. It is a topical antibacterial and antifungal agent, used as creams and ointments of skin infections.

DI-IODOHYDROXYQUINOLINE

It is an odourless, tasteless, pale yellowish to yellowish -brown crystalline powder. It is very slightly soluble in water, alcohol and ether. It should be stored in well closed containers protected from light.

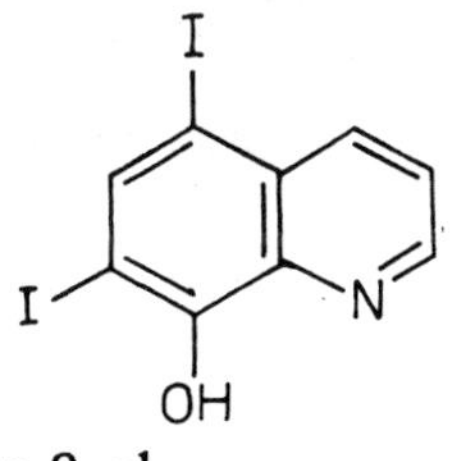

IUPAC Name : 5,7-Di-iodoquinolin-8-ol.

Actions and uses : This drug is used in the treatment of giardiasis and trichomonas infections. It produces rashes on skin, therefore it is used only in endemic area for prophylactic use. It is also used in the treatment of trichomonal and candidal vaginal infections.

Officials : Di-dohydroxy quinoline I.P.
Di-dohydroxy quinoline Tablets I.P.

DILOXANIDE FUROATE

It is an odourless, tasteless and white crystalline powder. It is very slightly soluble in water, alcohol and ether but soluble in chloroform.

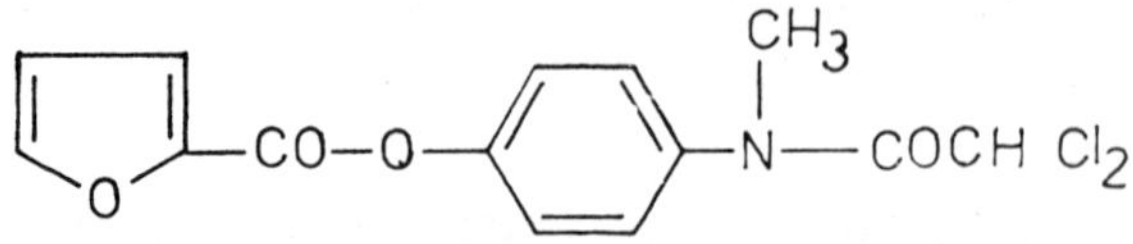

IUPAC Name : 4-[N-methyl-2,2-dichloro acetamido] Phenyl 2-furoate.

Actions and uses : It has a direct effect on amoeba present in the gut. It is used in the treatment of acute and chronic intestinal amoebiasis. It is also used to treat ameobic hepatitis in combination with chloroquine.

Officials : Diloxanide Furoate I.P.
Diloxanide Furoate Tablets I.P.

PAROMOMYCIN

It is a white amorphous powder which is soluble in water and methanol but sparingly soluble in ethanol. Paromomycin sulphate salt is a creamy-white, odourless, hygroscopic and water soluble compound. It should be stored in air tight containers.

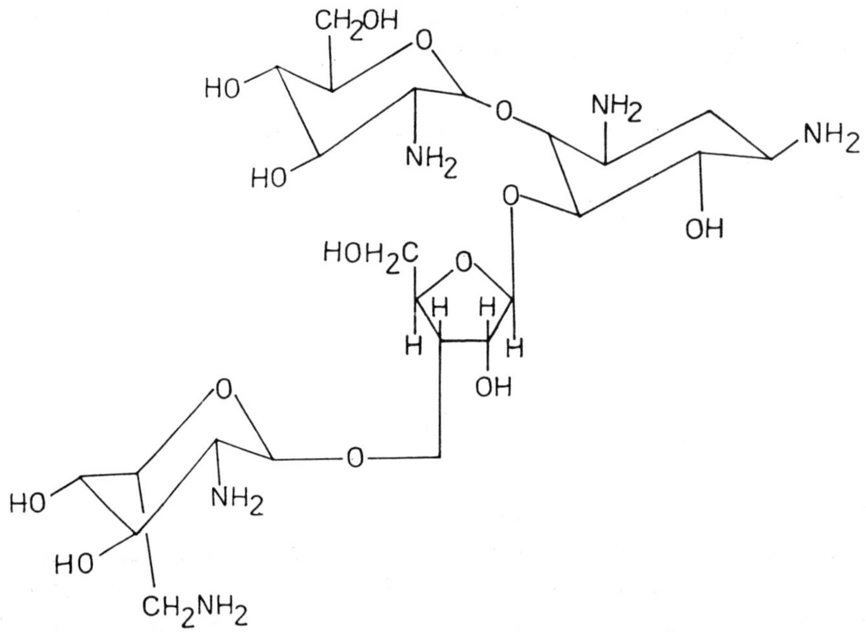

Actions and uses : It is an amino-glycoside type of antibiotic, obtained from the culture of *Streptomyces simosus* fungi. Its action is similar to neomycin. It is used in bacterial diarrhoea and intestinal amoebiasis.

PIPERAZINE

Piperazine is available as a colourless glossy deliquescent crystals with a faint characteristic odour. It is soluble in water and alcohol. It should be stored in air tight containers protected from light. The compound is available as piperazine citrate and piperazine adipate. The citrate salt is water soluble, very slightly soluble in alcohol and ether, but adipate salt is less soluble in water and alcohol.

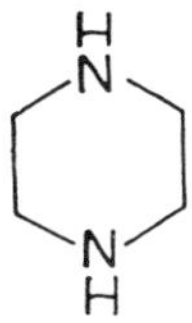

Actions and uses : It is an antihelmintic, effective against thread worm and round worms. The drug stimulates the muscular activity of round worm thereby expels them out of gut with fecal matter. It is the safest drug available for heavy infections.

The patients having thread worm infections over the age of 12 years are treated with this agent. It may act by blocking the action of acetylcholine. It does not have any significant action on hook worm or tapeworm. Prolonged therapy of this drug causes accumulation in tissues and may cause dizziness, muscular inco-ordination, vomiting and blurred vision.

Officials : Piperazine Adipate I.P.
Piperazine Adipate Tablets I.P.
Piperazine Citrate I.P.

MEBENDAZOLE

It is a white or slightly yellow powder, practically insoluble in water, chloroform, alcohol and ether. It should be stored in well closed containers protected from light.

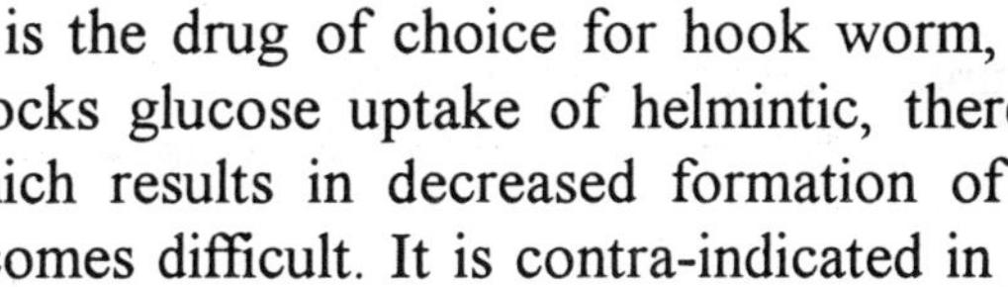

IUPAC Name : Carbamic acid, [5-benzoyl-1-benzimidazole-2-yl]-, methyl ester.

Actions and uses : It is the drug of choice for hook worm, pine worm, and round worm infections. It blocks glucose uptake of helmintic, thereby depleting glycogen stored in parasites which results in decreased formation of A.T.P.. Slowly their reproductive cycle becomes difficult. It is contra-indicated in hyper-sensitive patients and in pregnancy.

Officials : Mebendazole I.P.
Mebendazole Tablets I.P.

DIETHYLCARBAMAZINE [D.E.C.]

The drug is available as a citrate salt. It is an odourless, white crystalline powder with a bitter acid taste. It is very soluble in water, sparingly soluble in alcohol and practically insoluble in acetone, chloroform and ether. It should be stored in air tight containers.

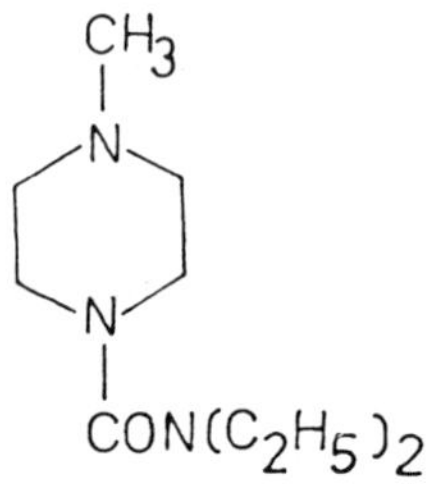

IUPAC Name : N,N-Diethyl-4-methyl-1 piperazine-1-carboxamide.
Actions and uses : Diethylcarbamazine is used as an anthelimenthic and antifilarial agent. It also helps to limit the spread of filarisis from insect vector.

(1) Emetine : Rothe : Dehydroemetinery : Adults : 10-20 mg. thrice daily.
Tablets India : Tilemetin : 1 mg/kg daily for days.

(2) Metronidazole : Rhohepounenc : Flagyl : 1-2 tab tid for 2-5 days.
Unique : Metrogyl : Adults : 200mg-400mg
Children : 100-200mg

(3) Halogenoted hydroxiquinalines : Jagsonpal : Quiss Oint.

(4) Diloxamide furoate : CFL : Amibartin : 1 tab tid for 5 days.
Both : Entamizole: 2 tab tid for 5 days.
Core : Cone : 2 tab b.i.d.

(5) Piperazine : Wellcome : Piperazine citrate Elixir

(6) Mebendazole : Torrent : Meberol : 1 tab only.
Clipa : Mebex : 1 tab bid for 3 days.

CHAPTER - 7

ANTIBIOTICS

Antibiotics are defined as chemical substances produced by various species of micro-organisms (fungi, actinomycetes, bacteria, yeast and moulds) that supress the growth of other organisms and may destroy them. These agents are either bacteriostatic or bacteriocidal. Some times their concentration brings their static or cidal effect on pathogenic organisms. These agents generally act on specific micro-organism but also act on several species and are then known as broad spectrum antibiotics. The ideal method to choose an antibiotic is to identify the type of infection in any patient. This can be done by identifying the infecting organism in culture and then determing antibiotic sensitivity.

Antibiotics are agents developed from various micro-organisms therefore they may develop bacterial resistance or patients may be hypersensitive to these drugs. All these problems should be supervised by a physician.

CLASSIFICATION :

Antibiotics can be classified as follows -

1. **According to source** : Antibiotics are classified according to the type of micro-organisms from which they are isolated.
   (a) **Antibiotics from fungi** : Penicillin from fungus *Penicilium-notatum*, and griseofulvin from *Penicillium griseofulvum*.
   (b) **Antibiotics from Actinomycetes** : Streptomycin from *Streptomyces griseus*, chlorctetracyclin from *Streptomyces aureofaciens.*
   (c) **Antibiotics from Bacteria** : Bacitracin from (*Bacillus subtilis*) polymycins from *Bacillus polymyxa*.
2. **According to the mode of action**:
   (a) **Bacterial cell wall synthesis inhibitors** : Penicillins; cephalosporins, bacitracin, Isoniazid.

(b) **Protein synthesis inhibitors** : Tetracycline, Chloramphenicol, aminoglycosides etc.

(c) **Bacterial cell membrane inhibitors** : Nystatin, Amphotericin ß, etc.

(d) **Nucleic acid metabolism inhibitors** : Griseofulvin, Actinomycin.

3. **According to the spectrum of antibacterial activity** :

(a) **Narrow spectrum antibiotics** :- Penicillin, streptomycin, Erythromycin, etc.

(b) **Broad spectrum antibiotics** : Chloroamphenicol, tetracyclines, cephalosporins.

4. **According to chemical nature** :

(a) **Amino acid Antibiotics** :

(i) Antibiotics containing one amino acid : Chloramphenicol, cycloserine, etc.

(ii) Antibiotics containing two amino acids : Penicillin, cephalosporins.

(iii) Antibiotics containing polypeptide chain : Bacitracin, polymyxin.

(b) **Aminoglycoside Antibiotics** : Streptomycin, kanamycin, paromomycin, Neomycin.

(c) **Polyene antibiotics** : Nystatin, Amphotericin B.

(d) **Compounds containing macrocyclic rings** : Erythromycin, spiramycin.

(e) **Miscellaneous** : Griseofulvin, Novobiocin.

PENICILLIN

Penicillin was discovered by **Alexander fleming** in 1929. It is obtained from the mould *Penicillium notatum*. Penicillin now designates a number of antibiotics obtained from various species of penicillium or semi synthetic derivative of 6-amino penicillinanic acid. Penicillin solution is very unstable at pH 5. The solution begins to detoriate upon extending for a few days, even in cold. Certain penicillins are more resistant to acid hydrolysis and therefore can be administered orally.

Penicillins are bacteriostatic at low concentration and bactericidal at high concentration. Penicillin-G, penicillin V, methicillin, etc. are narrow spectrum while ampicillin, amoxycillin are broad spectrum antibiotics. The bacterial cell wall consists of mucopeptide layer which is a support to lipo-protein cell membrane. Penicillin reaches the bacterial cell cytoplasm by penetrating these barriers. It also inhibits synthesis of mucopeptide and acts as bacteriostatic.

Bacterial resistance to penicilins is usually due to penicillinase (ß-lactomases). This is usually seen with staphylococci species. Potency of penicillin is expressed in units/mg. One international unit is equivalent to activity of 0.6 μg of pure crystalline sodium penicillin G.

Penicillins are effective against gram-positive bacteria such as staphylococcal, streptococci, pneumococcal, clostridia etc. The 6-amino penicilloic acid is a key compound in the synthesis of semisynthetic derivatives. A number of semisynthetic derivatives are prepared, among these few are very active. These compounds are classified as first generation penicillins, second generation, third generation and fourth-generation penicillin. This classification is in the increasing order of antibacterial activity and also reducing resistance to organisms. The fourth generation penicilins are very effective against gram-positive and gram-negative bacteria.

BENZYL PENICILLIN

Benzyl penicillin (penicillin G) is a white crystalline hygroscopic powder with a faint characteristic odour. It is very soluble in water but practically insoluble in fixed oils and liquid paraffin. It should be stored in air tight containers, below 30°c.

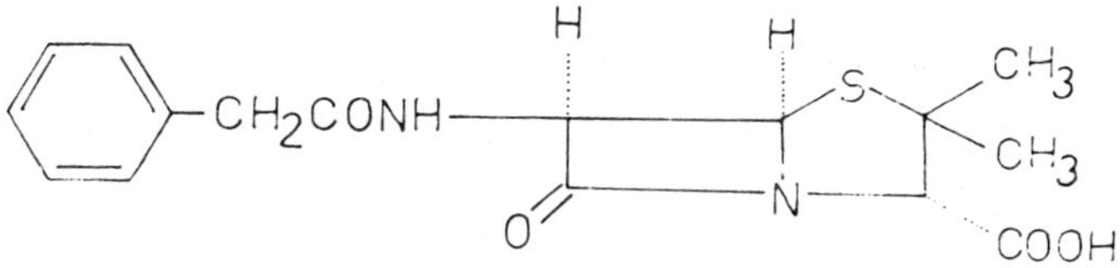

Actions and uses : It is used to treat infections by gram positive organisms (infection caused by actinomyces, bacillus anthracis, clostridium, spirochaetes, etc. species). It is given by intravenous injections and intramucular injections. This injection is administered only after testing hyper sensitivity to the drug.

PHENOXYMETHYL PENICILLIN

Phenoxymethyl penicillin (penicillin V) is a white fine crystalline powder. It is very slightly soluble in water, soluble in alcohol and insoluble in fixed oils. It should be stored in airtight containers.

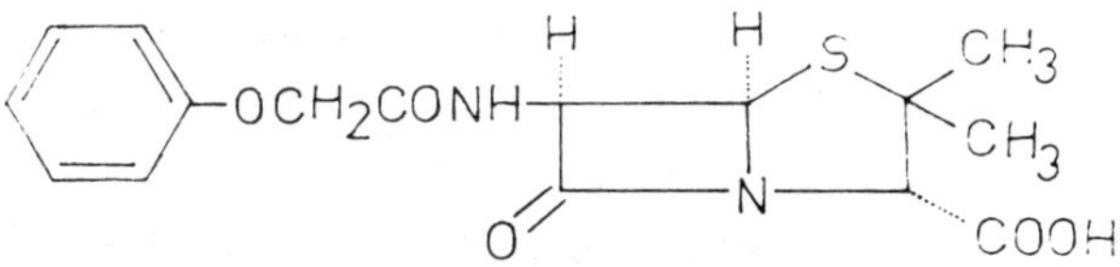

IUPAC Name: 6-(2- phenoxy acetoamido) penicillanic acid

Actions and uses: The compound is stable in acidic medium, therefore can be given orally. It is not used parenterally and topical, orally it is given half an hour before meal. It is indicated like benzylpenicillin in the treatment of susceptible gram-positive infections like meningitis, syphilis, etc.

BENZATHINE PENICILLIN

Benzathine penicillin **[PENIDURALA]** is an odourless, white hygroscopic powder; soluble in formamide and dimethyl-formamide (D.M.F.); very slightly soluble in water, alcohol, ether and chloroform. It should be stored in air tight containers protected from light below 25°C.

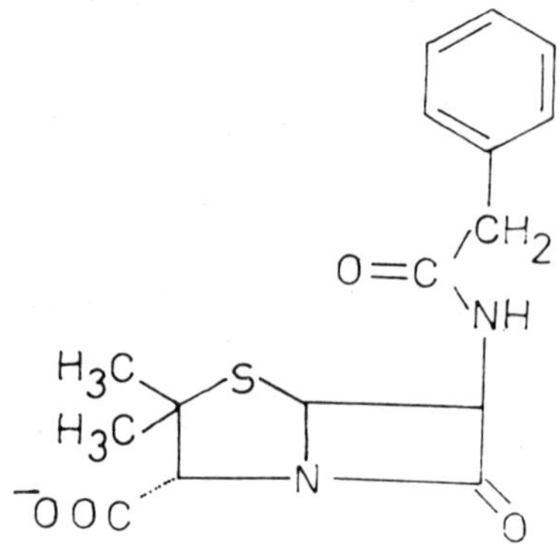

Actions and uses : It has a low solubility and prolonged action, and is therefore used for sustained action therapy. It maintains benzyl-penicillin level in blood. Its action and uses are similar to benzyl penicillin.

AMPICILLIN

Ampicillin is an odourless, white micro-crystalline powder with a bitter taste. It is slightly soluble in water and almost insoluble in alcohol, ether, chloroform and acetone. It should be stored in air tight containers below 25°C.

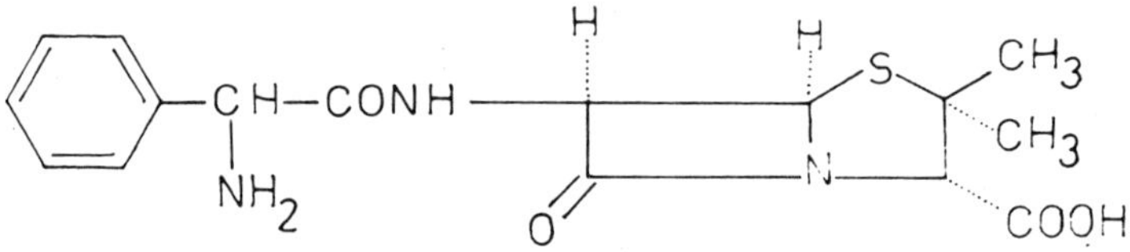

IUPAC Name : 6-(_-D-phenyl glycylamino) penicillinic acid.

Actions and uses: Ampicillin is a semisynthetic acid resistant compound which can be given orally, while its sodium salts are given parenterally. Ampicillin is also available as trihydrate. It is effective against gram-negative bacteria also. To certain extent it destroys bacterial penicilinase. It is useful against haemophilus-influenzae, and enterobacteriacae, etc. It should not be used in staphylococcal infections.

Officials : Ampicillin I.P.
Ampicillin Capsule I.P.
Ampicillin Sodium I.P.
Ampicillin Injection I.P.

CLOXACILLIN

Cloxacillin is an odourless, white , crystalline hygroscopic powder with bitter taste. It is soluble in water, sparingly soluble in alcohol and very slightly soluble in chloroform. It should be stored in air tight containers below 25°C. The compound hydrolyses in the presence of water.

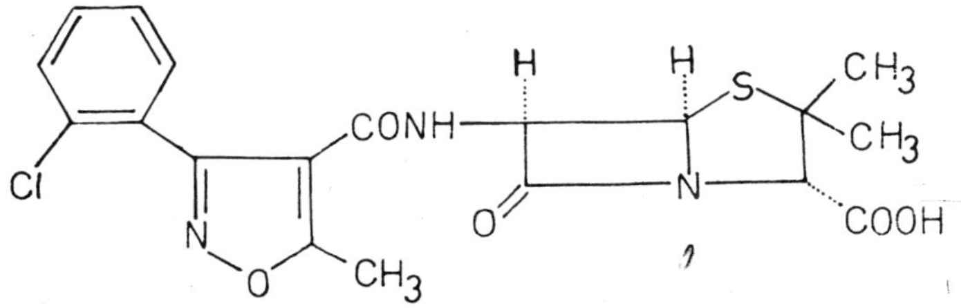

IUPAC Name : 6-[3-(2-chlorophenyl)-5-methylisoxazole-4-carboxamido) penicillanic acid.

Actions and uses : It is used in the treatment of penicillinase resistant staphylococcal infections. It is not effective against gram-negative organism, but in combination with Ampicillin it is used for gram-negative bacilli in urinary tract infection. It is stable in gastric acid and can be given orally.

Officials : Cloxacillin Sodium. I.P.
Cloxacillin Capsules Injection I.P.

CARBENICILLIN

Carbenicillin is an odourless, white , hygrosocpic powder, with a bitter taste. It is soluble in water and alcohol but practically insoluble in ether and chloroform. It should be stored in well closed containers, protected from light, below 5°C.

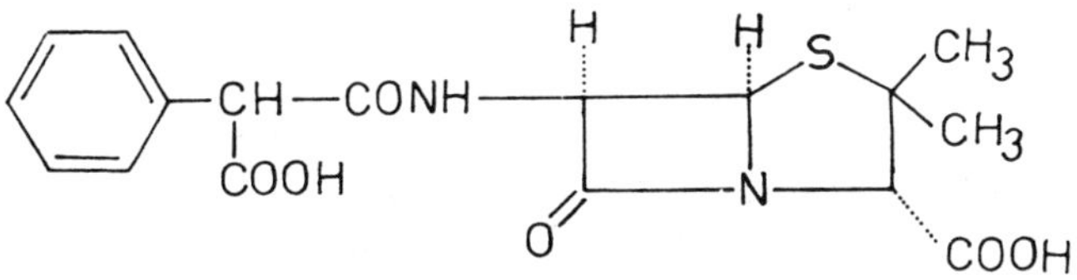

IUPAC Name :- 6 [2-carboxy-2-phenylacetamido] penicillanic acid.

Actions and uses: Carbenicillin is unstable in acid and hence it is not administered orally. An indanyl ester is more stable in gastric pH and is used for oral therapy. It is a IIIrd generation penicillin used in penicillin G resistant species and strains. It is used in the treatment of pseudomonas infections and urinary tract infections caused by gonorrhea, entero bacteriaceae, etc.

CEPHALEXIN

Cephalexin is also a beta-lactum antibiotic. Its antibacterial activity is similar to ampicillin. It is a white to cream coloured hygroscopic powder with a characteristic odour. It is slightly soluble in dilute hydrochloric acid and water; very slightly soluble in alcohol, ether and chloroform. It should be stored in air tight containers, protected from light, below 30°C.

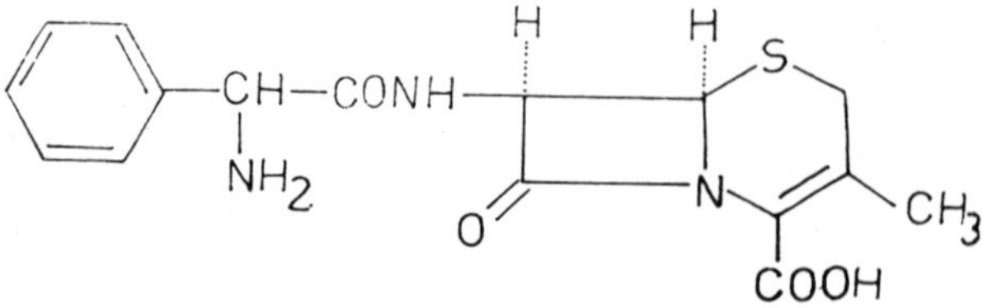

IUPAC Name : 3-methyl-7-[α-D phenyl glylcylamino] ceph-3-ene-4-Carboxylic acid.

Actions and uses: Cephalexin is a first generation cephalosporin. It is used against respiratory infections caused by pneumococcus, staphylococcus, streptococcus, H-influenza, bone and joint infections, skin infections, urinary tract infections, etc. The side effects of cephalexin are vomiting, diarrhoea, skin rashes, nausea, etc.

CEPHALOTHIN

Cephalothin is an odourless, white to off white crystalline, hygroscopic powder which decomposes on heating. It is freely soluble in water, saline and dextrose solution, slightly soluble in alcohol and insoluble in organic solvents. It should be stored in air tight containers protected from light below 25°C. Cephalothin is available as its sodium salt.

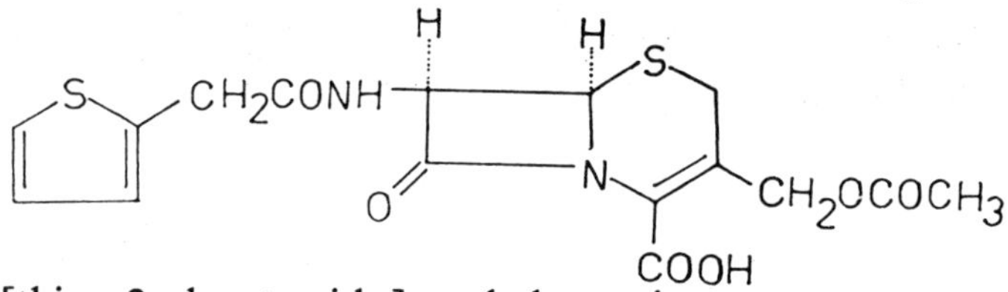

IUPAC Name : 7 [thien-2-ylacetamido] cephalosporin.

Actions and uses: It is not affected by penicillinase and hence used against pencillinase producing strains. It is recommended to those patients who are allergic to penicillin or does not respond to penicillin G . It is also used in the treatment of staphylococcal and pneumococcal .Side effects include eosinophillia, leukopenia, rashes and urticaria .

CEPHALORIDINE

Cephaloridine is a white crystalline powder having slightly pyridine like odour. It is soluble in water .

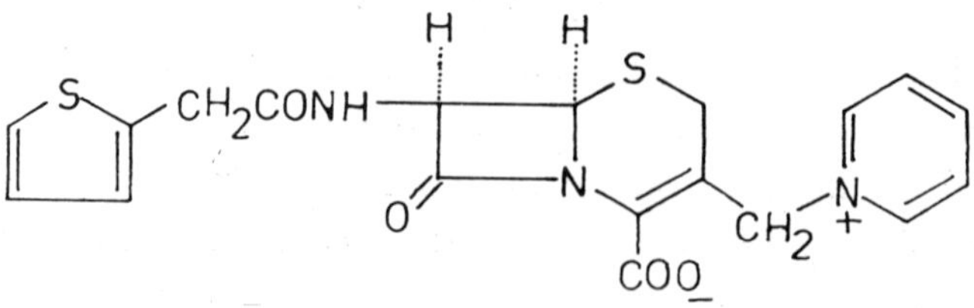

IUPAC Name : 7-(2 thienyl lactamido)-3-cephem-3 yl methyl pyridinium-4-carboxy acid.

Actions and uses: It is used in the treatment of urinary tract and respiratory infections caused by penicillin resistant staphylococci . Potency of this drug is reduced by the presence of penicillinase and abolished by cephalosporinase. It causes less renal damage as compared to other cephalosporins.

Official : Cephaloridine I.P.
Cephaloridine Injection I.P.

GENTAMYCIN

Gentamycin is a mixture of gentamicin C_1, gentamicin C_{1A} and gentamicin C_2. This mixture is produced by Micromonospora purpurea. It is closely related to aminoglycosides. It is official as gentamycin sulphate.

Gentamycin sulphate is an odourless, white powder, soluble in water and insoluble in alcohol, acetone and benzene. It should be stored in airtight containers.

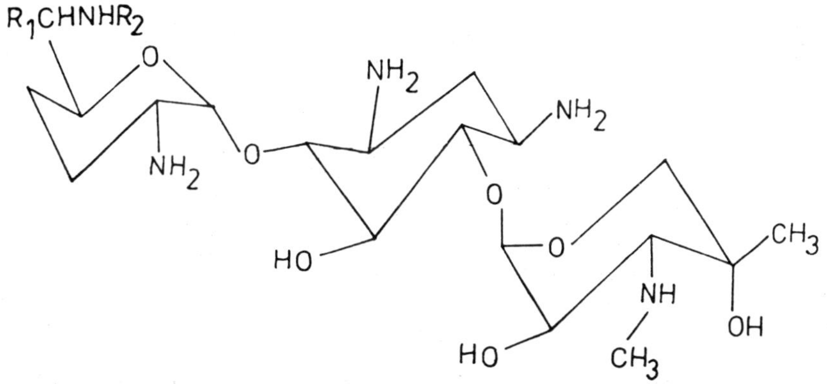

Actions and uses : It has a broad spectrum antibacterial activity. It is very useful in the treatment of Gram negative bacteria. Gentamycin is an effective antibiotic for pseudomonas infections. It is also used topically in the treatment of impetigo, bed sores, nasal staphylococcal infections etc.

Officials: Gentamycin Sulphate I.P.
Gentamycin Injection I.P.

NEOMYCIN

Neomycin is an aminoglycosidal antibiotic, produced by the growth of *Streptomyces fradiae*. It is also a mixture of three compounds neomycin B,C and A; out of which 'A' is inactive.

Neomycin sulphate is an odourless, hygroscopic and white to yellowish white powder. It is soluble in water, very slightly soluble in alcohol; and insoluble in acetone, chloroform and ether. It should be stored in airtight containers, protected from light, below 30°C.

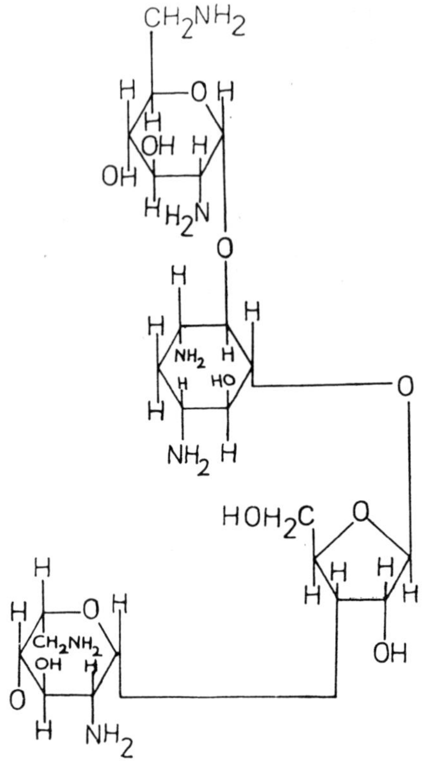

Actions and uses: Neomycin is a broad spectrum antibiotic. It is effective against gram positive infections like *C. diphtheriae, M.tuberculosis, S. aureus,* etc. and gram negative infections like *E.coli, Enterobacter, Bordetalla pertussis,* etc. as Gram negative organism. It is widely used on infected dermatoses, burns, wounds, ulcers, conjunctivitis, etc.

Officials : Neomycin Sulphate I.P

ERYTHROMYCIN

Erythromycin is a macrolide containing macrocyclic lactones containing 12-20 carbons antibiotic. It is produced by strains of *Streptomyces erythreus*. It is a mixture of erythromycin A, B and C; out of which 'A' is present in large quantity. Erythromycin readily forms salts with inorganic and organic acid and also forms esters. The official salts available are erythromycin estolate ,erythromycin ethyl-succinate and erythromycin stearate.

Erythromycin estolate is an odurless, tasteless and white crystalline powder. It is soluble in chloroform but very slightly soluble in water. It should be stored in airtight containers, protected from light.

Erythromycin ethylsuccinate and erythromycin stearates share all the properties of estolate salt but these compounds are yellow in colour and E. stearate salt is soluble in water and acetone. These salts are tasteless while erythromycin is bitter in taste, therefore its salts are recommended for oral therapy. They are stored in airtight containers, protected from light, below 30°C.

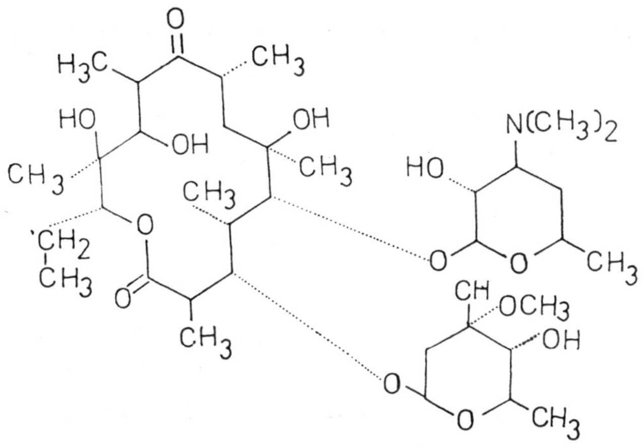

Actions and uses : Erythromycin has a similar spectrum as that of penicillin. The drug is effective against both penicillin sensitive and penicillin resistant strains. It serves mainly as a reserve drug for penicillin resistance or in penicillin allergic conditions .

It is effective against Gram -positive cocci such as enterococci, pneumococci, streptococci and S. aureus. It is also effective against N. meningitis,N. gonorrhoea, C. diphtheria, etc. The drug is an antibiotic of choice in Pneumonia, Diphtheria, Food poisoning, etc. It is also effective against Gram negative bacteria . Erythromycin is usually given as enteric coated tablets while its estolate and stearate salts are more stable in gastric juice.

Officials :

Erythromycin, I.P.
Erythromycin Tablet, I.P.
Erythromycin Estolate, I.P.
Erythromycin Estolate Tablet, I.P.
Erythromycin Sterate, I.P.
Erythromycin Sterate Tablets I.P.

TETRACYCLINES

Tetracyclines are broad spectrum bacteriostatic antibiotics. Chemically they are phenyl anthracence (naphthalene) derivatives. They bind 30" S ribosomal sub unit of the bacteria and prevent tRNA from combining with mRNA, therefore protein synthesis is inhibited. They are broad spectrum antibiotics, active against gram positive and gram negative bacteria, rickettsiae, etc. It forms a crystalline salt with strong acids and bases. They are yellow in colour and bitter in taste. Tetracyclins are produced by the growth of *Streptomyces aureofaciens*. Tetracyclines act as ligand to form a complex with various metal ions. It also forms complex with calcium, therefore it is not administered with calcium diet. e.g. Milk, Antacid containig calcium salt, etc.

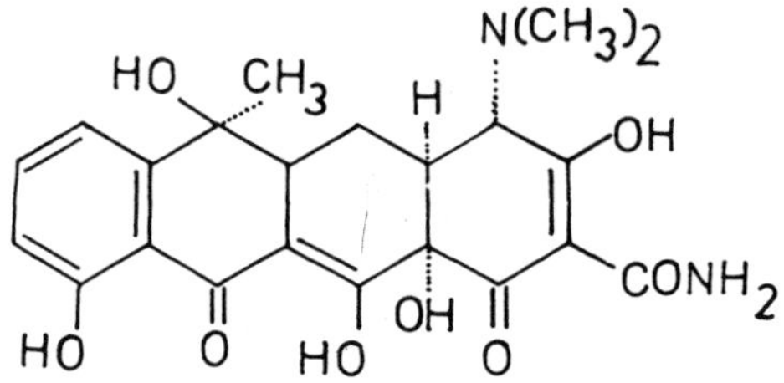

IUPAC Name : 4-dimethyl amino-1,4,4a,5,5a,6,11,12a-octahydro-octahydro-3,6,10,12,12a-pentahydrox-3,6,10,12,12a-penta hydroxy-6- methyl-1, 11,-dioxo naphthacene -2-carboxamide. (Tetracyclin)

Actions and uses : Tetracyclin alone is the drug of choice in the treatment of cholera relapsing fever and other infections like pneumonia and gonorrhea. It is a second choice of drug in the treatment of actinomycosis, rat bite fever, plague, syphilis, tetanus and staphylococcal infections. It is also a drug of choice in cholera and urinary tract infections.

Tetracyclins cause gastrointestinal toxicity by local irritation and alteration of intestinal flora leading to nausea, vomiting, diarrhoea and esophageal ulceration, etc. It may also cause hypersensitivity, hepatotoxicity, reversible cerebral toxicity, etc.

Officials :

Dimethyl chloro tetracycline Hydrochloride, I.P.
Dimethyl chloro tetracycline Capsules, I.P.
Doxycycline Hydrochloride, I.P.
Doxycycline Capsule, I.P.
Oxy-tetracycline, I.P.
Oxy-tetracycline Injection, I.P.
Oxy-tetracycline Hydrochloride, I.P.
Oxy-tetracycline Capsules, I.P.
Oxy-tetracycline Eye Ointment, I.P.
Oxy-tetracycline Hydrochloride Injection, I.P.
Tetracycline, I.P.

Tetracycline Hydrochloride, I.P.
Tetracycline Capsules, I.P.
Tetracycline Eye Ointment, I.P.
Tetracycline Injections, I.P.
Tetracycline Tablets, I.P.

CHLORAMPHENICOL

Chloramphenicol is obtained from the culture of *Streptomyces venezuleae*. It can also be synthesized chemically. It is available as odourless, fine white to greyish white or yellowish white, needle like crystals and bitter in taste. It is freely soluble in alcohol and sparingly soluble in water. It is soluble in water. It is rapidly destroyed in alkaline solution. It is also available as chloramphenicol palmitate and chloramphenicol sodium succinate. Both these salts are palatable in taste and hydrolysed in the body to chloramphenicol. The sodium succinate salt is freely soluble in water while palmitate salt is insoluble in water but soluble in acetone and chloroform. It should be stored in air tight containers protected from light.

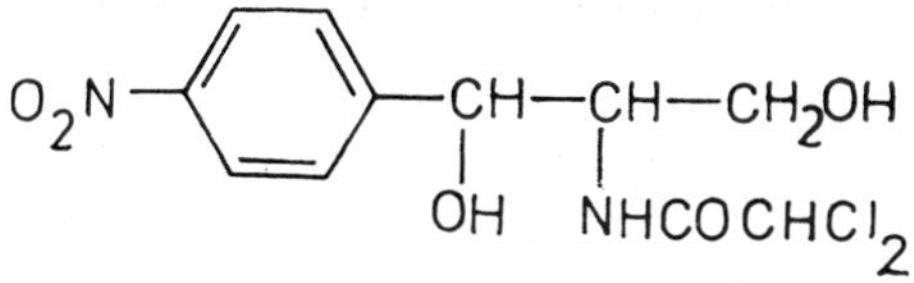

IUPAC Name : 2,2-dichloro-N-[(α- R, ßR)-ß-hydroxy--hydroxy methyl-4-nitro-phen ethyl] acetamide.

Actions and uses: Chloramphenicol is a wide spectrum antibactrial agent. The drug is effective in rickettsial infections and many other bacterial infections caused by *E.coli, K. pneumoniae, B. Pertussis, V.cholera, staphylococcus, streptococcous, actinomycetes*, etc.

The drug is still a choice for typhoid fever and, in combination with ampicillin for meningitis. Topically it is used in conjunctival infection.

Toxic effects of chloramphenicol are bone marrow injury, granulocytopenia and aplastic anemia. Aplastic anemia can also be precipitated even on topical application.

Officials :
Chloroamphenicol, I.P.
Chloroamphenicol, Capsules, I.P
Chloroamphenicol, Eye Ointment, I.P.
Chloroamphenicol, Palmitate, I.P.
Chloroamphenicol, Palmitate Oral Suspenison, I.p.
Chloroamphenicol, Sodium Succinate, I.P.
Chloroamphenicol, Sodium Succinate Injection, I.P.

(1) Benzyl penicillin : Alembic : Benzyl Penicillin : vials are given only as directed by the physician.

(2) Phenoxy methyl penicillin : HAL : Kaypentabs: Adults : 125-500mg 4-6 times daily.
Children : 10mg/kg/dose.

(3) Benzathine penicillin : Wyth : Penidure vials : Vials as directed by physician.
Alembic : Pencomvial : Vials as directed by physician.
Hal : Longacillin : Inj as directed by the physician.

(4) Cloxacillin : Biochem : Biocillin cap & vials.
PCI : Synthocillin cap & vials.
Torrent : Torcillin : vials.

(5) Ampicillin : Biochem : Ampilox : Cap & vials & syrup.
Bluecross : Blueclox : vials & cap. 250mg Ampicillin+250 mg (cloxacillin) for adults.

(6) Carbenicillin : Biochem : Biopence : 1-5gm IV or 1-2gm in every 4-6 hours upto 30gm in or 0gm daily.
German Remedes : Pyopen : vials.

(7) Gentamycin : Fulford : Garamycin vials : Adults : 3-5mg/kg body wt..
Core : Gentamycin vials : Children : 5-7.5mg/kg/24 hrs.

(8) Neomycin : Unichem : Neomycin sulphate cap. : Adults : 0.25-1gm four times.
Children : 12.5mg/kg/dose orally.

(9) Erythromycin : Alembic : Althrocin tabs, drops, liquids ; Adults : 250-500mg 3-4 times daily.
T.D.P.L. : Etomin tab, sus : Children : 30-50mg/kg/24 hrs.

(10) Tetracycline : Dabur : Tetracycline tab : Adults : 1gm daily in 2-4 divided doses.
IDPL : Threocycline cap : Children : 25-30mg/kg body wt. daily in 3 doses.

(11) Cephalexin : Searle : Nufex tab.: 1-4 gm. daily for 4 days on empty stomach.
Ranbaxy : Sporidex cap : Children : 25-30mg/kg body wt.daily for 4 days.

(12) Cephaloridne : Biochem .: Cephaxining : 500mg. IM or I.V. 2-3 times daily.
Children : 15-30 body wt.

(13) Griseafulvin : CFL : Cricactin terte : Adults : 250 mg. tid.
Children : 10mg/kg body wt daily.
Glaxo : Gnsovin F.P. : 500-1000 daily in 4 div doses with meals.

(14) Chloramphenicol : Boehringer M : Chloramphenicol syp : Adults : 50mg/kg body wt. daily.
Mac : Kemicitive cap vials : 50-100/kg body wt.

CHAPTER - 8

ANTIFUNGAL DRUGS

Fungi comprise five widely different class of flora. The variations in the cell physiology and in bio-chemistry are diverse. Most of the chemicals used as antifungal agents are narrow spectrum. Broad spectrum antifungal agents are generally toxic, irritant and have less absorption through epidermis. Most of the antifungal agents are fungistatic. The various fungal infections of hair mucous membrane, skin and nails are caused by genera" Candida [condidiasis] , Epidermophyton", Microsporum and Trichophyton (Tinea, ringworm). Certain antibiotics are also used for fungistatic action. e.g. Griseofulvin and amphotericin B.

CLASSIFICATION : Antifungal drugs can be classified as under :

(1) Antifungal Antibiotics
- (A) Griseofulvin.
- (B) Polyenes-Nystatin, Hamycin, Amphotericin, Hachimycin.

(2) Synthetic Antifungal agents
- (A) Dapsone.
- (B) Co-trimoxazole (Sulphomethoxazole-trimethoprim).
- (C) Imidazoles : Clotrimazole, Miconazole, Econazole, Ketoconazole.

(3) Miscellaneous Antifungal Agents :
- (A) Tolnaftate.
- (B) Undecylenic acid.

GRISEOFULVIN

It is an antifungal substance produced by the culture of *Penicillium griseofuluum*.It is a white to pink-cream colour odourless and tasteless powder. It is soluble in chloroform, sparingly soluble in alcohol and very slightly soluble in water. It should be stored in well closed containers.

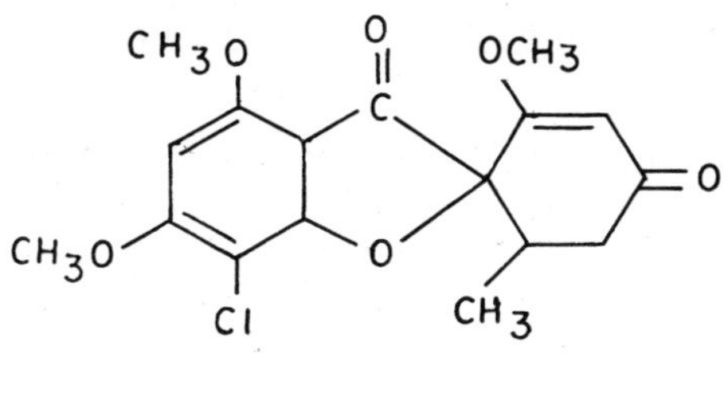

IUPAC Name : 7-chloro-2',4,6-trimethoxy-6'methyl benzofuran 2-spiro-1"-cyclohex- 2'-ene-3,4'-dione.

Actions and uses : Griseofulvin is a fungistatic and arrests reproduction of the organism. It is given systematically in the management of various species of Tinea and Microsporom. Treatment of fungal infections by griseofulvin may relapse frequently because it does not kill the fungi. It is also used in the management of cutaneous inflammatory conditions and several polyarthritis syndromes.

Officials : Griseofulvin I.P.
Griseofulvin Tablets I.P.

NYSTATIN

Nystatin is a polyene antifungal antibiotic. *Streptomyces noursei* strain is used to produce nystatin. It is a yellow to light brown hygroscopic powder with a characteristic odour. It is very slightly soluble in water, alcohol and methyl alcohol, practically insoluble in ether and chloroform. It should be stored in air tight containers protected from light below 5°C.

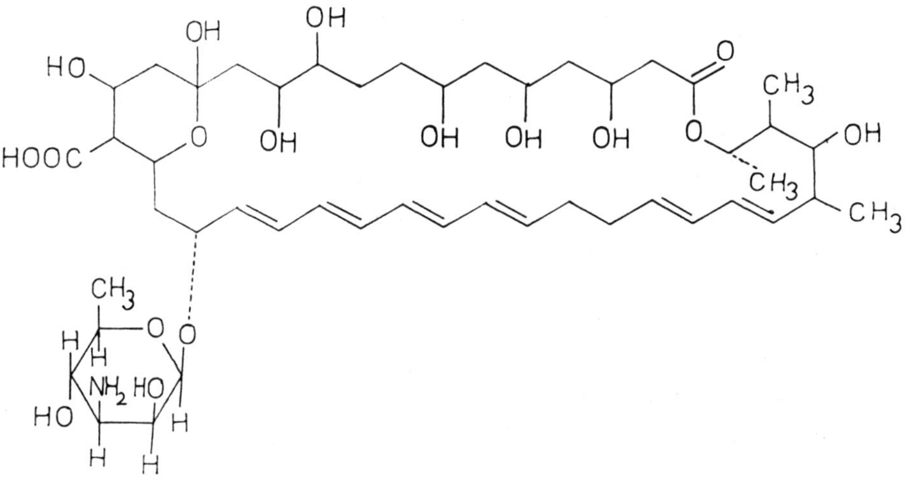

Actions and uses : It is active against a wide range of fungi and yeast. It is poorly absorbed after oral administration and is not absorbed through skin and mucosa. It is used in the treatment of candidal infection of mouth, skin and nails.

AMPHOTERICIN

It is a polyene antibiotic obtained from the strain of *(Streptomyces nodasus)*. It is an odorless, yellow to orange powder. It is insoluble in water, alcohol and ether. It should be stored in air tight containers protected from light and stored at a temperature between 2 to 10°C.

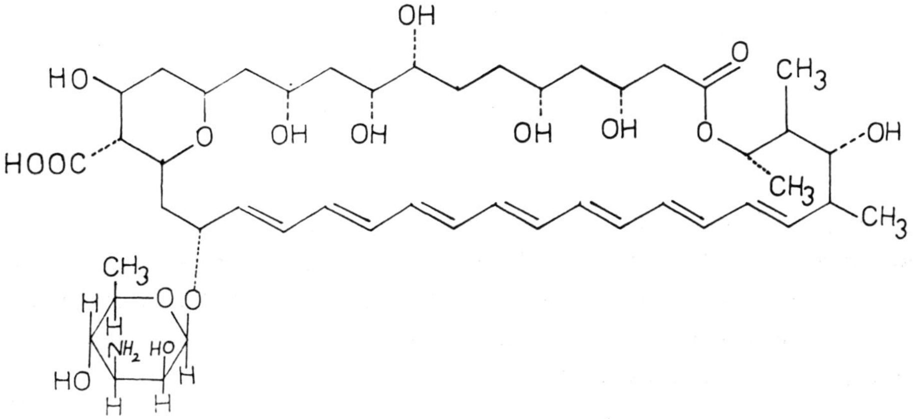

Actions and uses : It is a wide-spectrum antifungal. It acts systematically on various fungus like Coccididomycosis, systemic moniliasis, histoplosmosis, phycomycosis etc. This drug should not be given with saline dextrose injection because it is precipitated by sodium chloride. It is also incompatible with heparin (anticoagulant).

HAMYCIN

It is a polyene antifungal antibiotic obtained from the strains of *Streptomyces pimprina*. It is a yellow amorphous powder. It is practically insoluble in water, benzene, chloroform and ether, but soluble in basic solvents such as pyridine.

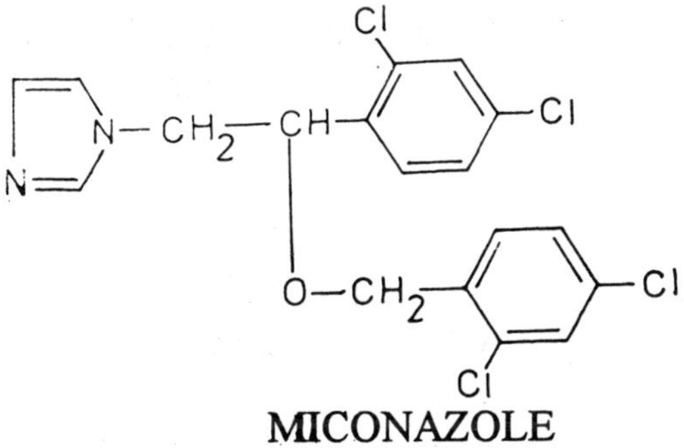

MICONAZOLE

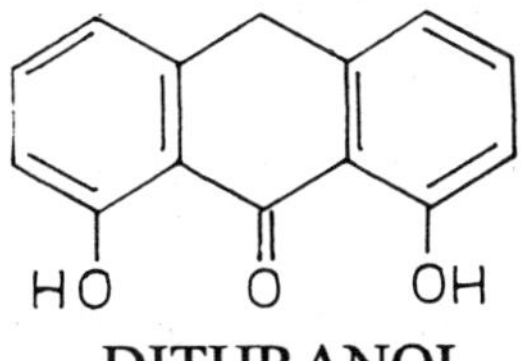

DITHRANOL

Actions and uses: Hamycin has been used as antifungal and anti-trichomonal properties. Structurally it was believed to be identical to trichomycene and candicidin.

TOLNAFTATE

It is an odourless, white to creamy white fine powder. It is freely soluble in chloroform, sparingly soluble in ether, slightly soluble in alcohol and insoluble in water.

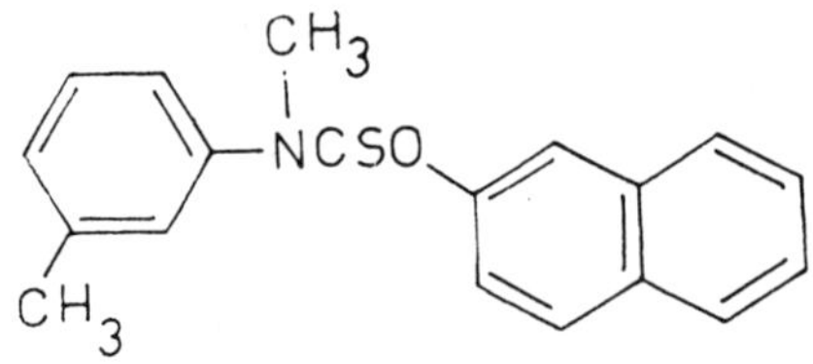

IUPAC Name : O-Naphth-2-yl N-Methyl-m-tolylthio-carbanilate.

Actions and uses : It is used in the superficial treatment of fungi like Tinea pedis [athlete foot] and other species of Tinea, epidermophyton floccosum. It is ineffective against infection of hairs and nails, and relapses are common. It is ineffective over the thick horny layers like soles and palms.

UNDECYLENIC ACID

It is a colourless or pale yellow liquid or a white or pale yellow crystalline mass with characteristic odour. It is miscible with alcohol, ether, chloroform, fixed and volatile oils but practically insoluble in water. It should be stored in air-tight containers protected from light.

$$CH_2=CH\text{-}CH_2\text{-}[CH_2]_7COOH$$

IUPAC Name : Undec-10-enoic acid.

Actions and uses : It is a pyrolysis derivative of ricinolic acid obtained from castor oil. It is employed in the treatment of dermatophytosis of head, ears, feet, axilla and Tinea capitis. It is mixed with astringents like zinc to reduce irritation. Some times it is also used in Tinea pedis (Athlete foot.)

Officials : Zinc undecylenate ointment I.P.

(1) Tolnaftate : Dabur : Tinavate cream & soln. : Apply evenly to affected area and rub gently 2-3 times daily.
Jagsonpal : Tolsol Soln.

(2) Nystatin : Sarabhai : Kenacomb ont. : With rubbing gently on the affected area.
Sarabhai : Mycostatin tab.

(3) Amphoterecin : Sarabhai : Talsutin vag. tab.: 1-2 tab. daily inserted deep in vagina using applicator.

(4) Hamycin : Hin.Anti.Ltd. : Hamycin sus : Apply to affected area with sterile cotton 2-3 times daily.

CHAPTER - 9

ANTIMALARIALS

Malaria is a widespread infectious disease caused by protozoan parasite (species of plasmodium). In human beings malaria may be caused by Plasmodium malariae (Quatran malaria), Plasmodium vivax (benign malaria), P.falciparum (malignant tertian malaria), P.ovale (ovale tertian malaria). These plasmodiums are found in female anaphales mosquito, which is a primary host of the protozoa . They are transmitted to human beings by the bite of mosquito (present in saliva of infected mosquito).

Man is a secondary host and during bite mosquito injects sporozoites into blood circulation. These sporozoites get attached to the parenchymal cells of liver and multiply vegetatively to forms merozoites. On maturity these merozoites are liberated in blood stream and enter in erythrocytes for erythrocytic cycle or schizogony. After schizogony haem is liberated from hemoglobin by the rupture of erythrocytes. This produces shivering and elevation in body temperature as well as reduction in R.B.C. count. At this stage symptoms of malaria arise.

In 1643 European countries used to import cinchona plant from peru, which is capable of suppressing the disease. Later various semisynthetic and synthetic derivatives are synthesized for the treatment of malaria.

CLASSIFICATION :

(1) Cinchona alkaloids : Quinine, cinchonine
(2) 4-amino quinolines : Amodiaquine, Chloroquine.
(3) 8-amino quinolines : Primaquine.
(4) Acridine derivative : Quinacrine.
(5) Biguanides : Proguanil, chloroproguanil.
(6) Diaminopyrimidine : pyrimethamine.
(7) Miscellaneous : Trimethoprim, Mefloquine.

QUININE

Quinine alkaloid are present in the bark of plant ***Cinchona officinales***. The plant is grown in Peru, Jawa and other parts of South America. This plant contains 6 to 10% of quinine alkaloid. Quinine is available as quinine sulphate. These are white fine needle like crystals which are odourless, very bitter in taste and when exposed to light become light brown. It is soluble in water and alcohol. The alkaloid quinine is insoluble in water but soluble in organic solvents. It should be stored in air tight containers.

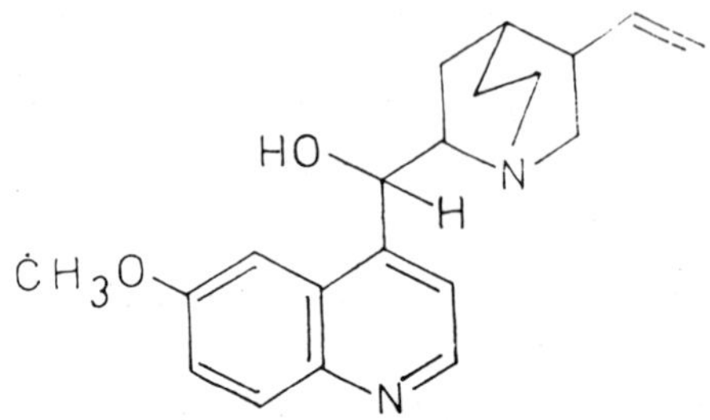

IUPAC Name : α -(6-methoxy-quinolin-4-yl)- α -[(2R,4S,5R)-(5-vinylquinuclidin-2-yl)]-methanol.

Actions and Uses : Quinine only affects the erythrocytic cycle of plasmodium and acts as schizonticidal. It is used as a suppressive in the management of acute attack of P. vivax, malariae, and ovale and also affects falciparum. Quinine in combination with pyrimethamine and sulfadiazine is the choice of treatment for chloroquine resistant cases. Quinine has been largely replaced by new drugs, but resistance to newer drugs makes quinine more superior. Quinine is also used in Thomsen's disease, nocturnal leg cramps,and as an abortifacient.

Officials : Quinine Bisulphate I.P.
Quinine Bisulphate, Tablets I.P.
Quinine Dihydrochloride I.P.
Quinine Dihydrochloride Injection I.P.
Quinine Sulphate I.P.
Quinine Sulphate Tablets I.P.
Quinine Ethyl Carbonate I.P.
Quinine Hydrochloride I.P.
Quinine Hydrochloride Tablet I.P.
Quinine and Urethane Injection I.P.

CHLOROQUINE

Chloroquine is available as a hydrochloride and phosphate salt. Chloroquine-phosphate is an odourless white powder with a bitter taste. It discolours on exposure to light. It is freely soluble in water, practically insoluble in alcohol, chloroform and in ether. It should be stored in well closed containers protected from light.

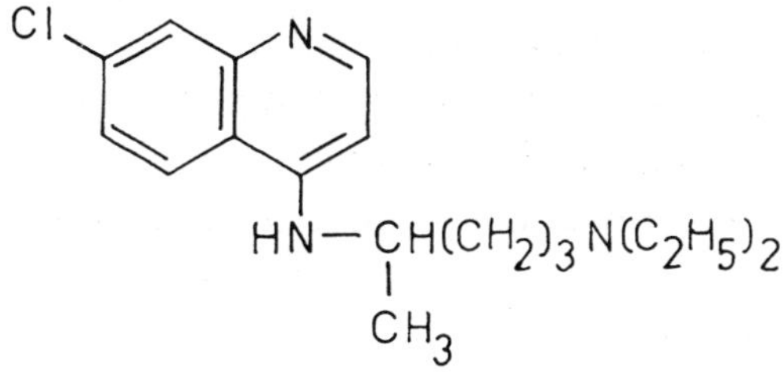

IUPAC Name : 7-chloro-4-(4-diethylamino-1-methyl-butylamino) quinoline.

Actions and uses: Chloroquine prevent or terminates clinical symptoms of malaria by suppressing or by killing malaria schizonts at all stages of erythrocytic cycle. It does not effect the sporozoites or merozoites present in liver. It is active against all species of plasmodium except falciparum. Chloroquine is also effective against extra intestinal amoebiasis especially amoebic hepatitis.

Officials : Chloroquine Phosphate I.P.
Chloroquine Sulphate I.P.
Chloroquine Sulphate Injection/Tablet I.P.
Chloroquine Sulphate Injection, I.P.
Chloroquine Sulphate Tablets, I.P.

AMODIAQUINE

Amodiaquine is available as amodiaquine hydrochloride. It is a yellow crystalline powder, odourless and bitter in taste. It is soluble in water, sparingly soluble in alcohol and very slightly soluble in chloroform and ether. It should be stored in air tight containers.

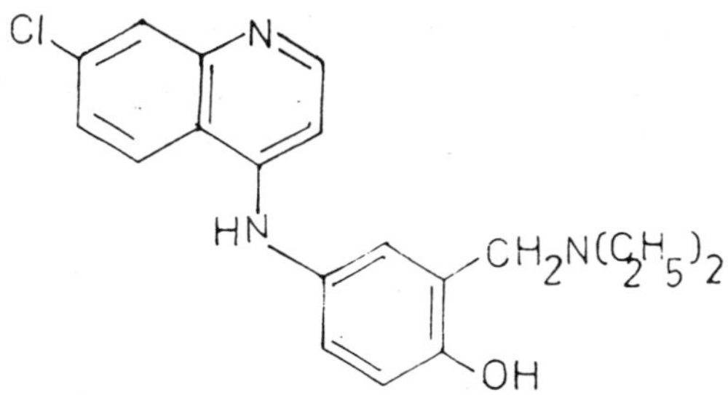

IUPAC Name : 4-(7-chloroquinol-4-ylamino)-2-(diethylaminomethyl)-phenol

Actions and uses: Amodiaquin has similar actions and uses as chloroquine. It can also cure malaria caused by *plasmodium falciparum* by eradicating parasites from erythrocytes. It is also used in the treatment of lupus erythematosus, giardiasis and extra intestinal amoebiasis.

Officials: Amodiaquine Hydrochloride I.P.
Amodiquine Tablets I.P.

PRIMAQUINE

Primaquine is a 8 aminoquinoline derivative and is available as a phosphate salt. It is an odourless orange red crystalline powder which is bitter in taste. It is slightly soluble in water, practically insoluble in alcohol, ether and chloroform. It should be stored in well closed containers protected from light.

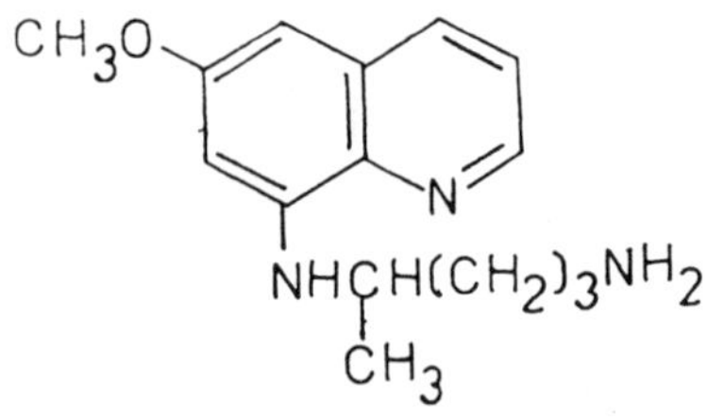

IUPAC Name : 8-(4-Amino-1-methylbutylamino)-6-methyoxyquinoline.

Actions and uses: It is used to prevent relapse of malaria. It is also used for the persons returning from malaria's area to cure plasmodium infections. It kills plasmodium at exo erythrocytic stage and also gametocytes but does not affect erthrocytic form. It affects erythrocytic stage of only P. falciparum. It is generally not recommended for acute infections. For this stage it is given in combination with chloroquin or amodiaquine. (schizonticidal).

Officials : Primaquine Phosphate I.P.
Primaquine Tablets I.P.

PROGUANIL

Proguanil is a biguanide derivative and available as hydrochloride salt. It is an odourless, white crystalline powder with a bitter taste. It is slightly soluble in alcohol water and very slightly soluble in ether and chloroform. It is a hygroscopic compound and should be stored in well closed containers.

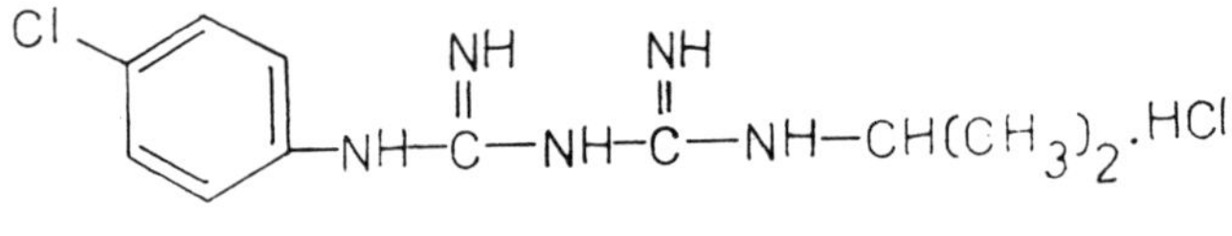

IUPAC Name : 1-(4-Chlorophenyl)-5-isopropyl biguanide.

Actions and uses: The action of proguanil depends upon the formation of active metabolic cycloguanil. It kills parasites undergoing schizogony in the red blood cells and tissue, therefore acts as causal prophylactic and cures radically. It does not kill gametocytes.

Officials : Proguanil Hydrochloride I.P.
Proguanil Tablets I.P.

PYRIMETHAMINE

Pyrimethamine is a diamino pyrimidine derivative. It is an odourless and white crystalline powder. It is soluble in warm, dilute mineral acids, slightly soluble in alcohol and chloroform and is insoluble in water. It should be stored in well closed containers.

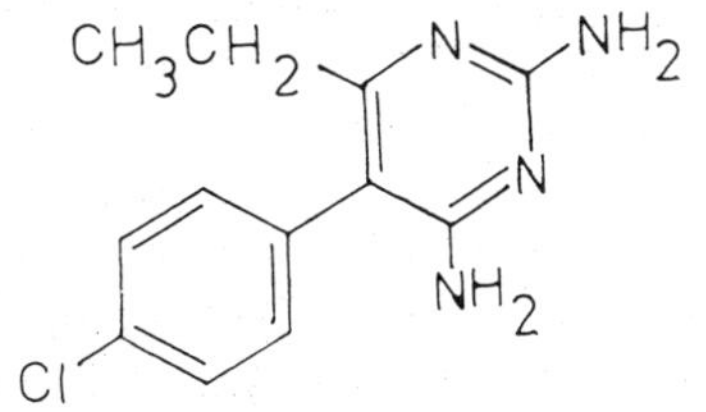

IUPAC Name : 5-(4-chlorophenyl)-6-ethylpyrimidine-2,4,-diamine.

Actions and uses: Pyrimethamine is an antimalarial drug with similar use as proguanil hydrochloride. It is slow to control a malarial attack. It affects the nucleoprotein metabolism of parasites by interfering in the folic-folinic acid system. It usually kills the primary exoerythrocytic stage and also effects gametocytes.

Officials : Pyrimethamine. I.P.
Pyrimethamine and Sulphadoxine Tablets I.P.

TRIMETHOPRIM

Trimethoprim is an odourless white powder with a bitter taste. It is slightly soluble in water, alcohol and chloroform insoluble in ether. It should be stored in well closed containers protected from light.

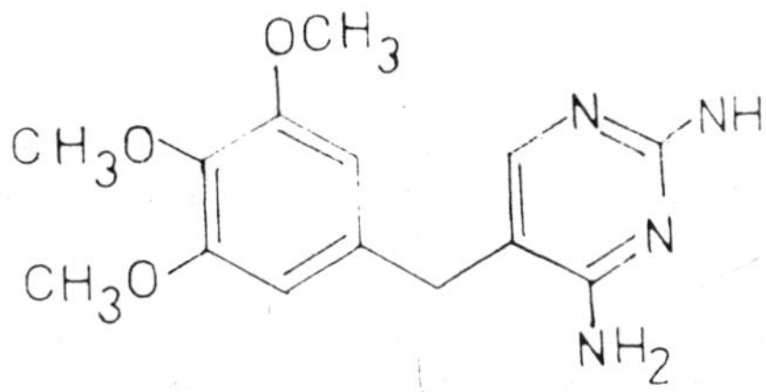

IUPAC Name : 5-(3,4,5-Trimethoxy benzyl) pyrimidine -2,4-diamine.

Actions and uses: Trimethoprim is an antibacterial agent similar to sulfonamides. It inhibits bacterial dihydrofolate reductases which neutralises the substrate. It is used in combination with sulfonamides in the treatment of malaria due to susceptible strains of plasmodium falciparum. It is an important ingredient of co-trimoxazole.

Officials : Trimethoprim I.P.

(1) Chloroquine : IPCA : Larigo tab. inj. susp.
Rhonepouletic : Nivaquine p tab. inj. susp.
P.C.I. : Malaquin tab. :

Adults : Initially 600mg, after 6 hours 300mg followed by 300mg daily for 2 days. inj. IM 10ml. after 6 hrs 5ml followed by 5ml daily for 2 days.

(2) Amodiaquine : Parke davis : Camoquin Tab.
Adults : 10mg/kg body wt. as a single dose. Children : 10mg/kg body wt.

(3) Primaquine : Unicure : Primaline tab. : 15ml daily for 14 days along with std. chloroquine therapy.

(4) Proguanil : Unicure : Laveran tab. : 200mg daily for adults.

(5) Pyrimethamine : Helics : Malicure tabs.
Plethico : Reziz tab. susp.
Adults : Prophylaxiz 1 tab. once a week; Treatment : 2 tabs. in single dose.
Children : 3/4 to 1 tab. depending upon the age as a single dose.

(6) Quinine : Clipa : Quinarsol.
P.C.I.: Rubiquin Tabs.
Adults : 300-600mg three times daily for 5-7 days.
Children : 25mg/kg/day div. every hour for 7 days.

CHAPTER - 10

TRANQUILIZERS

The term tranquilization or ataraxia can be defined in various ways but all are synonyms of "peace of mind". Originally the term was used for psychic effects of reserpine and chlorpromazine which makes a person calm without causing hypnosis or anesthesia. The main object in psychiatric therapy is to induce an improved mental state in mentally disturbed patients. These agents are effective in the condition of excitation, agitation, aggressiveness and impulsiveness by suppressing central nervous system.

CLASSIFICATION : Tranquilizers can be classified in two categories :

(1) **Major Tranquilizers or Anti-psychotics** - These drugs reduce agitation and disturbed behavior associated with hallucinations. These are classified as :

- (a) **Phenothiazines** : Chlorpromazine, Prochlorperazine
- (b) **Rauwolfia alkaloids** : Reserpine
- (c) **Butyrophenones** : Haloperidol, Trifluperidol
- (d) **Thioxanthines** : Thiothixene
- (e) **Indolic derivatives** : Molindone
- (f) **Miscellaneous** : Oxypertine

(2) **Minor Tranquilizers or Antianxiety drugs** : These drugs have a calming effect in anxiety states associated with neurotic personality or physical disease (situational crisis). These are classified as :

- (a) **Benzodiazepines** : Diazepam, Lorazepam, Chlordiazepoxide
- (b) **Miscellaneous** : Meprobamate, Buspirone

CHLORPROMAZINE

Chlorpromazine is an odourless white or creamy white powder or waxy solid. It is soluble in chloroform, ether, alcohol and practically insoluble in water. It should be stored in well closed container, protected from light. Its hydrochloride salt is soluble in water and is incompatible with phenobarbitone sodium.

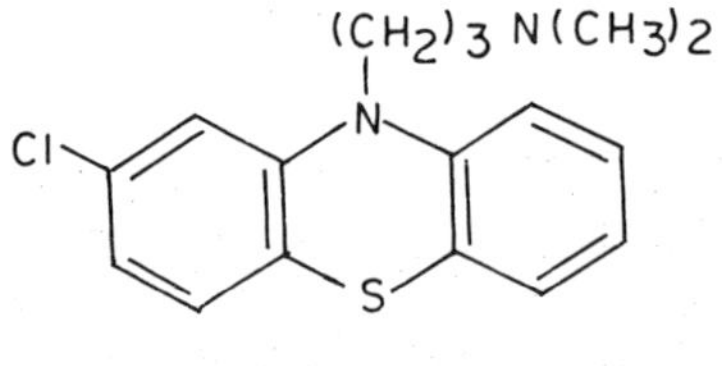

IUPAC Name : 2-Chloro-10-(3-dimethylaminopropyl) phenothiazine.

Actions and uses: Chlorpromazine is a central nervous depressant which blocks dopamine receptors. It has a weaker antihistaminic action and strong local anesthetic action. It reduces the efficiency of heat regulating centres so that vasodilatation produces a fall in blood pressure, but does not reduces cardiac output. It reduces salivary and gastric secretions and acts as a transient antiadrenergic. It is successfully used in several psychomotor excitements.

Officials : Chlorpromazine Hydrochloride, I.P.
Chlorpromazine Injection, I.P.
Chlorpromazine Tablets, I.P.

PROCHLORPERAZINE

Prochlorperazine is available as maleate salt. The salt is an almost odourless white or pale-yellow crystalline powder with a slightly bitter taste. The drug is practically insoluble in ether but very slightly soluble in water and alcohol. It should be stored in well closed containers, protected from light.

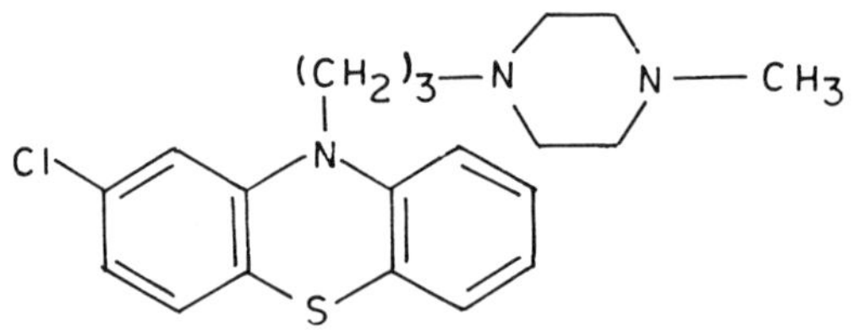

IUPAC Name : 2-Chloro-10-[3-(4-methyl-1-piperazin-1-yl) propyl]-10H-phenothiazine.

Actions and uses: Prochlorperazine has actions and uses similar to chlorpromazine hydrochloride. It is less sedative and more effective as an antiemetic drug, therefore it is used for the prevention and relief of vomiting. The side effects are parkinsonisms and drowsiness.

TRIFLUOPERAZINE

It is available as a hydrochloride salt. It is an odourless, hygroscopic, white to pale yellow, crystalline powder with a bitter taste. It is soluble in water, very slightly soluble in alcohol and practically insoluble in ether. It should be stored in air tight containers protected from light.

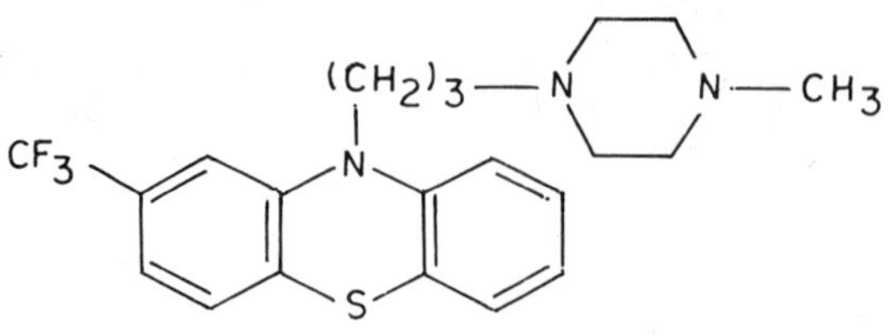

IUPAC Name : 10-[3-(4-Methyl piperazin-1-yl)-propyl]-2- (trifluoromethyl)-10H-phenothiazine.

Actions and uses: Its action and uses are similar to chlorpromazine hydrochloride but is effective in much smaller dose. It can be given to those patients who do not respond to chlorpromazine. It acts rapidly in blocking conditioned response and as an antiemetic. It may cause drowsiness and dizziness.

Officials : Trifluoperazine Hydrochloride, I.P.
Trifluoperazine Tablets, I.P.

HALOPERIDOL

Haloperidol is a butyrophenone. It is an odourless, tasteless, white to yellowish powder. It is soluble in chloroform, slightly soluble in chloroform and ether and practically insoluble in water. It should be stored in well closed containers.

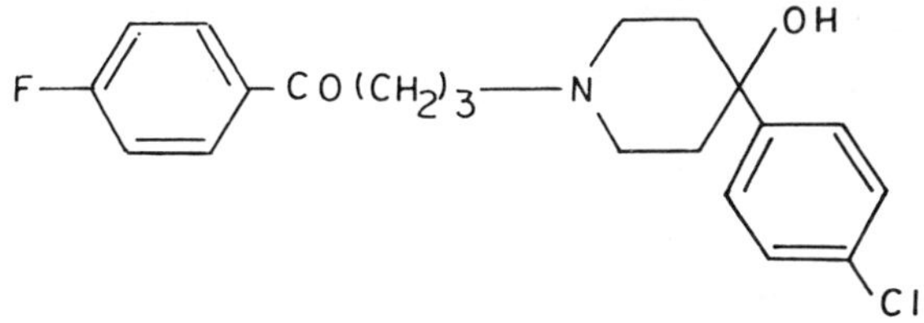

IUPAC Name : 4-[4-(p-Chlorophenyl)-4-hydroxy pipieridino]-4'-fluorobutyrophenone.

Actions and uses: Haloperidol is a selective central nervous system depressant. It is used in the management of severe agitation, anxiety, tension, hallucinations, hyperactivity, etc. Usually it is recommended in mania, hypomania and in chronic psychoses. It is a powerful antiemetic and enhances the action of barbiturates, analgesics and other central nervous system depressants.

Officials : Haloperidol Injection, I.P.
Haloperidol Tablets, I.P.

TRIPERIDOL

Triperidol is a white crystalline powder with a slight odour and is slightly soluble in water. It should be stored in well closed containers protected from light.

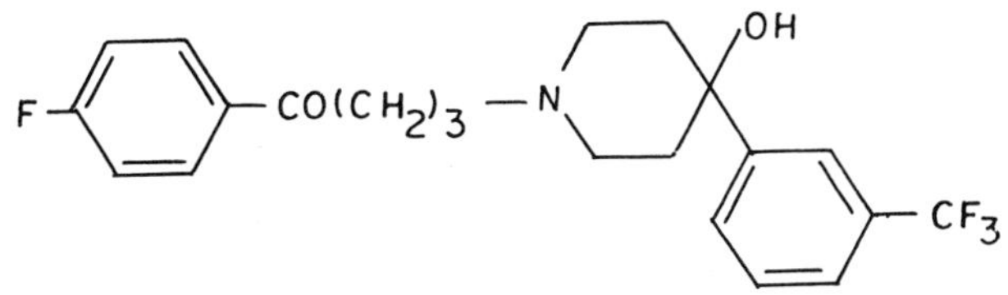

IUPAC Name : 4'-Fluoro-4-[4-hydroxy-4(α,α,α-trifluoro-m-tolyl) piperidino] butyrophenone.

Actions and uses: It has actions and uses similar to haloperidol.

THIOTHIXENE

Thiothixene is a white to tan coloured, almost odourless crystalline powder. It is slightly soluble in alcohol, ether and practically insoluble in water. It should be stored in air tight containers protected from light. It is available as hydrochloride salts. The salt is soluble in water.

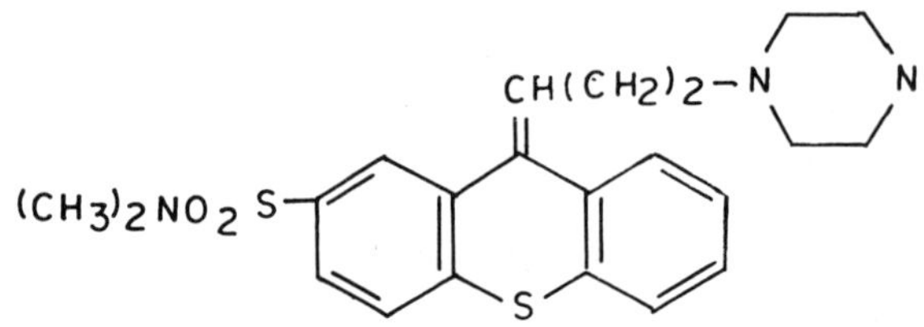

IUPAC Name: N,N-Dimethyl-9-[3-(4-methyl-piperazine-1-yl) propydine] thioxanthene- 2-sulphonamide.

Actions and uses: Thiothixene is a thioxanthene neuroleptic agent having action and uses similar to phenothiazine and chlorpromazine.

OXYPERTINE

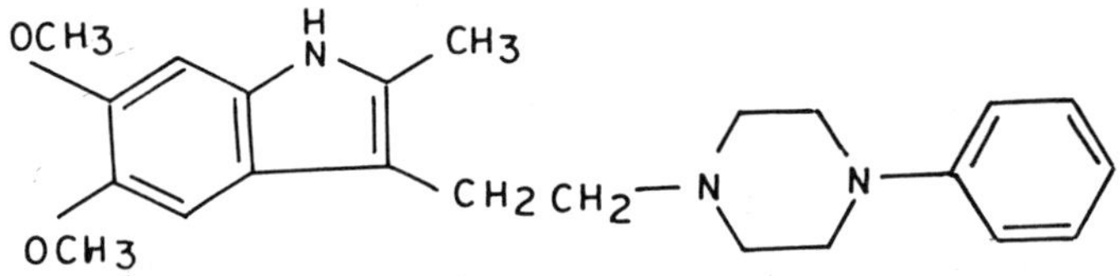

IUPAC Name : 5,6-Dimethoxy-2-methyl-3-[2-(4-phenyl-1-piperazinyl) ethyl]-1-H-indole.

Actions and uses: Oxypertine has similar neuroleptic actions as thiothıxene. It is used in the treatment of psychoses. The side effects are similar to phenothiazines.

CHLORDIAZEPOXIDE

Chlorodiazepoxide is available as a hydrochloride salt. It is a white crystalline powder, very bitter in taste and with a slight odour. It is soluble in water, sparingly soluble in alcohol and very slightly soluble in chloroform and ether. It should be stored in airtight containers protected from light.

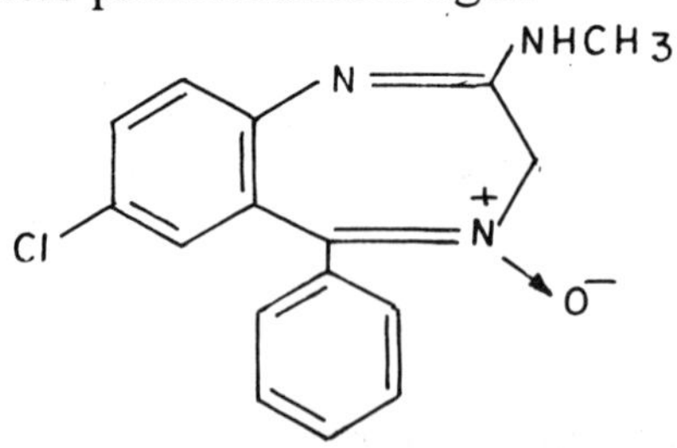

IUPAC Name: 7-Chloro-N-methyl-5-phenyl-3H-1,4-benzodiazepin-2-(1H)-one.

Actions and uses: Chlordiazepoxide relieves nervous tension and anxiety, thereby acts as a tranquilizer. It also possesses muscle relaxant activity. Its side effects are addiction and abuse.

Officials : Chlordiazepoxide, I.P.
Chlordiazepoxide, Tablets, I.P.

DIAZEPAM

It is a white crystalline, odourless powder. It is soluble in chloroform and alcohol, slightly soluble in ether and very slightly soluble in water. It should be stored in airtight containers protected from light.

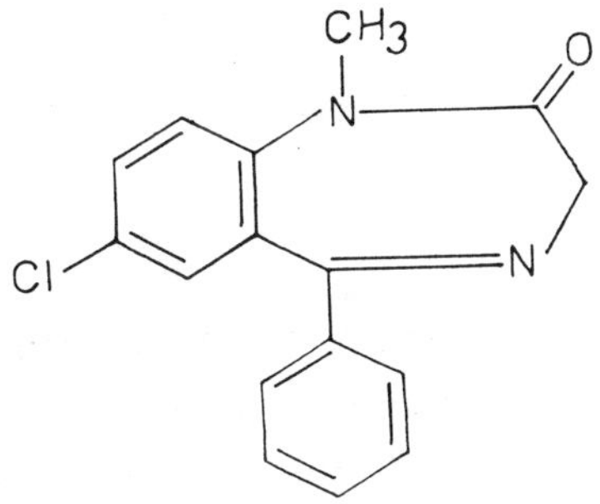

IUPAC Name : 7-Chloro-1,3-dihydro-1-methyl-5-phenyl-2H-1,4, benzodiazepin-2-one.

Actions and uses: Diazepam is a benzodiazepine derivative. Its actions and uses are similar to chlordiazepoxide. It is used to control muscle spasms in tetanus and in the management of alcohol withdrawl symptoms. It is also given in minor surgery to calm patients.

OFFICIALS : Diazepam, I.P.
Diazepam Capsule, I.P.
Diazepam Tablets, I.P.

LORAZEPAM

Lorazepam is a benzodiazepene derivative. It is an odourless, white to off white powder. It is slightly soluble in alcohol and chloroform, but practically insoluble in water. It should be stored in well closed containers.

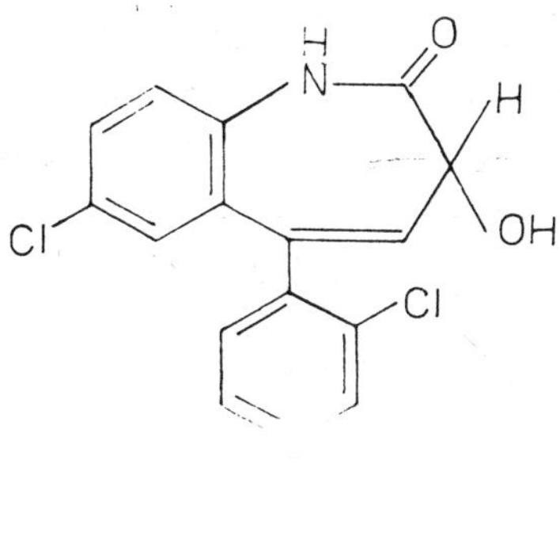

IUPAC Name : 7-Chloro-5[2-chlorophenyl] 1,3,-dihydro-3-hydroxy-2H-1,4-benzodiazepin-2-one.

Actions and uses: Lorazepam is a pre-anesthetic medication, produces sedation and decrease ability to recall events related to surgery. Other actions are similar to diazepam. Its side effects are weakness and dizziness.

MEPROBAMATE

Meprobamate is an odourless, white, granular crystalline aggregate with a bitter characteristic taste and soluble in alcohol, slightly soluble in ether and almost insoluble in water.

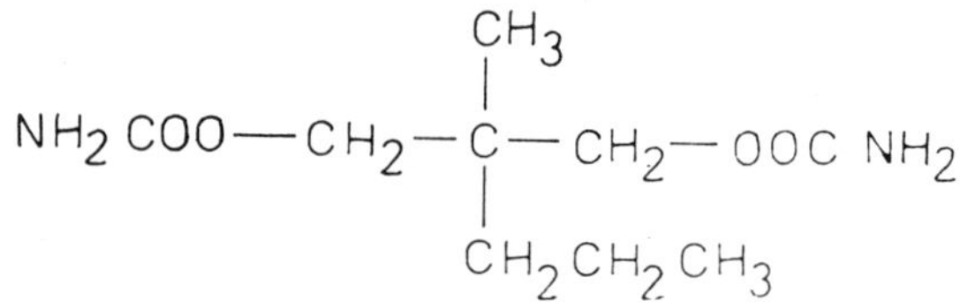

IUPAC Name : 2-methyl-2-propyl trimethylene dicarbamate.

Actions and uses: It is used in the treatment of psychoneuratic disorders when anxiety and nervous tensions are present. It also possesses anticonvulsant and muscle relaxant properties.

Officials : Meprobamate I.P.
Meprobamate Tablets, I.P.

(1) Chlorpromazine : Rheon Poulanc : Chlorpromazine tabs.
La Pharma : Emetil : Adults : 25 mg thrice daily.
Children : Depending upon the age.

(2) Prochlorperazine : Rheon poulanc : Stemetil : inj. are given 12.5mg deep.

(3)Trifuloperazine : Intas : Neocalm Plus tab.
Torrent : Trinicalm tab.
Adults : 5-10 mg daily orally 2.5 mg two times daily.
Children :6 years age and above : 1mg 1-2 times a day.

(4) Haloperidol : Searle : Serenace tab. liquid inj. : As directed by the physician.
La pharma : Benzydol 5mg, 10mg, 1.5mg tab.

(5) Chlordiazepoxide : Jagsonpal : Equarex Tabs.
Roche : Librium tabs. Adults : 20-40 mg daily.
Children : 5-10mg daily.

(6) Diazepam : Ranbaxy : Calmpose syp. inj.
Roche : Valium tabs. : Adults : 2-10 & 10-30mg at bed time.

CHAPTER - 11

HYPNOTICS AND SEDATIVES

Sedatives are drugs used to allay excitement and reduce motor activity without inducing sleep, while hypnotics help in production of sleep. Both sedative and hypnotic action may be present in the same drug. A small dose of a drug may act as sedative, where as a large dose may act as hypnotic.

Hypnotics have a common ability to induce a non-selective reversible depression of central nervous system. Hypnotics are generally used in insomnia, anxiety and restlessness.

CLASSIFICATION :

(I) Barbiturates	:Phenobarbitone, Butobarbitone, Cyclobarbitone.
(II) Aldehydes	: Paraldehyde, Choral hydrate.
(III) Acetylene derivative	: Ethchlorvynol
(IV) Acyclic compounds	: Ureides
(V) Piperidinediones	: Methyprylone, Glutethimide
(VI) Benzodiazepens	: Nitrazepam
(VII) Imidazopyridines	: Zolpidem, Alpidem

PHENOBARBITONE [Phenobarbital]

Phenobarbitone is an odourless white crystalline powder, slightly bitter in taste. It is soluble in alcohol, ether and chloroform but practically insoluble in water. It should be stored in air tight containers.

Barbiturates act on central synaptic transmission process of reticular activating system to depress cerebral cortex. Barbiturates calm the individual, whose normal electrical activity increases with emotions, tension, anxiety or use of C.N.S. stimulant.

IUPAC Name : 5-Ethyl-5-phenylbarbituric acid.

Actions and uses: Phenobarbitone is a long acting barbiturate. It has the basic property of barbitone and is also used in the treatment of migraine and epilepsy. It reduces the frequency of attacks. It is also available as a sodium salt that is soluble in water.

Officials : Phenobarbitone I.P.
Phenobarbitone Tablets I.P.
Phenobarbitone Sodium I.P.
Phenobarbitone Sodium Injection I.P.
Phenobarbitone Sodium Tablets I.P.

PENTOBARBITONE

Pentobarbitone is an odourless, hygroscopic, white crystalline powder. Its sodium salt is soluble in water. It should be stored in well-closed containers protected from light.

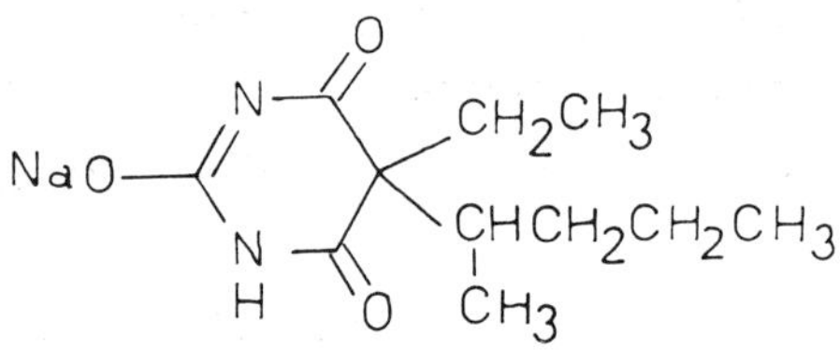

IUPAC Name : 5-Ethyl-5-(1-methyl butyl) barbiturate.

Actions and uses: Pentobarbitone sodium is an intermediate acting barbiturate. Its actions and uses are similar to barbiturates. It is uses as a basal anesthetic in pre-operative conditions.

Officials : Pentobarbitone I.P.
Pentobarbitone Sodium Tablets I.P.

BUTOBARBITONE

It is a colourless or white crystalline powder with a very slight odour and slightly bitter in taste. It is soluble in chloroform, ether and solutions of alkali hydroxides but poorly soluble in water. It is a hygroscopic compound and should be stored in well closed containers.

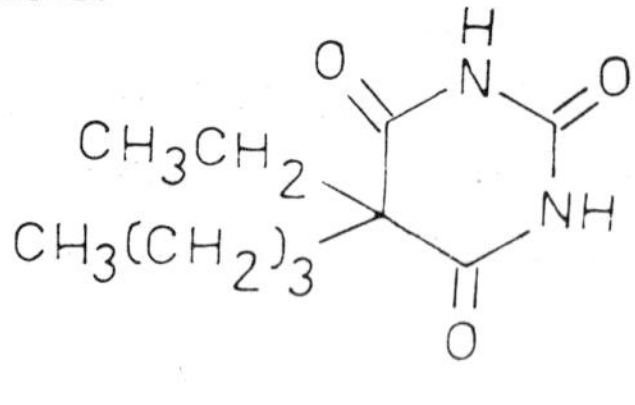

IUPAC Name : 5- Butyl-5-ethylbarbituric acid.

Actions and uses: Butobarbitone is an intermediate acting barbiturate. Its action and uses are similar to barbiturates.

CYCLOBARBITONE

Cyclobarbitone is available as a calcium salt. Its calcium salt is a white or slightly yellowish, odourless crystalline powder with a bitter taste. It is very slightly soluble in alcohol, ether and chloroform. It should be stored in air tight containers.

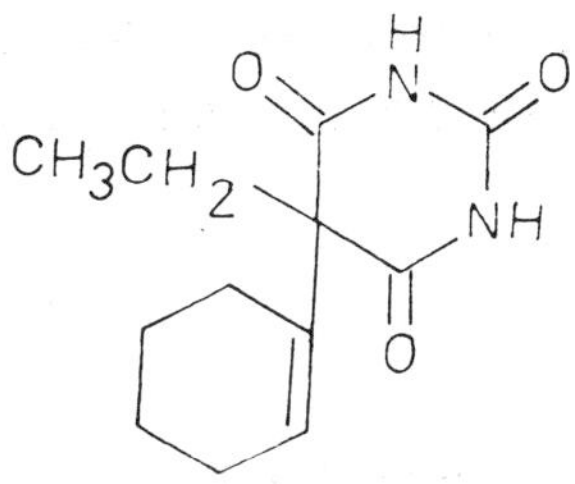

IUPAC Name : 5-[Cyclohex-1-enyl]-5-ethyl barbituric acid.

Actions and uses : Cyclobarbitone is also an intermediate acting barbiturate. Its actions and uses are similar to barbituric acid.

Officials : Cyclobarbitone I.P.
Cyclobarbitone Tablets I.P.
Cyclobarbitone calcium I.P.
Cyclobarbitone calcium Tablets I.P.

PARALDEHYDE

Paraldehyde is a polymer of acetaldehyde. It is soluble in water and miscible with alcohol, ether and chloroform. It should be stored in small well filled, air tight bottles in dark. If it is solidified then contents are mix by liquefaction with the help of gentle heat.

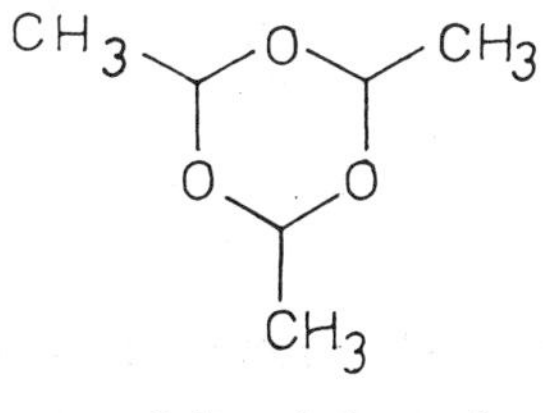

Paraldehyde is a powerful quick-acting hypnotic and anticonvulsant. It is an irritant to mucous membrane unless it has been well diluted.

METHYPRYLONE

Methyprylone is a white crystalline powder having characteristic odour. It is soluble in alcohol, chloroform and ether but sparingly soluble in water. It should be stored in well closed containers.

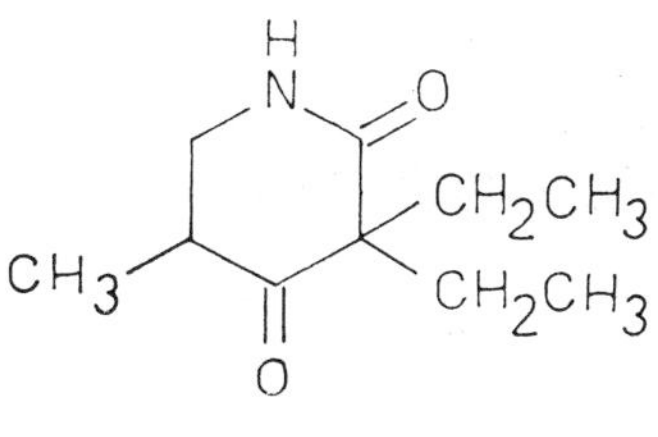

IUPAC Name : 3,3-Diethyl-2,4-dioxo-5-methylpiperidine.

Actions and uses: It is used as a hypnotic and sedative. It induces sleep for 5 to 8 hours and is given orally in the management of insomnia.

GLUTETHIMIDE

Glutethimide is an odourless, colourless or white crystalline powder with a bitter taste. It should be stored in air tight containers protected from light.

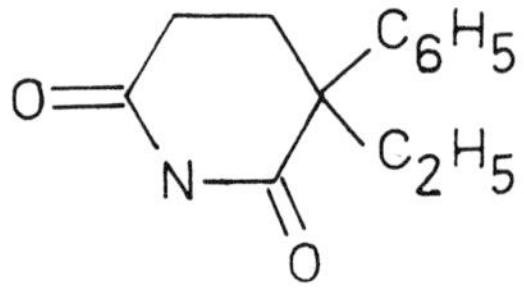

IUPAC Name : 2-Ethyl-2-phenylglutatrimide.

or

3-Ethyl-3-phenyl piperidine-2,6-dione.

Actions and uses: Glutethimide acts as inter-mediate acting barbiturate. It produces sleep that lasts for 4 to 6 hours.

NITRAZEPAM

Nitrazepam is an odourless yellow crystalline powder. It is slightly soluble in chloroform and alcohol but almost insoluble in water and ether. It should be stored in air tight containers protected from light.

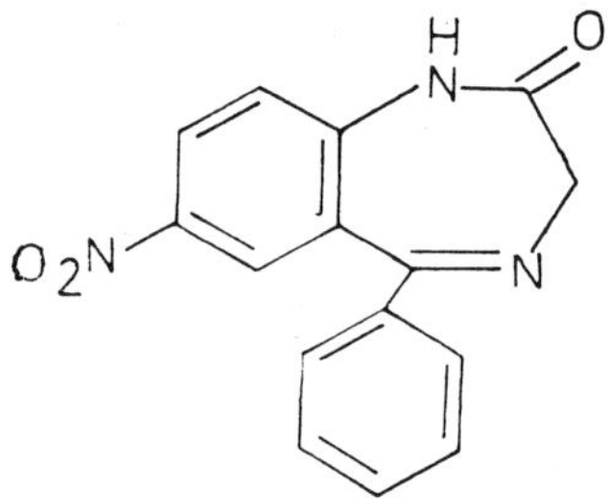

IUPAC Name : 1,3-Dihydro-7-nitro-5-phenyl-2H-1,4-benzodiazepin -2-one.

Actions and uses: Nitrazepam is a hypnotic-sedative but has similar properties as chlordiazepoxide. It produces sleep for 6 to 8 hours.

TRICLOFOS - SODIUM

Triclofos - sodium is an odourless, white hygroscopic powder with saline taste. It should be stored in air - tight containers. It is incompatible with calcium and magnesium salt of heavy metals and alkaloids.

$$CCl_3CH_2\text{-O-}\overset{\overset{\Large O}{\|}}{\underset{\underset{\Large OH}{|}}{P}}\text{-ONa}$$

IUPAC Name : 2,2,2- Trichloro ethyl sodium hydrogen phosphate.

Actions and uses: Trichlofos- sodium is a hypnotic and sedative, and suitable for domiciliary midwifery. The side effects are nausea, headache, and abdominal distension.

(1) **Phenobarbitone** : Rhone-poulanc : Gardenal tab. inj. : Adults:30-200mg per day in divided doses and as directed.
Bayer : Luminal tabs. : Adults : 1,2 tabs.3-4 times daily.

(2) **Nitrozepam** : PCI : Hypnex : Adults : 5-10mg at bed time.
Anglo french : Nitravel : 2.5-5mg at bed time.

(3) **Triclofos sodium** : Glaxo : Trichloryl liquid

CHAPTER - 12

GENERAL ANESTHETICS

The term anesthesia means loss of sensation. Local anesthetics abolish pain sensation in a localised area while general anesthetics bring about loss of all sensations particularly pain with reversible loss of consciousness. Anesthesia proceeds through following stages :

(I) **Stage of Analgesia** : This stage is also called as cortical stage. In this stage gradual depression of cortical centers makes patient sleepy but there is analgesia with retained consciousness.

(II) **Stage of delirium** : It is also called as excitement stage. In this stage depression of higher motor centres cause's excitement and loss of consciousness. In these stage pupils may dilate with marked hypertension.

(III) **Stage of surgical anesthesia** : In this stage smooth muscles are relaxed which is characterised by loss of reflexes, also relaxation of skeletal muscles with regular deep breathing starts. This stage is suitable for surgery.

(IV). **Stage of Medullary paralysis** : It is also called as respiratory paralysis. In this stage depression of respiratory function of medulla and brain stem take's place leading to vasomotor collapse and respiratory failure.

An ideal anesthetic agent should be inert non-inflammable, non-irritant to mucous membranes and non-toxic. It should be potent, produces rapid induction of anesthesia and be compatible with other anesthetics.

CLASSIFICATION : These are classified according to their nature of volatilisation.

(1) Inhalants (Volatile)

(A) **Volatile liquids** : Diethyl ether, Halothane, trichloroethylene.

(B) **Gases** : Cyclopropane, Nitrous-oxide.

(2) Non-volatile or intravenous anesthetics

(A) **Ultra short acting Barbiturates** : Thiopental sodium and methohexital sodium.

(B) **Non-Barbiturates** : Propanidid, ketamine.

HALOTHANE

Halothane is a colourless-mobile heavy liquid with a characteristic odour. It is miscible with dehydrated alcohol, ether and chloroform, but slightly soluble in water. Its boiling point is about 50°C, therefore volatilise in hot climate. It decomposes to halogen acids and free-halogens when exposed to UV-radiation. It should be stored in air-tight containers protected from light below 25°C.

CF_3-CHBrCl OR

```
   F Cl
   |  |
F -C--C-H
   |  |
   F Br
```

IUPAC Name :- 2-Bromo-2-chloro-1,1,1-trifluro ethane.

Actions and uses: Halothane is a volatile anesthetic and is more potent than chloroform and ether. It is non-inflammable, does not cause explosion with oxygen. It neither produces necrosis when spilt on tissue nor produces irritation on mucous-membrane nor skin. An adequate dose of atropine should be administered to the patient before its medication. Its induction is rapid, without signs of excitement, ventricular tachycardia and other cardiac irregularities. It produces moderate deep level of muscle relaxation. It blocks transmission of nerve impulses through ganglion

Officials : Halothane I.P.

DIETHYL ETHER

Diethyl ether contains 0.002% w/v propyl gallate or hydroquinone as stabilizer, to prevent the formation of ether peroxide. It is a clear, colourless, very mobile liquid with a characteristic odour and a sweet burning taste. It is soluble in water and insoluble in alcohol, chloroform, fixed and volatile oils. It is highly inflammable and with certain concentrations of oxygen it causes explosion. It should be stored in dry, air tight containers in a cool place, protected from light. The containers or closer should not contain metal foil.

$$CH_3\text{-}CH_2\text{—}O\text{—}CH_2\text{-}CH_3$$

IUPAC Name : Di-ethyl ether.

Actions and uses : It is less-depressant to medullary centers, causes less fall in blood pressure as well as less depression of respiration. Prolonged use of ether does not produce direct toxic action on the heart, but a transient toxic effect on liver and kidney is seen. It has a wide margin of safety and is given with atropine or hyoscine that inhibit bronchial secretions produced by respiratory stimulation of ether. Ether poisoning should be treated with artificial respiration and care must be taken to prevent collapse.

Official : Anesthetic Ether I.P.

TRICHLOROETHYLENE

Trichloroethylene contains blue colouring matter to distinguish from ether. It is a colourless or pale blue transparent mobile liquid with a characteristic odour resembling chloroform. It is very slightly soluble in water and miscible with dehydrated alcohol, chloroform and ether. It should be stored in air tight containers, in cool place, protected from light (It decomposes on exposure to air and bright light).

```
CH=C-Cl
|   |
Cl  Cl
```

IUPAC Name : 1,1,2-Trichloro ethene.

Actions and uses: It is least volatile but less potent than chloroform and ether. It is neither irritant nor-inflammable. It induces smooth and rapid anesthesia but does not produce deep anesthesia and full muscular relaxation. It may also increase respiratory rate and cardiac irregularities. Its poisoning should be treated by artificial respiration.

CYCLOPROPANE

Cyclopropane is a colourless inflammable gas having a characteristic odour. It is soluble in alcohol, ether, chloroform, water and fixed oils. It is stored in metallic cylinders. These cylinders should with-hold sufficient pressure of compressed gas. It should be stored in special cool room free from inflammable material. The whole cylinder should be painted with orange colour having a chemical symbol " C_3H_6 "of this gas.

```
CH2 ——— CH2
   \     /
     CH2
```

Cyclopropane

Actions and uses: It is a potent gaseous anesthetic and does not produce irritation. Its recovery and induction period are less. It can be administered with oxygen. It may cause respiratory depression, cardiac irregularities and bronchospasm.

METHOHEXITAL SODIUM

Methohexital sodium is a non-volatile anesthetic. Methohexital is available as a sodium salt. The salt is an odourless, white and hygroscopic powder. It is soluble in water. It should be stored in air-tight containers.

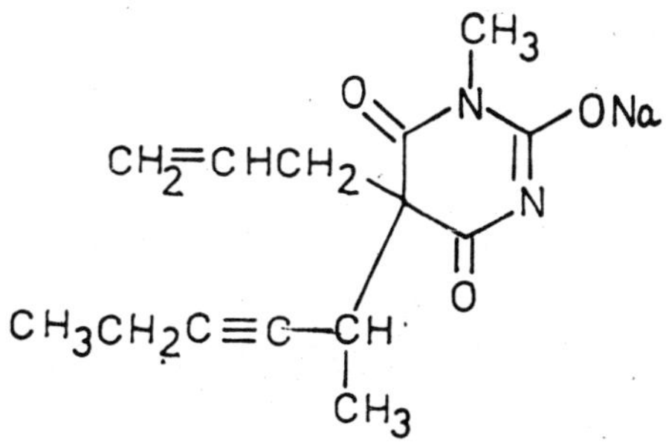

IUPAC Name : 1-methyl [5-allyl,5-(1-methylpent-2-ynyl) barbituric acid sodium.
Actions and uses: Methohexital is a very short acting barbiturate. It is used as an anesthetic for intravenous administration and its actions and uses are same as thiopentone sodium. It is incompatible with acidic substances or acidic solutions.

THIOPENTONE SODIUM

Thiopentone sodium is also non-volatile, barbiturate type of general anesthetic. It is available as a sodium salt. It is a hygroscopic yellowish - white powder with a characteristic alliaceous odour and bitter taste. It is soluble in water and alcohol but insoluble in ether. Its aqueous solution should not be stored more than 24 hours because salt decomposes vigorously. It should be stored in well closed air-tight containers.

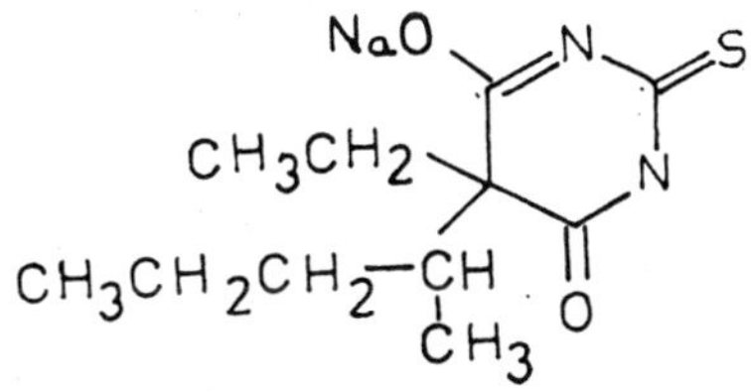

IUPAC Name : 5-Ethyl-5-[1-methylbutyl]-2-thiobarbiturate sodium.
Actions and uses: Thiopentone sodium is a very short acting barbiturate. It is administered intravenously for the induction of general anesthesia as a complete anesthesia for short duration and is therefore useful in short operation as in dental practice. Care should be taken so that none of the solution is injected outside the vein, because it may cause tissue necrosis.

Officials : Thipentone Sodium I.P.
Thiopentone Injection I.P.

(1) **Halothene** : ICI : Fluothane liquid : Adults Induction : Upto 5% in air, O_2 maint:

(2) **Thio pentol sodium** : May & Baker : Intraval Sodium

CHAPTER - 13

LOCAL ANAESTHETICS

Local anaesthetics prevent generation and conduction of nerve impulses. When they are applied to a nerve fibre, the threshold of excitation increases, impulse conduction slows and rate of rise in action potential and amplitude decreases and slowly abolishes generation of action potential. They also bind and block sodium channels which block propagation of impulse, in the nerve tissue. Local anaesthetics are of two types :

(1) Slightly soluble local anesthetics are used for topical application.[they are slowly absorbed and are safe for use on the ulcers, wounds and mucous surfaces].

(II) Soluble local anaesthetics : They are used to anesthetise local tissuse by a direct injection on the tissue or to the nerve supplying the tissue.

Classification

(I) Natural agents : Cocaine

(II) Synthetic nitrogenous compounds :

(A) Derivatives of PABA. : Procaine, benzocaine.

(B) Acetanilide derivative : Lignocaine [Lidocaine].

(C) Quinoline derivative : Cinchocaine.

(III) Synthetic non-nitrogenous compounds : Benzyl alcohol.

(IV) Miscellenous : Clove oil, phenol etc.

PROCAINE

Procaine is available as a hydrochloride salt. The salt is an odourless, colourless or white crystalline powder with a salty or bitter taste followed by numbness. It is soluble in water, slightly soluble in alcohol and very slightly soluble in chloroform. It should be stored in well closed containers protected from light.

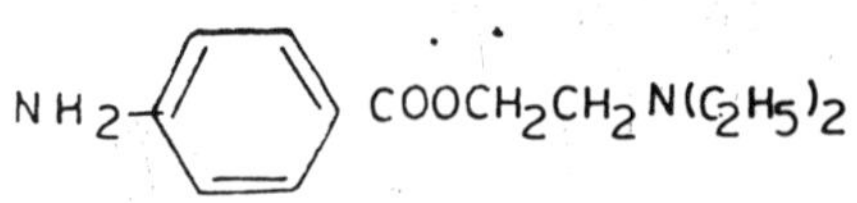

IUPAC Name : 2-Diethyl amino ethyl, 4-amino benzoate.

Actions and uses : Procaine is a short acting local anaesthetic. It is less toxic because of its poor penetration of intact mucous membrane. Procaine should not be given intravenously. It may produce dermatitis. Procaine poisoning should be treated with diazepam or with artificial respiration.

Officials : Procaine, I.P.
Procaine and Adrenaline Injection, I.P.

BENZOCAINE

Benzocaine is a colourless or white crystalline powder with a bitter taste followed by numbness of tongue. It is soluble in chloroform, ether and alcohol but very slightly soluble in water. It should be stored in air tight containers protected from light.

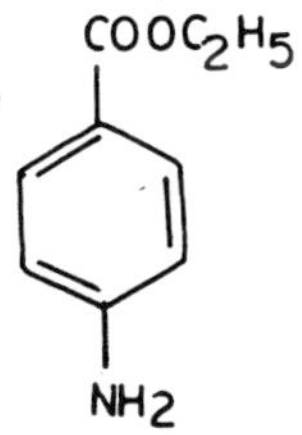

IUPAC Name : Ethyl 4-amino benzoate.

Actions and uses: It is a sparingly soluble salt with less toxicity than cocaine. It can be given orally to relieve pain of gastric carcinoma and in symptomatic treatment of tuberculous laryngitis. It is given as injections in the treatment of pruritus and anal fissure, lozenges are used to prevent nausea and vomiting while ointments are applied on burns and cancerous ulceration, etc.

Officials : Benzocaine Sulphate, I.P.
Benzocaine, I.P.

LIGNOCAINE

Lignocaine is available as lignocaine hydrochloride, which is an odourless, white crystalline powder with a slightly bitter taste followed by numbness. It is soluble in water, alcohol and chloroform and is practically insoluble in ether. It is precipitated in the presence of alkali. It is a hygroscopic compound and should be stored in well closed containers.

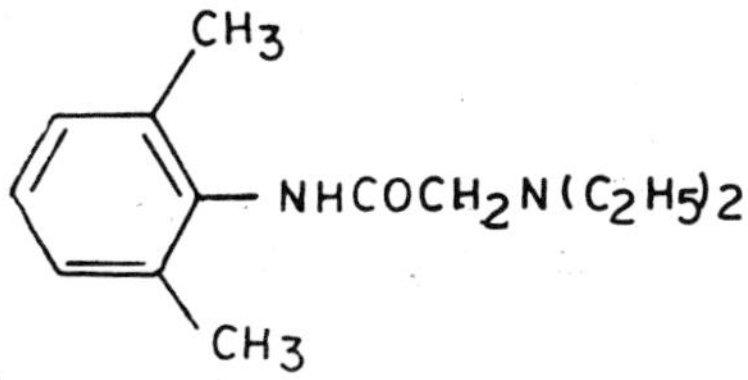

IUPAC Name : NN - Diethyl [(2,6-dimethyl phenyl) carbamoyl] methyl amine.

Actions and uses: Lignocaine is widely used as injections and for local application to mucous membranes. It is used for infiltration with adrenaline. It is also used in the treatment of cardiac arrhythmias and for epidural anaesthesia.

Officials : Lignocaine Hydrochloride, I.P.
Lignocaine and Adrenaline Injection, I.P.

(1) Lidocain : Astra IDL : Xylocard 2% Inj.
S.G. pharma : Gesicard

(2) Benzocain : Parke Davis : Chlormycetin Ear drop

CHAPTER -14

ANTIDEPRESSANTS

Antidepressant drugs are also called as psychic energizers. Antidepressant medication is used to treat endogeneous depression or are helpful in agitated depression and phobic anxiety states. Common symptoms of depression are anxiety, tension, guilty feeling and emotional withdrawls. Severe depression causes depression of C.N.S. and includes suicidal tendencies.

CLASSIFICATION

(I) Mono amine oxidase inhibitors (MAO)

(a) Hydrazine derivatives	:	Phenelzine
(b) Non-hydrazine derivatives	:	Tanycypromine
(II) Tricyclic compounds	:	Imipramine, Nortriptyline,Amitriptyline
(III) Lithium compounds	:	Lithium carbonate
(IV) Miscellaneous	:	Caffeine, Amphetamine.

PHENELZINE

Phenelzine is available as a hydrogen sulphate salt. It is a white powder or is present as pearly platelets with a pungent odour. It is soluble in water, slightly soluble in alcohol, and practically insoluble in ether and chloroform. It should be stored in airtight containers protected from light.

$$C_6H_5\ CH_2\ CH_2\ NHNH_2$$

IUPAC Name : Phenyl ethyl hydrazine.

Actions and uses : Phenelzine is an antidepressant drug. It inhibits monoamine oxidase (MAO) enzyme which influences the metabolism of transmitter substances (Eg. Noradrenaline, 5-hydroxy-treptamine) in the brain. It is used in the treatment of endogeneous depression. The drug should not be withdrawn abruptly because relapse may occur within two days.

TRANYLCYPROMINE

Tranylcypromine is available as a sulphated salt. It is odourless or has a faint odour of cinamaldehyde, and is a white crystalline powder with an acidic taste. It is slightly soluble in water, very slightly soluble in alcohol and ether but practically insoluble in chloroform. It should be stored in well closed containers.

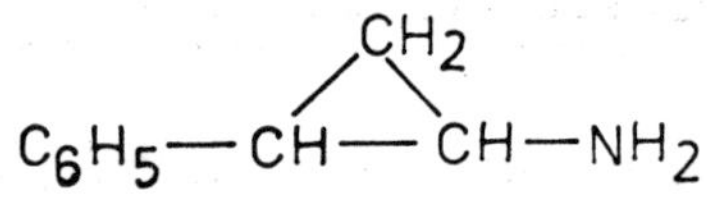

IUPAC Name : 2-phenyl cyclo propyl amine.

Actions and uses : It is also a MAO inhibito Its actions and uses are similar to phenelzine sulphate. It is used for endogeneous and psychoneurotic depression. The side effects are insomnia, dizziness, muscular-weakness, dryness of mouth, etc.

IMIPRAMINE

Imipramine is available as a hydrochloride salt. The salt is an odourless, white or slightly yellow crystalline powder with a bitter taste followed by numbness. It is soluble in chloroform, alcohol and water but very slightly soluble in ether. It is a hygroscopic compound. It is very sensitive to moisture and light. Its degradation increases in the presence of oxygen and water. It should be stored in airtight containers protected from light.

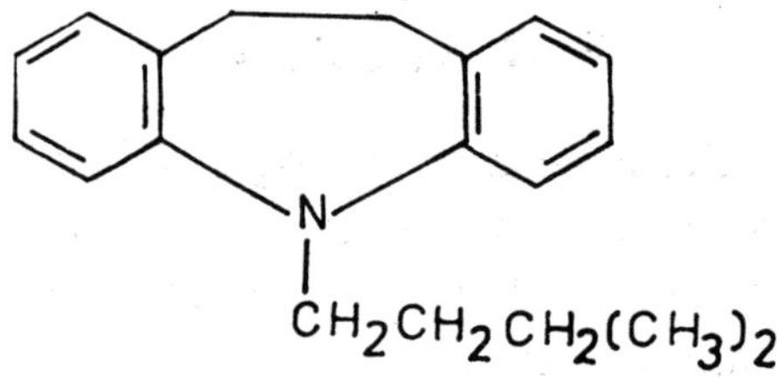

IUPAC Name : 10,11-Dihydro-5-(3-dimethyl amino propyl)- 5H-dibenz-[b,f] azepine

Actions and uses : It is a tricyclic antidepressant. It has weaker anticholinergic activity and less tranquillizing action. It is used to control nocturnal enuresis. This drug should be gradually withdrawn to prevent relapse.

Officials : Imipramine Hydrochloride, I.P.
Imipramine Tablets, I.P.

AMITRIPTYLINE

Amitriptyline is available as hydrochloride and embonate salt. Its hydrochloride salt is an odourless, colourless or white crystalline powder with a bitter burning taste. It is soluble in water, alcohol, chloroform, methanol and insoluble in ether. Its aqueous solution is oxidized in the presence of metal ions for which a chelating agent (Disodium EDTA) is used. It should be stored in airtight containers protected from light.

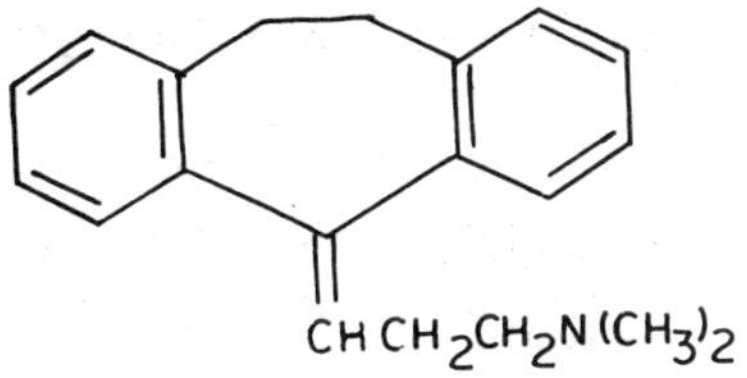

IUPAC Name : 3- (10,11-Dihydro-5H-dibenzo [a,d] cyclohepten-5-yl-idene) propyl-NN-dimethyl amine.

Actions and uses : It is a tricyclic antidepressant. It does not inhibit MAO but blocks the re-uptake of released monoamines into pre-synaptic nerve ending. It also reduces incidence of bed wetting in some children. It may impair alertness when driving car or operating dangerous machinery, so these drugs should be avoided.

Officials : Amitriptyline Hydrochloride, I.P.
Amitriptyline Tablets, I.P.

NORTRYPTYLINE

Nortryptyline is a tricyclic antidepressant. It is available as hydrochloride salt. It is a white powder with slightly characterstic odour, and has a burning and bitter taste followed by numbness. It is soluble in chloroform and alcohol, slightly soluble in water and practically insoluble in ether.It should be stored in well closed containers protected from light.

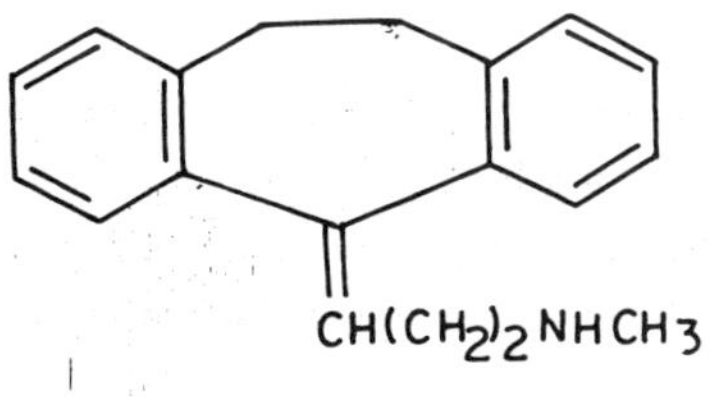

IUPAC Name : N-10,11-Dihydro-5H dibenzo [a,d] chclohepten-5-ylidenepropyl-N-methylamine.

Actions and uses :Its actions and uses are similar to amitriptyline hydrochloride but is less sedative. Its side effects, contra-indications and other properties are also similar to amitriptyline.

(1) Amitriptyline : Merind : Libotryp tab.
Torrent: Amitol
Adults : 10-25mg initially thrice daily increased by 10-25mg every 2nd and 3rd day till opt.

(2) Nortryptyline : Sun pharma : Primox tab.
Wallace : Sensival tab.
Adults : 50-150mg daily in single or divided dose.
Children : Depending upon the age. 6-20mg and as reqd.

(3) Imipramine : SG pharma : Depsonil tab.
Torrent : Antidep tab.
Adults : Initially 75mg a day which is gradually increased to 300mg a day in single bed time dose and as directed.

CHAPTER - 15

ANALEPTICS

Central nervous system stimulants can increase excitability either by blocking inhibition or by enhancing excitation. The agents that enhance excitation are known as analeptics. They stimulate respiratory centre and also increase flow of blood. Analeptic acts upon sensory area of brain and increase alertness, brighten spirits and combat mental fatigue. These drugs are classified as

(1) **Natural agents** : Caffeine, Theophylline.

(2) **Synthetic agents** : Dextro-amphetamine coramine.

CAFFEINE

Caffeine is an alkaloid obtained from tea and coffee. It is an odourless, white or silky white crystalline powder, having a bitter taste. It is soluble in chloroform, slightly soluble in water and very slightly soluble in alcohol. It should be stored in air-tight containers. It is also available as caffeine citrate and caffeine hydrate.

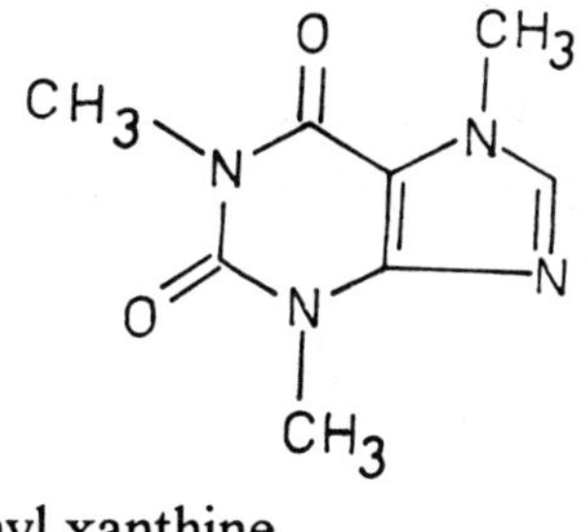

IUPAC Name : 1,3,7-Trimethyl xanthine.

Actions and uses : It is a central nervous system stimulant and a weak diuretic, because it increases renal blood flow. Generally it is given with aspirin, codeine or with ergotamine for the treatment of migraine.

Officials : Caffeine I.P.
Caffeine Citrate, I.P.

THEOPHYLLINE

Theophylline is also a xanthine derivative [alkaloid]. The drug is isolated from tea, coffee and coco plant. It is an odourless, white crystalline powder with a bitter taste.

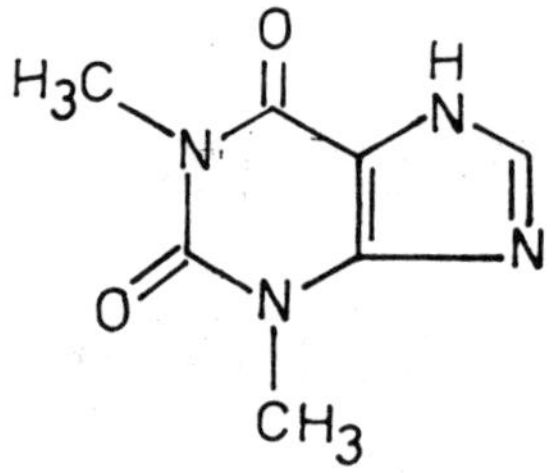

IUPAC Name : 1,3 -Dimethyl xanthine.

Actions and uses: Theophylline has actions similar to caffeine but it has stronger diuretic action and is a powerful involuntary muscle relaxant but it causes gastric irritation, nausea and vomiting.

CORAMINE OR NIKETHAMIDE

Coramine is a colourless or slightly yellow oily liquid or crystalline mass with a characteristic odour and a slight bitter taste followed by burning warm sensation on tongue. It is miscible with water, alcohol and ether. It should be stored in well closed containers.

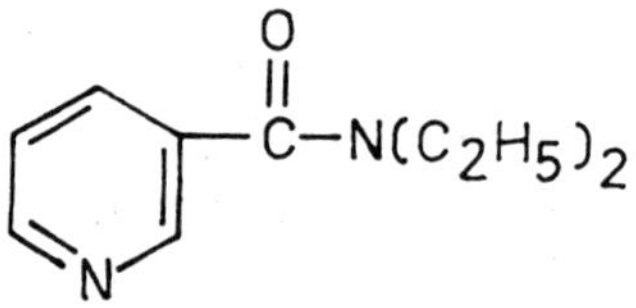

IUPAC Name : N-N- Diethylpyridine-3-carboxamide.

Actions and uses : It is a respiratory stimulant. It acts on the medullary centers of the brain to increase the rate and depth of respiration.

Officials : Nikethamide I.P.
Nikethamide Injection, I.P.

DEXTROAMPHETAMINE

Dextroamphetamine is available as a sulphated salt. It is an odourless, white crystalline powder having slightly bitter taste. It is soluble in water and practically insoluble in alcohol and ether. It should be stored in well-closed containers.

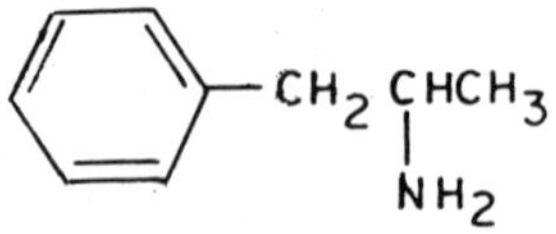

IUPAC Name : α-Methyl phenethylamine.

Actions and uses : It is a sympathomimetic drug with uses and actions similar to amphetamine but has an active twice of amphetamine. It is used in the treatment of obesity.

(1) **Theophylline** : Germen Remedia : Deriphyllin syp., tab., inj. : Adults: 1-2 spoon b.i.d., 1-2amp b.i.d and 1-3 tab. daily.

Cipla : Theo asthalin : Adults: 1 tablet tid.

Alembic : Theo SR : Adults: 1-2 tabs b.i.d.

(2) **Caffeine** : John wyeth : Dristan Tab.

Nicholas Piramal : Micropyrin

CHAPTER - 16

ADRENERGIC - DRUGS

The medulla of adrenal gland secretes adrenal hormone. This hormone stimulates heart, increases blood pressure, stimulates central nervous system and relaxes bronchial muscles. The main uses of adrenergic drugs are :

(1) Used to increase blood pressure.
(2) Used as central nervous system stimulants (amphetamine).
(3) Used in allergic reactions (Adrenaline).
(4) Used as smooth muscle relaxants (adrenaline and salbutamol).
(5) Used for local vaso constriction. (Adrenaline and phenyl-ephedrine) and
(6) Used as anorectic [suppress appetite. - fenfluramine].

Classification :

Sympathetic drugs [adrenergic or sympathomimmetics] are classified on the basis of presence or absence of catechol nucleus.

(1) **Catecholamines** : Adrenaline, Nor-adrenaline, Iso-prenaline.
(2) **Non-catecholamines** : Ephedrine, Phenyl ephedrine, Pseudo ephedrine, Salbutamol, Terbutaline.

ADRENALINE

Adrenaline is a white or creamy white ,sphaero -crystalline and odourless powder. It is very slightly soluble in water, insoluble in alcohol, ether and chloroform, but readily soluble in mineral acids and alkali hydroxides. Adrenaline darkens slowly when exposed to air, light and in solution form it is converted to inactive racemic form. Adrenaline is available as adrenaline acid tartarate. The drug and its salt are incompatible with oxidising agents, alkalis, tannins, gum and metals like copper, iron, zinc ,etc. It should be stored in air tight containers preferably in nitrogen atmosphere, protected from light.

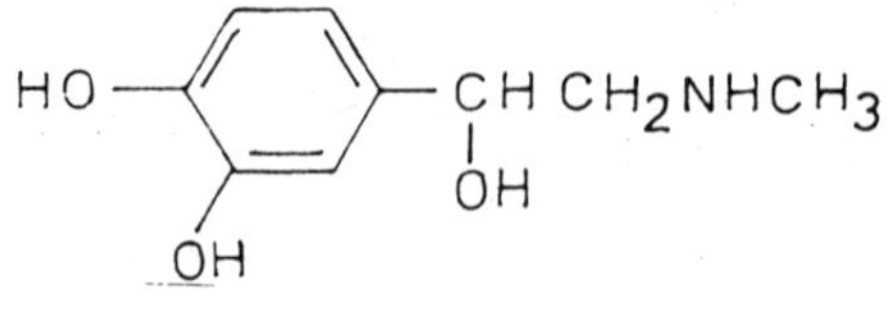

IUPAC Name : 1-(3,4-Dihydroxyphenyl)-2-methyl amino ethanol

or

3,4 -Dihydroxy-α- methylaminomethylbenzyl alcohol.

Actions and uses : Adrenaline is life saving in the treatment of bronchial asthma. It relaxes constricted bronchial musculature and reduces bronchial oedema. It is also a vital drug oedema in allergic states and in anaphylactic shock. Adrenaline acts upon both α and ß receptors. Adrenaline acts upon both α- and ß receptors. It is also used in cardiac arrest as cardiac stimulants and in the enhancement of the activity of local anesthetics.

Officials : Adrenaline Bi-tartarate I.P.
Adrenaline Tartarate Injection I.P.
Adrenaline I.P.
Adrenaline Maleate I.P.

NORADRENALINE

Noradrenaline is available as acid tartarate salt. The salt is an odourless white, crystalline powder, having a bitter taste. It is soluble in water, slightly soluble in alcohol, and very slightly soluble in ether. It slowly darkens on exposure to air and light. It should be stored in air tight containers protected from light.

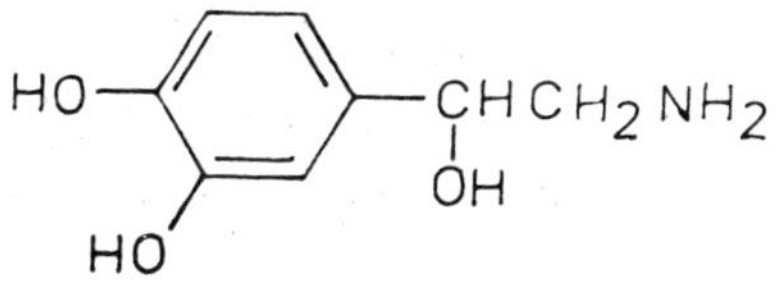

IUPAC Name : ß,3,4 Trihydroxyphenyl ethyl amine

Actions and uses : Noradrenaline is a neurohormone, released at the termination of post-ganglionic adrenergic nerve fibers. It acts on α receptors, thereby causes dilatation of pupils, inhibition of gastric ,intestinal, bladder, smooth musculature. It doesn't act as a bronchodilator or a vosodilator[ß-effects].

Officials : Noradrenaline Acid Tartarate I.P.

ISOPRENALINE

Isoprenaline is available as hydrochloride and sulphated salts. Its hydrochloride salt is an odourless, white crystalline powder. It is soluble in water, slightly soluble in alcohol, and practically insoluble in ether. Isoprenaline sulphate has similar properties as that of hydrochloride salt. It should be stored in air tight containers protected from light.

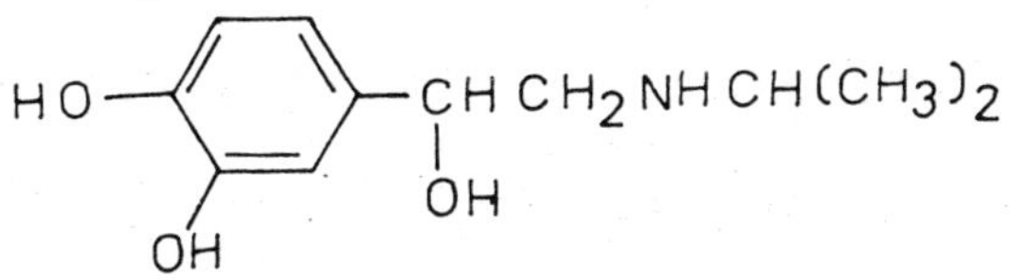

IUPAC Name : N-[2-(3,4-Dihydroxy phenyl)-2-hydroxy ethyl]-N-isopropyl amine.

Actions and uses : Isoprenaline acts mainly on ß-receptors. It is used in the treatment of bronchial asthma. Isoprenaline is a very potent cardiac stimulant and is given in cardiac surgery to combat heart block. It is contra-indicated in the patients suffering from hyper-thyroidism and cardiac patients.

Officials : Isoprenaline sulphate I.P.
Isoprenaline Tablets I.P.

EPHEDRINE

Ephedrine is an alkaloid obtained from various species of *ephedra.* Ephedrine is present as colourless, hexagonal, prismatic crystals or a white crystalline powder; having a bitter taste, and odourless or slight aromatic odour. It is soluble in alcohol, and slightly soluble in water or glycerol. It should be stored in air tight containers protected from light. It is also available as a hydrochloride salt that is soluble in water.

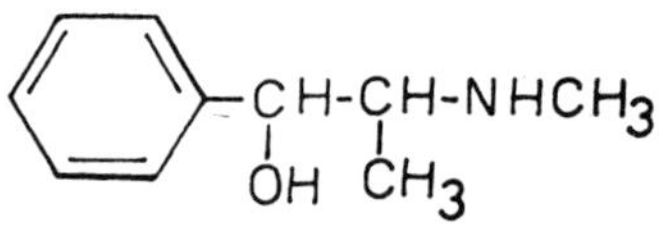

IUPAC Name : 2-Methylamino-1-phenylpropan-1-ol.

Actions and uses : Ephedrine has an indirect effect on adreno-receptors. It increases blood pressure, relaxes bronchioles and decreases peristaltic movements. It dilates the pupil [mydriasis] and constricts the sphincter but relaxes muscles of the bladder. It is a C.N.S. stimulant.

Officials : Ephedrine Tablets I.P.
Ephedrine Hydrochloride Tablets I.P.

PSEUDOEPHEDRINE

Pseudoephedrine is also an alkaloid obtained from species of Ephedra. It is available as a hydrochloride salt. The salt is an almost odourless, white crystalline powder with bitter taste. It is soluble in water, alcohol and slightly soluble in chloroform.

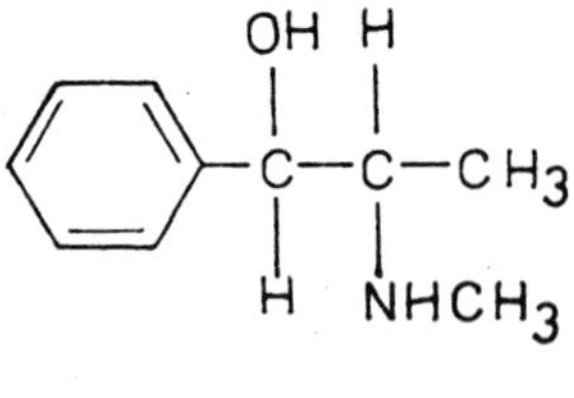

IUPAC Name : N-ß-Hydroxy-α-methyl phen ethyl-N-methyl amine.

Actions and uses : It is used as a broncho-dilators to relieve nasal and bronchial congestion in bronchial asthma. Its actions are similar to ephedrine.

PHENYLEPHRINE

Phenylephrine is available as a hydrochloride salt. The salt is an odourless, white crystalline powder with bitter taste. It is soluble in water, alcohol, and glycerol. It should be stored in air tight containers protected from light. Its aqueous solution gradually oxidises and is decolourised.

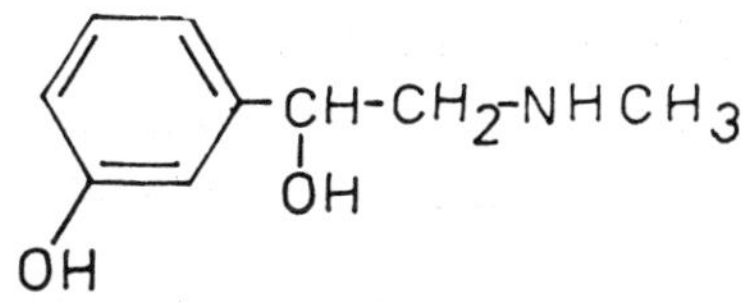

IUPAC Name : N-[3-ß-Dihydroxy phenyl ethyl] N-methyl amine.
Actions and uses : Phenylephrine has actions similar to nor-adrenaline but it has weaker pressor activity and longer duration of action than nor-adrenaline. It is used in the treatment of hypotensive state, drug induced [cyclopropane] hypotensions or in nasal decongestion as bronchodilator.

Officials : Phenylephrine Injection I.P.
Phenylephrine Hydrochloride I.P.

SALBUTAMOL

Salbutamol is an odourless, tasteless and white crystalline powder. It is slightly soluble in alcohol and very slightly soluble in ether. It should be stored in well closed containers protected from light. Salbutamol is also available as a sulphated salt that is soluble in water, alcohol, ether and chloroform.

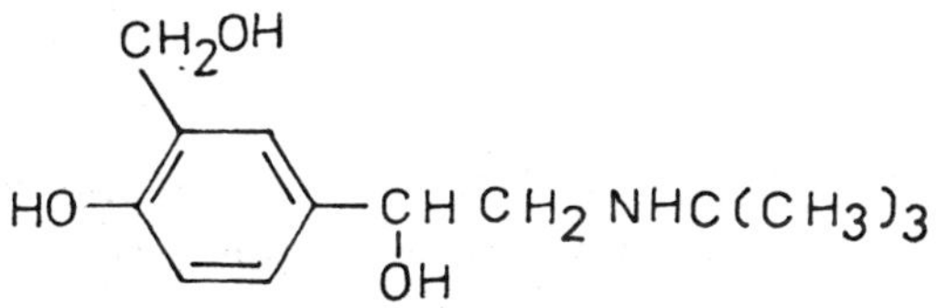

IUPAC Name : 1-[4-Hydroxy -3-hydroxymethyl phenyl]-2-[tert-butyl amino] ethanol.

Actions and uses : Salbutamol is a direct acting sympathomimetic agent. Its actions are similar to isoprenaline. It is used in the treatment of asthma, chronic bronchitis and broncho-pulmonary disorders involving bronchospasm.

It may cause palpitations and tachycardia and is therefore contra-indicated to the patients suffering from hypertension and hyperthyroidism .

Officials : Salbutamol I.P.
Salbutamol Injection I.P.
Salbutamol Inhaler I.P.

Salbutamol Sulphate I.P.
Salbutamol Syrup I.P.
Salbutamol Tablets I.P.

TERBUTALINE

Terbutaline is available as a sulphated salt. It is an odourless, white to grayish white crystalline powder with a bitter taste. It is soluble in water, slightly soluble in alcohol, practically insoluble in ether and chloroform. It should be stored in well closed containers protected from light.

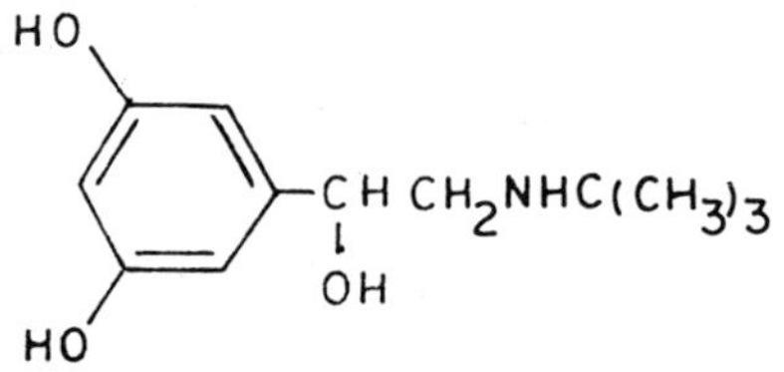

IUPAC Name : N-tert-Butyl-N-[2-(3,5-dihydroxy phenyl)-2-hydroxy ethyl] amine
Actions and uses : Terbutaline sulphate is a direct acting sympathomimetic agent. It is used in the treatment of asthma, chronic bronchitis and other bronchopulmonary disorders involving bronchospasm. Its other actions are similar to salbutamol.
Officials : Terbutaline Sulphate I.P.
Terbutaline Injection I.P.
Terbutaline Tablets I.P.

(1) **Adrenaline** : Biddle sawyer : Brovon inhalant : 10 drops at a time. Two times during the day.
FDC : Midricin inj. : 0.3 ml oralused for subconjunctival inj. only.

(2) **Noradrenaline** : Unicbery : Nodrin inj. : Contents of 1-2 ml or more 2ml. ampoules diluted in 500ml normal saline or 5% glucose soln. Infusion of drop-rate. 0.5 to 1ml/minute.

(3) **Isoprenaline** : Unichem : Isoprin inj. : infused by drip in 500ml normal saline or glucose saline solution.
Wellcome: Neo Epinine tab. : Adults : Sublingually 1 tab. t.i.d.

(4) **Phenylephrine** : Alembic : Wikoryl tab. : 1-2 tab. tid.

(5) **Salbutamol** : Cipla : Asthalin , syrup inhater : tabs. 2-4 times a day.
Franco Indian : Grinlinctus BM : 3-4 mg 3-4 times a day.

(6) **Terbutaline** : Astra IDL : Bricanyl Tab.

(7) **Ephedrine** : B-Wellcome: Actified tabs : Adults & children above 12 days : 1 tab b.i.d.
Rhone-poulenc : Zedex

(8) **Pseudo ephedrine** : Protec : Phencedyl liquid : 5-10 ml t.i.d. Children 2-3 times daily.
Adults & children above 12 yrs : 10ml t.i.d.
Plethico : Recofast plus tabs : 1 tab. 2-3 times daily.

CHAPTER - 17

ADRENERGIC ANTAGONISTS

Adrenergic blocking agents are those that block the adrenergic neuro effecter receptor by competitive antagonism. They do not prevent the action of catacholamines but act as classical adrenergic blocking agents. This agent's block either α (ergot alkaloids and benzodioxaines) or ß-blockers i.e. Propanalol, Practelol, etc.

TOLAZOLINE

Tolazoline is available as its hydrochloride salt . It is an odourless, white to creamy white crystalline powder. It is soluble in water, chloroform and alcohol but practically insoluble in ether. It should be stored in air tight containers protected from light.

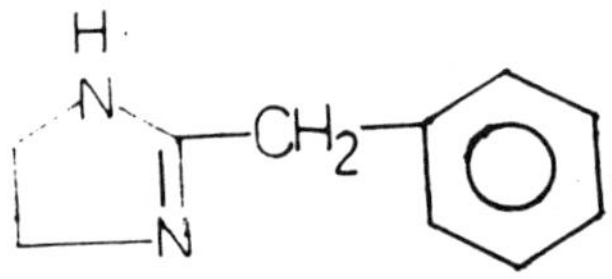

IUPAC Name : 2-Benzyl-2-Imidazoline.

Actions and uses: Tolazoline is an α receptor blocking agent and is used for the treatment of vascular disorders, Raynauds disease and in the treatment of local vascular disorders. The side effects are nausea, vomiting, diarrhoea and postural hypotension.

PROPRANOLOL

Propranolol is available as propranolol hydrochloride. It is an odourless, white powder having bitter taste. It is slightly soluble in water and alcohol and very slightly soluble in chloroform. It is a hygroscopic compound therefore it should be stored in air tight containers protected from light.

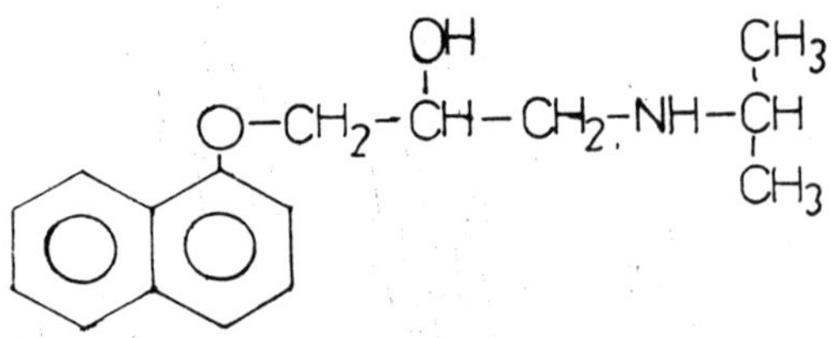

IUPAC Name : N-[2-Hydroxy-3-Naphth-1-yl oxypropyl]—N-isopropyl amine.
Actions and uses : It is a specific adrenergic ß-blocker. It inhibits sympathetic stimulation of the heart. It is used in the treatment of cardiac arrhythmia's associated with heart disease, anesthesia or digitalis intoxication and in auricular fibrillation, it is also used in hyperthyroidism.
Officials : Propranolol Tablets I.P.

PRACTOLOL

Practolol is an odourless, fine, white powder with a bitter taste. It is slightly soluble in alcohol. It is a hygroscopic compound and should be stored in air tight containers protected from light.

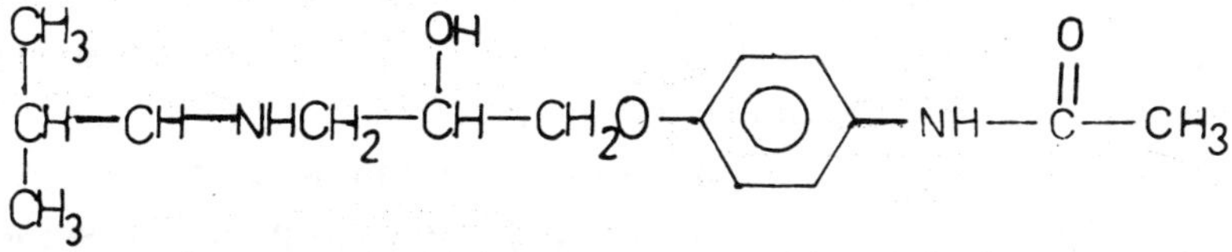

IUPAC Name : 4'-(2-Hydroxy-3-isopropylaminopropoxy) acetanilide.
Actions and uses : Practolol has actions and uses similar to propranolol but has more specific cardiac actions and less respiratory actions. It can be recommended for long term therapy and also in the emergency treatment of cardiac arrthymias.

(1) **Propalonol** : M.M. labs : Betazine Tab. : 1 tab. once or twice a day gradually increase upto 5 tabs.
Cipla : Clipar Tab : tab. 80-160mg daily in divided doses; inj. 1-2 mg. i.v. 1ml per minute.

CHAPTER -18

CHOLINERGIC DRUGS

The terms' cholinomimetic (cholinergic) and Parasympathomimetic are not equivalent but are popularly treated as synonyms. Acetylcholine is liberated not only at parasympathetic postganglinoic nerve endings but also at autonomic pre-ganglinoic nerve endings, at central synapses or at somatic motor nerve ending. They exert two types of effects nicotinic action and muscarinic actions.

Most of the therapeutic cholinomimetic drugs are used for their muscarinic actions. These agents stimulate gastro-intestinal smooth muscles and increase peristalsis, contract smooth muscle of urinary bladder, stimulate exocrine glands and produce miosis (pupillary constriction) of eyes.

Accumulation of acetylchloline at cholinergic sites is due to inhibition of enzyme acetylcholinesterase that inactivates acetylcholine.

CLASSIFICATION

(1) **Reversible cholinergic drugs** : Neostigmine, Physostigmine, pyridostigmine.

(2) **Irreversible cholinergic drugs :** Di isopropyl fluorophosphate, Echothiophate

NEOSTIGMINE

Neostigmine is available as a bromide and methylsulphate salt. Bromide salt is an odourless, colourless to white crystalline powder, soluble in water, alcohol and ether. It should be stored in airtight containers, protected from light.

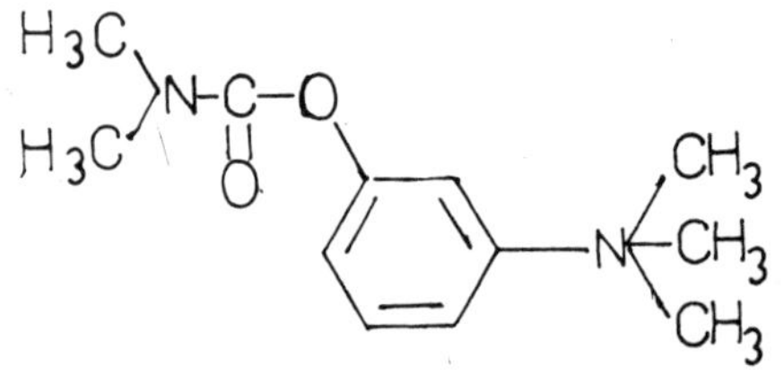

IUPAC Name : 3-(Dimethylcarbamoxyloxy)-NNN tri-methylaniline.

Actions and uses : Neostigmine inhibits the activity of enzyme cholinesterase. It is used mainly for its actions on voluntary muscles and less frequently to increase the activity of involuntary muscles. It is used in the treatment of myasthenia gravis.

It is also used to curtail the muscular relaxation produced by non depolarising neuromuscular blocking drugs like gallamine triethiodide and d-tubocurarine.

Officials : Neostigmine Bromide I.P.
Neostigmine Tablet/ Injection I.P.
Neostigmine Methylsulphate I.P.

PYRIDOSTIGMINE

Pyridostigmine is available as a bromide salt. The salt is a white, deliquescent, crystalline powder with an agreeable characteristic odour and bitter taste. It is soluble in water, alcohol, chloroform but very slightly soluble in ether and petroleum. It should be stored in air tight containers protected from light.

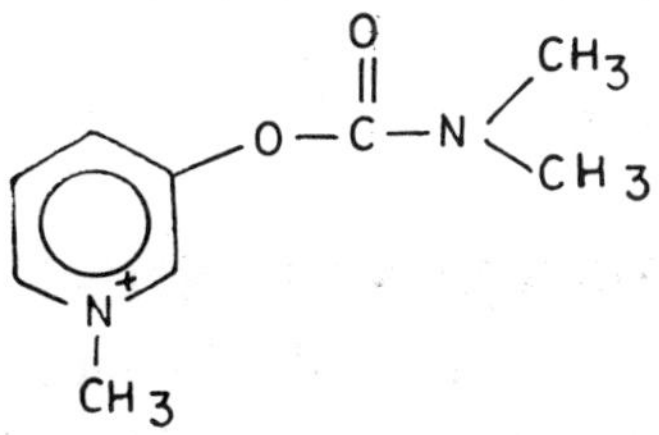

IUPAC Name : 3-Dimethyl carbamoyloxy-1-methylpyridinium.

Actions and uses : Pyridostigmine is less-active than neostigmine but its actions and uses are similar. It is used in the treatment of myasthenia gravis, but it dose not cure the disease completely.

PRALIDOXINE

Pralidoxine is available as a chloride salt. The salt is an odourless, white to pale yellow crystalline powder. It is soluble in water and slightly soluble in alcohol. It should be stored in well-closed containers.

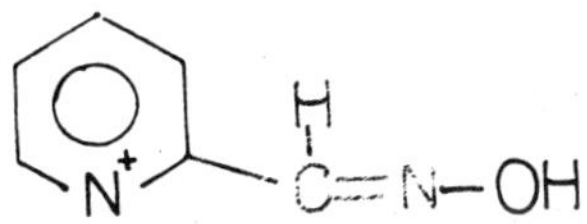

IUPAC Name : 2-Hydroxy iminomethyl-1-methyl pyridinium.

Actions and uses : It is a reactivator of cholinesterase and is used in the treatment of poisoning of organophosphorus compounds, except carbamate pesticides. It may give rise to nausea, headache, dizziness, tachycardia, muscular weakness, etc. .

PILOCARPINE

Pilocarpine is available as a hydrochloride and nitrate salt. It is an alkaloid obtained from leaves of *Pilocarpus microphyllus*. Its hydrochloride salt is an odourless colourless or white crystalline powder. It is soluble in water and alcohol and very slightly soluble in chloroform and ether. It is a hygroscopic compound and should be stored in air tight containers protected from light. Hydrochloride salt is incompatible with chlorohexidine acetate and phenyl mercuric salt, while nitrate salt is incompatible with chlorhexidene acetate and benzylkonium chloride.

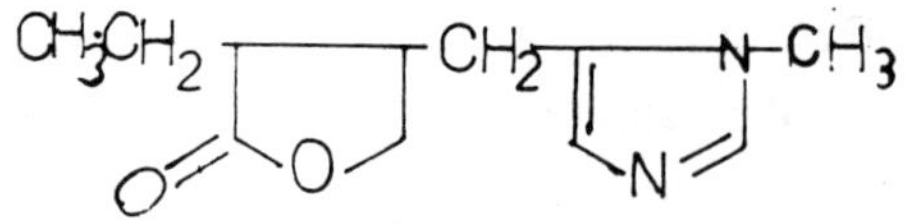

IUPAC name : Ethyl -ß-[1-methyl imidazol-5-ylmethyl] α-butyrolactone.

or

3-Ethyl Dihydro-4-[(Methyl-1H-imidazol-5-yl)]-2(3H)-Furanone.

Actions and uses : Pilocarpine act on muscarinic receptors. It has been used to decrease intra-ocular pressure in glaucoma and to constrict the pupil. The side effects are dryness of mouth, constipation and impaired vision. Pilocarpine poisoning is treated by gastric lavage.

Officials : Pilocarpine Nitrate I.P.

PHYSOSTIGMINE

Physostigmine is an alkaloid obtained from seeds of *Physostigma venenosum.* Physostigmine is available as odourless, colourless crystals. It becomes pink on exposure to air and light. It is soluble in chloroform, slightly soluble in alcohol, ether and water . It should be stored in air tight containers protected from light. It is also available as physostigmine salicylate and physostigmine sulphate. The sulphated salt is soluble in water and alcohol.

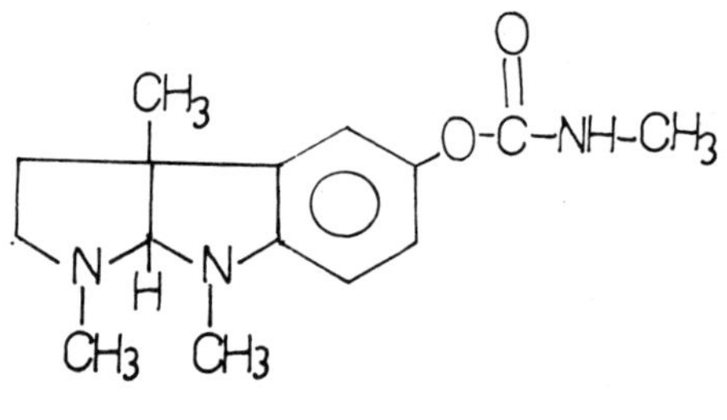

IUPAC Name : 1,2, 3,3a,8,8a-Hexahydro-1,3a,8-trimethyl-Pyrrolo [2,3-b] indol-5-yl methylcarbamate [ester].

Actions and uses : Physostigmine inhibits cholinesterase activity and prevents destruction of acetylcholine. Its effects are antagonistic to atropine. It increases salivary , bronchial and gastric secretions and slows the heart rate. It is mainly used as a mitotic or to counteract homatropine or cocaine effect on eye. It reduces intra-ocular pressure in glaucoma. Its side effects are nausea, vomiting, etc.

Official : Physostigmine salicylate I.P.
Physostigmine Injection I.P.

(1) **Neostigmine** : Roche : Prostigmin tab. : 15-30 mg. daily.
Prostigmininj. 1-5mg in with atropine or as directed by physcian.
Tablets India : Tilstigmin tab : 5-20 spread over the day.

(2) **Pralidoxime** : Shree Ganesh : PAMA-Korea inj.

(3) **Pilocarpine** : FDC : Pilocardrops : 1-2 drops or as reqd.

(4) **Physostigmine** : Bell pharma : Bi-miotic.

CHAPTER -19

CHOLINERGIC ANTAGONISTS

Cholinergic blocking agents block or interfere with the action of acetylcholine at the post-ganglionic parasympathetic nerve endings. These agents are also called as parasympatholytic or anticholinergics or muscarinic receptor blocking agents or antimusacarinic drugs.

Classification :

1. Natural agents : Atropine, Hyoscine (scopolamine).
2. Synthetic agents :
   - (A) Atropine like drugs : Homatropine.
   - (B) Antispasmodic - Antisecretory : Propantheline
   - (C) Antiparkinsonism drugs : Benztropine, Benzhexol

ATROPINE

Atropine is a solanaceous alkaloid (Tropane alkaloid) obtained from plant *Atropa belladona* and different species of *Hyoscyamus niger*. Atropine is an odourless, colourless to white crystalline powder. It is soluble in chloroform and alcohol, and insoluble in water. Its sulphated salt is soluble in water but insoluble in organic solvents. Atropine sulphate is unstable in aqueous solution. It is incompatible with bromides, iodides, quinine, tannic acid and salts of mercury.

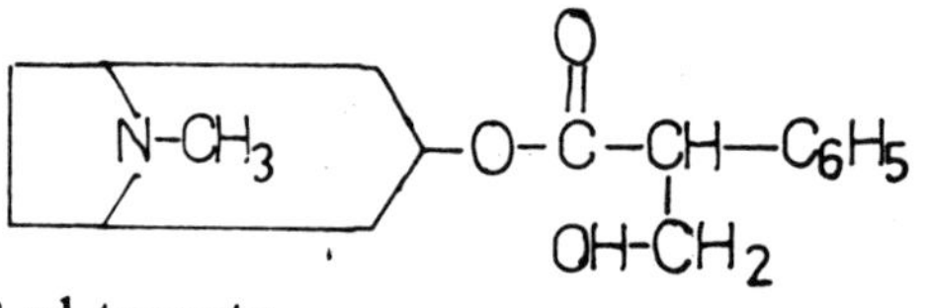

IUPAC Name : Tropane-3-yl-tropate.

Actions and uses : It antagonises the muscarinic actions of acetylcholine. It stimulates central nervous system causing excitement and restlessness but in large doses produces depression. It acts on lower motor centers and diminishes muscular rigidity. It also reduces secretions of salivary and sweat glands. It dilates the pupil and paralyses accommodation. It is given before volatile anesthesia. It is used in the treatment of biliarycolic, gastric and duodenal ulcers, etc. It is also used in the treatment of rheumatism, neuralgia and sciatica.

Officials : Atropine I.P.
Atropine Sulphate I.P
Atropine Sulphate Injection/Tablets I.P.
Atropine Eye Ointment I.P.

HYOSCINE or SCOPOLAMINE

Hyoscine is an alkaloid obtained from various species of DHATURA. It is available as a hydrobromide salt. The hydrobromide salt is an odourless, slightly effervescent, colourless or white crystalline powder. It is soluble in water, slightly soluble in alcohol and very slightly soluble in choloroform. It should be stored in air tight containers protected from light.

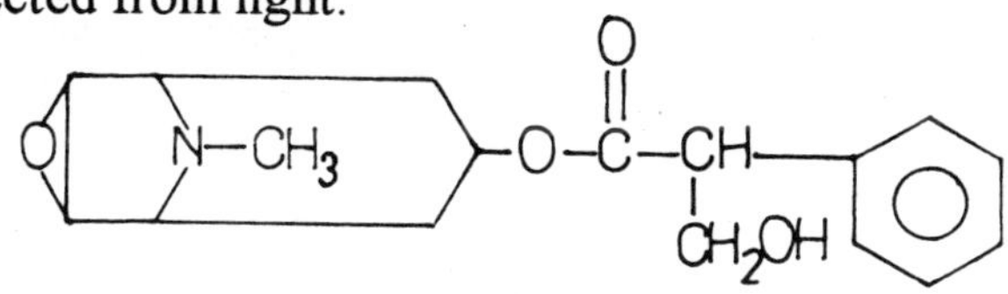

IUPAC Name : 6,7-Epoxy-3-[Tropoyloxy] Tropanium.

Actions and uses : Hyoscine is an antagonist to acetylcholine. It produces mydriasis and other actions similar to atropine. It is effective in mania, cerebral excitement, delirium and alcoholism. It is also used for the prevention and treatment of motion sickness.

Official : Hyoscine hydrobromide I.P.
Hyoscine Injection I.P.
Scopolamine hydrobromine Tablet I.P.

HOMATROPINE

Homatropine is available as a hydrobromide salt. It is an odourless, colourless or white crystalline powder. The salt is soluble in water and slightly soluble in alcohol. It should be stored in well closed containers protected from light.

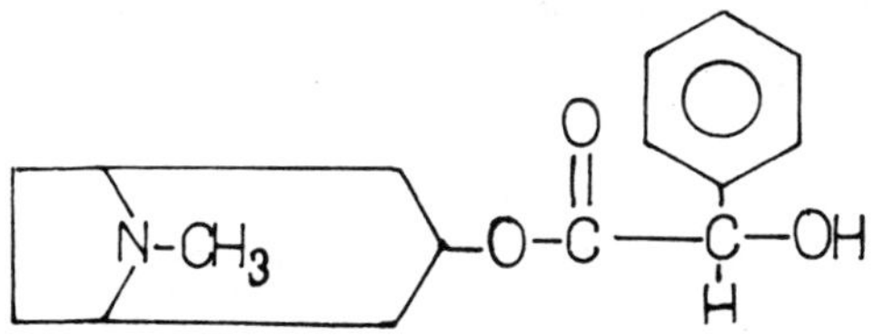

IUPAC Name : 3-[2-Hydroxy-2-phenylacetyloxy] Tropanium.

Actions and uses : Homatropine has actions and uses similar to atropine. It is a powerful mydriatic and has less tendency to increase intra-ocular pressure.

PROPANTHELINE

Propantheline is available as prupantheline bromide. It is an odourless, slightly hygroscopic, white or yellowish white powder with a bitter taste. It is soluble in water, alcohol and chloroform but practically insoluble in ether. It should be stored in air-tight containers.

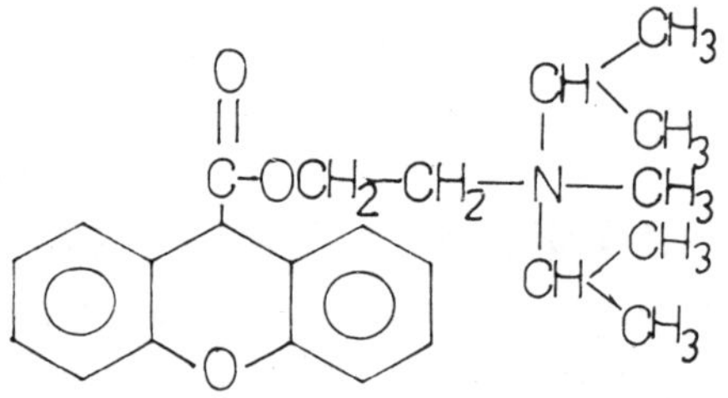

IUPAC Name : N,N-Di isopropyl-N-methyl-N-2-[xanthen-9-ylcarbonyl oxy] ethylamine.

Actions and uses : Propantheline has only peripheral actions similar to atropine. It reduces gastric secretions and intestinal motility. It also diminishes biliary and ureteric spasm. It can also be used to control sweating, salivation, etc.

BENZTROPINE

Benztropine is available as a mesylate salt. The salt is an odourless, white crystalline powder with a bitter taste. It is soluble in water and alcohol, and practically insoluble in ether. It should be stored in air tight containers.

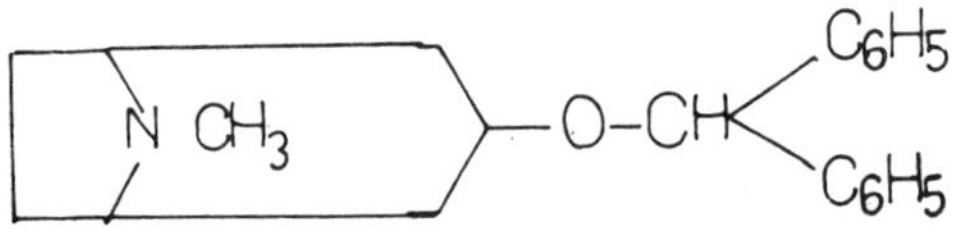

IUPAC Name : 3-Benzhydryloxytropanium

Actions and uses : Benztropine depresses motor cortex and also has antihistaminic actions. It reduces spasm and tremors of voluntary muscles and is used in the treatment of parkinsonism.

TROPICAMIDE

Tropicamide is an odourless, white crystalline powder. It is soluble in choroform and alcohol, and, slightly soluble in water. It should be stored in well closed containers protected from light.

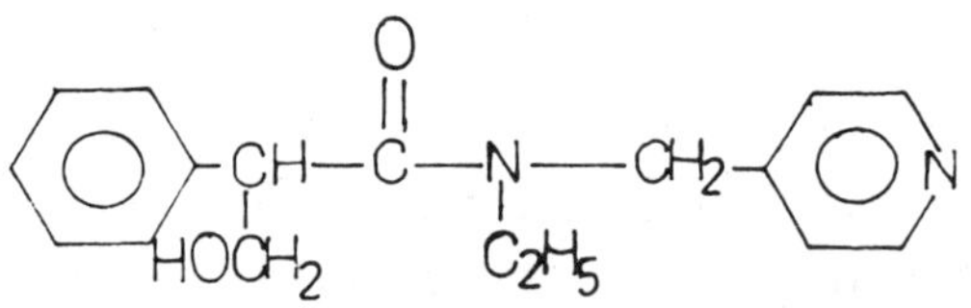

IUPAC Name : N-Ethyl-N-[Pyrid-4-yl methyl] tropamide.

Actions and uses :Tropicamide has cycloplegic and mydriatic properties similar to atropine.

BIPERIDEN

Biperiden is an odourless white crystalline powder. It is soluble in chloroform; sparingly soluble in ether, slightly soluble in alcohol and almost insoluble in water. It is stored in well-closed container protected from light.

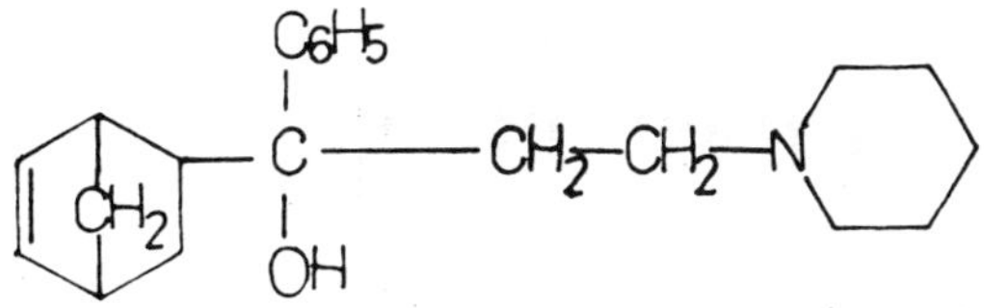

IUPAC Name : 1-[Bicyclo(2.2.1) hept-5-en-2-yl]-1-phenyl-3-piperidino propan-1-ol.
Actions and uses : A Biperiden is used in the treatment of idiopathic, encephalitic and arteriosclerotic type of parkinsonism. It is also used in the treatment of dystonic reactions.

(1) **Atropine** : Searle : Lomafen tab. : 2 tabs every 6 hrs.
Searle : Lomotil tab. : 2 tabs every 6 hrs.

(2) **Hyoscine** : German Remedies : Buscopan Tab.

(3) **Homatropine** : Plethico : Lumingy plus cap. : 2 caps b.i.d.
Akil pharma: Methozyne liquid : 2-10 ml b.i.d. or as reqd.

(4) **Propenthaline** : Sun pharma : pepcer tab. : 1 tab tid or as reqd.
Sun pharma : spastheline tab. : According to clinical requirements.

(5) **Tropicamide** : Mepla : Tropisyn drops : As directed by the doctor.

(6)**Propentheline** : Sarle India : Probanthine Tab.

CHAPTER 20

DIURETIC DRUGS

Diuretics are drugs used to increase the volume of urine excreted by the kidneys. These drugs are used for the relief of oedema or ascites that are caused by heart, kidney and liver diseases. These are also effective in the treatment of cardiac oedema and other oedema caused by pregnancy and to reduce raised intraocular pressure. They are also used in glaucoma, epilepsy, migraine hyperkalemia, anginal syndrome, etc. These agents are classified according to their mode of action.

1. **Osmotic Diuretics** :Urea and mannitol.
2. **High ceiling or Loop Diuretics** :Furesemide and ethacrynic acid.
3. **Thiazides** :Chlorthiazide,Hydrochlorthiazide, Benzthiazide.
4. **Potassium sparing or Aldosterone antagonists** : Spironolactone.

UREA

Urea is an odourless, colourless, transparent, slightly hygroscopic crystalline salt having cooling and saline taste. It is soluble in water and boiling alcohol; slightly soluble in alcohol; and practically insoluble in ether and chloroform. It should be stored in well closed containers protected from light.

$$H_2N—\underset{\underset{O}{\|}}{C}—NH_2$$

UREA

Actions and uses : When urea is given orally, it is rapidly excreted with an increasing urinary output thus acting as a diuretic. The solution is irritant and care must be taken to avoid extravasation during injection. The cream of urea is used as a keratolytic agent in hyperkeratotic skin conditions.

Officials : Urea I.P.

MANNITOL

Mannitol is an odourless, white crystalline powder with a sweetish taste. It is soluble in water and slightly soluble in alcohol. It should be stored in well-closed containers protected from light.

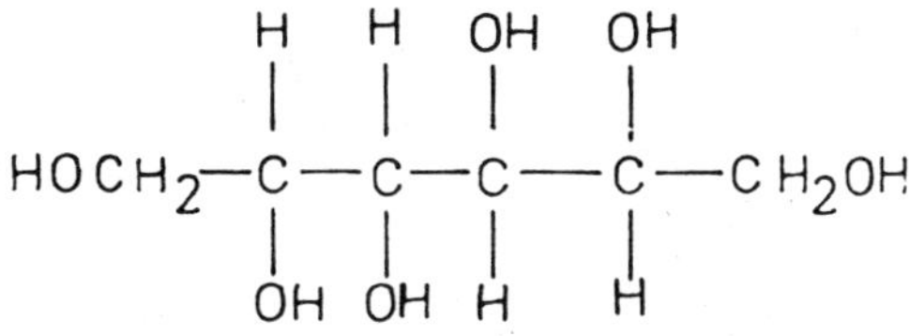

IUPAC Name : 1,2,3,4,5,6-Hexane hexa ol. OR Mannose OR sorbitol

Actions and uses : Mannitol is an osmotic diuretic. It is given intravenously for diuretic purposes. It is used for irrigation of bladder, in cerebral injury and as a base in glyceryl trinitrate tablets.

Officials : Mannitol I.P.
Mannitol Injection I.P.

FRUSEMIDE

Frusemide is an odourless, tasteless and white crystalline powder. It is soluble in alkali hydroxides, slightly soluble in alcohol, and very slightly soluble in water and chloroform. It should be stored in well-closed containers.

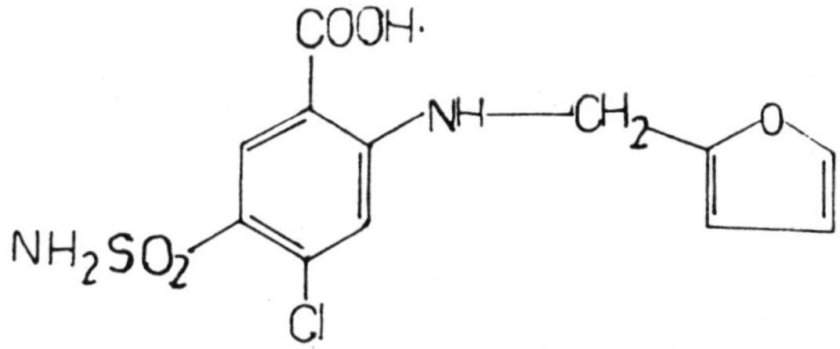

IUPAC Name : 4-Chloro-N-furfuryl-5-sulphamoylanthranilic acid.

Actions and uses : It is a loop diuretic and reduces reabsorption of electrolytes by proximal and distal renal tubules and loop of henle. The excretion of sodium, potassium and chloride ions is increased but serum uric acid concentration will increase in blood. It is used in the treatment of acute renal failure and also in the treatment of hypertension and cerebral oedma.

Officials : Frusemide I.P.
Frusemide Injection I.P.
Frusemide Tablets I.P.

CHLORTHIAZIDE

Chlorthiazide is an odourless, white crystalline powder with a bitter taste. It is slightly soluble in acetone; very slightly soluble in water and alcohol; and practically insoluble in ether and chloroform. It should be stored in air-tight containers.

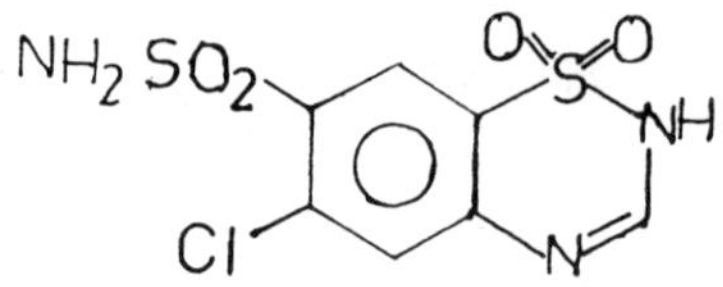

IUPAC Name : 6-Chloro-2H-benzo-1,2,4-thiadiazine-7-sulphonamide 1,1 dioxide.

Actions and uses : It's actions and uses are similar to frusemide. It also inhibits carbonic anhydrases. It is used in the treatment of oedma and toxaemia of pregnancy. It is also given with hypotensive agents in the treatment of hypertension.

HYDROCHLORTHIAZIDE

Hydrochlorthiazide is an odourless, white crystalline powder with bitter taste. It is soluble in alkali hydroxides, slightly soluble in acetone and alcohol, but insoluble in water, ether and chloroform. It should be stored in air-tight containers.

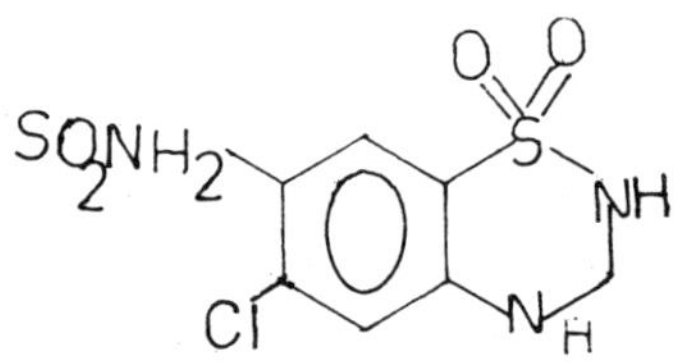

IUPAC Name : 6-Chloro-3,4-dihydro-2H-benzo-1,2,4-thiadiazine-7- sulfonamide-1,1-dioxide.

Actions and uses : Hydrochlorthiazide has a similar action and uses as of other thiazides but it is more effective even in smaller doses.

Official : Hydrochlorthiazide I.P.
Hydrochlorthiazide Tablets I.P.

BENZTHIAZIDE

Benzthiazide has a characteristic odour and taste, and is a white crystalline powder. It is slightly soluble in alcohol, and insoluble in water, chloroform and ether. It should be stored in air-tight containers.

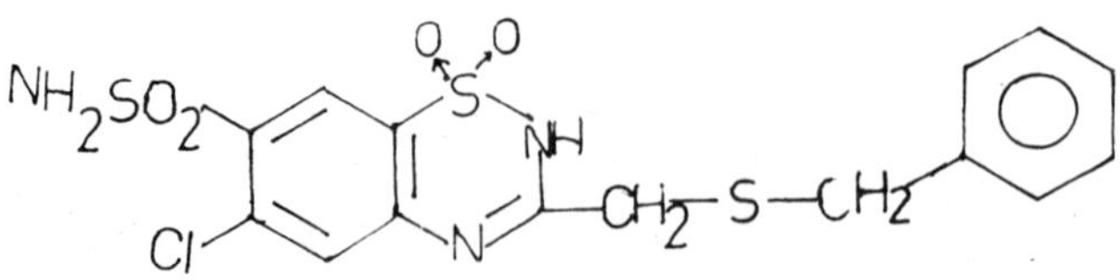

IUPAC Name : 6-Chloro-3-[{(Phenyl methyl)thio }methyl]-2H-benzo-1,2,4 - thiadiazine-7-sulfonamide-1,1-dioxide.

Actions and uses : Benzthiazide has action and uses similar to chlorthiazide. It is used as a diuretic and also as an antihypertensive.

ETHACRYNIC ACID

Ethacrynic acid is an odourless, white crystalline powder. It forms soluble salts with hydroxides and is soluble in alcohol, ether and chloroform but very slightly soluble in water. It should be stored in air-tight containers.

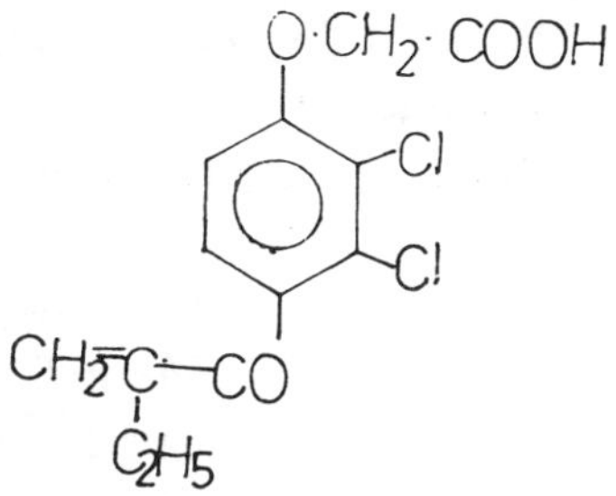

IUPAC Name :2,3-Dichloro-4-(2-ethylacryloyl) Phenoxyacetic acid.

Actions and uses : Ethacrynic acid is a loop diuretic and increases the excretion of sodium, potassium and chlorides. It decreases the urinary pH as well as the excretion of bicarbonates.

Officials : Ethacrynic acid I.P.
Ethacrynic acid Tablets I.P.

(1)**Urea**	: FDC Ltd.	: Cotaryl
(2)**Mannitol**	: Krishna Keshav Ltd.	: Mannitol 5%
(3)**Frusemide**	: Hoechst	: Lasix Tab.
(4)**Hydro chlorthiazide**	: Ciba - Geigy	: Esidrex Tab.

CHAPTER - 21

CARDIOVASCULAR DRUGS

Cardiovascular drugs are the drugs that effect heart or blood vessels or circulatory system directly or indirectly. Generally those drugs that effect the cardiac system directly are called cardiovascular drugs. All the adrenergic drugs, diuretics and anticoagulants are also used in the treatment of cardiac diseases. These agents can be further classified into

(1) Cardiac glycosides : Digitalis,
(2) Antihypertensive agents : Methyldopa, guanithidine
(3) Antianginal agents : Ethyl nitrite, glyceryl trinitrate
(4) Antiarrhythmic agents : Quinine, ethyl alcohol
(5) Antihypercholesterolemic (lipid lowering)agents : Clofibrate.

ETHYL NITRITE

Ethyl nitrite is a colourless to yellowish clear, volatile liquid with characteristic ethereal(Fruity) odour and sweet burning taste. It is miscible with alcohol and ether, and slightly soluble in water. Air, light, moisture and presence of acid or alkali activates decomposition of drug to form oxides of nitrogen and acids. It should be stored in well closed containers protected from light.

$$C_2H_5\text{-}NO_2$$

Ethyl nitrite

Actions and uses :Ethyl nitrite is used as a diaphoretic and cardiovascular agent. The side effects of this drug are hypotension and methaemoglobinimea and narcosis.

GLYCERYL TRINITRATE

Glyceryl trinitrate is a clear colourless oily liquid. It is explosive on rapid heating. It is miscible with Chloroform, ether and acetone. It is soluble in glycerol, light petroleum, alcohol, almond oil and very slightly soluble in water. It is a very unstable compound may deteriorate and in the presence of cotton, cork, paper, plastic, rubber, wool and elevated temperature. It should be stored in air-tight containers protected from light below 25°C.

$$\begin{array}{l} CH_2\text{-}ONO_2 \\ | \\ CH\text{-}ONO_2 \\ | \\ CH_2\text{-}ONO_2 \end{array}$$

IUPAC Name : 1,2,3-propane trinitrite.

Actions and uses : Glyceryltrinitrate relaxes involuntary muscles leading to dilatation of arterioles. It is used in the prophylactic and treatment of angina and to relieve colic of renal and gall bladder.

ALPHA-METHYLDOPA

Alpha-Methyldopa is an odourless, tasteless white to yellowish white powder. It is soluble in dilute hydrochloric acid, slightly soluble in water and alcohol, and very slightly soluble in ether. It should be stored in air-tight containers protected from light.

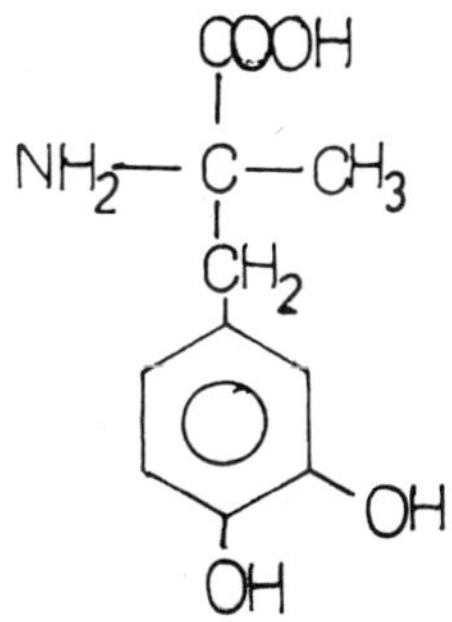

IUPAC Name : 3-(3,4-Dihydroxy phenyl)-2-methyl-L-alanine.

Actions and uses : Alpha methyldopa inhibits conversion of dopa to dopamine by competing for the enzyme dopa-decarboxylase and reduction in the formation of noradrenaline. It is used as an antihypertensive agent and as a CNS depressant. The side effects include depression, dryness of mouth, diarrhoea, liver damage, etc.

Officials : Methyldopa I.P.
Methyldopa Tablets I.P.

ANTI-HYPERTENSIVE AGENTS

Hypertension is a disease characterised by abnormally high blood pressure. The syndrome of essential hypertension is characterised by elevation of diastolic blood pressure .Hypertension is classified into:

(A) Primary [Essential or Idiopathic] hypertension : For which the exact cause is not known.

(B) Secondary hypertension : This may be due to renal, endocrine or vascular lesions. Antihypertensive drugs are classified according to the site of action. It is calssified as :

(1) Drugs acting on CNS : Clonidine, Alpha methyl dopa
(2) Drugs acting on ANS
    (A) Ganglion blockers : Hexamethonium, Pentolinium, Pempidine
    (B) Adrenergic receptor blockers : Phenoxybenzamine, Phenoxy ,Propronolol
    (C) Adrenergic neurone blockers : Guenethidine, Bethenidine ,Debrisoquine
(3) Catecholamine depletors : Reserpine
(4) Vasodilators : Diazoxide
(5) Oral diuretics : Thiazides
(6) Renin angiotensin antagonists : Seralasin
(7) Drugs acting reflexly : Veratrum alkaloids
(8) Miscellaneous drugs : Pargylline

GUANETHIDINE

Guanethidine is available as its monosulphate salt. The salt is an odourless, colourless crystalline powder. It is soluble in water, very slightly soluble in alcohol, and practically insoluble in ether and chloroform. It should be stored in air tight containers proteced from light.

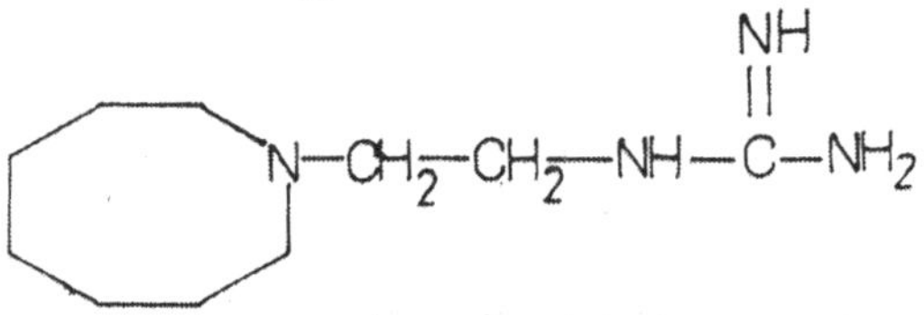

IUPAC Name : 1-[2-(perhydroazocin-1-yl)ethyl] guanidine

Actions and uses : Guanethidine is a hypotensive agent that lowers the blood pressure by blocking transmission in post ganglionic adrenergic nerve. It is also useful to reduce blood pressure in patients with phaeochromocytoma. Its eye drops were used for mydriasis and to reduce intra-ocular pressure. The side effects of this drug include diarrhoea.

Officials : Guanethidine Sulphate I.P.
Guanethidine Tablets I.P.

CLOFIBRATE

Clofibrate is a colourless liquid ,with characteristic faint acrid odour. The taste is acrid that turns sweet. It is very slightly soluble in water, and miscible with alcohol, ether and chloroform. It should be stored in well closed containers.

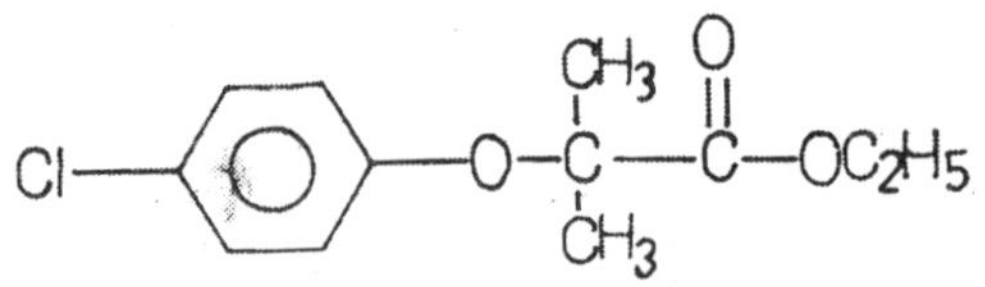

IUPAC Name : Ethyl-2-[4-Chlorophenoxy]-2-methyl propionate

Actions and uses : Clofibrate reduces elevated levels of triglycerides, phospholipids and plasmocholestrol concentration. It also reduces platelet sickness and fibrinogen concentration thereby causing fibrinolysis. It is used in hyper-triglyceridema, hyper-cholesterolemia. Its side effects are nausea, diarrhoea and pain in muscles.

Officials : Clofibrate I.P.
Clofibrate Capsules I.P.

CARDIAC ARRHYTHMIA'S

Disturbances in cardiac rhythm are called as cardiac arrhythmia's. Mortarlity rate in acute myocardial infarction can be decreased by the urgent treatment of various arrhythmia's. Antifibrillatory drugs are compounds which prevents the development of atrial or ventricular fibrillation.

Cardiac arrhythmia's may be due to either disorders of impu!se formation or disorders of impulse conduction. Tachyarrhythmias are due to disturbed impulse formation or irregular and rhythmic discharge from ectopic pace-maker. The drugs used in the treatment of cardiac arrhythmia's are :

(I) Myocardial depressants :
- (A) Electro-physiological depressants : Quinidine, procanamide.
- (B) Electro-physiologically partial depressants : Lignocain, Phenytoin

(II) Drugs acting on A.N.S.[Beta adrenergic blockers] : Propranolol.
(III) Calcium Channel blocker : Verapamil
(IV) Digitalis and analogues
(V) Drugs which prolong repolarisation.

QUINIDINE

Quinidine is an alkaloid obtained from the bark of various species of cinchona. It is an odourless, neddle like white crystalline substance possessing very bitter taste. It is insoluble in water but soluble in organic solvents. It is also available as quinine sulphate that is soluble in water and insoluble in organic solvents. It should be stored in air tight containers protected from light.

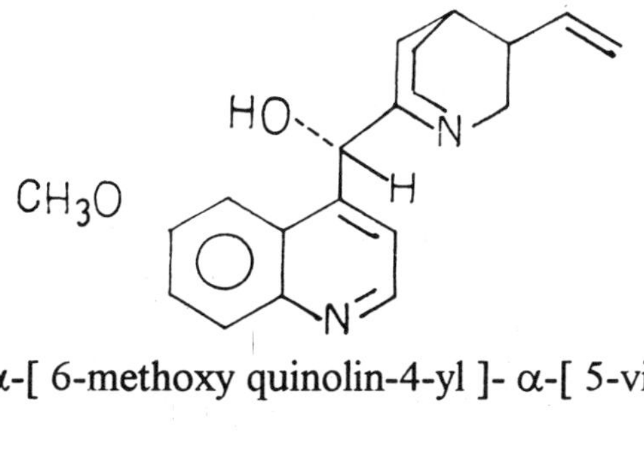

IUPAC Name : α-[6-methoxy quinolin-4-yl]- α-[5-vinyl quinuclidin-2-yl] methanol.

Actions and uses : Quinidine acts on cardiac muscles and increases the refractory period of contraction thereby decreases rate of contractions. It is used in the treatment of auricular fibrillation and paroxysmal ventricular tachycardia. The side effects of this drug include are palpitation, diminution of vision, headache, nausea, vomiting etc.

Officials : Quinidine Sulphate I.P.
Quinidine Tablets I.P.

CARDIOTONICS OR CARDIAC GLYCOSIDES

The Cardiac glycosides are sweet compounds containing sugar moiety (Glycon) and non-sugar moiety (aglycon). The aglycon is responsible for the different actions of glycosides. The cardiac glycosides contain steroidal (Cyclo pentophenanthrene) nucleus of C-23 carbon. In these aglycon ring C & D junction is in cis-Configuration. The lactone ring is attached to the C-17 position of steroidal skeleton which is important for cardiac activity. The sugar moiety is attached at C-3 by an ethereal linkage. The sugar attached is either ribose, digitoxose, glucose, cymarose, etc. These are further classified into two types.

(A) Cardenolides : These glycosides contain five membered lactone ring attached to C-17 of steroidal nucleus the example of cardenolides : digitoxigenin, gitoxigenin, digoxigenin and ovabagenin

(B) Bufadienolides: These are C-24 homologues of cardenolides containing six membered lactone ring attached to C-17 of steroidal nucleus. It also possesses a double bond. It has low therapeutic index. The example of bufadienalides are scillaren A and scillaren B obtained from *Urginea maritima.* These cardenolides increase the tone of cardiac muscles and are used in the treatment of congestive heart failure and cardiac tachyarrhythmia. It is also used in cardiac failure by increased force of myocardial contraction. Scillaren is a bufadienolide. It is a white or yellowish white, odourless, granular and bitter in taste. It is soluble in alcohol and methanol, and slightly soluble in water. It contains rhamnose and glucose as glycon moiety. It has similar action and used as cardenolides but it is less potent.

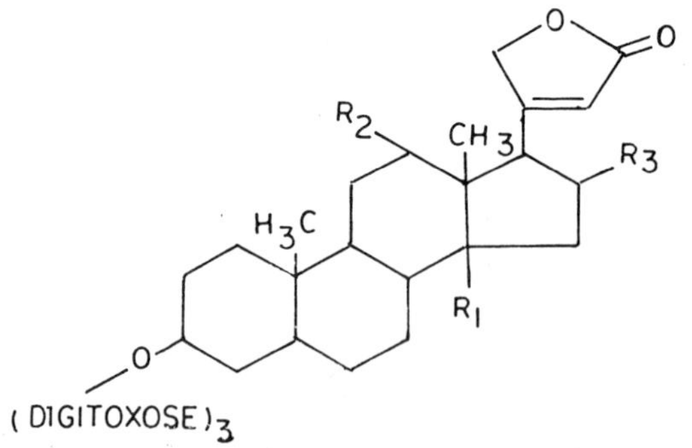

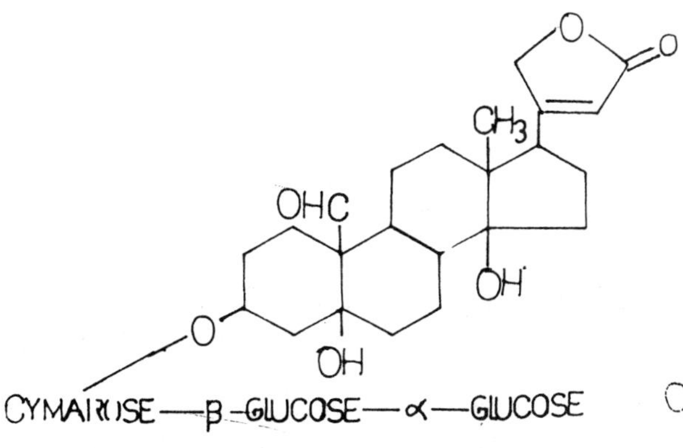

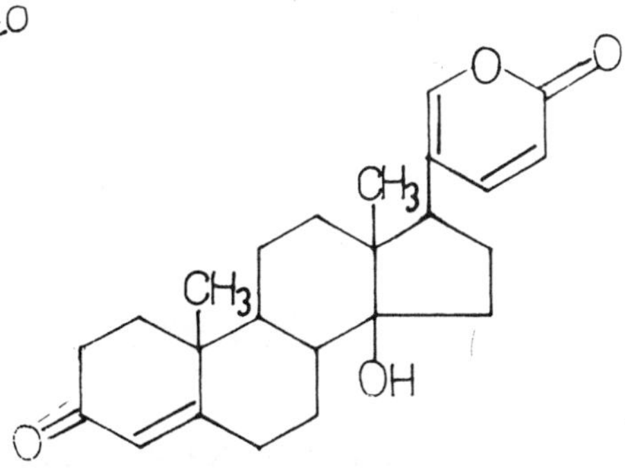

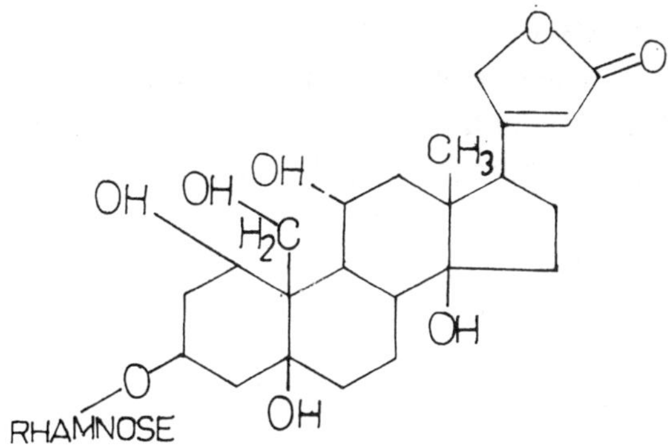

(1) **Glyceryl trinitrite** : Wellcome : Angised tabs : 0.5 mg every 3 minutes till pain appears.
Cadila : Myovin oint : 1.5-3.5 cm rub thrice daily.
(2) **Alpha methyldopa** : Merind : Alphadopa : 0.5-2 gm daily in divided doses.
IDPL : Emdopa : 0.5-2 gm daily in divided doses.
(3) **Clofibrate** :Sigma Lab.: Clofert tabs : 1-3 cap 3-4 times daily.
(4) **Quinidine** : Frano india : Natcardine tab : 200-300 mg 3-4 times daily.
Wellcome : Quinidine tabs : 200-300 mg 3-4 times daily.

CHAPTER - 22

HYPOGLYCEMIC AGENTS

Pancreas consists of glandular tissue. It secretes digestive enzymes, glucagon and insulin. An isolated group of cells within pancreas is called as islets of langerhons. These cells are divided into two parts as per their secretary nature. The cells secreting glucagon are called α-cells and cells secreting insulin are called ß-cells.

Insulin plays an important role in digestion and utilisation (Catabolism) of food material. It is essential for the phosphorylation of glucose to glucose-6-phosphate. Glucose-6-phosphate is further catabolised to give energy. In certain individuals glucose level in blood increases due to lack of sufficient insulin. This condition is called hyperglycemia. The disease is called diabetes mellitus. Hypoglycemic agents can be classified as :

(1) Insulin and its preparations :

(2) Synthetic compounds :

(A) Sulfonyl ureas : Chlorpropamide,Tolbutamide,Glibenclamide

(B) Biguanides : Phenformin , Metformin

INSULIN

Insulin is a polypetide hormone secreted by ß-cells of islets of langerhans present in pancreas of all vertebrates. It is the first protein whose chemical structure and molecular weight was determined. It contains 51 amino acids having a molecular weight of six thousand. Insulin comprises of a polypeptide chain. The 51 amino acids are present in two chains. Chain A contains 21 amino acids and chain B contains 30 amino acids and both these chains are united by two disulfide (-s-s-) linkage. It is present as a macromolecule of molecular weight 12 to 36 thousands depending on the pH of the solution. The iso-electric point of insulin is 5.3.

Commercially insulin is obtained by the extraction from bovine or porcine pancreas or as a mixture of both these pancreas purified by recrystallisation. Human insulin is produced by enzymatic modification of insulin obtained from porcine pancreas. Human insulin is also produced by the chemical combination of A & B chains obtained by genetically modified technology of DNA recombination in bacteria. Insulin obtained by this technology is called biosynthetic human insulin.

Crystalline insulin preparation contains small amounts of heavy metals such as cadmium ,cobalt, nickel and zinc. Insulin is available as amorphous as well as crystalline powder in combination with heavy metal salts.

Insulin plays an important role in transport of glucose through cell membrane; protein synthesis in muscles, fatty acid synthesis and increase in deposition of fats in liver and adipose tissue.

Insulin also helps in oxidative phosphorylation, oxidation in T.C.A. (Tricarboxylic acid) cycle and conversion of glucose to glucose-6-phosphate with utilisation of energy (ATP). This conversion is followed by reversible transport of glucose through cell membrane. Pure insulin has a rapid onset and short duration of action. Amorphous form of insulin is having more rapid action and less duration of action as compared to crystalline form. The duration of action can be increased by esterification of insulin with metal or with protein (globin or protamine). These esterified products have a longer duration of action and onset of action is also fast.

Insulin therapy is given by admixturing various amorphous and crystalline forms as per the dose requirement of individual patient. It is a protein and is destroyed by G.I.T.secretions, therefore it should not be given orally. It should be given subcutaneously or intramuscularly. The market preparation has a potency not less than 95%. The potency is 40, 80, 100 or 500 insulin units in each ml.

Insulin is used in the treatment of Diabetes Mellitus. Side effects of insulin therapy are sweating, palpitation, anxiety and hunger.

Officials : Globin Zinc Insulin Injection I.P.
Insulin Zinc Suspension I.P.
Protamine Zinc Insulin Injection I.P.
Insulin Injection I.P.
Isophane Insulin Injection I.P.

CHLORPROPAMIDE

Chlorpropamide is an odourless, tasteless and white crystalline powder. It is soluble in alkali hydroxides, acetone and chloroform, slightly soluble in ether, and insoluble in water. It should be stored in well closed containers protected from light.

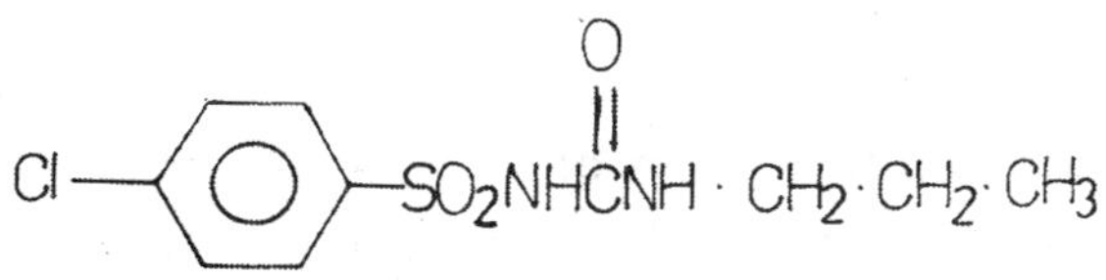

IUPAC Name : 1-[4-Chloro benzene sulfony]-3-propyl urea

Actions and uses : Chlorpropamide is an oral hypoglycemic agent. It acts by stimulating beta-cells of islets of langerhans, which stimulates release of insulin. It is only effective when islets tissue is functional. It is used in non Insulin dependent Diabetes. It is unsuitable for the patients with Diabetic ketosis. The side effects include gastro-intestinal disturbances, intolerance to alcohol, skin sensitization etc.

Officials : Chlorpropamide I.P.
Chlorpropamide Tablets I.P.

TOLBUTAMIDE

Tolbutamide is an odourless white crystalline powder. It is soluble in alkali, mineral acids, acetone and alcohol but insoluble in water. It should be stored in well closed containers protected from light.

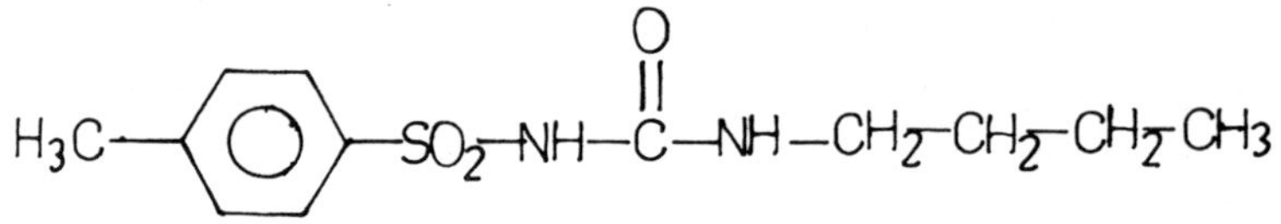

IUPAC Name : 1-Butyl-3-tosylurea.

Actions and uses : Tolbutamide has actions and uses similar to chlorpropamide but has shorter duration of action.

Officials : Tolbutamide I.P.
Tolbutamide Tablets I.P.

GLIBENCLAMIDE

Glibenclamide is an odourless, white crystalline powder. It is slightly soluble in chloroform, methanol and alcohol but very slightly soluble in water and ether. It should be stored in well closed containers protected from light.

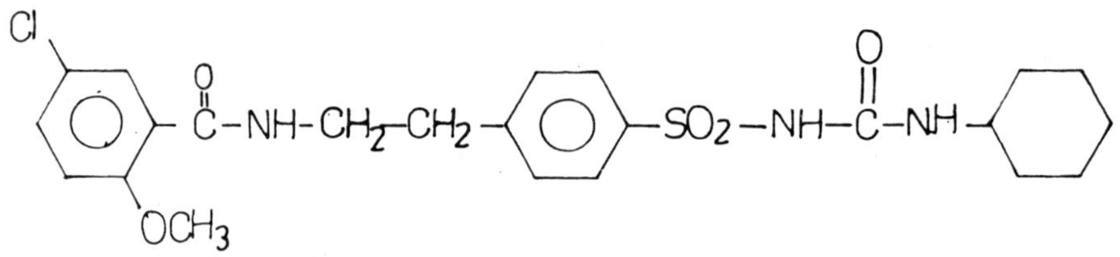

IUPAC Name : 1-[4-{ 2-(5-Chloro-2-methoxy benzamido) ethyl }benzene sulphonyl]-3- cyclohexyl urea.

Actions and uses : Glibenclamide is an oral hypoglycemic agent. It has actions and uses similar to chorpropamide. Patients who fail to respond to other hypoglycemic agents may sometimes respond to it or in combination with biguanides.

Officials : Glibenclamide I.P.
Glibenclamide Tablets I.P.

PHENFORMIN

Phenformin is available as a hydrochloride salt. It is an odourless, white crystalline powder with a bitter taste. It is soluble in water and alcohol but insoluble in ether and chloroform. It should be stored in air tight containers.

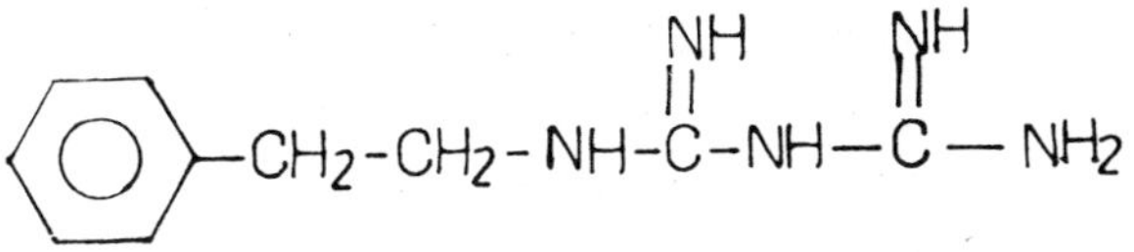

IUPAC Name : 1-Phen ethyl biguanide.

Actions and uses : Phenformin is a biguanide derivative. It acts by increasing the peripheral utilisation of glucose and inhibits gluco-neogenesis in Diabetes. These agents usually give rise to gain in weight and does not encourage lipogenesis. It reduces insulin requirements of young Diabetics The side effects include nausea, vomiting, diarrhoea and anorexia.

Officials : Phenformin Hydrochloride I.P.
Phenformin Tablets I.P.

METFORMIN

Metformin is available as a hydrochloride salt. It is an odourless, white crystalline powder with bitter taste. The salt is soluble in water, sparingly soluble in alcohol, and insoluble in ether and chloroform. It is a hygroscopic compound. It should be stored in air tight containers.

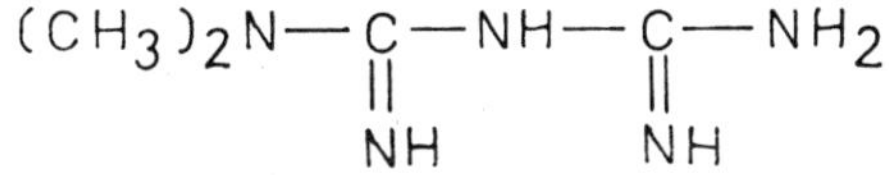

IUPAC Name: 1,1-dimethyl biguanide.

Actions and uses : Metformin is an oral hypoglycemic agent having actions and uses similar to phenformin. It is unsuitable for the treatment of young diabetics. It should not be given to patients suffering from diabeties with severe acidosis, hepatic and renal diseases, etc.

Officials : Metformin Hydrochloride I.P.
Metformin Tablets I.P.

(1) **Insulin**: Torrent : Human Actrapld

(2) **Chlorpropamide** : Deys : Copamide tab : Dose Adults initially 100-250 mg once .
Pfizer : Diabinese tab : daily after breakfast.

(3) **Tolbutamide** : Hoechst : Rastinon tab: Daily 0.5-200 gm.

(4) **Glibenclamide** : Heochst : Daonil tabs : Dose·: initially 2.5mg daily at breakfast.
Medopharm: Gluhic tabs.

(5) **Phenformin** : USV : DBI: Adults : 25 mg 1-4 times daily.
(6) **Metformin** : Franco India : Glyciphage tab : Adults : 250 mg 2-3 times daily.
Wallace : Walaphage tab

CHAPTER - 23

COAGULANTS AND ANTICOAGULANTS

Coagulation is a complex phenomenon. In this process prothrombin is converted to thrombin and fibrinogen is converted to fibrin. Fibrin forms a net in which blood cells get entangled to block the bleeding. The conversion of prothrombin to thrombin is achieved by factor X in the presence of calcium, phospholipids and factor V. Activated factor X may initiate coagulation place either by intrinsic system or by extrinsic system. Formation of factor X by intrinsic system takes more time as compared to extrinsic factor (Twenty-four seconds). This formation of thrombin splits fibrinogen molecules into small fibres. These fibres unite end to end and side to side to form an insoluble net of fibrin. The clot or fibrin can be destroyed with the help of plasma components called antithrombin. If clots are formed in the vascular system, it can be removed by proteolytic enzyme fibrinolysin or plasmin.

ANTICOAGULANTS

These agents are used in the treatment of cardiovascular disease such as myocardial infarction, venous thrombosis and to prevent thrombosis after operation. These agents prolong the duration of coagulation of blood.

HEPARIN

Heparin is available as calcium and sodium salt. Heparin sodium is a white crystalline and hygroscopic powder. It is soluble in water. It should be stored in sealed containers protected from micro-organisms.

Actions and uses : Heparin sodium inhibits blood clotting in vivo and in vitro by combining with certain fractions of plasma protein. It inhibits conversion of prothrombin to thrombin, antagonises thromboplastin and prevents formation of thrombin. Heparin is ineffective when taken orally but very well effective by intravenous injection. It is used as an anticoagulant in vascular surgery and in blood transfusions. It is also used in the treatment of arterial and venous thrombosis. It prevents coagulation during dialysis and as an adjunct to thrombolytic therapy. The side effects include haemorrhage, thrombocytopenia and allergic reactions.

Officials : Heparin sodium I.P.

Heparin sodium Injection I.P.

THROMBIN

Thrombin is cream coloured and is readily soluble in saline and forms a cloudy pale yellow solution. It should be stored in nitrogen atmosphere, in a sterile sealed container below 25°C and protected from light.

Thrombin solution in sodium chloride is used in conjuction with fibrinogen and human fibrin. A care should be taken when dried human thrombin is used which may transmit viral hepatitis.

MENADIONE [Vit.K]

Menadione is a bright yellow, crystalline and odourless powder. It is soluble in vegetable oils, benzene, sparingly soluble in chloroform and practically insoluble in water. It should be stored in well closed containers protected from light.

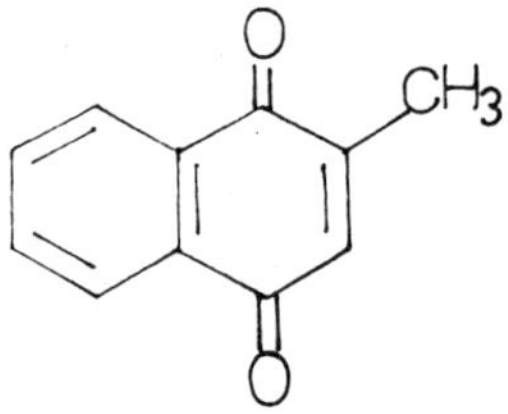

IUPAC Name : 2-Methyl naphthalene-1,4-dione.
Actions and uses : Menadione has an antihaemorrhagic action and also inhibits glucose metabolism. The side effects are irritation to skin and respiratory tract.
Officials : Menadione I.P.

BISHYDROXYCOUMARIN

Bishydroxycoumarin is also called Di-CUMAROL. It is a white crystalline powder, faint pleasant odour and slightly bitter in taste. It is soluble in alkali hydroxides; slightly soluble in chloroform ; and insoluble in water, alcohol and ether. It should be stored in well closed containers.

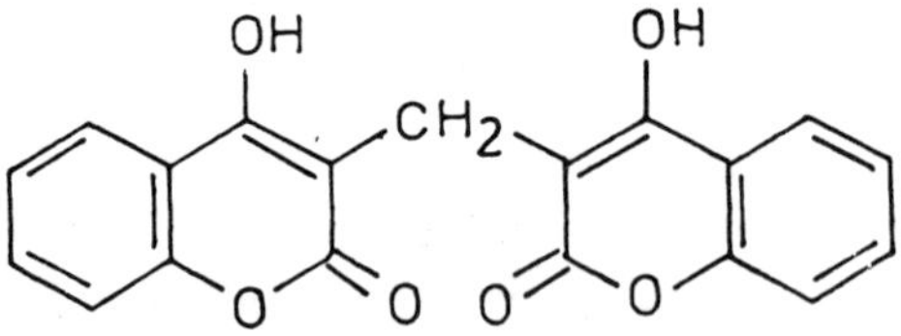

IUPAC Name : 3,3'-methylenebis [4-hydroxy coumarin]
Actions and uses : Bishydroxycoumarin is a prothrombopenic anticoagulant depresses hepatic production of prothrombin. It competes with vitamin K, therefore lowers the blood level of prothrombin and less blood is coagulable. It can be used for long term anticoagulant therapy and is effective orally .

It is used in the treatment of pulmonary embolism, post operative thrombo phlebitics, prophylaxis of post operative venous thrombosis, etc.

WARFARIN

Warfarin is available as warfarin sodium. It is an odourless, white crystalline powder having slightly bitter taste. It is soluble in water, alcohol and very slightly soluble in ether and chloroform. It should be stored in air tight containers protected from light.

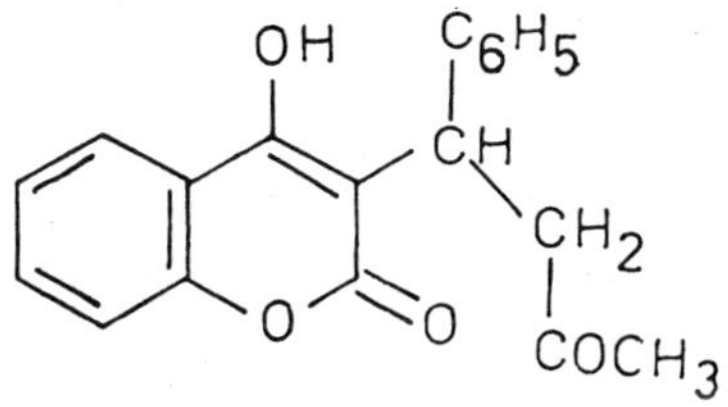

IUPAC Name : 4-Hydroxy-3-[3-oxo-1-phenylbutyl] coumarin.

Actions and uses : Warfarin is a prolong prothrombin time inhibiting anticoagulant. It acts by inhibiting the formation of factor VII. An intra-venous heparin is given for immediate blood coagulation effect. It is used in the treatment of thrombosis in veins or arteries. It reduces the risk of embolism and given in the treatment of post operative thrombosis. It should not be used in the treatment of cerebral thrombosis. It is also used as rodenticides.

(1) **Heparin** : Biological C : Beparine inj : Adults : IV 10,000-12500 i.v. state.
Pecon : Delcot inj.

(2) **Menadeone** : Sterling tabs : Gynae c.v.p. : 1-3 caps daily in divided doses.
Indon : Styptindon tab : 1-2 tab 3 times daily.

(3) **Warfarin sodium** : Unichem : Uniwarfin tab : 10-15 mg daily.

CHAPTER - 24

HISTAMINE AND ANTIHISTAMINIC AGENTS

Histamine is a potent biogenic amine, formed by decarboxylation of amino acids [Histidine] by the presence of enzyme histidine decarboxylase. Histidine is present in platelets, leucocytes, basophills, mast cells, biological fluid, lungs and gastrointestinal mucosa. Histamine acts on three type of receptors, H_1, H_2 and H_3.

Stimulation of H_1, receptors is associated with increased intra cellular cyclic guanosine 3,5 monophosphate [CGMP]. It stimulates smooth muscle contraction, vascular permeability and mucous secretion.

Activation of H_2 receptors is associated with decreasing CGMP. It increases gastric acid secretion. Both H_1 and H_2 receptors are involved in the vascular dilatation and in edema formation.

Antihistaminic are the drugs which antagonise the actions of histamine. These drugs are classified as.

(1) H_1 receptor antagonists :

- (A) Ethanolamine derivative : Diphenhydramine.
- (B) Ethelene Di amine derivative : Mepyramine.
- (C) Alkylamine derivative : Chlorpheniramine.
- (D) Piperazine derivative : Chlorcyclizine, Meclizine,Buclizine, Cyclizine, Cyproheptadine.
- (E) Phenothiazines : Promethazine.
- (F) Newer non sedating H_1 Antihistaminics : Cetrizine,Loratidine, Astemizole

(2) H_2 receptor antagonists : Cimetidine, Ranitidine, Famotidine, Oxmetidine.

HISTAMINE

Histamine is a crystalline compound. It is soluble in water, alcohol and chloroform but sparingly soluble in ether. It is available as histamine dihydrochloride salt. The salt is hygroscopic in nature. It should be stored in well closed containers protected from light.

IUPAC Name : Imidazole-4-ethylamine.

Actions and uses : Histamine is present in abundance and is formed in the tissues. The various actions of H_1 receptors and H_2 receptors have already been discussed above. It is used to diagnose impairment of the acid producing cells of the stomach and in hyposensitization.

The side effects of histamin therapy are headache fall in blood pressure tachycardia, visual disturbances, vomiting, diarrhoea, flushing of skin, etc.

Officials : Histamine Acid Phosphate I.P.
Histamine Acid Phosphate Injection I.P.

DIPHENHYDRAMINE

Diphenhydramine is available as diphenhydramine hydrochloride. The salt is an odourless, white crystalline powder with a bitter taste followed by sensation of numbness. It is soluble in water and alcohol, slightly in acetone and ether. It should be stored in air tight containers protected from light.

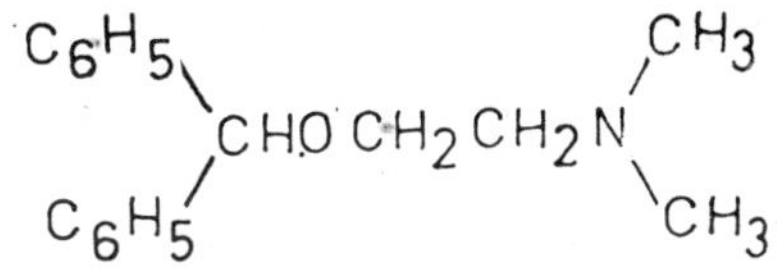

IUPAC Name : 2-Benzhydroxy ethyl-N N-dimethyl amine.

Actions and uses : Diphenhydramine is an H_1 antagonist. It causes sedation and possesses antiemetic and antimuscarinic effects. It is used in the treatment of nausea, vomiting, motion sickness and parkinsonian symptoms. It is also added in cough and cold preparations.

Officials : Diphenhydramine Hydrochloride I.P.
Diphenhydramine Capsules I.P.

MEPYRAMINE

Mepyramine is available as mepyramine maleate. The salt is an odourless, white or creamy powder and is bitter in taste. It is freely soluble in water, alcohol and chloroform. It should be stored in well closed containers protected from light.

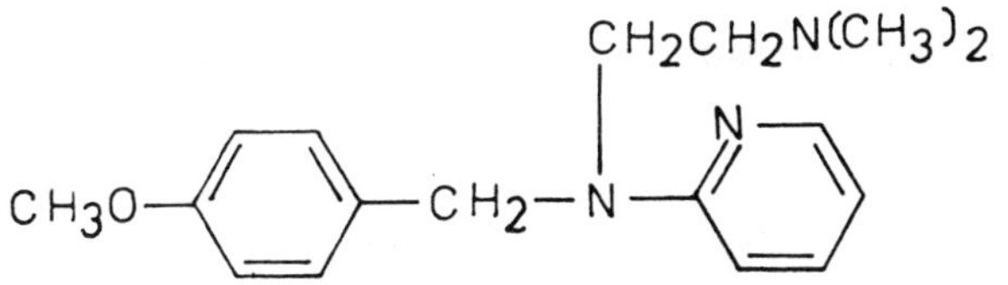

IUPAC Name: 2-[N-p-Anisyl-N-2-pyridyl amino]ethyl di methylamine.

Actions and uses : Mepyramine is mainly used in the treatment of allergy, anaphylactic condition, hay fever, urticaria, etc.

Officials : Mepyramine Maleate I.P.
Mepyramine Tablets I.P.

PROMETHAZINE

Promethazine is available as hydrochloride salt. The salt is an odourless white or faintly yellowish crystalline powder with a bitter taste. It is soluble in water, chloroform and alcohol. The compound is unstable in aqueous solutions when exposed to heat, light, air or oxygen. It should therefore be stored in well closed containers protected from light.

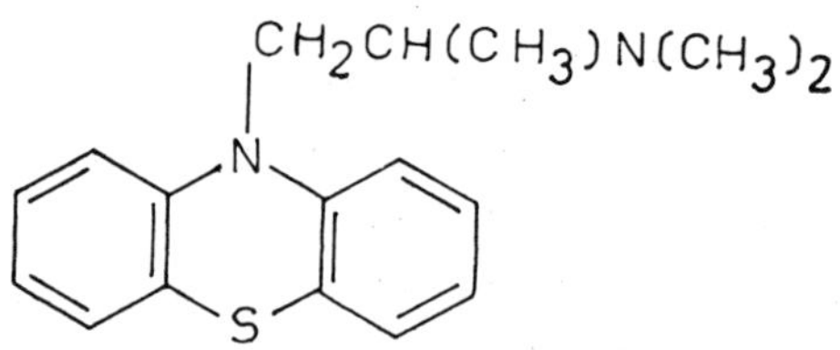

IUPAC Name : 10-[2-Dimethyl aminopropyl] phenothiazine.

Actions and uses : Promethazine is a powerful long acting H_1 antagonist. It has effects on involuntary muscles of intestine, bladder, uterus and bronchioles. It also antagonises vasodilatory and vasoconstrictor action of histamine. The duration of action is long (20 hours) therefore its use is restricted.

It is used in the treatment of allergic reactions of skin and mucous membrane. It is also used for prevention and treatment of vomiting, motion-sickness, nausea and radiation sickness.

Officials : Promethazine Hydrochloride I.P.
Promethazine Injection I.P.
Promethazine Syrup I.P.
Promethazine Tablets I.P.
Promethazin Theoclate I.P.

CHLORPHENIRAMINE

Chlorpheniramine is available as maleate salt. The salt is an odourless, white crystalline powder with a bitter taste. It is soluble in water, alcohol and chloroform but very slightly soluble in ether. It should be stored in well closed containers protected from light.

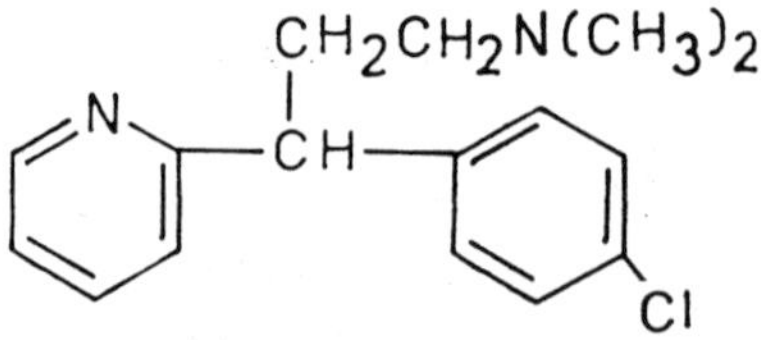

IUPAC Name : 3-[4-Chlorophenyl]-3-[pyrid-2-yl]-N,N-dimethyl propyl amine.

Actions and uses : Chlorpheniramine has actions and uses similar to promethazine hydrochloride but it is effective in smaller doses and does not produce antiemetic effect.

Officials : Chlorpheniramine Maleate I.P.
Chlorpheniramine Elixir/Tablets I.P.

CYPROHEPTADINE

Cyproheptadine is available as a hydrochloride salt. The salt is an odourless, white yellow crystalline powder with a bitter taste. It should be stored in air tight containers.

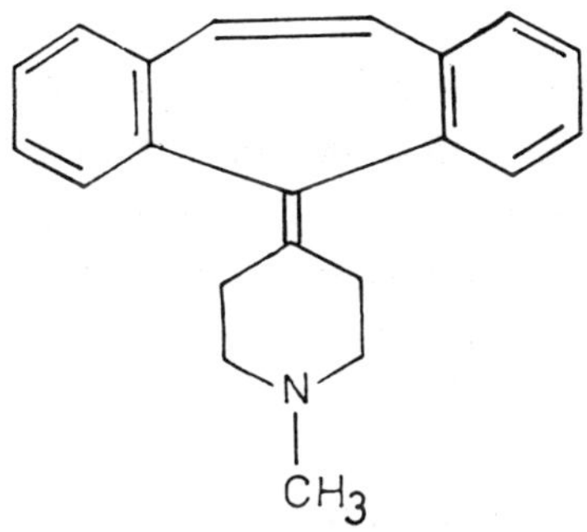

IUPAC Name: 4-[5H-Dibenzo (a,d) cyclohepten-5-ylidene] -1-methyl piperidine.

Actions and uses : Cyproheptidine has actions and uses similar to promethazine. It is also used to stimulate appetite and in treatment of migraine, headache, cushing's disease and allergic reactions.

Officials : Cyproheptadine Hydrochloride I.P.
Cyproheptadine Hydrochloride Syrup I.P.
Cyproheptadine Tablet I.P.

(1) **Histamine** : John wyeth : Algipan : Apply cream in affected areas.

(2) **Diphehydramine** : Parke davis : Benadryl syp. : Adults : 10-25ml 3-4 times daily.
Astra\Idl : Mucosol syp. 5-10ml 2-3 times daily.

(3) **Promethazine** : Rhone poulenc: Phenergan tab./ Ellixir/ syp. : 25mg at night 6-10ml during day.
Rhone poulnec: Phenseryl syp. : 5-10ml b.i.d.

(4) **Cyproheptadine** : Merind : Practin Tab.

(5) **Chlorpheniramine** : Glaxo : Piriton expectorant.

CHAPTER - 25

ANALGESICS AND ANTIPYRETICS

Analgesics are agents which relieve pain without loss of consciousness. Pain is an unpleasant sensation and cannot be defined objectively. Clinically pain can be of superficial pain, deep non-visceral pain from muscles, joints, ligaments and bones; visceral pain, and functional pain. Important analgesics include morphine and related compounds. Some synthetic compounds are also active as analgesics e.g. butorphanol, methadone, buprenorphine.

MORPHINE

Morphine is an alkaloid obtained from unripe fruit of *Papaver somniferum*. It is available as morphine hydrochloride and morphine sulphate. Its hydrochloride salt is an odourless, colourless, silky crystalline powder having bitter taste. It is soluble in glycerol and water, slightly soluble in alcohol and insoluble in chloroform. It is incompatible with ammonia. It should be stored in air tight containers, protected from light.

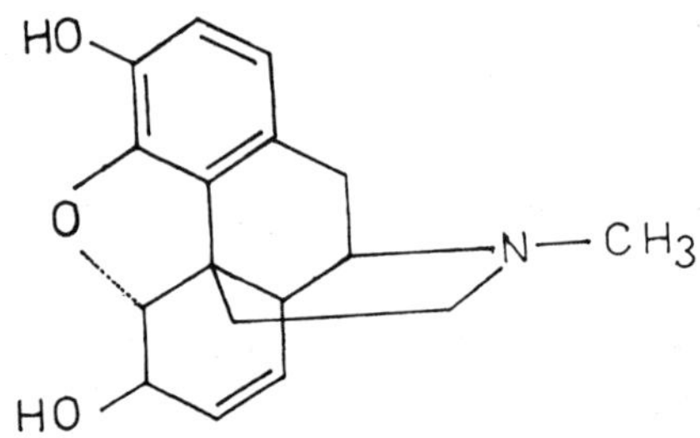

IUPAC Name : 4a,5,7a,8,9,9c Hexahydro-12-methyl-8, 9c-imino ethophenanthrol(4,5 b cd) furan-3,5-diol.

Actions and uses : Morphine is a powerful analgesic and narcotic. It is a central nervous system stimulant. It depresses thalamus, sensory cortex, respiratory and cough centres. It stimulates spinal cord, vagous and vomiting centre. Morphine increases tone of involuntary muscles like sphincters of gastro-intestinal track. It reduces secretions and dilates skin vessels. It is used to relieve pain, anxiety and sleeplessness due to pain.

The major drawback of morphine is to make person dependent on the drug and produces marked euphoria. In morphine poisoning cases saline purgatives are given to reduce rate of absorption of drug and 0.2% potassium permanganate solution is used for gastric lavage.

Officials : Morphine Hydrochloride I.P.
Morphine Hydrochloride Solution I.P.
Morphine Sulphate I.P.
Morphine and Atropine Injection I.P.
Ethyl Morphine Hydrochloride I.P.

PETHIDINE

Pethidine is available as pethidine hydrochloride. The salt is an odourless, white crystalline powder with a slightly acidic bitter taste. It is soluble in water, alcohol and chloroform but very slightly soluble in acetone. It should be stored in well closed containers protected from light.

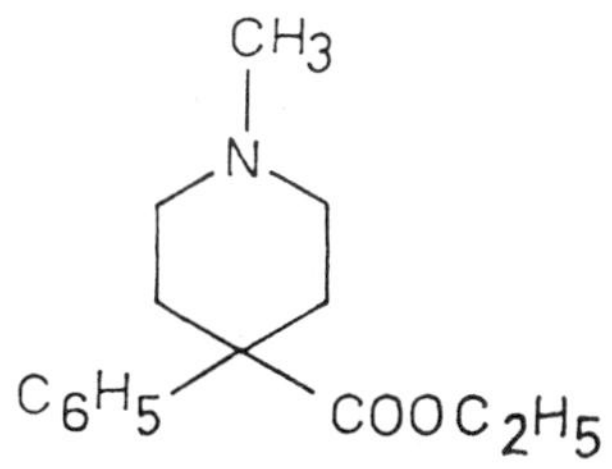

IUPAC Name : 4-Ethoxycarbonyl-1-methyl-4-phenyl piperidin.

Actions and uses : It has local effect on nerve fibres and nerve endings. It is used to relieve more severe types of pain. Its spasmolytic action is less important. It is used to relieve pain in most medical or surgical conditions post operative conditions. It is a useful alternate to morphine for control of pain. Barbiturates or hyoscine may be given concurrently to enhance sedation and to depress memory. Diphenoxylate and Fentanyl are pethidine analogeses having similar actions to pethidine.

Officials : Pethidine Hydrochloride I.P.
Pethidine Injection I.P.
Pethidine Tablets I.P.

CODEINE

Codeine is an alkaloid obtained from latex of unripe fruit of *Papaverum somniferum.* It is available as codeine phosphate. The salt is an odourless, colourless or white crystalline powder with a bitter taste. It should be stored in air tight containers protected from light.

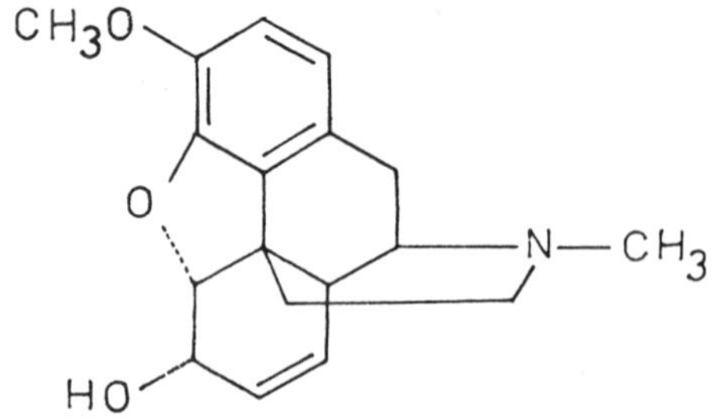

IUPAC Name : 3-O-Methyal morphine

or

4a,5,7a,8,9,9c -Hexahydro- 12-methyl-8, 9c-imino ethanophenanthrol (4,5bcd) furan-3-methoxy-5-ol.

Actions and uses : Codeine is a modrate analgesic and has cough suppressant effect. It is less depressant to respiratory centre.

Officials : Codeine Phosphate I.P
Codeine Phosphate Syrup I.P.

METHADONE

Methadone is available as methadone hydrochloride. The salt is an odourless, colourless to white crystalline powder with bitter taste. It is soluble in chloroform, alcohol and water but practically insoluble in ether. It is incompatible with certain dyes. It should be stored in well closed containers.

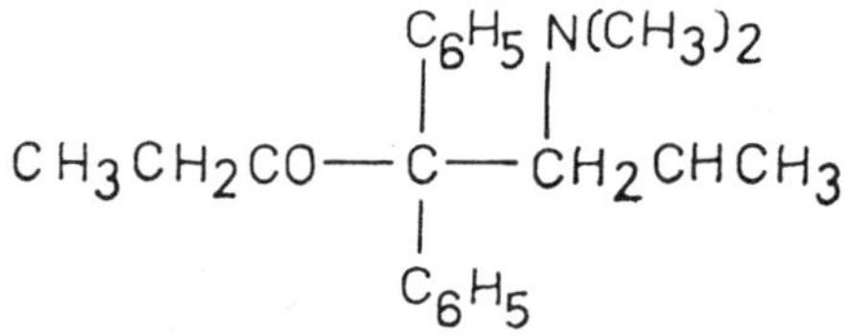

IUPAC Name : N,N-Dimethyl-N-[5-oxo-4,4-diphenyl heptane-2-yl] amine.

Actions and uses : Methadone has similar actions and uses as morphine hydrochloride. It is a less potent analgesic but has a delayed onset of action. It is not used as a pre-anaesthetic agent because of less sedative action. It depresses cough centre and respiratory centre therefore it is undesirable for as an obstetric analgesic. It is used to treat morphine addicts as therepuiic substitutent.

Officials : Methadone Injection I.P.
Methadone Tablets I.P.
Methadone Hydrochloride I.P.

ANTIPYRETICS

Fever is defined as an increase in body temperature because of abnormal hypothalamic thermostat. Hypothalamus plays an important role in regulating body temperature and also to increase or decrease secretion of sweat glands.

Antipyretics are the agents which reduce increased body temperature to normal. Common examples are aspirin, paracetamol, analgin, etc.

ASPIRIN

Aspirin is an odourless, colourless or white crystalline powder with a slightly acidic taste. It is soluble in solutions of acetate and citrates, slightly soluble in alcohol, ether and chloroform and practically insoluble in water. In presence of moisture, aspirin hydrolyses salicylic acid and acetic acid. It should be stored in air tight containers.

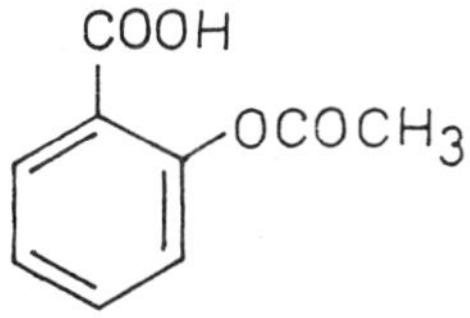

IUPAC Name : 2-Acetoxy benzoic acid.

Actions and uses : Aspirin has analgesic, anti inflammatory and anti pyretic action by inhibiting prostaglandin synthatase. It is rapidly absorbed from the upper gastro intestinal tract. It is used in the treatment of chronic rheumatic state. Its use in the children should be avoided.

Side effects of aspirin therapy are gastrointestinal disorders like nausea, vomiting, irritation of gastric mucosa, etc. It also increases bleeding time.

Officials : Acetylsalicylic Acid, Tablets I.P.
Compound Acetylsalicylic Acid, Tablets I.P.
Methyl Salicylate I.P.
Sodium Salicylate I.P.
Aspirin Tablets I.P.
Soluble Aspirin Tablets I.P.

PARACETAMOL

Paracetamol is an odourless, white crystalline powder with a bitter taste. It is soluble in alkali hydroxides, alcohol and acetone, slightly soluble in glycerol and water. It should be stored in air tight containers.

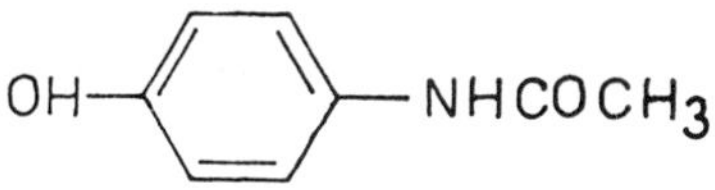

IUPAC Name : 4-Hydroxyacetanilide. or
N-para aceto amino phenol.

Actions and uses : Paracetamol has similar antipyretic action as that of aspirin but it is weaker than aspirin. It has also anti-inflammatory activity. It is used in the treatment of pain such as headache, toothache, rheumatism and neuralgia. Long term use may lead to renal and hepatic damage.

Officials : Paracetamol I.P.
Paracetamol Tablets I.P.
Paracetamol Syrup I.P.

ANALGIN

Analgin is an odourless, white to yellowish crystalline powder with a bitter taste. It is freely soluble in water, slightly soluble in alcohol, practically insoluble in chloroform and solvent ether. It should be stored in air tight containers.

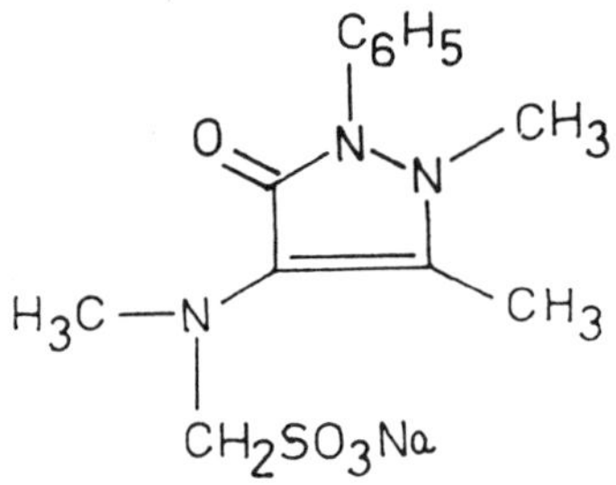

IUPAC Name : 1,5-Dimethyl, 2-phenyl, 4-[N-methyl, N-sodium methyl sulphonate] amine, 3-oxo, 4-pyrazoline.

Actions and uses : Analgin is used to relieve headache, muscle pain, and post-operative pain etc. It is also used as an antipyretic. Nausea, vomiting, rashes, aganulocytosis, etc. are side effects of analgin.

Officials : Analgin I.P.
Analgin Tablets I.P.

DEXTROPROPOXYPHENE

Dextropropoxyphene is available as dextropropoxyphene hydrochloride. The salt is an odourless, white yellowish powder with a bitter taste. It is soluble in water, alcohol and chloroform but insoluble ether. It should be stored in air tight containers.

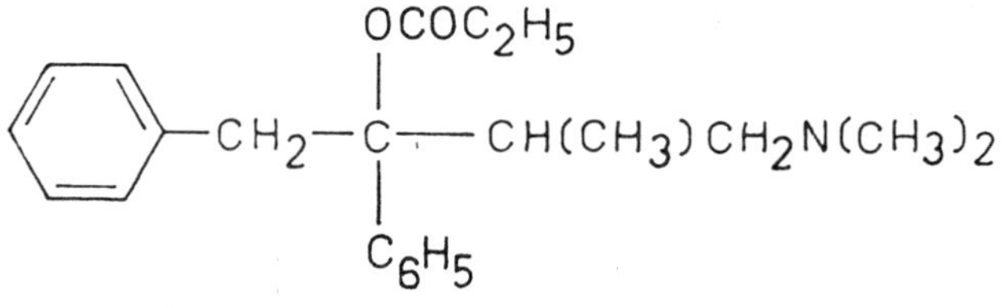

IUPAC Name : 4-Dimethyl amino-3- methyl-1,2-diphenyl but-2-yl propionate hydrochloride

or

Dimethyl [(2R,3S)2-methyl-3,4-diphenyl-3-propionyloxybutyl] amine.

Actions and uses : Dextropropoxyphene is a potent analgesic similar to codeine but produces less constipation. It develops rapid analgesia. It may cause nausea, vomiting, drowsiness and irritation to mucous membrane

Dextropropoxyphene napsylate is less bitter and irritant to mucous membrane as compared to its hydrochloride salt. The other properties are similar to Dextropropoxyphene hydrochloride.

Officials : Dextropropoxyphene Hydrochloride I.P.
Dextropropoxyphene Napsylate I.P.

PENTAZOCINE

Pentazocine is an odourless, white or creamy white powder. It is soluble in chloroform, slightly soluble in alcohol and ether and very slightly soluble in water. Pentazocine salt is slightly soluble in water. It should be stored in air tight containers protected from light.

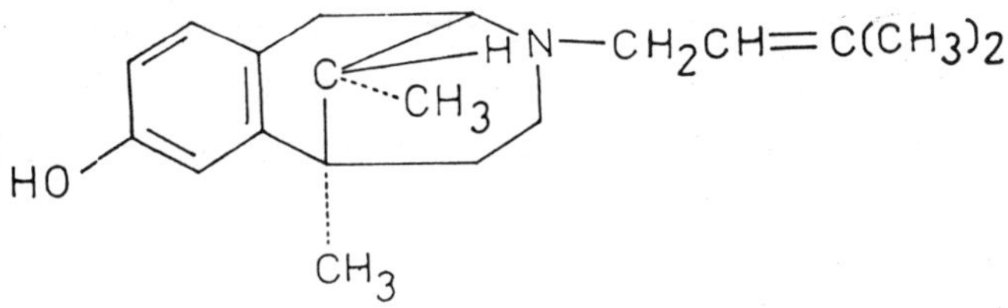

IUPAC Name : 1,2,3,4,5,6-Hexahydro-6,11-dimethyl-3-(3-methyl-but-2 enyl]-2,6-methano-3-benzazocin

Actions and uses : Pentazocine hydrochloride is a narcotic antagonist having sedation and analgesia. It depresses respiratory centre and fall in blood pressure.

Officials :

(1) **Morphine** : Modi Mundi Pharma : Morticontin (C.R.) continus Tab.
morphine sulphate C.R Tab.10,30,60,100mg.

(2) **Codein** : Indon : Codeine sulphate Tab 25 mg. : Pfizer : Corex Sy. -10mg/5ml.

(3) **Aspirin** : Reckitt columan : Disprin Tab. 350mg. 300 to 600mg./day.
: US vitamins : Ecospirin Tab. 150 to 325mg.

(4) **Paracetamol** : B. Wellcome : Calpol Tab./Sy. :
Themis : Metacin Tab./Sy./Drops.

(5) **Analgin** : IDPL : Analgin Tab. I.P. 30-60mg/kg./day.
: Hoechst : Novalgin Tab./Inj. 500mg. 0.8ml/day.

(6) **Dextropropoxyphene** : Roussel : Corbutyl Tab. 60 to 120mg. daily.
Whokhardt : Ibu-Proxyvon 65mg. Capsules.

(7) **Pentazocine** : Ranbaxy : Fortwin 25mg Tab. as HCl.
: Ranbaxy : Fortwin 30mg/mlInj. as Lactate.
: Indoco : Susewin inj. 30mg/ml Inj. as lactate.

CHAPTER - 26

NON STEROIDAL ANTIINFLAMMATORY AGENTS

Antiinflamnatory agents are the drugs which reduce inflammation and pain arising from it. Glucocorticoids (hydrocortisone and cortisone) are steroidal antiinflammatory agents but are not recommended for their various undesirable effects. The non-steroidal anti inflammatory agents also have analgesic and antipyretic properties. These drugs are used in the treatment of arthritis, rheumatism and ankylosing, spondylitis. They have weaker analgesic actions as compared to opoid derivatives. They are classified as :

(i)	Salicyclic acid derivatives	:	Aspirin
(ii)	N-arylanthranilic acid derivatives	:	Mefenamic acid.
(iii)	Indolyl or aryl acetic acid derivatives	:	Indomethacin.
(iv)	Pyrazole derivatives	:	Phenyl butazone, oxyphen butazone.

INDOMETHACIN

Indomethacin is an odourless, tasteless, pale yellow, crystalline powder. It is slightly soluble in chloroform and ether. It should be stored in air tight containers protected from light.

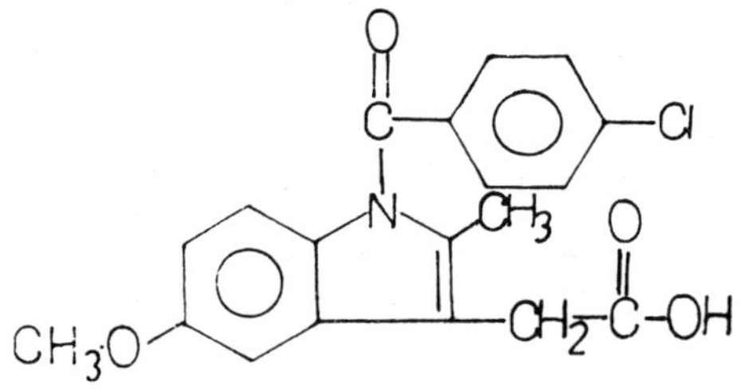

IUPAC Name : 1-(4-Chlorobenzoyl)-5-methoxy-2-methyl indol -3-yl-acetic acid.

Action and uses : Indomethacin is an anti-inflammatory, antipyretic and analgesic. It is effective in reducing swelling in cases of gout and rheumatoid arthritis, osteoarthritis and ankylosing spondylitis. The side effects are dizziness, dyspepsia and peptic ulceration.

PHENYLBUTAZONE

Phenyl butazone is an odourless white crystalline powder having bitter taste. It is soluble in alkali hydroxides, and chloroform; slightly soluble in alcohol and ether and insoluble in water. It should be stored in air tight containers protected from light.

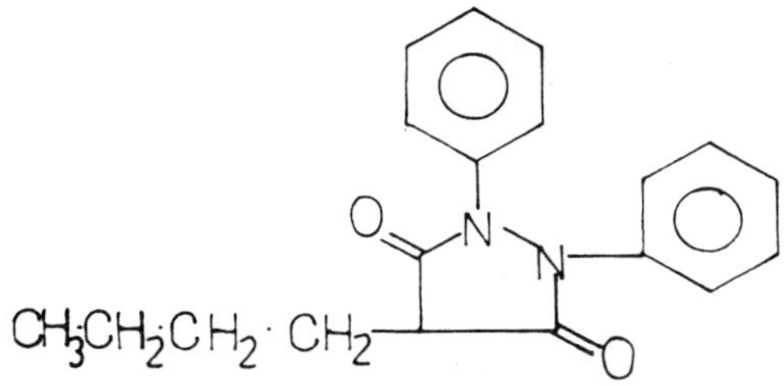

IUPAC Name : 4-Butyl-1,2-diphenylpyrazolidine -3,5-dione.

Action and uses : Phenylbutazone is an antiinflammatory agent similar to aspirin. It exhibits uricosuric and sodium retention properties and blocks the iodine uptake by thyroid gland. It is a long acting anti inflammatory agent used in rheumatic disorders. The important side effects are gastric upset, rashes, mucosal ulceration of mouth and other parts of G.I.T.

Officials : Phenylbutazone I.P.
Phenylbutazone Tablets I.P.

OXYPHENBUTAZONE

Oxyphenbutazone is an odourless white crystalline powder with a bitter taste. It is soluble in alkali hydroxides, acetone and alcohol, slightly soluble in chloroform and ether, and very slightly soluble in water. It should be stored in air tight containers.

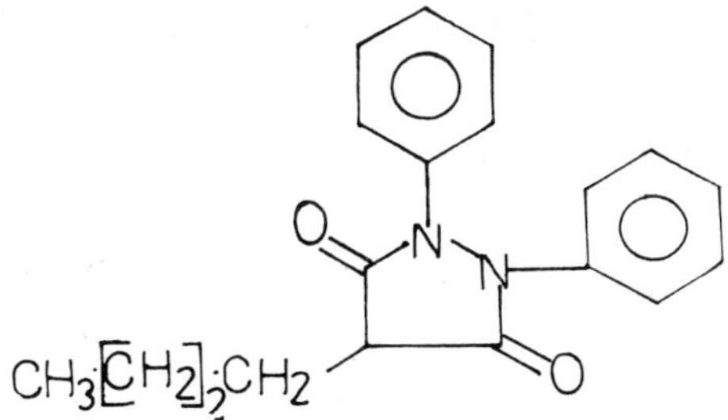

IUPAC Name : 4-Butyl-2-(4-hydroxyphenyl)-1-phenyl pyrazolidine-3,5 dione.

Action and uses : Oxyphenbutazone has actions, uses and side effects similar to phenylbutazone. It is used in the treatment of acute gout, active rheumatoid arthritis and other disorders. Its ophthalmic preparation is used in inflammatory conditions of eye.

Officials : Oxyphenbutazone I.P.
Oxyphenbutazone Tablets I.P.

IBUPROFEN

Ibuprofen is a white crystalline powder with a characteristic odour. It is soluble in alcohol, ether, chloroform, and acetone but slightly soluble in water. It should be stored in air tight containers protected from light.

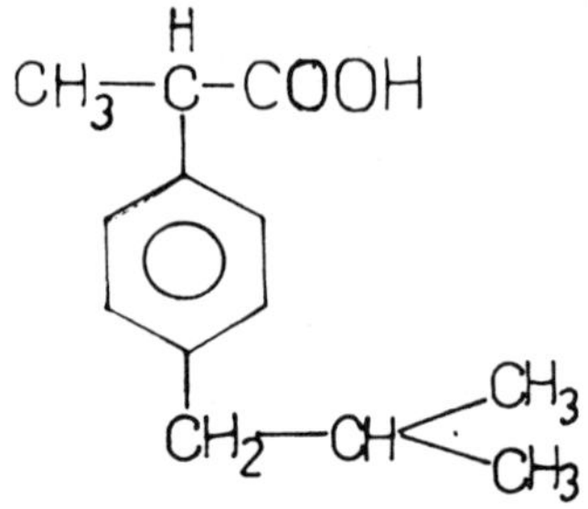

IUPAC Name : 2-(4-Isobutylphenyl) propionic acid.

Action and uses : Ibuprofen is an analgesic with a lesser anti inflammatory property as compared to aspirin. It is used to relieve pain or inflammation in rheumatic diseases. It may cause bronchospasm in patients of bronchial asthma or allergic persons.

Officials : Ibuprofen I.P
Ibuprofen Tablets I.P.

(1) **Indomethacin** : Jagsonpal : Indocap Cap. 25 mg.
: Jagsonpal : Indocap SR Cap. 75 mg. Sustained Release.

(2) **Phenyl Butazone** : SG pharma : Zolandin Tab. 100 to 200 mg TID.
: Pharmed : Actimol Tab. 50mg.

(3) **Oxyphenbutazone** : IDPL : Phenabid Tab. 100mg. - 100 to 200mg. 2 to 3 times daily.
: Albert David : Siorll Tab. 100mg.

(4) **Ibuprofen** : Knoll : Brofen 200/400/600mg. Tab. 200 to 600 mg twice daily.
: Knoll : Febrilix Sy 100mg/5ml.
: Cipla : Ibugesic Tab. 200/400/600mg.
: Ibugesic Susp. 100mg/5ml.

CHAPTER - 27

THYROXINE AND ANTITHYROIDS

Thyroid gland is an endocrine gland which utilises inorganic iodides present in blood plasma to synthesise and secrete, thyroxine and tri-iodo thyronine. These hormones are stored as bound to thyroglobulin. These hormones are responsible for basal metabolic rate (BMR). In absence of these glands BMR can reduce to 50%, while in excessive secretion (hyperthyroidism) it may increase to 160%. The deficiency of thyroid hormones leads to myxedema (hypothyroidism) and, affects growth and development of brain. Excessive secretion of thyroid hormones is called hyperthyroidism (thyrotoxicosis). In this condition metabolic rate, heart rate, anxiety and restlessness are increased.

THYROXINE

Thyroxine is official as thyroxine sodium. It is an odourless white to pale brownish yellow powder. It is soluble in alkali hydroxides, slightly soluble in alcohol and water, and very slightly soluble in ether and chloroform. It should be stored in air tight containers, protected from light.

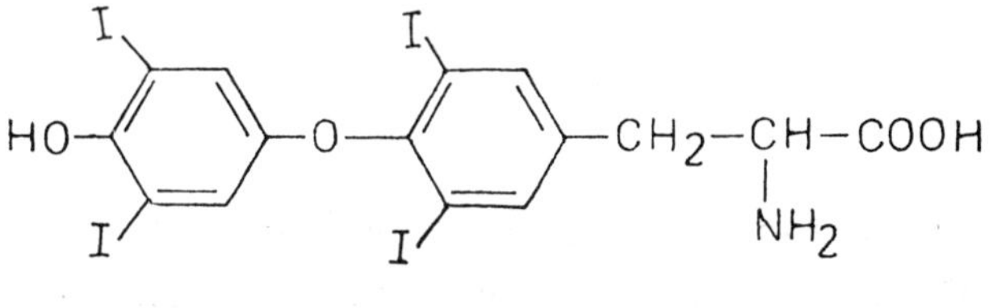

IUPAC Name : 3-[4-(4-hydroxy-3,5-di-iodophenoxy)-3,5-di iodo phenyl]-L-alanine.

Actions and uses : Thyroxine sodium is used in the treatment of thyroid deficiency states and cretinism. It should not be given to the patients with normal functioning of the gland, because intrinsic secretion of the hormone is destroyed by the drug. It increases oxygen consumption and stimulates general metabolism associated with increased excretion of nitrogen, calcium, water and urine. Side effects of thyroxine include sweating, tachycardia, diarrhoea, restlessness and excitability.

Officials : Thyroid I.P.
Thyroid Tablets I.P.
Thyroxine Sodium I.P.
Thyroxin Tablets I.P.

METHIMAZOLE

Methimazole is a white to pale buff coloured crystalline powder, with a faint characteristic odour. It is soluble in chloroform, water and alcohol; and sparingly soluble in ether.

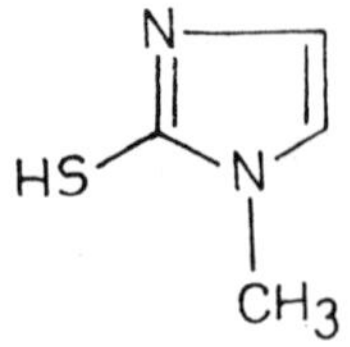

IUPAC Name : 1-methyl, 2-thione, 1,3-dihydro-2-imidazole

or

1-Methylimidazol-2-thiol

Actions and uses : Methimazole is an antithyroid drug and is used in the treatment of hyperthyroidism. It is a potent, prolonged acting antithyroidal drug. It lowers metabolic rate.

METHYLTHIOURACIL

Methylthiouracil is an odourless white crystalline powder. It is soluble in boiling water, sparingly soluble in alcohol, chloroform and ether; and freely soluble in alkali hydroxides. It is stored in well closed containers protected from light.

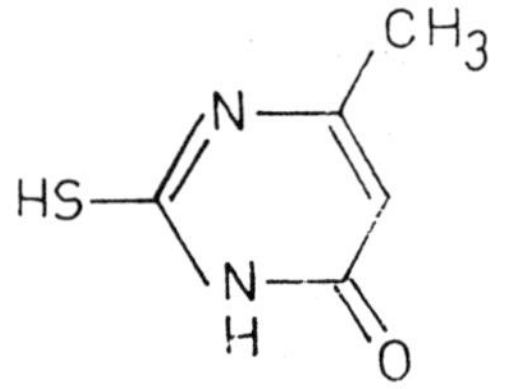

IUPAC Name : 2,3-Dihydro-6-methyl-2-thioxo-4-{1H}-pyrimidinone

Actions and uses : Methylthiouracil is a homologue of thiouracil. It is an antithyroidal agent used in the treatment of hyperthyroidism. Common side effects are headache, vomiting, nausea and skin-rashes.

PROPYLTHIOURACIL

Propylthiouracil is a white crystalline powder and bitter in taste. It is soluble in alkali hydroxides; sparingly soluble in alcohol; and slightly soluble in water, chloroform and ether.

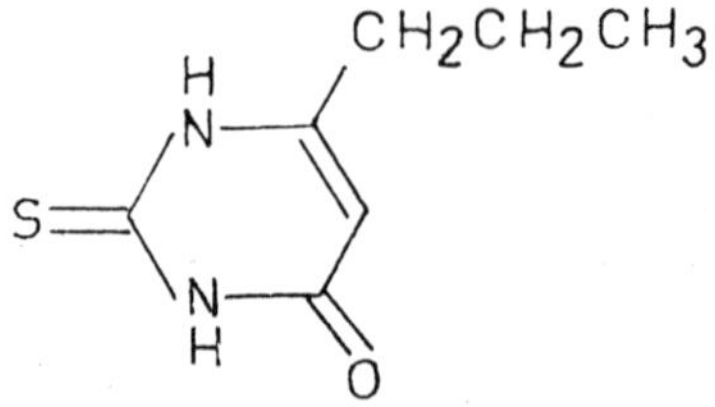

IUPAC Name : 2,3-Dihydro-6-propyl-2-thioxo-4[1H] pyrimididione.
Actions and uses : Propylthiouracil is used in the management of hyperthyroidism. It blocks extrathyroidal conversion of thyroxin to liothyronine [Triiodothyroxine]. It decreases hypermetabolic conditions. Side effects are granulocytopenia, leucopenia, dermatitis etc. It may cause pro-sensitivity to other thiouracils.

Officials : Propylthiouracil I.P.
Propylthiouracil Tablets I.P.

CHAPTER - 28

DIAGNOSTIC AGENTS

There are certain agents which do not play any role in the treatment and prevention of diseases, but they are essential for the identification or diagnosis of certain diseases. These agents are called diagnostic agents. Certain radio-pharmaceuticals and inorganic ions are also helpful in the diagnosis of diseases Inorganic diagnostic agents have already been in the pharmaceutical chemistry -I. Organic diagnostic agents are classified into four major groups.

I **Drugs used as X-ray contrast media** : Iopanoic acid, Propylidone.
II **Drugs used for organ function test** : Sulphobromophthalein sodium, Indiogatin disulphonate sodium.
III **Drugs used to determine blood volume** : Evans blue
IV **Miscellaneous compounds** : Congo red, fluorescein sodium

Drugs used as X-ray contrast media
OR
Radio opaque contrast media

These agents have the ability to absorb x - rays. These agents are used for the evaluation of gastro-intestinal tract, gall bladder, ureter, fallopian tubes, bile duct and renal system. These drugs are administered in various ways to visualize with the help of fluoroscopy or x-ray.

These drugs are usually radioopaque and therefore provide a shadow of positive x-ray contrast.

IOPANOIC ACID

Iopanoic acid is a cream coloured, tasteless powder containing characteristic odour. It is soluble in alcohol, chloroform, ether and solution of alkali hydroxides and carbonates. It should be stored in well closed containers protected from light.

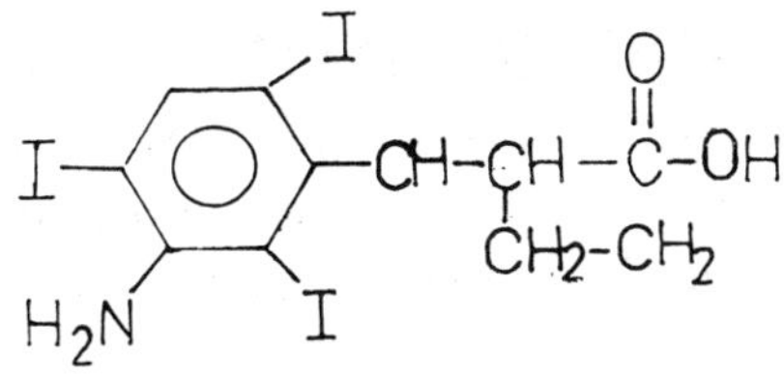

IUPAC Name : 3-Amino- α-ethyl-2,4,6-tri iodo benzene propanoic acid

Actions and uses : Iopanoic acid is used for roentgenography. It is given to the patients with a fat free evening meal. It is promptly absorbed from the gastro-intestinal tract and concentrated in gall-bladder. It visualizes the gall bladder and extra-hepatic ducts.

It is relatively free from toxicity but may cause . The hypersensitivity reactions involving skin, mucous membranes and systemic serum sickness. It should not be used in patients with acute nephritis and uremia. After roentgenography patients are given a high fat meal to excrete the drug.

Dose : 3-6 gm.

PROPYLIODONE

Propyliodone is a white crystalline and odourless powder. It is slightly soluble in alcohol and chloroform, very slightly soluble in ether; and practically insoluble in water. It should be stored in air tight containers protected from light.

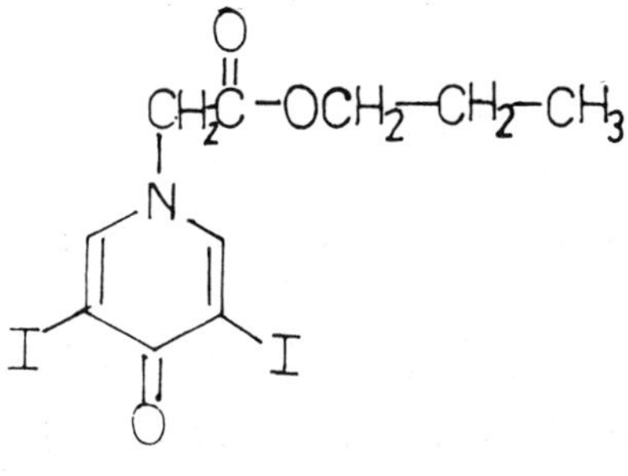

IUPAC Name: Propyl-(1,4-dihydro-3,5-di-iodo-4-oxopyrid-1-yl) acetate.

Actions and uses : Propyliodone is used as a radio-opaque contrast media for the examination of bronchial tract. It's aseptic aqueous or 60% oily suspension is used for diagnostic purposes.

Drugs used for organ function test

In the year 1909 Abed and Rowntree worked on liver excretory functions using phenolitetra chlorophthalein and other similar compounds. These compounds are excreted from certain organs e.g. 8 phenol sulfophthalin is excreted in urine by the kidney. These findings help in determining the function of a particular organ. Such drugs are used to test liver, kidney and gastric functions.

SULPHOBROMOPHTHALEIN SODIUM

Sulphobromophthalein is an odourless, white, crystalline powder which is bitter in taste. It is soluble in water but insoluble in alcohol and acetone. It is a hygroscopic compound and should be stored in air tight containers.

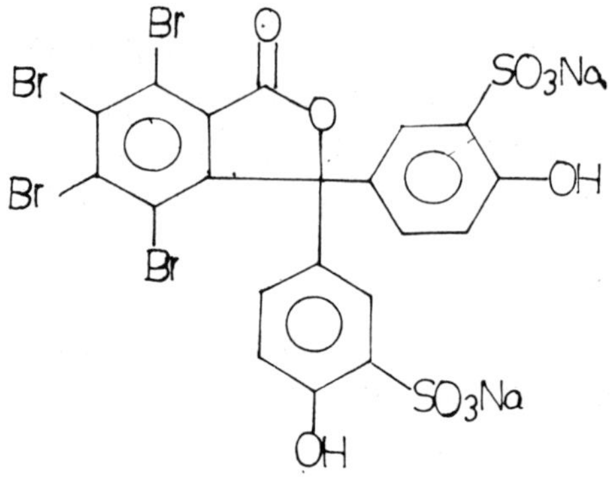

IUPAC Name : 3,3'- [4,5,6,7-tetrabromo-3-oxy-1-(3H)-isobenzo-furanylidene] bis [6-hydroxybenzene sulfonic acid] disodium salt.

Actions and uses : Sulphobromophthalein is used for testing liver functions. A fat free break fast is provided to the patients in the morning before performing this test. If there is a normal liver excretion most of the dye is excreted in a period of 30 minutes. Precautions should be taken in the asthmatic patients and in patient with a history of urticaria or allergy.

Dose : 5 mg/kg not more than 500 mg. body wt.

Official : Sulphobromophthalein sodium I.P.
Sulphobromophthalein sodium Injection I.P.

INDIGOTIN DISULPHONATE SODIUM or INDIGO CARMINE or INDIGO BLUE

Indigotin disulphonate sodium is available as purple blue coppery lusturous granules. It is slightly soluble in water and alcohol, and practically insoluble in organic solvents. It is sensitive to light. It should be stored in air tight containers protected from light.

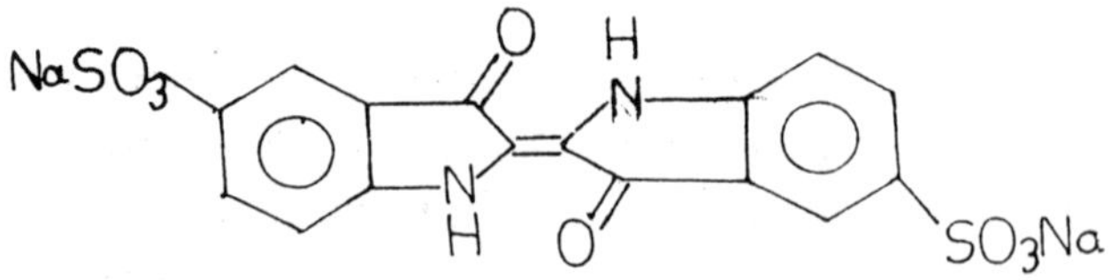

IUPAC Name : Disodium 5,5'-indigotin disulphonate

Actions and uses : Indigo caramine is a dye used for renal functions to locate urethral orifices. The dye is entirely excreted within three hours after an intravenous injection. The rate of excretion is determined colorimetrically. Indigo caramine is also useful in colouring nylon, surgical sutures, testing of milk and as a food colour. The patient should be tested for sensitivity before the drug is given.

Officials : Indigocarmine I.P.

Drugs used to determine blood volume

Estimation of blood volume is an important test to guide physician for the treatment of shock. This test provides amount of plasma and other fluids. The drugs used for determination of blood volume are Evans blue, Indocyanine green and fluorescien sodium.

EVANS BLUE

Evans blue is an odourless, green or blue green powder. It is very soluble in water, very slightly soluble in alcohol, and practically insoluble in benzene, chloroform and ether. It is a hygroscopic compound and should be stored in air tight containers.

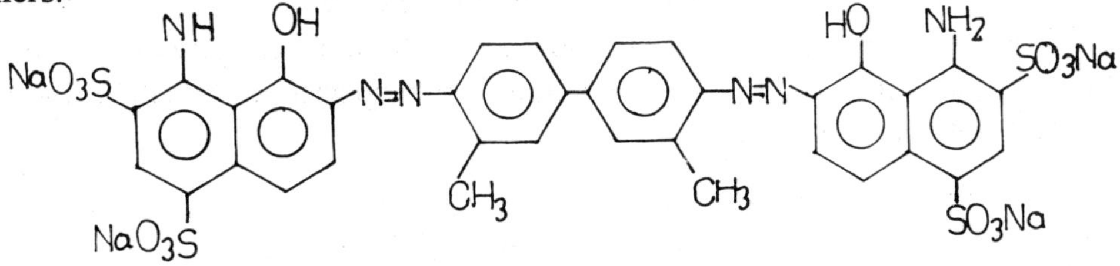

IUPAC Name : 6,6'- [(3,3'-Dimethyl{1,1'-biphenyl}-4-4'-diyl) bis{ azo}] bis(4-amino-5- hydroxy-1,3-naphthalenedisulphonic acid] tetrasodium salt.

Actions and uses : Evans blue is used as a diagnostic agent for blood volume estimation. A known quantity of the dye is injected into blood. After sometime when the dye is thoroughly mixed in blood, a sample of blood is withdrawn. The concentration of this dye in blood determines the volume of blood. The dye is not excreted via kindney and does not escape into extracellular fluid.

Dose : 4.52 mg/ml of 5 ml. injection.

Officials : Evans Blue I.P.

MISCELLANEOUS COMPOUNDS

A number of other drugs are useful for diagnostic purposes. Fluorescein sodium is useful to detect foreign bodies or corneal ulcers and amyloidosis is detected with the help of congo red These are certain reagents when come in contact with urine provide diagnostic clues e.g. Gravindex and pregnosis for pregnancy, sodium nitroprusside for ketone bodies, etc.

CONGO RED

Congo red is an odourless, reddish brown powder. It is soluble in water and slightly soluble in alcohol. The compound decomposes to acid fumes. It should be stored in well closed containers.

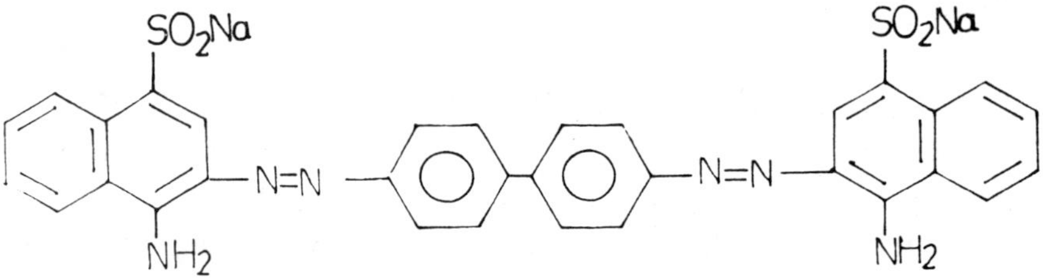

IUPAC Name: 1-Napthalenesulfonic acid, 3,3'-[(1,1'-biphenyl)-4,4'-diyl bis (azo) bis 4-amino

Actions and uses : It is used in the detection of amyloidosis. Amyloid collections in liver are stained by this dye. If amyloid growth is in kindney, a small amount appears in the urine.

FLUORESCEIN SODIUM

Fluorescein sodium is an odourless, orange-red powder. It is freely soluble in water and sparingly soluble in alcohol. It is hygroscopic in nature and should be stored in air tight containers.

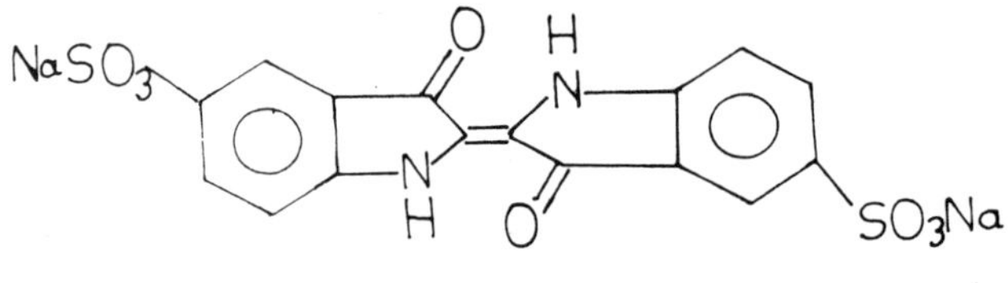

IUPAC Name : Spiro [isobenzofuran -1 (3H), 9'-(9H) xanthene] -3-one,3,6' dihydroxy, disodium salt.

OR

2-(6-hydroxy-3-oxo-xanthen-9-yl) benzoic acid

Actions and uses : Fluorescein sodium is used for detection of corneal lesions and foreign bodies in eyes. An intravenous injection may produce nausea , vomiting and other allergic reactions. Skin and urine may become transiently yellow.

Official : Fluorescein sodium I.P.

Dose : 0.1 to 0.3 ml of 2% solution.

CHAPTER - 29

ANTICONVULSANT AGENTS

Epilepsy is a collective term for chronic convulsive disorders characterised by sudden episodes of seizures with or without loss of consciousness. The seizure always correlates with an abnormal electro encephalo gram (E.E.G.).

Convulsions may occur at any time with or without warming signal (aura). Common features include increase in muscle tone, locked jaw, frothing of mouth and upward movement of eye-ball.

Convulsions can be prevented by the depression of motor cortex. Sleep may also be induced by these drugs. Epileptic seizures can be classified into :

(I) **Grand mal epilepsy (major epilepsy)** : This type of epilepsy is characterised by sudden loss of consciousness and comprises of chronic spasms of whole body. These are followed by depression of central nervous system.This epilepsy may be either idiopathic or secondary to progressive (Non-progressive) organic brain disease. It may be associated with petitmal epilepsy.

(II) **Petitmal epilepsy** : This type of epilepsy is associated with bilateral motor activity such as blinking of eyelid . Petitmal is always idiopathic and may either disappeared completely or may be converted to grandmal epilepsy.

(III)**Temporal lobe epilepsy** : It is also called as psychomotor epilepsy. In these type convulsions are absent but their is change in behavior of the patients.

(IV) **Minor epilepsy** : This type of epilepsy leads to sudden loss of consciousness with or without fall. They may resemble petitmal epilepsy.

CLASSIFICATION : Different types of epilepsy's can be treated with following drugs :

(I) Hydantoin derivative	:	Phenytoin, Methoin.
(II) Barbiturate derivatives	:	Phenobarbitone, Mephobarbitone.
(III) Acetyl urea derivatives	:	Phenecemide.
(IV) Oxazolinedione derivatives	:	Trimethadione, Paramethadione
(V) Succimides derivatives	:	Phenosuximides, Ethosuximide.
(VI) Miscellaneous	:	Carbamezapin, Sodium valproate, Diazepam

PHENYTOIN
OR
DIPHENYL HYDANTOIN

Phenytoin is available as phenytoin sodium. Phenytoin is an odourless, white crystalline powder. It is soluble in alkali hydroxides, slightly soluble in alcohol and very slightly soluble in ether, chloroform and water. Its sodium salt is soluble in water and alcohol but insoluble in ether and chloroform. It should be stored in air tight containers.

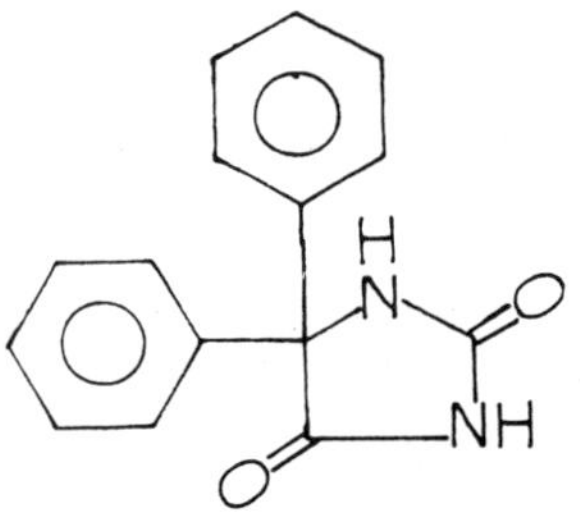

IUPAC Name : 5,5-Diphenyl imidazolidine-2,4 dione.

Actions and uses : Phenytoin has an anticonvulsant action but relatively a lesser hypnotic effect. It is effective in controling grand mal epilepsy and prophylactic control of seizures, developed after neurosugery but ineffective in petit mal epilepsy.

The side effects of this drug include nausea, rashes and dizziness. It may cause hallucinations, muscular tremors and mental confusion.

Officials : Phenytoin Sodium, I.P.
Phenytoin Tablets, I.P.
Phenytoin Capsule, I.P.
Phenytoin Injection, I.P.
Phenytoin Sodium Tablets, I.P.

METHOIN

Methoin is an odourless, tasteless, colourless and lustrous compound. It is soluble in chloroform and alkali hydroxides, sparingly soluble in alcohol, slightly soluble in ether, and very slightly soluble in water. It should be stored in air-tight containers.

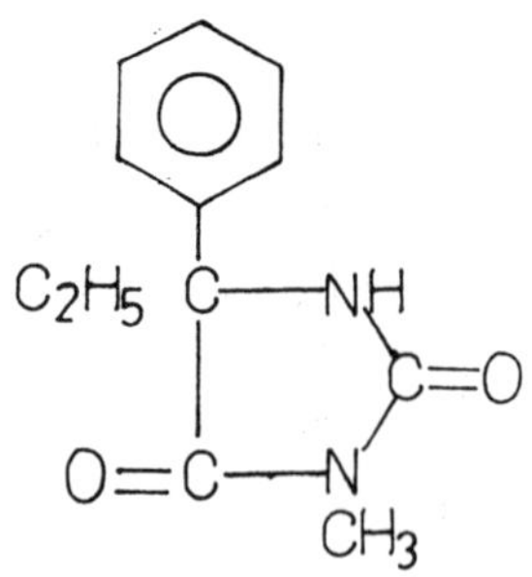

IUPAC Name : 5-Ethyl-3-methyl-5-phenyl imidazolidine 2,4,-dione.
Actions and uses : Methoin has similar action as that of phenytoin sodium . It is used in the treatment of grand mal, psychomotor and jacksonian epilepsy and behavioral disorders.

PHENOBARBITONE

Phenobarbitone is an odourless, colourless white crystalline powder with a slightly bitter taste. It is soluble in ether, chloroform and solutions of alkali hydroxides, slightly soluble in alcohol and insoluble in water. It is also available as phenobarbitone sodium which is soluble in water and practically insoluble in organic solvents. It should be stored in air-tight containers protected from light.

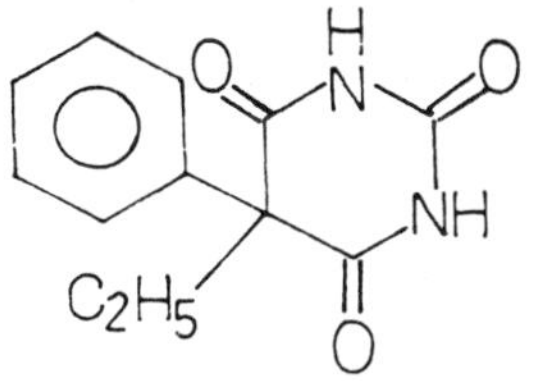

IUPAC Name : 5- Ethyl-5-phenyl barbituric acid.
Actions and uses : Phenobarbitone is a long acting sedative and hypnotic. It has been used as a sedative in anxiety disorders, neurasthenia, dysmenorrhoea and thyrotoxicosis.
Officials : Phenobarbitone Sodium I.P.

PHENECEMIDE

Phenecemide is an odourless white, crystalline powder. It is soluble in acetone and methanol; and slightly soluble in water, alcohol and ether. It should be stored in air-tight containers.

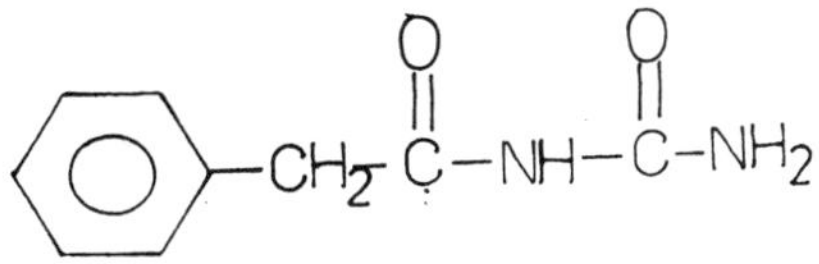

IUPAC Name : N-[Aminocarbonyl] benzene ethanamide.
Actions and uses : Phenecemide is used in psychomotor epilepsy. Its toxic effects are aplastic anemia, change in personality and damage to kidney and liver, therefore its use is restricted.

TRIMETHADIONE [TROXIDONE]

Trimethadione is available as colourless, granular crystals with a slightly camphoraceous odour. It is soluble in ether, chloroform and alcohol and slightly soluble in water. It should be stored in air tight containers in a cool place.

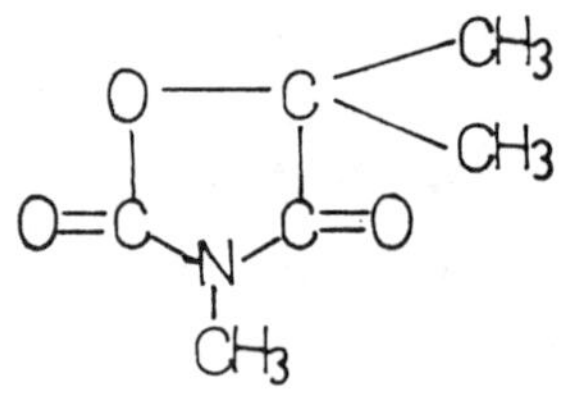

IUPAC Name : 3,5,5-Trimethyl-2,4,-oxazolidinedione.
Actions and uses : Trimethadione is used in the treatment of true petit mal epilepsy. In animals it prevents convulsions induced by leptazol without causing depression of C.N.S. The side effects include photophobia,glare effect, nausea, headache, fatigue and muscular weakness.
Officials : Troxidone I.P.
Troxidone Capsules, I.P.

PARAMETHADIONE

Paramethadione is a colourless liquid with a characteristic odour. It is soluble in water, alcohol ether and chloroform. It should be stored in air tight containers.

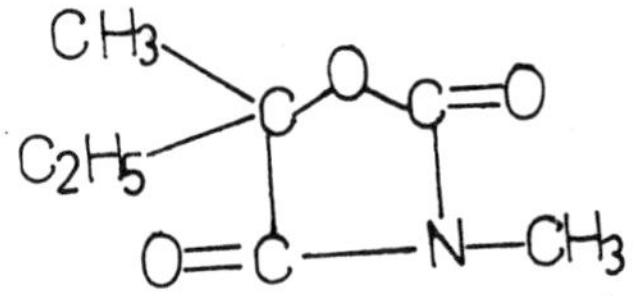

IUPAC Name : 5-Ethyl-3,5-dimethyl-2,4-oxazolidine dione.
Actions and uses : Paramethadione has anticonvulsant actions similar to troxidone but less potent to control attack of petit mal epilepsy.
Officials : Paramethadione I.P.

PHENSUXIMIDE

Phensuximide is an odourless, white crystalline powder. It is soluble in water, alcohol, chloroform and ether. It should be stored in air tight containers.

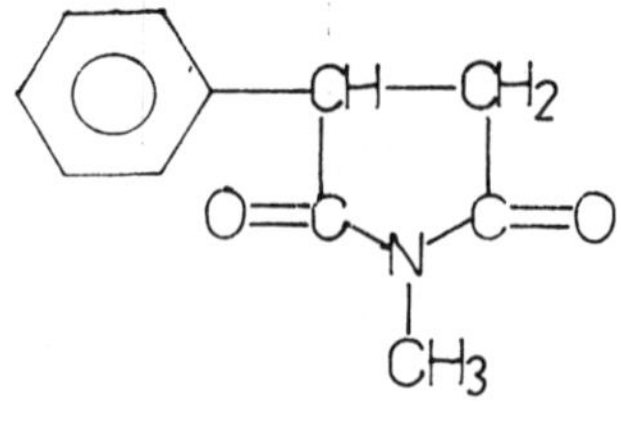

IUPAC Name : N-methyl-2-phenyl succinimide.

or

3- phenyl-1-methyl pyralidine 2,5-dione.

Actions and uses : Phensoximide is an anticonvulsant used in the treatment of pure petitmal epilepsy. It is given with other agents to treat petit mal with grand mal epilepsy. The side effects of this drug include gastric-upsets, drowsiness, headache and skin rashes.

ETHOSUXIMIDE

Ethosuximide is an odourless, white waxy solid with slightly bitter taste. It is soluble in alcohol, ether, chloroform and water. It should be stored in air tight containers.

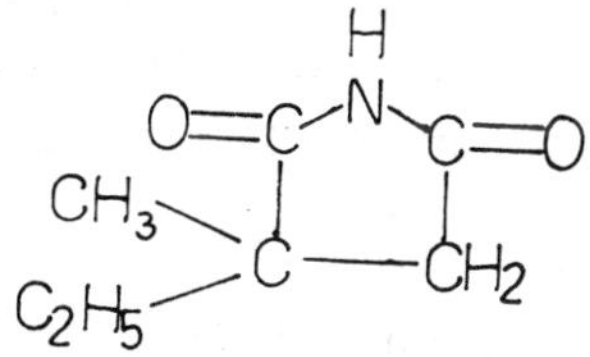

IUPAC Name: 3-Ethyl-3-methyl-2,5-pyrolidinedione.

Actions and uses : Ethosuximide has similar actions and uses as that of phensuximide but it is a more potent anticonvulsant.

Officials : Ethosuximide I.P.
Ethosuximide Capsules/Syrup I.P.

CARBAMAZEPINE

Carbamazepine is an odourless, white to yellowish crystalline, tasteless or slightly bitter powder. It is soluble in alcohol and chloroform but very slightly soluble in water and ether. It should be stored in air-tight containers.

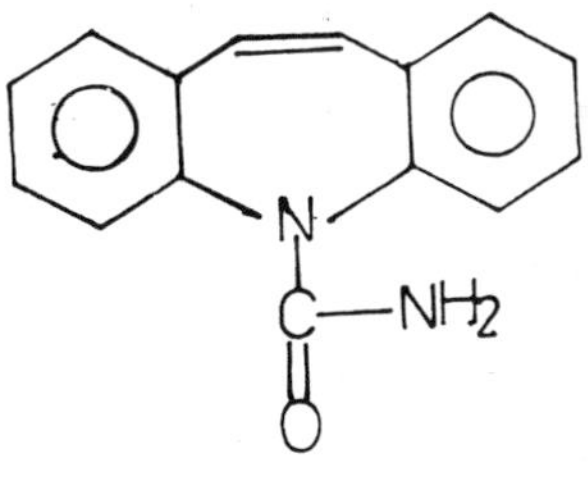

IUPAC Name : 5H-Dibenz [b,f] azepine-5-carboxamide.

Actions and uses : Carbamazepine is used in the treatment of grand mal and temporal lobe epilepsy. Side effects of this drug include dizziness, diarrhoea, dryness of mouth, nausea, aplastic anemia and jaundice.

Officials : Carbazepine I.P.
Carbazepine Tablets I.P.

SODIUM VALPROATE

Sodium valproate is an odourless, white or crystalline powder having a saline taste. It is soluble in water and alcohol. It should be stored in air-tight containers.

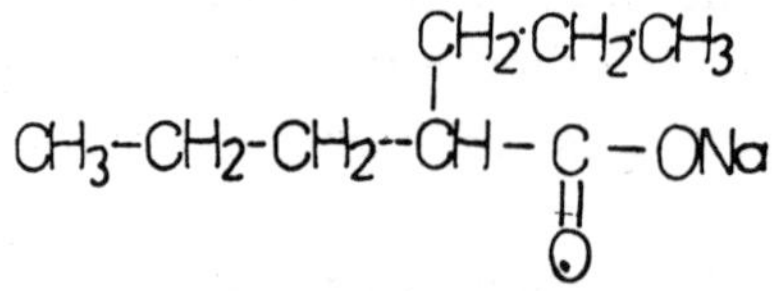

IUPAC Name : Sodium -2-propylpentanoate.

Actions and uses : Sodium valproate is used in the treatment of petit mal and grand mal epilepsy and may also used in the treatment of temporal lobe epilepsy. It increases the concentration of gamma-aminobutyric acid in the brain. Its action is potentiated the presence of MAO inhibitors. The side effects of this drug are gastro intestinal disturbances, nausea and alopecia.

(1)**Phenobarbitone** : Bayer : Luminal 300 mg
R. Poulenc : Gardenal 30 mg
R. Poulenc : Gardenal 30/60 mg Tab.

(2) **Phenytoin** : Parke Davis : Dilanti Cap. 100 mg/4 ml.

(3) **Carbemezepine** : Ciba Gegy : Tagretol 100/200/400 mg. dose 100 mg/day daily.
SG pharma : Mazetol 10/200/ Sy. 20 mg/5 ml.

(4) **Sodium valproate** : Torrent : Valparin Alkalets 200 mg. Valparin inj. 200 mg/5 ml.

CHAPTER - 30

VITAMINS

The terms Vitamin means **vita**, i.e., vital for life, these compounds are **amine**-compounds containing-NH_2 group, i.e., vital amines required for life. Later it was discovered that some non amino compounds are also essential for life. The term vitamin is used for such compounds. These compounds are required by the body in a very small amount for the normal growth of the body. They regulate some of the metabolic activities or act as enzyme or co-enzymes [enzyme activators].

Vitamin deficiency may give rise to various diseases. Most of the vitamins are present in normal diet. Excessive fat soluble vitamins are accumulated in the body and are potentially dangerous while excessive in water soluble vitamins are excreted in urine.

Classification of vitamins :

(I) **Fat soluble vitamins** : Vit-A, Vit-D, Vit-E, Vit-K.

(II) **Water soluble vitamins** : Vit. C and Vitamin B complex.

Vitamin B complex is a group of vitamins which includes [thiamine (B_1) riboflavin (B_2), nicotinic acid (B_3), Biotin (B_4 or vit H), Pantothenic acid (B_5), pyridoxin (B_6), folic acid, inositol, para-amino benzoic acid and cyanocobalamin (B_{12}).

VITAMIN A

The richest source of vitamin A is liver oils of fish ,cod-liver oil, halibut liver oil and shark liver oil. It is also available in green leafy vegetables, carrots, apricots, milk and egg yolk. It may present as esters or as provitamin.

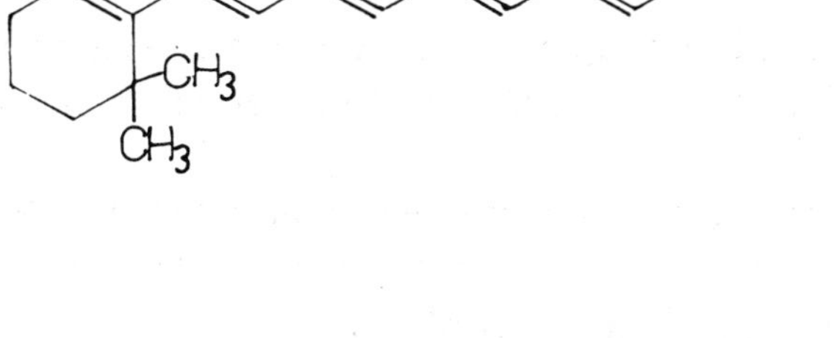

Vitamin A is a yellow oil which may solidify on cooling; it has a slight odour. Vitamin A is stable to heat [necessary for cooking]. It is freely soluble in alcohol and fixed oils but insoluble in water. It should be stored in air-tight nitrogenous atmosphere, light resistant containers in a cool place. The different forms of naturally occurring vitamin A are isomer of retinol [vit. A1].

Vitamin A is essential for dark adaptation. Deficiency of vitamin A leads to night-blindness which may lead to xeropthalmia. It helps in epithelial regeneration and keratinisation.

Officials : Concentrated vitamin A solution I.P.
Concentrated vitamin A and D solution I.P.
Shark liver oil I.P.
Vitamin A, I.P.
Shark -liver oil with vitamin D, I.P.

Dose : 5000 units prophylactic and 10,000 to 2,00,000 units therapeutic.

VITAMIN D

Vitamin D is a sterol derivative. It exists as calciferol, cholecalciferol and dihydrotachysterol.

Ergosterol is a yeast sterol that gives vitamin D_2 (ergocalciferol) on exposure to sun light. The naturally occurring vitamin D is cholecalciferol (D_3) present in fresh liver oils.

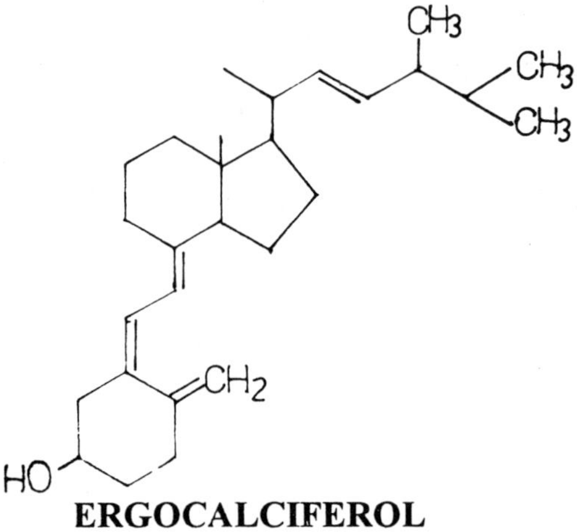

ERGOCALCIFEROL

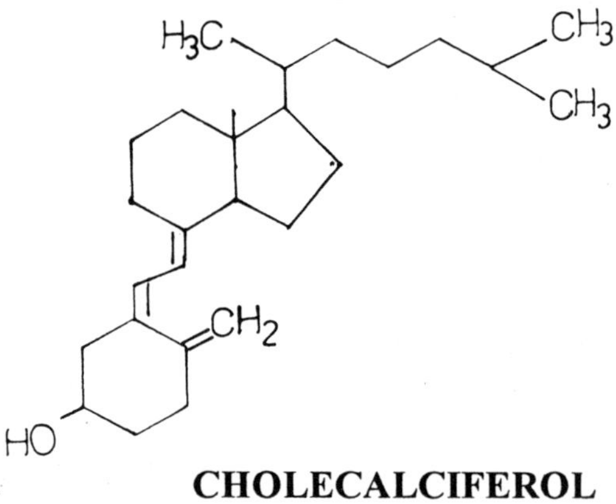

CHOLECALCIFEROL

Ergocalciferol is a colourless to white crystalline powder. It is soluble in fixed oils and insoluble in water. It is stored in thermally sealed containers, protected from light, below 15°C.

Cholecalciferol is a white crystalline substance. It is also soluble in fixed oil but insoluble in water. It is also stored in hermeticlly sealed containers in nitrogen atmosphere, protected from light in a cool place.

Major source of vitamin D include shark, cod and Halibut liver oils. Vitamin D is essential for the absorption and transport of calcium and phosphorous. Deficiency of vitamin D causes rickets in children and oestomalacia in adults that may lead to tetany.

Officials : Cholecalciferol I.P.
Concentrated vitamin D solution I.P.
Concentrated vitamin A & D solution I.P.
Dilute shark liver oil I.P.
Shark liver oil with vitamin D I.P.
Vitamin A and D capsules I.P.

VITAMIN E

Vitamin E is available as α-tocopheryl acetate salt. It is present in sunflower seed, rapseed, soybean oil, wheat germ, etc.

Alpha tocopheryl is an odourless, yellowish green viscous liquid. It is soluble in alcohol, chloroform and solvent ether but insoluble in water. It should be stored in air tight containers protected from light.

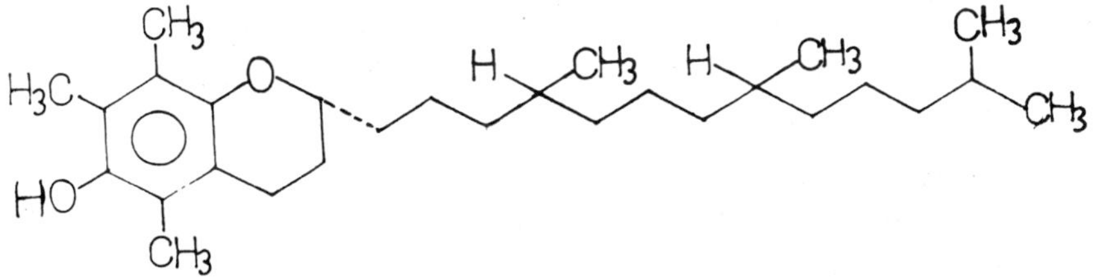

Vitamin E is involved in metabolic reactions and its deficiency leads to neurological syndrome. An excessive dose of vitamin E may cause diarrhoea, abdominal pain, weakness and fatigue.

Officials : Tocopheryl acetate I.P.

VITAMIN K

Vitamin K is a group of naphthoquinone compounds. These are phytomenadione, menadione, actomenaphthone and menatetrenone.This vitamin is responsible for clotting of blood.

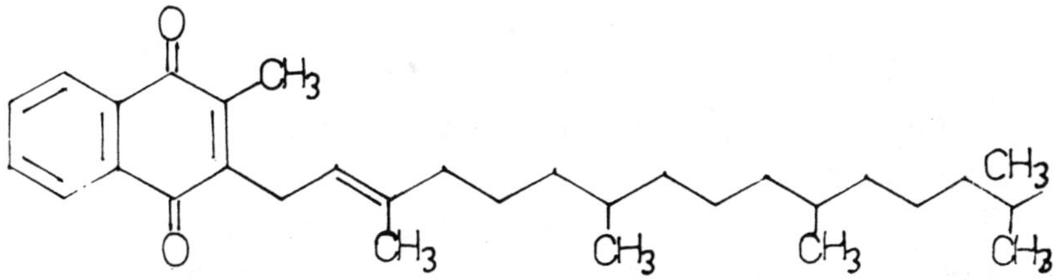

PHYTOMENADIONE

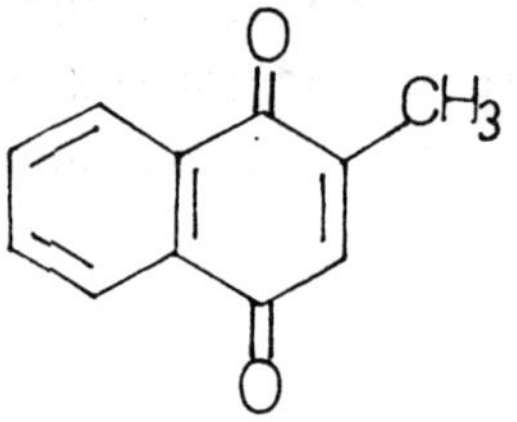

MENADIONE

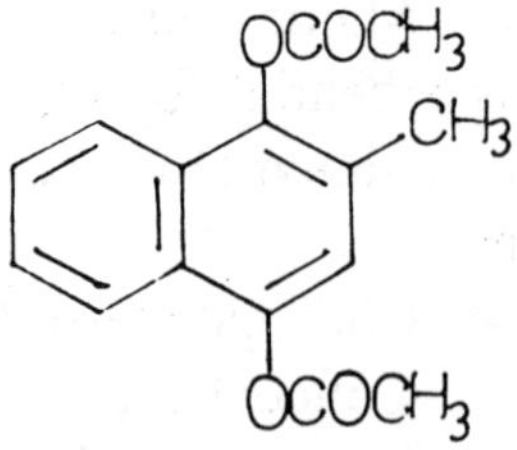

ACTOMENAPHTHONE

Phytomenadione is an odourless, clear to deep yellow oil. It is soluble in ether, chloroform and insoluble in water. It should be stored in airtight containers, protected from light.

IUPAC Name : 2methyl-3-phytyl-1,4-naphthoquinone.

OR

2 methyl-1,4 naphthoquinone

OR

2 methyl-1,4 bis (aceto) naphthanate

Actions and uses: It is a naturally occurring vitamin K. The production of coagulation factors prothrombin and factors VII, IX and X is controlled by vitamin K. A deficiency of vitamin K reduces prothrombin level and ability to clot.

Officials : Acetomenadione I.P.
Acetomenadione Tablet I.P.
Menadione I.P.
Menadione Sodium Bisulphite I.P.

THIAMINE HYDROCHLORIDE (B1)

Thiamine hydrochloride is a member of B complex. Rich sources of thiamine include yeast, milk, rice-polishing and liver. It is a colourless or white crystalline powder with a characteristic odour. It is soluble in water, slightly soluble in glycerol and alcohol and very slightly soluble in ether and acetone. It should be stored in airtight containers, protected from light and contact with metal should be avoided.

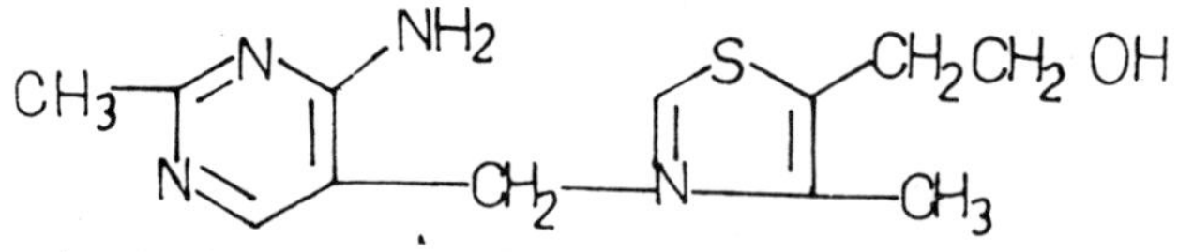

IUPAC Name : 3-(4-Amino-2-methylpyrimidin-5-ylmethyl)-5-(2-hydroxyethyl)-4-methylthiazolium.

Actions and uses : Thiamine is present as thamine pyrophosphate (TPP) in the body. TPP is a prosthetic group for the enzymes involved in the decarboxylation of pyruvic acid and α- keto-glutaric acid in the carbohydrate (glucose) metabolism.

Thiamine deficiency gives rise to beriberi. It is also given for the treatment of neuritis. The daily requirement of thiamine is increased during pregnancy, lactation, hyperthyroidism, pyrexia and diuresis.

Dose : Prophylactic dose : 2 to 5 mg.
Therapeutic dose : 25 to 100 mg.

Officials : Thiamin Hydrochloride I.P.
Thiamin Hydrochloride Injection I.P.
Thiamine Hydrochloride Tablet I.P.
Thiamine Hydrochloride Mononitrate I.P.

RIBOFLAVINE (B_2)

Liver, kidney, egg, yeast, green vegetables and milk are rich sources of dietary vitamin B_2 (riboflavine). A small amount of vitamin is lost during cooking. Deficiency of riboflavin gives rise to ariboflavinosis.

Riboflavin is a yellow to orange coloured crystalline powder, with slight odour and persistently bitter taste. It is soluble in saline water and 10% urea solution, very slightly soluble in water and alcohol and practically insoluble in chloroform.

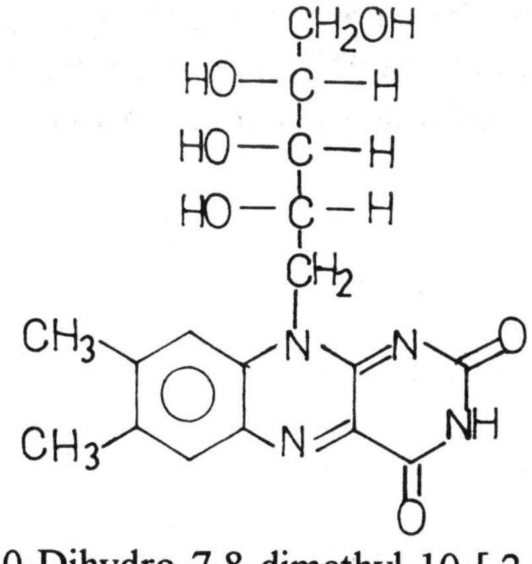

IUPAC Name : 3,10-Dihydro-7,8-dimethyl-10-[2,3,4,5, tetrahydroxy pentyl] benzopteridine -2,4,dione.

or

7,8 dimethyl-10-(D-ribit-1-yl) isoalloxazine.

Actions and uses : Riboflavin is a component of flavin mono nucleotide (FMN) and flavin adenin dinucleotide (FAD). These are useful in carbohydrate & protein metabolism. Deficiency of vitamin B_2 is characterised by stomatitis, glossitis, reddened, shiny and denuded lips, etc.

Dose : Prophylactic : 1.5 to 3 mg
Therapeutic : 2 to 10 mg

Officials : Riboflavin injection I.P.

NIACIN AND NIACINAMIDE

Dietary sources of niacin include liver, adrenal glands, white meat, yeast, milk, legumes, corn and whole cereals. It is an odourless, white crystalline powder. It is freely soluble in water, hot alcohol and dilute alkali hydroxides; very slightly soluble in chloroform and practically insoluble in ether. It is stored in well closed containers, protected from light.

Nicotinamide is a colourless to white crystalline powder with a faint characteristic odour and bitter taste. It is soluble in water, alcohol and glycerol but very slightly soluble in ether. It should be stored in well closed containers.

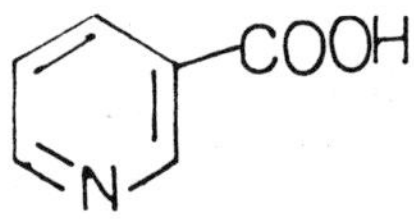

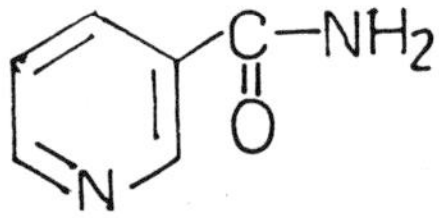

Niacin and nicotinamide have similar actions and uses. Deficiency of nicotinic acid leads to pellagra, characterised by dermatitis, red swollen tongue and enteritis.

Niacin is a constituent of coenzyme diphospho-pyridine nucleotide (DPN) and triphosphopyridine nucleotide (TPN). These co-enzymes are associated with hydrogen transport in biological oxidation reduction process.

Dose : Prophylactic dose : 50 mg.
Therapeutic dose : 500 mg.

Officials : Nicotinamide I.P.
Nicotinamide Tablet I.P.
Nicotinamide Injection I.P.
Nicotinic Acid I.P.
Nicotinic Acid Tablet I.P.

BIOTIN

Dietary sources of biotin are liver, kidney, yeast and milk. This is also called as anti-egg white injury factor because it forms a complex with avidin present in egg white and makes it inactive. It is a white crystalline powder, soluble in hot water, very slightly soluble in water and alcohol and insoluble in other organic solvents. It should be stored in air tight containers.

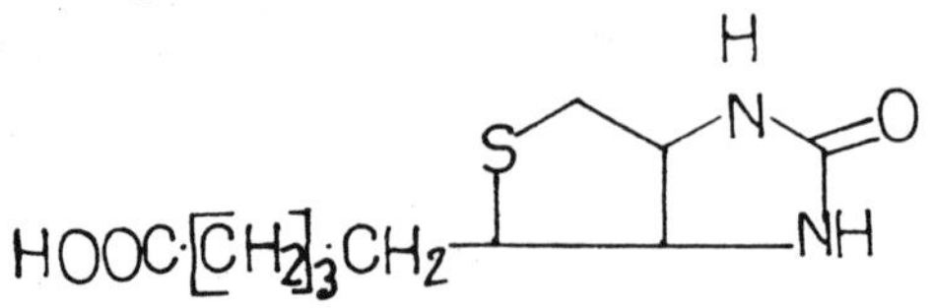

IUPAC Name : Hexahydro-2-oxo-1H thieno (3,4-d) imidazole-4-pentanoic acid.

Actions and uses : Biotin is a cofactor in the carboxylation reactions taking place in the body. It is also responsible for baldness in persons due to seborrheic conditions.

PANTOTHENIC ACID

Dietary sources of pantothenic acid include meat, egg, yeast, milk and fresh vegetables. It is available as calcium pantothenate. Calcium pantothenate is an odourless, white crystalline powder. It is freely soluble in water. It should be stored in well closed containers protected from light.

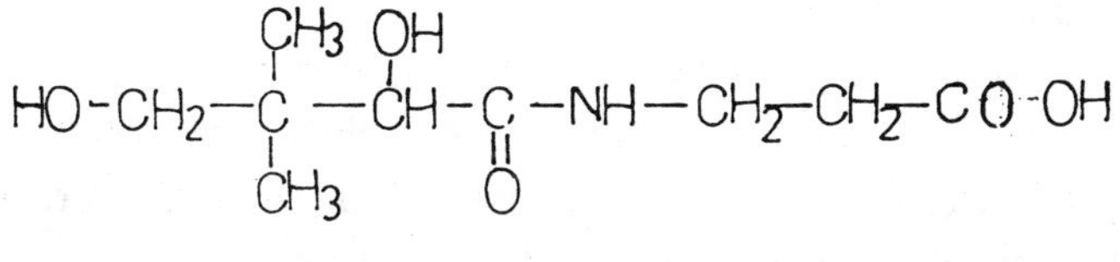

IUPAC Name : 3-[2,4-dihydroxy-3,3-dimethyl butyroamido] propinic acid.
Actions and uses : It is a component of vitamin B complex. It is essential for the metabolism of carbohydrate, protein and fat.
Officials : Calcium Pantothenate I.P.

PYRIDOXINE

Pyridoxine, pyridoxal and pyridoxamine are the forms of vitamin B_6. Rich dietary sources include liver, meat, yeast and cereals. Pyridoxine hydrochloride is an odourless, white crystalline powder with a saline bitter taste. It is soluble in water, slightly soluble in alcohol, and very slightly soluble in ether. It should be stored in airtight containers.

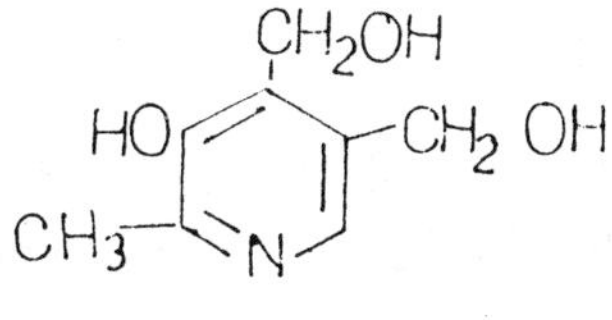

IUPAC Name : 4,5 Bis (hyroxy methyl)-3 hydroxy-2-methyl pyridinium chloride.
Actions and uses : Pyridoxal phosphate is a coenzyme for various metabolic reactions like transamination, racemization and decarboxylation. It is used in the treatment of convulsions and hypochromic anemia.
Officials : Pyridoxine Hydrochloride I.P.
Pyridoxine Tablets I.P.

FOLIC ACID

Dietary sources of folic acid are liver, yeast and leafy vegetables. It is an odourless, tasteless, orange to yellowish crystalline powder. It is soluble in sodium hydroxide and practically insoluble in water and alcohol. It should be stored in airtight containers, protected from light.

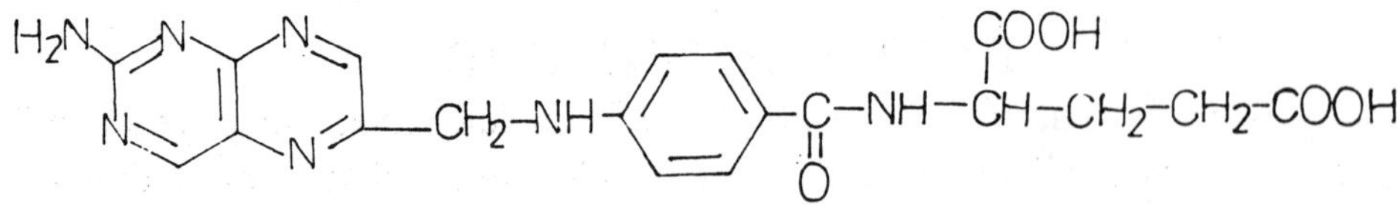

IUPAC Name : N-4-[2-Amino-4-hydroxypterid-6-ylmethylamino] benzoyl -L-glutamic acid.

Actions and uses: Folic acid is converted into tetrahydrofolic acid, which acts as a coenzyme in the synthesis of purine and pyrimidine nucleotide. Cell division arrest at metaphase stage in absence of folic acid. It is necessary for the production of red-blood cells. Deficiency of folic acid may cause megaloblastic anemia.

Officials : Folic acid I.P.
Folic Acid Tablet I.P.

PARA AMINO BENZOIC ACID

Para amino benzoic acid is an odourless, white to yellowish crystalline powder. It is soluble in alcohol and solution of alkali hydroxides but slightly soluble in water. It should be stored in airtight containers, protected from light.

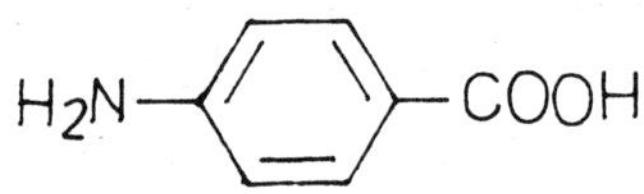

IUPAC Name : 4- Aminobenzoic acid.

Actions and uses: Para aminobenzoic acid (PABA) is essential for the synthesis of purine and pyrimidine bases. It is also useful as a sunscreen.

CYANOCOBALAMIN (B_{12})

Liver, kidney, egg, muscle tissue and milk are the dietary sources of cyanocobalamin. It is a freeze dried solid available as odourless, dark red crystalline powder. It is slightly soluble in water. It should be stored in air tight containers, protected from light, below 10°C.

Cyanocobalamin is useful in pernicious anemia and its neurological complications. Radio labeled cyanocobalamin is used to identify megaloblastic anemia and pernicious anemia.

Officials : Cyanocobalamin I.P.
Cyanocobalamin Injection I.P.

Hydroxocobalamin I.P.
Hydroxocobalamin Injection I.P.

ASCORBIC ACID [VITAMIN C]

Ascorbic acid is present in fresh citrus fruits and vegetables. It can be extracted from juice of citrus fruits and ripe fruit of *Capsicum annum*. It is an almost odourless, colourless to pale yellow crystalline powder with acidic taste. It is soluble in water and alcohol; slightly soluble in methanol and practically insoluble in ether. It should be stored in airtight containers free from contact with metal and protected from light.

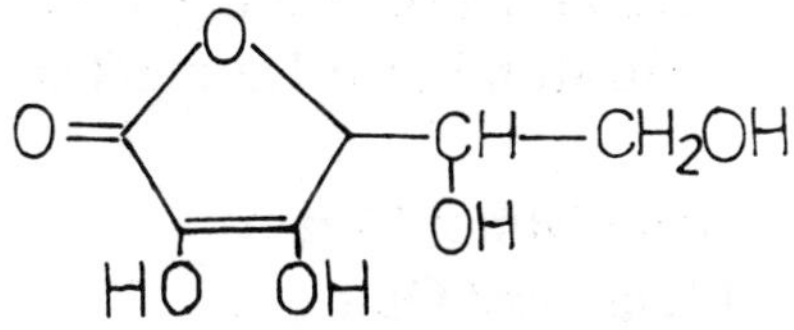

IUPAC Name : 3-oxo-L-gulofuranolactone.

Actions and uses :Ascorbic acid is essential for the formation of folinic acid, maturation of erythrocytes and absorption of iron from gut. Ascorbic acid is essential for the formation of intercellular material like collagen, cartilage, bone, teeth and healing of wounds.

Officials: Ascorbic acid I.P.
Ascorbic acid Injection I.P.
Ascorbic acid Tablets I.P.

(1) **Vitamin A** : US vitamins : Aquasol-A. Cap. 50,000 I.U.
US vittamins: Inj. Aquasol-A. 2/ml-50,000 I.V/ml.
Roche : Arovit Drops 150,000 I.V./ml.

(2) **Vitamin D** : Cadila : Calcirol Grannules (Vit.D_3 cholcalciferd)
Duphar : Arachitol inj. 300,000 & 600,000 I.V/ml

(3) **Vitamin K** : Merck : Evion Cap. 100/200/400/600 mg.
Merck : Evion Drops (paed) 50 mg/ml.

(4) **Thiamine HCl (B_1)** : Franco Indian : Benalgis Tab. 75mg.
: Franco Indian : Beneuron Cap. 5mg.

(5) **Riboflavin (B_2)** : Modi mundi Pharma : Pyricontin continus Tab.100 mg
controlled Relax Tab.

(6) **Niacin** : Whockhard : Recupex Powder 5.5 mg/50 gm sachet.

(7) **Niacinamide** : Pfizer : Protinex powder
or contains 15 mg/30gm. Nicotinic acid
: Raptakos : Heptaglobine Sy.
or Nicotinic acid 22.5 mg/15ml.Naicinamide

(8) **Biotin** (vitt.H) : Roche : Supradyn Tab. contain 0.25 mg/Tab.

(9) **Pentothenic acid** : Sigma Lab. : Calcium pentothinate Tab.25 mg/Tab.

(10) **Folic acid** : Comtack Labs. : Rubifol Tab. 1.5 mg/Tab.
: Sarabhai : Basiton Forte 1.5 mg/Tab.

(11) **PABA** : Franco India : Para Minol Cream
Melanocyl Oint.

(12) **Cyanocobalamine (B_{12})** : Rallis : Imferon B_{12} Inj. 500 mg/ml.
:Geno : Ferz Cap. 15 mcq/Cap.

(13) **Ascorbic acid** :Sarabhai : Limcee Tab. 500 mg.
(Vit. C) : Glaxo : Celin Tab. 500 mg.
: East India : Sorvicin Drops 100 mg/ml.

CHAPTER - 31

STEROIDAL DRUGS

Steroidal drugs act as hormones. These hormones are secreted by endocrine glands having specific physiological actions. These hormones reach the effector organ by blood stream.

Steroids are derivatives of perhydro-1,2-cyclopento-phenanthrene [Tetra cyclic] nucleus. The three cyclic rings of phenanthrene are called A, B, C, D rings and cyclopento is a D ring. Rings C & D is united by cis-arrangement.

The cortex of adrenal gland secretes three types of steroids-gluco-corticoids, mineralo-corticoids and sex hormones. The sex hormones include oestrogen and androgens. Gluco-corticoids are cortisone and hydrocortisone and mineralocorticoids are aldosterone and deoxycortisone.

Sex hormones influence the maintenance and development of reproductive organs. Oestrogens and progesoteron influence female sex physiology and androgen has a role in male sex physiology.

Gluco-corticoids help in gluconeogenesis and their by act on glycogen storage and also in metabolism of protein and calcium. Mineralo-corticoids cause sodium retention and potassium excretion.

BETAMETHASONE

Betamethasone is an odourless, white to creamy white powder. It is slightly soluble in alcohol and very slightly soluble in water and chloroform. It is also available as betamethasone sodium phosphate and betamethasone valerate. The sodium phosphate salt is soluble in water and insoluble in organic solvents while and valerate salt is soluble in organic solvents and insoluble in water. It should be stored in air tight containers protected from light.

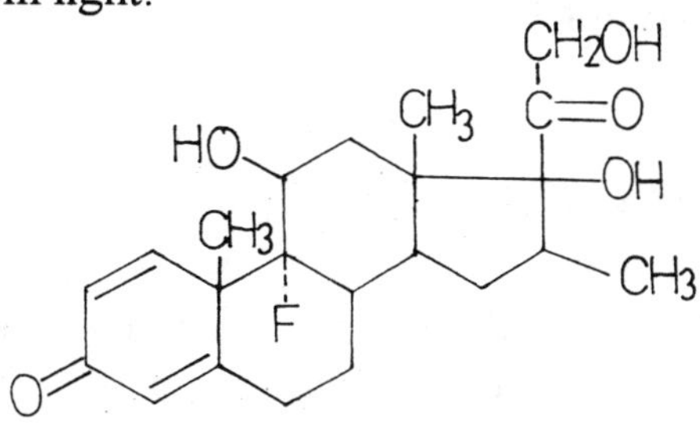

IUPAC Name : 7 α-Fluoro-11ß, 17 α, 21-trihydroxy-16ß methyl pregna-1,4-diene-3,20 dione.

Actions and uses : Betamethasone and prednisolone are having similar actions and uses. It is used in the treatment of rheumatoid arthritis, and bronchial asthma.

Officials : Betamethasone I.P.
Betamethasone Tablet I.P.
Betamethasone Sodium phosphate I.P.
Betamethasone Sodium phosphate Injection I.P.
Betamethasone Valerate I.P.
Bethamethasone Valerate Ointment I.P.

CORTISONE

Cortisone is available as cortisone acetate. This salt is an odourless, white crystalline powder. It is soluble in ether, chloroform, acetone and methyl alcohol, slightly soluble in alcohol and very slightly soluble in water. It should be stored in well closed containers, protected from light.

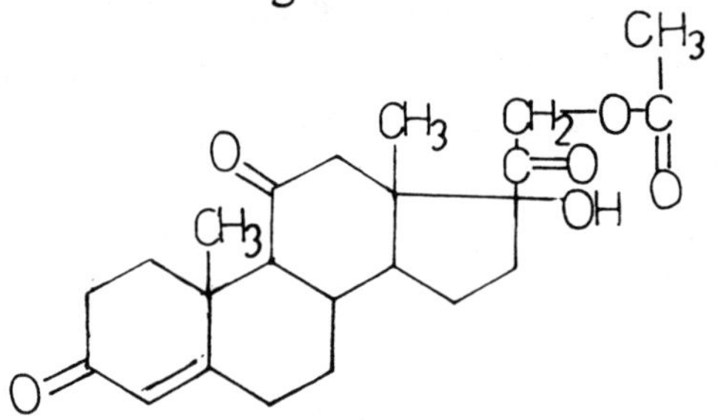

IUPAC Name : 17 α, 21-dihydroxy pregn-4-ene-3,11,20-trione 21-acetate.

Actions and uses : Cortisone has actions and uses similar to adrenocortical hormone hydrocortisone. It is used in the treatment of inflammation. It is more effective orally than parenterally or topically. It is given in the treatment of rheumatoid arthritis, asthma, colitis, pulmonary granulomatosis and alcoholism.

It causes increase in urinary potassium level (hypokalemia), metabolic alkalosis, muscular weakness and glycosuria.

Officials : Cortisone Acetate I.P.
Cortisone Injection I.P.
Cortisone Tablets I.P

HYDROCORTISONE

Hydrocortisone is an odourless, white crystalline powder. It is slightly soluble in alcohol and acetone but practically insoluble in water, chloroform and ether. It should be stored in well closed containers protected from light. Hydrocortisone is available as hydrocortisone acetate, hydrocortisone hydrogen succinate and hydrocortisone succinate.

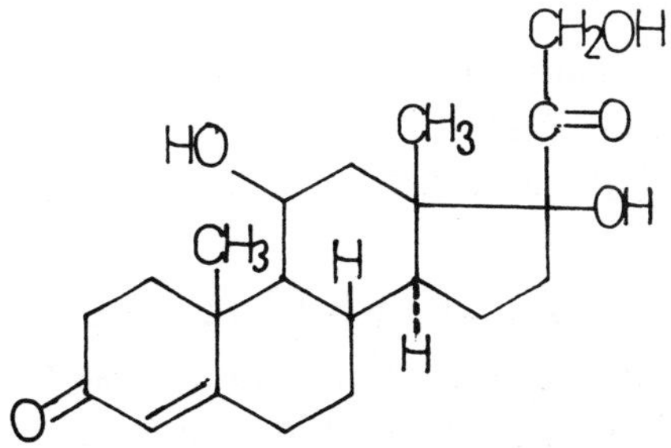

IUPAC Name : 11 ß, 17α, 21 - Trihydroxy pregen-4-ene-3,20-dione.

Actions and uses : Hydrocortisone has actions and uses similar to glucocorticoids. It is used in the treatment of addisonians or post-ardrnalectomy crises and ulcerative colitis. Its acetate salt is used in the inflammatory conditions of eye and in the treatment of arthritis.

Officials : Hydrocortisone Acetate I.P.
Hydrocortisone Acetate Injection I.P.
Hydrocortisone Eye Ointment I.P.
Hydrocortisone Hydrogen Succinate I.P.
Hydrocortisone Sodium Succinate Injection I.P.

PREDNISOLONE

Prednisolone is an odourless, white crystalline powder. It is soluble in alcohol, dioxone, and methanol but very slightly soluble in water. It is a hygroscopic compound and should be stored in air -tight containers protected from light.It is available as prednisolone acetate, prednisolone sodium phosphate and prednisolone pivalate.

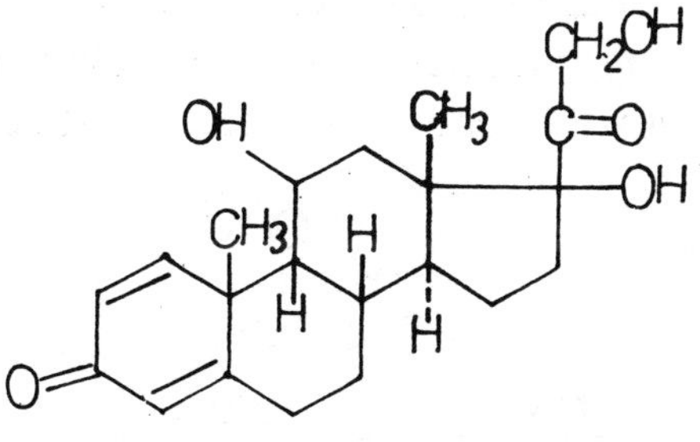

IUPAC Name : 11ß, 17α, 21-Trihydroxy pregna- 1,4-diene 3,20 dione.

Actions and uses : Prednisolone has glucocorticoid actions and is used as an anti-infammatory drug. It is four times more potent than hydrocortisone but its mineralo-corticoid activity is lesser (weaker sodium retaining effect). It is preferred for the treatment of rheumatoid arthritis, rheumatic fever, status asthmaticus and ulcerative colitis. The side effects include cushing's syndrome and dyspepsia in peptic ulceration.

Officials: Prednisolone I.P.
Prednisolone Tablet I.P.
Prednisolone Acetate I.P.
Prednisolone Pivalate I.P.

PROGESTERONE

Progesterone is an odourless, colourless to white crystalline powder. It is soluble in alcohol and ether, slightly soluble in arachis oil and ethyl oleate; practically insoluble in water and soluble in chloroform. It should be stored in air tight containers protected from light.

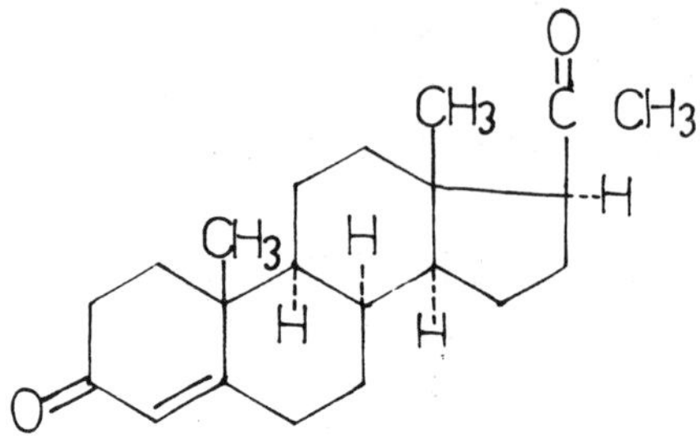

IUPAC Name : Pregn-4-ene-3, 20-dione

Actions and uses : Progesterone is secreted by *Corpus luteum* and converts the proliferative endometrium into a secretory phase. If pregnancy ensues it helps to maintain the decidua. Progesterone is used in the treatment of functional uterine haemorrhage and in intra-uterine devices for prevention of conception. It is responsible for development of breasts.The side effects of progesterone include gain in weight, mental depression and allergic skin rashes.

TESTOSTERONE

Testosterone is an odourless, white crystalline powder. It is soluble in alcohol, very slightly soluble in water and ethyl oleate. It should be stored in air tight containers protected from light.

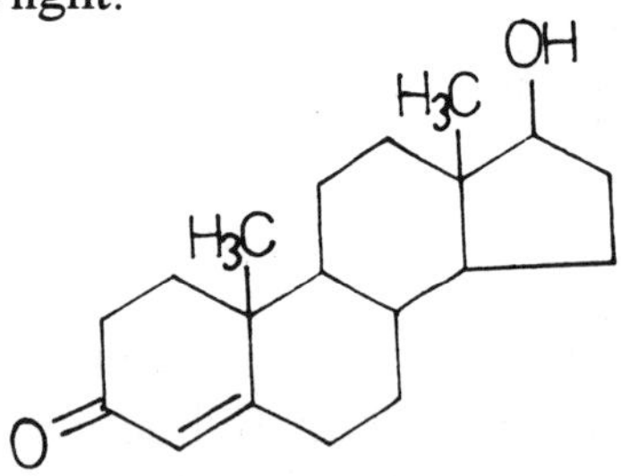

IUPAC Name: 17ß -Hydroxyandrost -4- en-3-one.

Actions and uses : Testosterone is an androgenic hormone. It controls the development and maintenance of male-sex organs and male secondary sex-characters. In adolescent males it increses size of sex-organs and increases sexual activity. In small dose it increases spermatozoa production. These hormones are used in the treatment of mal developed testies, absent or delayed secondary sex-characters and in the treatment of gynaecomostia.

In females, testosterone and its derivatives are used in the treatment of dysmenorrhoea, uterine bleeding, releif of after-pains in labour and palliative treatment of carcinoma of the breast.

Officials : Testosterone Propionate I.P.
Testosterone Propionate Injection I.P.

OESTRADIOL

Oestradiol is available as oestradiol benzoate. The salt is an odourless, colourless to white crystalline powder. This salt is slightly soluble in acetone, alcohol and ethyl oleate but practically insoluble in water. It should be stored in well closed containers protected from light.

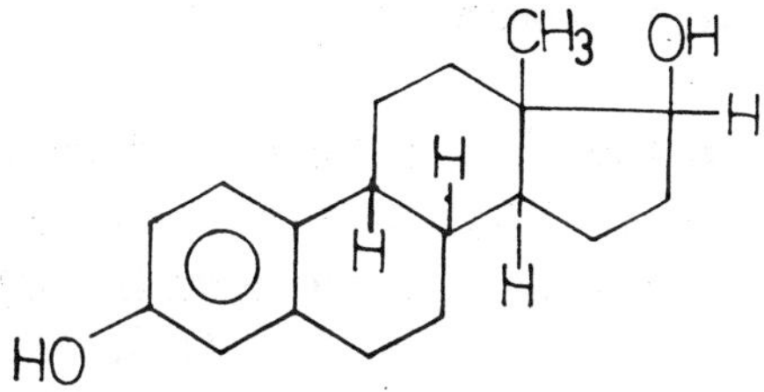

IUPAC Name :Estra-1,3,5-(10)-triene-3,17 ß - diol.

Actions and uses : Oestradiol is the most active naturally occuring oestrogen. It controls the functions of human uterus, particularly proliferation of endometrium, development of decidua and cyclic changes in the cervix and vagina. It also influences secondary sex characters, development of mammary glands and contractility of uterus.

It is used in the treatment of menopausal syndrome, senile vaginitis, vulvitis and to inhibit lactation.

Officials : Oestradiol Benzoate I.P.
Oestradiol Dipropionate I.P.
Oestradiol Propionate Injection I.P.

NANDROLONE

Nandrolone is available as decanoate, laurate and phenyl propionate salt. Nandrolone decaonate is a white crystalline powder with a faint characterstic odour. It is soluble in alcohol, ether, chloroform and very slightly soluble in water. It should be stored in nitrogen atmosphere in sealed containers protected from light below 10°C.

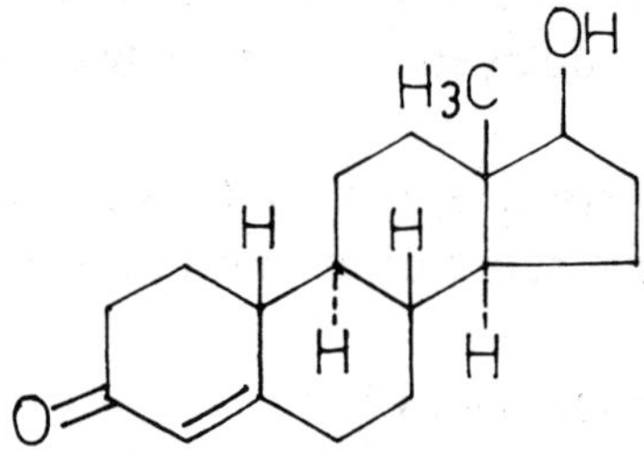

IUPAC Name : 4-Ene, 17ß-hydroxy-estra-3-one.

Actions and uses : Nandrolone has actions and uses similar to testosterone. Its anabolic properties are more than androgenic properties. It is used in the treatment of in-operable mammary carcinoma, acute renal failure and prevents nitrogen loss after severe burns.

Officials : Nandrolone Decanoate I.P.
Nandrolone Decanoate Injection I.P.
Nandrolone Phenylpropionate I.P.

(1) **Betamethasone** : Glaxo : Betnesol Tabs, Inj. O.5.- 6 mg daily.
(2) **Cortisone** : Indrsuifta : stemin Tab., Inj.:O.5.- 6 mg. daily
(3) **Hydrocortisone** : Hydrocortison sodium & succinate Inj. -Macleods : Prima cost
Dose : 100 ml gm. in inj or i.v.

(4) **Prednisolone** : Wyeth : Wysolone Tabs : 60mg/day and as required.
(5) **Progesterone** : Unichem : Uniprogestin Ing.: As reqd. & as directed.
(6) **Testosterone** : Intercase : Nuvircops 120-60 mg as initial increasing to 40-120 inj.
German ramedis : Testovindepoting : 250 mg 1 gm every 2-3 weeks.

(7) **Oestradiol** : Infar :Evalon Tab. : German remedise : Progynon Depot Inj.
Dose: As directed by physcian

(8) **Nadrolone** : Infer:Decadurabolin Inj.
Cadilla : Decaneurabol Inj. : Dose : 25-50 mg. in weekly to 3 weekly.

CHAPTER - 32

ANTINEOPLASTIC DRUGS

Neoplasm is also called as cancer or tumor. It means a relatively autonomous growth of tissue. Tumor indicates any abnormal mass or growth of tissue. Cancerous tumor is a malignant neoplasm with potential danger. Malignant neoplasm is the beginning of metastasis. These tumors have a rapid growth of cells but the rate of cell death is less and therefore a tumor is formed. Primary tumors can be treated by cytotoxic agents or exposure to radiation or by surgery but it is very difficult to treat secondary tumor.

Classification of antineoplastic agents :

(A) **Alkylating agents** : Azathioprine, Busulphan, Cisplatinum, Chloranmbucil, Cyclophosphamide.

(B) **Antimetabolites** : 5-Fluoro-uracil, 6-Mercapto-purine, Methotrexate.

(C) **Antibiotics** : Mitomycin, Daunorubicin and Actinomycin.

ACTINOMYCIN

Actinomycin D is also called dactinomycin. It is isolated from *streptomyces parvullus*. It is a powerful bacteriostatic and cytostatic agent. It is used for the treatment of wilms tumor [a kidney tumor of children] and gastrointestinal trophoblastic disease.

Dactinomycin binds with D.N.A by intercalation and interferes with synthesis of R.N.A and with protein synthesis.

Actinomycin is a bright red crystalline powder. It is soluble in water, freely soluble in alcohol, and very slightly soluble in ether. It is a hygroscopic compound and should be stored in air-tight containers protected from light below 40°C.

It is a tricyclic phenoxazine-3-one chromophore and has two identical penta petide lactone rings. It is the only agent which shows preference for purine-primidine D.N.A base sequence. It is also used in the treatment of tumors of uterus and testis, esterogenic sarcoma and other solid tumors.

MITOMYCIN

Mitomycin is isolated from *Streptomyces verticillatus* or *Streptomyces caespisosus*. It is a blue violet crystalline powder soluble in water, acetone, methanol and cyclohexanone. It should be stored in air-tight containers protected from light.

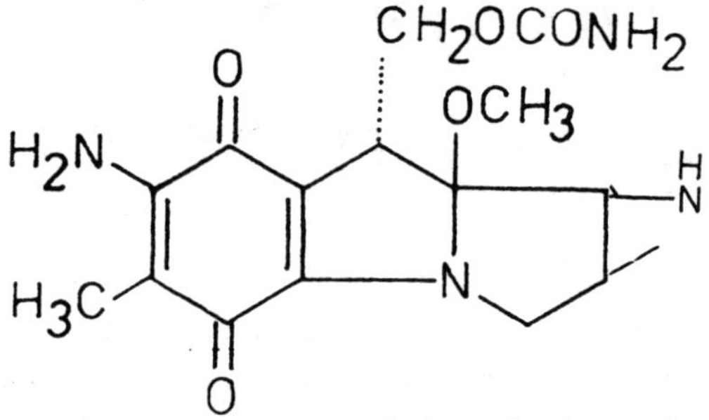

IUPAC Name : 6-Amino-1,1a,2,8,8a,8b-hexahydro-8-hydroxymethyl-8a-methoxy-5-methylazirino [2',3' : 3,4] -pyrrolo [1,2-a] indole-4,7-dione carbomate.

Actions and uses : Mitomycin binds preferentially to guanine and cytosine moieties of D.N.A, leading to cross-linkage to D.N.A and inhibits synthesis and functions of D.N.A. It is used in the treatment of carcinomas of bladder, breast, cervix, stomach, liver and prostate.

DAUNORUBICIN

Daunorubicin is available as hydrochloride salt. It is an orange-crystalline powder. It is freely soluble in water and methanol, slightly soluble in chloroform and practically insoluble in acetone. It is hygroscopic compound and stored in air-tight containers below 40°C.

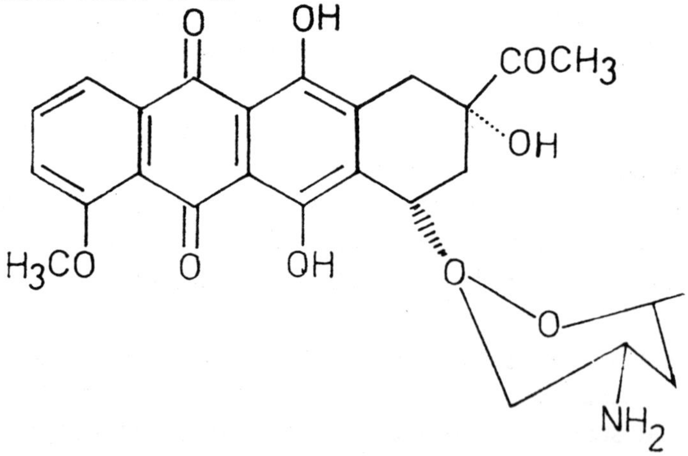

IUPAC Name : 8- [Acetyl-10-[3-amino-2,3,6,-trideoxy-α-L-lyxohexopyanosyl) oxy] -7,8,9,10-tetrahydro-6,8,11-trihydroxy-1-methoxy-5-12-naphtacenedione.

Actions and uses : Daunorubicin forms a stable complex with D.N.A and interferes with synthesis of nucleic acid. It is given in the treatment of acute lymphoblastic leukaemia in combination with vincristine and prednisone.

AZATHIOPRINE

Azathioprine is a pale yellow, odourless-powder. It is soluble in alkali hydroxides, sparingly soluble in mineral acids and practically insoluble in alcohol and chloroform and should be stored in air-tight containers protected from light below 30°C.

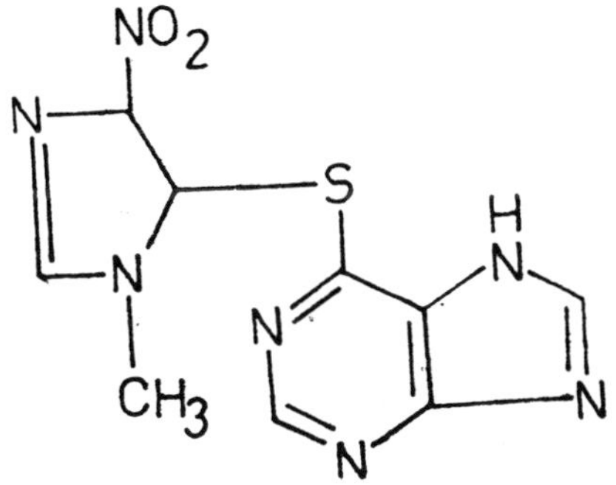

IUPAC Name : 6-[(1-methyl-4-nitro-1H-imidazol-5-yl) thio]-1H-purine.

Actions and uses : Azathioprine is a cytotoxic and immunosuppressant agent. It is converted into another cytotoxic drug mercaptopurine, thus providing prolonged action. It is used in the treatment of acute leukaemia and as immunosuppressive in organ transplantation. It is also used as immunosuppressive in lupus erythomatosus and polyarthertis nodosa. It is also useful in severe rheumatoid arthritis, ulcerative colitis, various nephritis, etc.The side effect are gastro-intestinal disorder pain in joints, liver damage, etc.

BUSULPHAN

Busulphan is an odourless white crystalline powder, freely soluble in acetone and chloroform, and very slightly soluble in water, alcohol and ether. It should be stored in air-tight containers protected from light.

$$CH_3\text{-}SO_2\text{-}O(CH_2)_4\text{-}O\text{-}SO_2\text{-}CH_3$$

IUPAC Name : 1,4-Bis { methane sulfonoxy } butane.

Actions and uses : Busulphan is a cell-cyclic, non-specific alkylating agent and inihibits cell division. Its main action is on bone-marrow granulocyte production and platelet production. It is given orally in the treatment of chronic myeloid leukaemia. It reduces size of the spleen.

The undesirable effects are hyperpigmentation and amenorrhoea. Blood infusion should be given along the drug every week and a check on platelets counts and granulocyte count should be stable.

CISPLATIN

Cisplatin is a yellow or orange yellow crystallin powder. It is slightly soluble in water; sparingly soluble in dimethyl formamide and practically insoluble in alcohol. It should be protected from light.

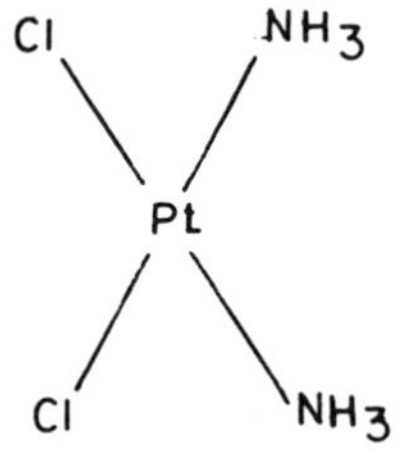

IUPAC Name : Cis - Diammine dichloro platinum.

Actions and uses : Cisplatin is a cell-cyclic, non specific antineoplastic drug. It is used in the treatment of metastatic tumours of testis, ovary and advanced bladder cancer. It is given by intravenous infusion.

The adverse effects are nephrotoxicity, myeloid suppression and neurotoxicity. It may cause nausea and vomitting.

CHLORAMBUCIL

Chlorambucil is a white crystalline powder with a slight odour. It is soluble in alcohol chloroform and acetone but practically insoluble in water. It should be stored in air-tight containers protected from light.Chlorambucil is an irritant; avoid contact with skin and mucous membrane.

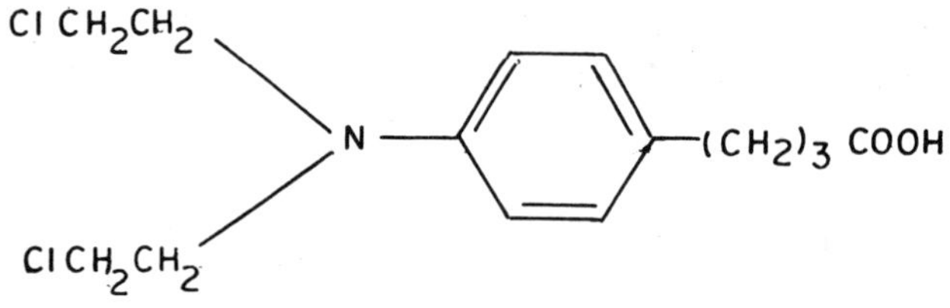

IUPAC Name : 4-[4-Bis {(2-chloro ethyl)amino}phenyl] butyric acid.

Actions and uses : Chlorambucil is a cytotoxic agent which damages cells by fragmentation of nuclear chromosomes. It is used in the treatment of follicular lymphoma, lymphocytic lymphoma with or without leukaemia, hodgkin's disease, reticulum-cell,sarcoma, chronic myelocytic leukaemias, rheumatoid arthritis and systemic lupus erythematosus.

It may produce severve neutropenia, thromobocytopenia and irreversible damage to bone morrow.

CYCLOPHOSPHAMIDE

Cyclophosphamide is an odourless white crystalline fine powder with a slightly bitter taste. It is freely soluble in alcohol, soluble in water and very slightly soluble in ether. It should be stored in air tight containers below 30°C.

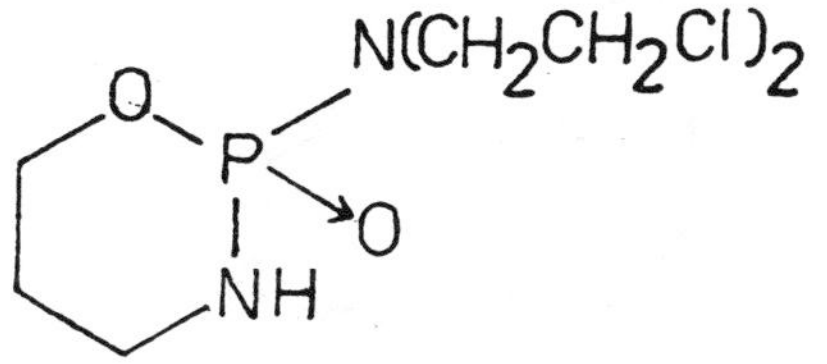

IUPAC Name : 2-[Bis (2-chloro ethyl)amino]perhydro-2H-1,3,2,-oxazaphosporine 2-oxide.

Actions and uses : Cyclophosphamide is a cyto-toxic drug. It probabİy broken down at nitrogen phosphorus linkage and act as alkylating agent in liver.It is used in the treatment of hodgkins disease, multiple myeloma, lymphosarcoma, lymphatic leukaemia, ovarian tumour and other tumors. It is also used in the treatment of inoperable breast and bronchial cancers. The side effects are cardiac toxicity, gastro intestional, pulmonary disturbances, etc.

Officials : Cyclophosphamide I.P.
Cyclophoamide Injection I.P.
Cyclophosphamide Tablets I.P.

FLUOROURACIL

Flurouracil is an odourless-white crystalline powder. It is soluble in water, very slightly soluble in alcohol and practically insoluble in chloroform and ether. It should be stored in air-tight containers protected from light.

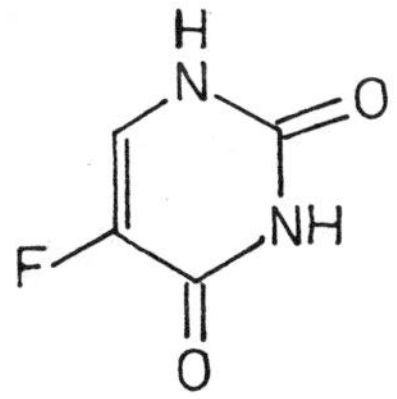

IUPAC Name : 5-Fluro pyrimidine-2,4-[1H,3H]- dione.

Actions and uses : Flurouracil is an analouge of uracil. It competitively blocks biosynthesis of ribonucleic acid. It is used in the treatment of respiratory tract, gastro intestinal tract and breast cancer. It is also used in the treatment of solar keratoses on the skin. The side effects are nausea, vomiting, diarrhoea, depression in bone marrow, etc.

Officials : Flurouracil I.P.
Flurouracil Injections I.P.

MERCAPTOPURINE

Mercaptopurine is an odourless yellow crystalline powder. It is soluble in alkali hydroxide, very slightly soluble in water, alcohol, ether and acetone. It should be stored in air tight containers protected from light.

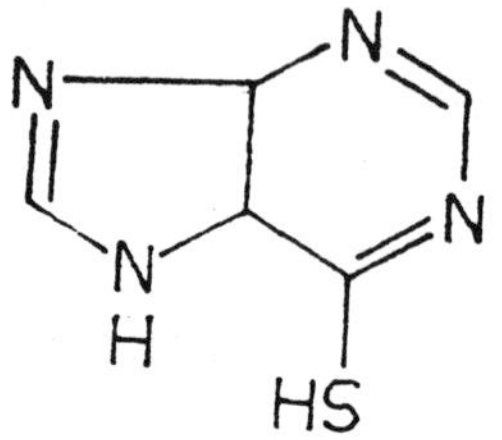

IUPAC Name : 6-mercaptopurine.

Actions and uses : Mercaptopurine is a analogue of adenine and blocks the components of nucleic acid,it interfere with nucleic acid biosynthesis. It is used in the treatment of acute leukaemia or chronic myeloid leukaemia. It is also immuno-suppressant in the treatment of nephrotic syndrome and auto-immuno haemolytic anaemia.

Officials : Mercaptopurine I.P.
Mercaptopurine Tablets I.P.

METHOTREXATE

Methotrexate is a yellow to orange crystalline powder. It is soluble in alkali hydroxides, very slightly soluble in water, alcohol, ether and chloroform. It should be stored in air tight containers protected from light.

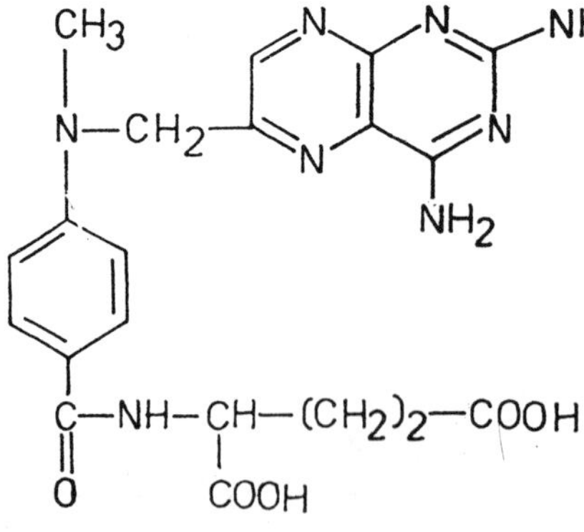

IUPAC Name : N-{4-[(2,4-diaminopteridin-6-ylmethyl)methylamino] benzoyl} L-glutamic acid.

Actions and uses : Methotraxate is a cyto-toxic and folic acid antagonist. It combines irreversible with dihydrfolate reductase and inhibits nucleic acid synthasis, thereby stops cell division. It is used in the treatment of leukaemia and meningial leukaemia. It should be given intrathecally because it can not cross blood-brain barrier. It is also used in the treatment of choriocarcinoma, testicular cancer and breast cancer. Its immunosuppressive action is used in the treatment of dermatomyositis. The side effects are nausea, vomiting, diarrhoea, ulceration, abdominal cramp, etc.

Officials : Methotrxate I.P.
Methtrexate Tables I.P

(1) **Actinomycins** : Actinomycin-D Inj. 15 μg/kq I.V. daily Inj. for 5 days.

(2) **Busulphan** : B.Wellcome: myleran Tab. : Dose depends on condition-4-8 mg/day.

(3) **Chlorambusil** : B.wellcome : Leukeran Tabs : As directed.

(4) **Cisplatin** : Biochem : Cisplatin Inj.: Dose depend upon the type of tumour.

(5) **Cyclophosphamide** : Biochem : Cycloxan Tab., Inj.: 40-50 mg/kg. in div. doses.

(6) **Flurouracil** : Biochem : Fluracil Inj., Cap. : 12 mg/kg. wt.once daily.

(7) **Mercaptopurine** : B. Wellcome : Nenthol Tabs : As directed and reqd.

(8) **Methotrexate** : Biochem : Biotrexate Inj., Tab : 12 mg/m^2 max. upto 15 mg.

(9) **Mytomycin** : Biochem : Mitomycin-C-Kyowa : 6-10 mg. i.v.Inj. twice weekly

(10) **Azathioprine** : Searle : Azoran Tab. 50 mg
B.Wellcome : Imuran 0.5 mg

(11)**Daunorobicin** : Sigma Lab. : Rubidomycin Inj.
Dabur : Adrim Inj.

INDEX

Collector Bro

ISBN 978-93-5457-088-9

Authored by Prasanth Nair
Illustrations by Nithya Deepak
Layout and design by Ranjith Ramadasan

Published by Lekshmy Sankar
Compassionate India, 1/574, Ambadi, Kallara
Thiruvananthapuram, Kerala, India

Printed by Akshara Offset
Thiruvananthapuram, Kerala, India

COLLECTOR Bro

The quixotic thallals of a civil servant

ABOUT THE AUTHOR

Prasanth, son of Dr. N Radha and PV Balakrishnan hails from Thalassery. He did his studies in Loyola School, Mar Ivanios College and Government Law College, Thiruvananthapuram and got enrolled as an advocate before the High Court of Kerala.

Prasanth joined the Indian Administrative Service (IAS) in 2007 and he served in various capacities in different sectors including tourism, taxation, roads, water supply, shipping, energy, skill development, irrigation etc. He headed two World Bank projects.

As District Magistrate in Kozhikode he earned the moniker of Collector Bro for his citizen friendly and participative approach in governance. Internationale Tourismus-Börse Berlin chose his Compassionate Kozhikode as one of the 50 inspirational projects from around the world. Digital Empowerment Foundation and the Friedrich Naumann Foundation selected it for the Social Media for Empowerment (SM4E) award. Prasanth is considered a pioneer in using social media for governance.

An avid film buff, Prasanth has co-scripted and acted in Malayalam movies, directed short films, documentaries and musicals. His short film, Daivakanam was premiered at Cannes Film Festival in 2018.

Prasanth lives in Kochi with his wife, children and cat.

To the Universal Mother

HEAPS OF LOVE

My sincere thanks to Dr B Ashok, Prof. Vinayakumar, Neetu, Arun, Hari, Gopika, Noufal, Saiju and scores of others close to me, who spared their time to make this book a reality. I also have to thank the hundreds of unsolicited advisors, both the busy and the jobless, and their sustained critical scrutiny on how to conduct myself as an officer, that has equipped me over time to ignore them in toto and write this book. My thanks to Amma who taught me not to become someone else's football to be kicked around in all directions to please the beholders; to my Achan who made me understand what classy perseverance is; and to Lekshmy, Ammu, Varshan and Vasu for their immense patience and love.

TABLE OF CONTENTS

FOREWORD

Filled with warm humour and no little wisdom, Collector Bro, the memoirs (or "quixotic thallals", as he eloquently puts it!) of Prasanth Nair, are a fascinating look into the world of a young and hard-working IAS officer. A life that is sometimes frustrating, often uplifting, and certainly never boring, comes alive on the page. Aspiring civil servants, serving officers, and lovers of storytelling should all enjoy this book.

Dr Shashi Tharoor

INTRODUCTION

Often imitated, but never duplicated is what comes to my mind when I think of Prasanth. Most of Kerala knows Prasanth Nair, IAS as The Collector Bro. He has made his presence felt through his remarkable career and being a massive social persona, but what sets him apart is his compassion for fellow humans and his boldness to drive positive change.

This book by Prasanth is his tribute to the everyday heroes, during his tenure as the Collector of Kozhikode - a must read for aspiring and current administrators and for those hoping to make a social impact. It is a roadmap on how to build a visible and sustainable brand and leverage social media effectively, making it a nice read for anyone in the marketing and management spectrum. The real-life examples of crowd-sourcing to drive community projects, how empowered common folks created major social changes, are worthy of case studies at Civil Service Academies and Business Schools. Above all, this book is a testament to the goodness of the average human being that when pooled together miracles are created. One of the most remarkable aspects of the incidents narrated here is the strategy adopted to find many solutions - as an early adopter leveraging the massive power of technology and social media.

With his penchant for doing good, Prasanth used his influencing skills to tap into the power of people and bring positive change to the society instead of being burdened by the weight of bureaucracy. He made volunteering mainstream and with his humble approach, he has proved that all effective organizations are inverted pyramids, where the most ordinary will become the true leaders when those at the tip of the pyramid act as selfless enablers. In the end, we are left with the positive feeling that bureaucracy is not about hiding away from people behind a mountain of files, but a chance to make lives around us better by standing together in support to each other.

I cannot think of a better way to conclude other than quoting a Sanskrit Shloka from Samayochitapadya Maalikaa:

"amaṃtramakṣaraṃ nāsti nāsti mūlamanauṣadham

ayogyaḥ puruṣo nāsti yojakastatra durlabhaḥ."

that translates to

"There is no letter which doesn't have a charm, there is no root which doesn't have medicinal property.

There is no person who is not able, but rare is the one who knows how to make proper use of all these."

Collector Bro, with the hand that he's dealt with, created a sense of purpose for many around him and created incredible positive change. I am sure this book will be a lesson to many of us today and an inspiration to future generations.

Tony Thomas

PREFACE

This book is something that has been in the offing for long. Friends, colleagues and elders had asked me to write down the inside story of the years that I spent as District Collector for academic purposes. Many senior officers advised me to document events and experiences for the benefit of others. Some advised that I do it for posterity. A senior bureaucrat turned politician said I should do it for vanity. But I shied away from writing the book for various reasons.

The main problem was that it is terribly embarrassing for me to write in first person about my own experiences as a bureaucrat. When you do that, you invariably tend to overestimate your importance in the unfolding of the events described and your contribution to the end result. "When I was District Collector..." signals the prelude to the umpteen boring stories narrated by many senior officers. How I detest hearing that and imagine me doing precisely that! However, as a student of psychology, I am also cognizant that as one grows older and moves away from the events, the recollection of facts becomes more inaccurate and one's own centrality and significance in the story become dear and profound. So, finally, I decided to write down at least a few pages of reminiscences, before things get worse and memory becomes increasingly tainted with my self-esteem! Now, isn't that a good excuse? I've a better one - my better half, Lekshmy, wanted me to write a book than write on social media!

In this collection I seek to capture the emotional roller-coaster experienced during my stint as a District Collector - not a bundle of pages about 'I did this' but one on 'I went through this'. Therefore, you can expect descriptions of incidents which had an impact on me, at a deeply personal level, rather than a chronicle of everything that happened during the tenure. May I also clarify that this is not a 'service story' but only a memoir of incidents, ideas and memories that can be loosely tied with a single theme called compassion. And, as a statutory warning, I would request readers to discount the importance attached to me or my contribution in the events described. It is basic psychology that each human being tends to exaggerate his own worth in any anecdote; and I confess that I am human, all too human, in this and in everything else.

This book seeks to trace a short journey that was personally enriching and emotionally draining but nevertheless a journey undertaken in one of those exciting phases in life when you realise what you are, what you can do and what you should do: the learnings from outside the typical government systems, of a District Collector posted in the northern Malabar district of Kozhikode between 2015 and 2017 in the south Indian state of Kerala, laced in with a bit of nostalgia and zeal.

Some say that Indians are quicker to find fault with a failed experiment than to learn from the failure. Hence, we are scared of experimenting, innovating and taking risks. At Kozhikode, we took abundant, calculated risks. We carved out new paths and adventured. In the following pages you will find accounts of many things that worked brilliantly and many that ended as a failure. Some projects were running well then and are doing well even now, and have been proven to be sustainable. Some immaculately designed schemes which functioned smoothly during those days hit a dead end of late. I hope this book will shed some light on the 'whys' and the 'why nots' of such success and failure.

I prefer not to follow a particular pattern in my writing that would force to divide my thoughts into chapters or fragment them into distinct segments. Thoughts are best presented as they flow and kept as unedited as possible, especially so when they are emotionally rich. That way I may succeed in capturing the essence and preserving the life of life-experiences as they occurred. Though this book would touch upon governance, it isn't at all about government. In fact, 'anything other than government' would be a better description. This book may be treated as a poorly attempted literary work with artistic content thrown in, ably aided by Nithya the illustrator and Ranjith the designer, in deep pursuit of a scientific character and squarely in conformity with the provisions of Rule 6(2) of All India Service (AIS) Conduct Rules, 1969! Perhaps you will find the book similar to a long essay or a compilation of stories or anecdotes.

Over the last few years, our family has been trying to support the education of the less fortunate children around us, at a very personal level, without much fanfare. The proceeds from the sale of this book is intended to augment that cause.

I share any achievement with all my well-wishers. The short falls are entirely mine.

Prasanth Nair

ASHOKA the GREAT

Many Indians seem to think that Indian Administrative Service (IAS) officers know everything under the sun. Nothing could be farther from truth. But all the same, as an IAS officer, you could be handed any assignment overnight, expected to take charge and start delivering results immediately. You could be in charge of Tourism one day and you could be shifted to Education the next day. Someone who has been serving in the Excise Department could be transferred and assigned the charge of the Health Department within a day or two. The Ports Director could become the Labour Commissioner in the blink of an eye, and vice versa. Unlike the private sector where even the Chief Executive Officer (CEO) goes through a period of induction training before taking over the reins of the company, the assumption in government is that the officer comes into the organisation equipped with superior knowledge. There is no need to elaborate on how illogical this premise is. Experience and sufficient time to get a grasp over the subject are paramount to make any meaningful impact. Equally important are the aptitude and interest of the particular officer in the assigned job, though such considerations are immaterial from the government's point of view. So, generally speaking, an IAS officer is expected to land on all fours wherever he or she is dropped into an assignment. And then break into a lovely salsa.

If that's not enough, the officer would have virtually no control over the recruitment of members of his staff or on matters pertaining to their discipline. The recruitment is mostly done by the Public Service Commission (PSC) while the transfers and postings are administered by political bosses and unions. And dismissal - well, what does that even mean in government services?

In 2011, while I was posted as the Executive Director of Jalanidhi[1], a World Bank project, my good friend and senior schoolmate, Ashok Chandran sent me a probing email. Unlike me, he is a Bujji[2] and hence, his observations are thought-provoking, crafted, teasing and even intriguing at times. A highly accomplished academician, he is an alumnus of the London School of Economics who chose to tread a path of his own instead of getting into the rat-race of corporate money-making.

In the email I received from him, Ashok was expressing shock over the lack of career planning or planned career-grooming in the IAS cadre. The preparation an officer undergoes for the task that he is about to take up is very basic and minimal. Ashok found this extremely shocking. In his view, it accounted for virtually no preparation! And political expediency did not provide any security of tenure either. But the most burning question in his mail was this - "Isn't there any post or assignment for which you could prepare yourself mentally, do proper homework in advance and deliver results professionally? 'Enthuvaadei ithu?' "[3]

It was embarrassing for me to divulge the state secret that our career planning and human resource management amounted next to nothing. All the IAS postings are a result of choices made by the political powerhouses and are unpredictable. There is no opportunity for officers to prepare themselves for any task that is assigned to them. They can only begin learning on the

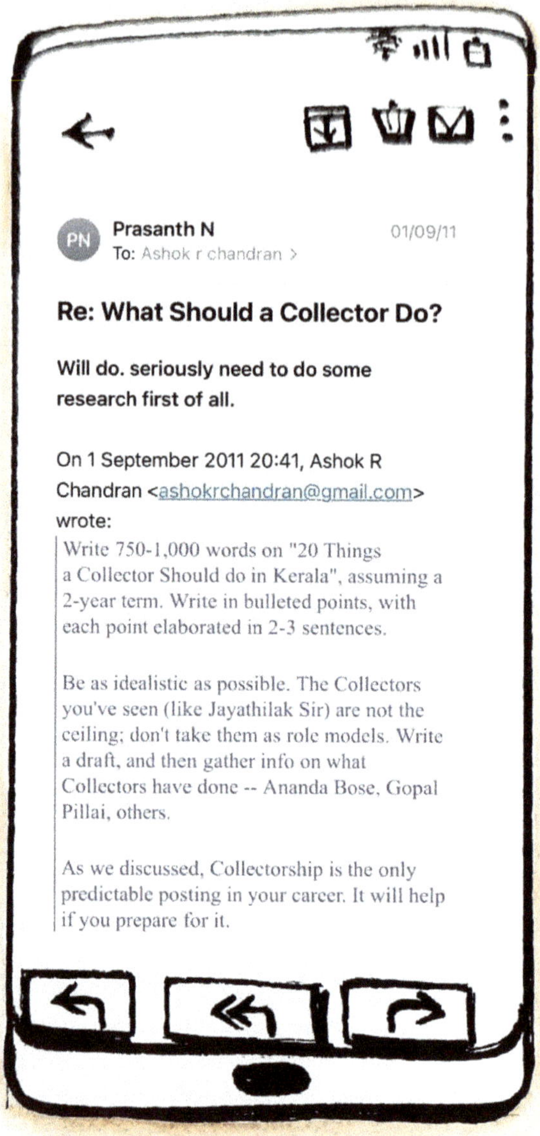

Prasanth N 01/09/11
To: Ashok r chandran >

Re: What Should a Collector Do?

Will do. seriously need to do some research first of all.

On 1 September 2011 20:41, Ashok R Chandran <ashokrchandran@gmail.com> wrote:

> Write 750-1,000 words on "20 Things a Collector Should do in Kerala", assuming a 2-year term. Write in bulleted points, with each point elaborated in 2-3 sentences.
>
> Be as idealistic as possible. The Collectors you've seen (like Jayathilak Sir) are not the ceiling; don't take them as role models. Write a draft, and then gather info on what Collectors have done -- Ananda Bose, Gopal Pillai, others.
>
> As we discussed, Collectorship is the only predictable posting in your career. It will help if you prepare for it.

job. The faster they learned, the better they would become as officers. I was about to send this reply when I suddenly remembered that every IAS officer is expected to work as a District Collector for a minimum of two years. Of course they wouldn't know in which district, but a district assignment was bound to happen. It dawned upon me that this is one posting of an IAS officer that is clearly predictable. I mailed back to Ashok about my newfound knowledge. He replied and called me up, "Wakke[4]... agreed that you are unable to know beforehand about your postings and prepare for it. But you now admit that you know in advance about one upcoming job for sure - that of the District Collector. And if you indeed know that, have you prepared yourself for that?" This was on 1st of September 2011. He suggested that I send him a write-up in around 750-1000 words about the preparation that I would do for the inevitable forthcoming assignment. Django njaan pettu[5].

It was the process of drafting my response to his mail that made me think hard about the role that a Collector should play in a state like Kerala. A state that is advanced in many respects has different needs and unique problems, and one needs novel approaches to tackle those unique problems. Official intervention of the type taken for granted in other parts of India may not be necessary or appropriate in the context of Kerala and the officer in charge has to be constantly aware of this fact. The District Collector's post that was originally designed as 'land tax collector' had evolved over the centuries to become that of the CEO representing the state government in the district[6]. The officer doesn't belong to any one department; but is expected to dabble in and orchestrate all departments.

I sent a reply to Ashok after seven days. It was this mental churning that made me realise that my heart was profoundly in the social sector. The high ideals of social service and helping the poor and the underprivileged, about which every civil service aspirant writes essays and talks eloquently in the selection interview stirred within me. The very purpose of joining the civil service, and Gandhi's Talisman, started making a lot of sense. It was as if all of a sudden I was able to see the huge elephant that had been there in the room throughout. I am forever thankful to Ashok for helping me clarify my priorities as an administrator and as a human being.

THODA HAT-ke

This chapter is about me - within the me - speaking of me - to the me - as observed by me.

I have been asked many times - what makes me different from other IAS officers? The assumption in the question being that I am indeed different and that it is an established fact. Honestly, I would not consider myself any different from other IAS/IPS/IRS/IFS officers. It could be the new generation shift that was inevitable as far as the resultant public discussions and hype were concerned, and I might have just been there at the right moment. Like a church mouse who happened to be on the stage when the spotlight got switched on.

Again, not a novelty on its own, but perhaps the only characteristic I would agree that I possess to a certain extent could be my obsession in finding solutions, in whatever bizarre ways. However, what got hyped about yours truly was the extensive use of technology. Looking back, I would rather call it a case of luck as I just happened to be one of the early adopters in the younger generation of officers who understood technology. It was bound to happen. And as Bhagavad Gita says, "Whatever happened, happened for the good". For me!

From 1999 to 2006, as part of cost-cutting exercises in the government, there was very little direct recruitment to the IAS cadre with barely one officer joining Kerala every year. Generally, the scene was dominated by officers promoted from the ranks, who were quite senior in age and outlook. It is in this context that a young directly recruited officer armed with technology and inexperience enters. And anything that happens for the first time is hyped and celebrated in the media, more so in social media. In a nutshell, that explains the Collector Bro phenomenon to a large extent.

Given that this chapter is all about me, I will immodestly disclose that the psychometric analysis done as part of the mid-career training in Mussoorie to assess the risk-taking mentality and decision making skills of the officers, projected me as somewhat deviant with out-of-the-box thinking style and relatively higher risk-taking nature, both of which were completely opposite to the traditional bureaucratic way of relying on precedence. I remember standing out as a loner in that batch of about 110 with the results from the psychometric test. I do not know whether it reassured me or declared me as officially deviant - a misfit in a job where adherence to precedents and conformity is expected. Whatever be the case, it is a fact that I enjoy trying to problem-solve, creatively-ideate, conceptualise, system-design or roll out new projects. I have immense respect for those who excel in regular maintenance tasks and everyday chores, because I find them incredibly boring and difficult.

Then comes the question of the weird humour sense. Being a 'funny', not so serious IAS officer has its fair share of problems. Because I am (almost) always accessible and (almost) always try to handle things with a pinch of humour, some people tend to take me for granted or stretch the boundaries. In fact, I like that. There is banter in that too. You are insecure about yourself when you don't know your legitimate authority, statutory powers or how to exercise it. Only then will you be

worried. If you know your boundaries, you can set them. If you can set them, people won't cross them.

The conclusion here is that we have to live with our individual personality type after all - some good, some not so much. Just like anyone, I try to leverage my traits in a positive manner as far as possible and perhaps that's why people find it different. In the interest of transparency, here's a caveat: I get emotional, all too often, and all too quickly. Sometimes, I tend to empathise more than what is needed. You would be better off learning from a well-written book on psychology, but I can personally vouch one thing: you do get into trouble if you're emotionally vulnerable.

Having said that, one emotion that has never made me regret in whatsoever manner, is compassion. For me, compassion is a human emotion prompted by the pain of others. More vigorous and impactful than empathy, it gives rise to an active desire to lessen another's suffering. Compassion is not about charity but sharing your luck with someone who isn't as fortunate as you. Exploring this phenomenon led to the creation of a platform called Compassionate Kozhikode[7]. It is rooted in the principle enunciated in Gandhi's Talisman.

I found this to be the most powerful administrative tool ever invented. Yet, it is one of the most underrated and under-utilised mechanisms. If you have been to the Collectorate at Kozhikode, you will find this talisman displayed boldly near the staircase leading to the Collector's chamber. Once you realise the magnitude of this unbelievably simple tool it is hard to let go of it. It is this tool, coupled with the possibilities of modern communication that transformed an ordinary civil servant, a mere District Collector, hitherto an unknown entity to the public, into a brotherly Collector Bro. It was a social capital or social brand that evolved organically without any prior design. There was an element of honest effort and genuine emotional content in that evolutionary voyage. Throughout my tenure in Kozhikode, the effort was to remain truthful to the emotions and conscience which powered every initiative under the umbrella of Compassionate Kozhikode. This reminiscing is also a narrative on how I got seriously obsessed with compassion.

Having read this chapter, do take away the concept of Gandhi's talisman; the rest was nothing but a bit of thallal[8] .

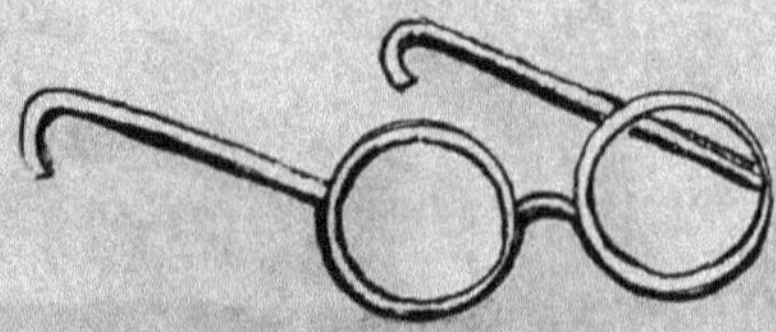

I will give you a talisman. Whenever you are in doubt, or when the self becomes too much with you, apply the following test. Recall the face of the poorest and the weakest man whom you may have seen, and ask yourself, if the step you contemplate is going to be of any use to him. Will he gain anything by it? Will it restore him to a control over his own life and destiny? In other words, will it lead to swaraj for the hungry and spiritually starving millions? Then you will find your doubts and your self melt away.

Mahatma Gandhi –
The Last Phase, Vol. II (1958), p.65

A shady CHARACTER

Viral conjunctivitis is one of the most irritating of diseases. I had just recovered from one when my posting orders as District Collector of Kozhikode came out. I was to take charge on 23rd of February 2015 and exactly the night before, my eyes started troubling me again. The next day, I had the kismet to take over the District Administration with my dark shades on, in full-on Bollywood style. Though it was not any intentional fashion statement, the public of Kozhikode, with their great fascination for fashion, put up with my shady looks for almost a week.

During the customary interaction with the media after taking over as the District Collector, I was asked about the new developmental projects that I was going to bring to the district. I said none as far as I knew. "I come with no preconceived notions or magic wand for development. The idea of development itself needs to be deconstructed. I would like to be known as a collector who presided over a district of peaceful people wholeheartedly helping one another and displaying love and fraternity than a district with lots of flyovers, metro lines and growing concrete jungles lacking humanity. There will always be enough people to lobby for and fund huge projects. Every new piece of infrastructure - be it road, bridge or flyover - will have beneficiaries all the way from the contractor to the real estate owners and everyone in between, whose pockets would bulge over time. Unfortunately, there are sections of the population for whom there is nobody to support or be their voice - they would be my priority." That morning, I had incidentally read about a place called Balika Sadanam in the newspapers[9]. Apparently, the civil society of Kozhikode observed the 67th anniversary of the preservation of the mortal remains of Gandhiji at this building, a noble legacy that it carried all those years. Maybe my thoughts had unknowingly meandered to Gandhiji and his Talisman. I don't think anyone was particularly happy with my answers that day, except perhaps my parents. Parents are the only ones who think whatever their children do or say is brilliant!

Having successfully antagonised the press and the commercial magnates of Kozhikode within the first week, I got going with what I was supposed to do. Thanks to my friend Ashok, the priorities in the district were clear in my mind. The ball started rolling, and one thing led to another. In March 2015, we brainstormed the idea of developing marginalized groups with specific tasks and goals in the District. We devised plans to enable them once they were operational. Although completely informal, I saw commitment and passion in everyone who took effort to be part of these initiatives. Within a month of taking charge, I started seeing early traction, got acquainted with new people, and found solid ground support. To be frank, these developments had nothing official about them. Perhaps, what was official about forming this network - as my wife would vouch - were the empty jokes we cracked, the bottomless cups of tea and coffee we savoured, and the abundant supply of the best Porottas in town during those informal meetings. A blue-print was born! Dr. Suresh Kumar, former Director of the Institute of Palliative Medicine (IPM)[10], Kozhikode, along with the student volunteers of the palliative care centre were central to the teams formed.

The District Legal Services Authority (DLSA) under the able leadership of the Sub Judge RL Baiju gave us the right legal framework and judicial support for all interventions. (Oftentimes, I heard through the grapevine of the judiciary office that I spoiled him whereas on the executive side, the murmur was that he was the one who spoiled me!) Dr. Saji Gopinath of the Indian Institute of Management (IIM), Kozhikode, was the management brain in the team. Amandeep Kaur IFoS, the young District Forest Officer (DFO), gave us the gender balance and the 'non-Malayali' perspective. People like Dr. Krishnakumar, Director of IMHANS, Dr. Anwar and many others became integral to these gatherings. But in my opinion the fulcrum of all these meetings was Dr. Nijeesh, Personal Assistant (PA) to the District Collector. While I let loose Nijeesh into the wilderness of volunteering and social sector activities in the district, I remain indebted to Babu, my Confidential Assistant (CA) who held the fort for me in the traditional official functions of the District Collector. Add to this a bunch of crazy youngsters like Arun, Sabith, Snehaj and Binoy - the recipe for a mad roller-coaster ride was ready.

An efficient team of Deputy Collectors led by Jenilkumar, Abdul Nasser and Shamin Sabastain to whom I delegated heavily the routine work of administration never disappointed me. It was more of a management by exception principle that I adopted there. In revenue collection, land acquisition, distribution of Patta, resolving long pending land-tax issues, declaring the district as open defecation-free - you name it, Kozhikode out-performed all other districts[11]. There is a misconception that if you focus more on public and participatory programmes, the traditional revenue administration would get neglected. On the contrary, I experienced that it actually gets extremely strong.

In fact, we discovered that even law and order issues had solutions in compassion and empathy. In 2015, a few weeks before I joined Kozhikode, Hindu-Muslim riots broke out in Tuneri, Nadapuram in the northern part of the district. As the new District Magistrate, one of the primary tasks that I had at hand was to pacify people and get things back to normalcy in Nadapuram. Visiting the locality, I talked to the many innocent men and women whose houses were burnt down and livelihoods destroyed. It was an emotionally shaking experience listening to old frail women whose houses were destroyed by their own neighbours. For a moment I felt fortunate that I had conjunctivitis and had goggles to cover my wet eyes.

Communal riots and conflicts have a never ending cycle associated with it. The communities try to keep track of the 'score' and keep perpetrating violence as and when they get an opportunity to outsmart the 'other' community. There was a long history of retaliations dating from 2000 behind the latest riots of 2015. We badly needed to break this cycle. The intervention was a patient and painstaking one that went on for more than a year.

As part of the rehabilitation package, the State government declared compensation amounts to all the victims, irrespective of their community or religion. On the day of distribution of the cheques signed by the Collector, we planned and executed a small social experiment. I drove down to Nadapuram and distributed the cheques personally, one after the other, talking and listening to each one of them. It went on well into late night. When each person was to collect his or her cheque, they had to recollect and name at least one person of the other community with whom they had an excellent bonding prior to the riots. They were to then tell me privately whether they are willing to forgive them. Or at least think about forgiving them. Only then would I hand over the cheque. At least half a dozen of them broke down as they recollected the love and bonding they had with their neighbours. Some of them wept and wondered how their close friends got transformed into devils in the name of religion. They recollected how their kids used to play together and how they supported each other in times of difficulty. Some of them admitted that they themselves got carried away by the evil. There were some who were not at all remorseful.

After that tiring long day of 'listening/counselling therapy', as we drove back home, I was hoping that the little bit of empathy and compassion that we might have had ignited in their minds would reduce the mental conflict and the resultant violence. Violence starts and ends in the mind. I don't know whether our unplanned social experiment was any success, but it is a fact that after 2016, we did not have any major untoward incident in Nadapuram, till date. Touchwood.

A full-fledged programme called Compassionate Kozhikode was formally announced in April 2015.

The thought of designing it originated from the realisation that there were people in Kozhikode who were willing to give and there were many who needed help. It was the culmination of several brainstorming sessions by a group of dedicated souls during the many evenings we had at the Collector's residence. Citizens with the right intentions and even the right plan were reluctant to take the right action at the right time. Compassionate Kozhikode sought to ignite those people and serve as a platform through which they could overcome their inhibitions and break the shell that restricted them. All the schemes under Compassionate Kozhikode were voluntary and crowd sourced. A plethora of initiatives were launched by the District Administration in partnership with civil society, government agencies and citizen volunteers. The Administration was essentially a facilitator and to some extent a match-maker. The Collector was an aggregator and Compassionate Kozhikode was the Collectorate. It is my strong belief that the aggregator model that has revolutionised private business has its due application in the public sector as well.

Now, that was the theory. What actually got me into doing all these is a rather long and emotional story. A few weeks into the job, I had an opportunity to visit the Government Mental Health Centre[12], Kuthiravattam. The mental health facility was set up in 1872 by the British with just nine beds. In 1886, it was upgraded to accommodate 84 patients. It expanded further when more and more mental patients were dumped in asylums. The local termed it the Bhranthan Jail (Lunatic Jail). The purpose was to isolate the mentally deranged British soldiers and the violent, mentally ill native patients from the civilian population. The language and tenor of the building and infrastructure still maintain that character. The Inspector General (IG) of Jails who was in charge, regularly visited the asylum and gave necessary directions in those days. Sadly, I found that the hospital still maintained the same levels of insensitivity right in the heart of a prosperous, 21st century city.

Catering to the six northern districts of Kerala and the adjacent districts of Tamil Nadu, the hospital was spread over 19.6 acres of land. More than 800 inmates were housed in a facility made for less than 500 patients. Around 150 of the inmates were no longer ill and were ready for rehabilitation. However they continued to languish in the hospital because either they had no place to return to or their homes could not be located. One should understand that most of the inmates in such facilities are abandoned by their relatives. More disturbingly, there were patients with intellectual disabilities and other developmental anomalies placed in the facility, although only patients with mental illness were supposed to be admitted and treated. I do not know how many amongst the public understand the difference between mental illnesses and intellectual disabilities, but let me assure you the more you know about the nuances, the more disturbed you would be as a person.

It is in the dark alleys of this hospital that I discovered the seeds of Compassionate Kozhikode. I will come back to the mental hospital many times in this book. This hospital continued throughout as the centre of all our activities and it still remains so. It is this hospital that I regard as the heart of Kozhikode.

THE MAPS of KUNNAMKULAM

Another parallel story in giving greater leverage to the activities of the District Administration was the use of social media which was perhaps done on this scale for the first time in India. It wasn't any Newton's Apple that fell from above, but a simple idea that managed to grow bigger and showed some gravitas in the months that followed. It had its advantages and an equal share of complications too. For one, there was an element of novelty in the whole exercise which grabbed a lot of eyeballs. This helped us reach out to a wider audience and made the change more visible and popular. On the flip side, many found it difficult to accept that social media and the tools of technology could benefit the underprivileged. Unfair criticism for the use of social media for governance naturally followed, on the assumption that Facebook is something designed solely for the entertainment of the rich. Unfortunately, this popular perception, that social media cater exclusively to the elite still prevails, although it is not true.

On 23rd February 2015, the day I joined as the District Collector, the official Facebook page of the Administration - Collector Kozhikode - was launched[13], which within a year became (and it still continues to be) the largest followed official page of any District Collector in India. We grew from zero to over 3 lakh followers within a few months without any paid promotions or campaigns. The growth was entirely organic. The page later became the voice of the Compassionate Kozhikode project. It’s a no-brainer that for any social media page to be effective it should have sufficient reach. However, having a large followership in itself is not the target. The target is to utilise this large reach for positive engagement with the public. It is this subtle difference that often gets forgotten. When it is forgotten, we see 'likes' and 'number of followers' being cheered for, instead of celebrating the successful delivery of service or the objectives being achieved through this medium.

I’m no influencer by any means to give you a refresher course on the optimal ways of using social media, but I'll share what I’ve learned from my own humble exploration into its deep corridors.

As you can imagine, you become popular in social media due to various reasons. A celebrity page garners a lot of followers and ‘likes’ simply because of the stardom associated with the person. Being glamorous or controversial or famous or “currently in the news” - these adjectives matter a lot to get scroll-stopping attention. But an impersonal page of a district official that is not glamorous or famous, cannot afford to make controversial political statements simply to become noticed! So, what remains? It should engage with the public. It should talk. It should laugh. It should reply, interact, respond and live like any other human being on social media. In short, the mantra is - go, get a life!

The phenomenal experience of engagement with the public through Facebook was invaluable. Instead of making posts in a "transmission mode", the Collector Kozhikode page adopted a multipronged communication strategy. The idea was to avoid treating the Facebook page like a notice board. The key was to be eternally conscious that your one sentence could provoke a multi-directional resonance. Often in such communication, you don't have to say everything. Nonetheless, you have to convey the important message clearly. Adding the spice of humour and allowing a space for discussion among the followers is what makes it lively. Adopting an informal language that connects with the social media platform is also important. For example, the lingo that is popular on Facebook may not exactly suit Twitter. The language that you use on an official file will definitely not gel in either of these platforms. Though it may be technology-enabled, here exists a subtle element of art, rather than one of science in this communication. And while you're at it, having a bit of fun is no crime either.

The government and government servants need not be shy or scared of communicating freely with the public. Citizens are out there on social media, so they need to be there. It's as simple as that. Pasting memos on the notice boards of the village office is no longer the way to reach out to the public nor is it the efficient way to disseminate information in the modern world I've proof, and I do believe social media as a platform makes administration more transparent, seamless, fast, approachable and publicly accountable.

A basic rule when communicating through social media is not to lose your temper. Humour is crucial. The more self-deprecating it is, the better. Malayalis are known to be extra sarcastic and cynical and I am no exception. However, not everyone in this world shares the same type of sense of humour.

A senior politician often has a bunch of close followers who keep invoking the name of their boss to get things done and interfere in governance, in the name of democracy. There was this curious case of an extraordinary interest taken by one such fellow in a certain contractor's work bills to be cleared from the finance section of the Collectorate. I warned about him to his godfather-politician a couple of times but he feigned ignorance of this person's doings. I got confidential information that the work was not even completed by the contractor when the bills were presented. From the files it was seen that the mandatory inspections on at least 10% of the works which were to be conducted had not been done. I instructed that these works be inspected and reported back within two weeks. This was a standard practice in government administration. The moment the inspection is ordered, the contractor makes amends and ensures the work was completed decently. However, the next day, the senior politician burst out in the media against the inspections saying it would cause delay in releasing payment to the contractor. Evidently, his guy had fed him something. Unfortunately, this serious and aggressive rhetoric tickled my funny bone and a humorous chain of events followed. I wondered aloud why the otherwise soft-spoken politician was angry and upset about a two weeks' delay of payment to some unknown contractor. This made him angrier.

He demanded that I, a lowly bureaucrat, should publicly apologise to him for hurting the prestige of an elected representative. Asking mappu[14] for doing my duty was contrary to my convictions and this further amused me because I had never heard of any official procedure or rule or law where an officer was asked to apologise publicly to satisfy the ego of a politician. I confounded the problems by unabashedly posting a 'map' of Kunnamkulam[14a][14b] on my personal Facebook account. To be honest, I felt very satisfied with my wicked sense of humour, but not everyone was just as humoured. The ping-pong of comments (oh, how much fun I had!) went on for a while until my mother intervened and asked me to shut up.

Upon watching the politician conducting aggressive, targeted press meets on a daily basis, my parents drove down from Thalassery to Kozhikode on 'Mission Killjoy'. My mother worried that the frail gentleman would suffer some health issues if I kept driving him mad like this. She knew that I had this singularly weird sense of humour which could spur the game till eternity. Well, she had a point. I needed to be more compassionate (no pun intended) in understanding the constraints and difficulties of any politician than make a joke out of it. Amma wanted me to empathise with even someone who is playing against you! Not only did I empathise, I let go of my ego, and patched up the episode with him.

Humour can get you into trouble, but it is this very same humour that gets you some fresh breath at times in life. Of course, the best form of humour is when you don't hurt anyone. Then again, if you try to be light-hearted and the recipient is hell bent on picking a fight, your weird humour sense will only work as rubbing salt on the wound. My Amma was right on this and I admit it.

However, it is most illogical and false to associate immaturity and superficiality with being funny. In my opinion, a well-developed sense of humour is one of the highest forms of intelligence and I usually pay close attention to opinions given by humorous people. A sense of humour also makes you young at heart, and in appearance too, which can further compound the problem because a youngster would never be taken seriously. Despite all these odds, with a heavy heart, let me admit that I'm willing to live a young life even when all my classmates turn into oldies.

A MERE FB-Collector

The rule of not reacting to an irritating comment or post for twenty four hours immediately following it is a standard strategy advocated by many. I also subscribe to that. It's not that I don't lose my temper ever. Sometimes one has to put on a show of being angry for expressing displeasure or to get the job done from subordinates. I've observed more than once that throwing your weight around is the only way to get some people to respond. I usually try not to get hyper-excited with anger as an emotion. The key is not to allow anger to control us. As the wise say, anger should be used as a tool like scissors, and put it back in your pocket after use. This is important not only when you dabble in social media but also in life in general.

Going back to Kozhikode, there were certain ground rules that were laid at the very beginning for social media interaction through the official Facebook account. The District Collector's "face" would not be shown anywhere on this page other than as the profile picture. This meant that the daily inaugurations and meetings the Collector attends would never be featured on this page. The page would not be used as a propaganda platform or for gaining publicity for the Collector. Every post was to be personally made by the Collector himself with his personal touch. Even though I loved delegation, the responsibility of official communication to the general public was not something that could be delegated unscrupulously. However, maintaining a team that could provide me with sufficient data and decent drafts with relevant content was important. High priority posts that needed to connect well with the public were done personally, from scratch, without following a template. Having an efficient back-end office that could promptly take action on the grievances reported by the public made the engagement meaningful.

I also wanted the public to access the internet freely so that they could communicate. Around the same time, the mobile phone carriers were having trouble setting up their service-towers because of protests from the local community who were apprehensive of the radiation emitted. The Collector chaired a committee to permit construction of these towers after they were certified as technically safe by assessing the radiation levels. During one of these meetings with the service providers, I made them agree to provide one hour free WiFi service for every mobile phone in major locations, just as you have in the airports[15]. In early 2015, this was not just revolutionary, it was blasphemy! After the service was launched, I started getting complaints from 'concerned' citizens about young boys and girls spending time at these locations to access complimentary WiFi. The principal of Government Medical College at Kozhikode formally requested me to disable or restrict the service in his campus but I stayed determined. My simple logic was that you have to steadily increase the supply of WiFi spots rather than get restless with the sight of crowded happy youngsters.

In July 2015, KC Abu, the District Congress Committee (DCC) President of Kozhikode publicly made a statement that the District Collector is wasting time on social media. Though I was initially surprised at the lack of understanding the senior leaders had about mass communication and modern technology, we quickly got around it by staying on course and not deferring from our principles or purpose. I used to joke that even though my face could be seen gleaming on Facebook 24 x 7, it didn't mean that I was live on camera every single minute. It is just a picture, for God's sake! You don't need more than a few moments in a day to put out posts and write comments.

In July 2016, Facebook officially acknowledged the Kozhikode Administration's experiment as a model worth emulating and they posted an official video[16] on their timeline[17][18]. It was indeed a proud moment for the entire team. The Kozhikode experience is now being used as official study material for government departments and officers on how to engage with the public using social media platforms.

To put things in perspective, the official Facebook account of the Kerala Chief Minister's[19] office came into existence on 20th June 2016. It was only from then onwards many officials dealing with the public - Sub Collectors, District Collectors, District Police Chiefs etc. - started using social media freely in Kerala. Time flies in the digital realm. Today it is unimaginable for politicians and officials to keep away from social media. Constructive use of social media is now recognised as a legitimate administrative tool. Not so in 2015, when I took all the brickbats for the transgression into digital space! It was only an instance of poetic justice when the very same people who were mocking and criticising me for making use of social media to engage with the public started doing the same. Imagine my surprise when the man KC Abu himself started a Facebook page in March 2016. We had become good friends by then.

Being as self-effacing as possible, without pandering to traditional media was our team's hallmark achievement. We consciously avoided interaction with mainstream media too. The desired, right communication at the right time would proceed in measured terms, only from the official Facebook page. You should have a clear reason as to why you are putting out a post in the first place. We in Kozhikode, definitely had a purpose, that of furthering the cause of compassion.

I don't like to find fault, but I have observed something regressive in the conduct of many 'official' Facebook users. In most of these pages, the handle is used merely for transmission and personal propaganda instead of meaningful dialogue with the public. The difference is not so subtle as to be missed. Politicians are sometimes known to specialise in self-marketing but to find officials doing the same is disappointing. Not only young officers but even senior officers who have recently started their pilgrimage to social media platforms indulge in it. News from local Madison Avenues is that some officers even engage professional PR and advertising agencies for preparing heroic content to publish their personal hogwash. I can only affirm that there is nothing more hilarious than printing official pamphlets and advertisements with your smiling face photoshopped right in the centre.

I wouldn't have cared less, had it not been for one thing: this awkward behaviour of some officers gets blamed on me, as I am the one who started using social media for engaging with the public as far the records can find out, and it worries me. Only if I knew I was teaching them how to self-promote, the social media way! Obviously, those who blame me for spoiling the younger generations of civil servants haven't studied how Collector Kozhikode as a social media page functioned and how different it was from the personal schemes you come across these days[20].

To sum it up, here's my cheat sheet for using social media even today: one, have a purpose for every single post. If you don't have one, don't post. Two, the right dose of humour in communication is essential but don't end up looking like a joker and get trolled every other day. Three, you can't satisfy everyone, nor should you try to. Four, do not post your personal stories on an official account, however amazing they are.

The VIP CULTURE

In India, everyone wants to become a VIP (Very Important Person). It is a sad fact that only a VIP or someone recommended by someone important gets a fair deal or gets ahead faster in many circles. This is felt more acutely in government offices. So the aspiration of a common man to become a VIP perhaps stems from an innate psychology to be treated fairly and with dignity more than from anything else. The restricted channels of communication with those in power also set apart a common man from a VIP. Utilising the possibilities of social media, if an administrator establishes lines of communication with everyone, the intermediary power-brokers have no role to play and the common man can access an official just as any VIP can.

On the other hand, the more you explore the possibilities of social media, the more independent and powerful an administrator you become. You have direct feedback from the public without any mediation. Your immediate subordinates cannot deceive or misguide you because anyone can communicate with you and let the cat out. For the public, they don't have to depend on intermediary channels or politicians to 'get things done'. With technology enabled free access to the chief executive, common citizens do not have to depend on any version of service given by the 'gatekeepers' of power.

Relying largely on social media for communicating with the public doesn't mean that you are entirely ignoring traditional media. If your social media post is sufficiently relevant and has news value, the traditional media will certainly carry it. But you don't need to pander to local journalists, which I feel is a thoroughly corrupt practice. There was this absurd tradition of the District Collector of Kozhikode sponsoring a vacation trip for the local journalists in December / January to the resorts of Wayanad using government funds. As a Collector, I put an end to that customary 'goodwill' practice. There were reportedly some highly influential journalists in Kozhikode who could get any order out from the Collectorate - they were more dealers than journalists, I would say. Some even specialised in subjects like illegal sand-mining and building-permits for making "effective" interventions. After sunset, the Collector's residence was supposed to be the den of such powerful entities with ghazals and drinks. It became apparent that cleansing the collector's residence from the stains of these VIP visitors had to be a top priority. Easier said than done.

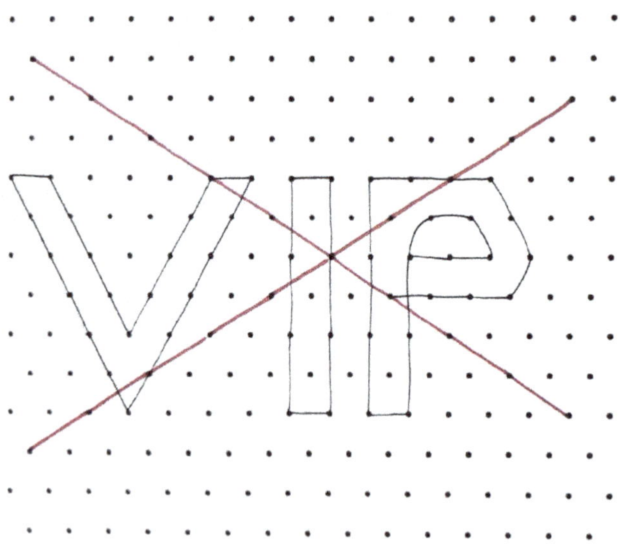

When I made clear that I wouldn't be entertaining two classes of visitors, the VIP category at the official residence and the ordinary 'cattle class' at the Collectorate, all hell broke loose. The rich, famous and influential who were used to coming to the "camp office" (as the collector's residence was called) to meet the

Collector suddenly found it very uncomfortable to visit and wait alongside the ordinary folk at the Civil Station. Except for people's representatives, the differently-abled or exceptional and genuine cases, all visitors were treated alike. I recollect the friendly advice I received those days from various quarters to not antagonise the 'powers' of the district. But the blame for my behaviour rests with my mother, who brought me up to value self-respect over prudence - a trait which others might perceive as arrogance. Having spent enough time on the other side of the desk, meeting bureaucrats and officials as an ordinary citizen, I had come to value fair treatment from them over everything else. As a law graduate the sense of justice got even more embedded in my thinking. Being young also didn't particularly help. I just didn't care about the consequences.

As a citizen, as a common man, as a human being, everyone wants to be treated with dignity. It hurts when you don't get a fair treatment or someone else gets an unfairly privileged treatment. The feeling of injustice or indignity hurts everyone. For a child who is sensitive, this could be a powerful experience.

That takes me back to my childhood when the thought of joining the civil service first entered my mind. My mother is a doctor and she was working in the government medical college service at that time. She wanted to meet the principal of the Government Medical College, Thiruvananthapuram for sorting out some official business and as a kid I went along with her. I presume it was something to do with her promotion or transfer or some service-related matter, which obviously I couldn't understand. But something that I clearly understood was the plain arrogance on the face of the principal who would not even look at our faces while talking, nor offer us a seat out of courtesy.

Not being able to find a solution with the principal, we continued our trip to the office of the Director of Medical Education (DME). Yet another senior doctor, hierarchically much above the principal. Alas, we were treated with the same demeanour, perhaps a bit more imperious. Not offering a seat to the visitors seemed to be the norm in these offices to say the least. Not looking into the eyes or even acknowledging the presence of the person in your room while talking seemed to be some sort of style they inherited. For the kid that I was, this was not just interesting but a tad irritating. I was witnessing well educated people occupying powerful positions behaving extremely rudely, in total variance to what was taught to us in school. And usually you don't find people behaving rudely towards kids. Despite the presence of a child, how could they behave so badly? I couldn't understand it. Even now I don't get it. My mother knew the government system but for me this was a new experience. I felt pretty upset about it.

That evening we went to the Secretariat to meet the Secretary to the government health department. We waited for him in his office. After winding up an emergency meeting with the then Minister of Health, a bearded gentleman, the Secretary, rushed into his chamber and called us in. He offered us seats and ordered coffee. His radiant smile and the gentle and pleasant conversation made up for the other experiences earlier in the day. I do not know whether my mother's official problem got resolved or not. But when we emerged from his room we were pleased.

That last person we met had been the busiest and the most powerful person in the hierarchy. Yet, he was the humblest, best-behaved and most dignified of the lot. There was something about him that made me aspire to become like him. As we got out of his room and walked through the corridors of the Secretariat, I asked my mother who that person was. "He is the government Secretary, an IAS officer", she said. I turned back and looked at the name board. At the end of his name were three bold letters inscribed - IAS.

I wanted to become an IAS officer.

THE SOUL of KOZHIKODE

A District Collector has certain duties and responsibilities placed on him under the Mental Health Act, 1987[21]. So when I visited the Government Mental Health Centre (GMHC) along with the Sub Judge RL Baiju, I was discharging a legally mandated function. That day however changed the way I saw and understood the world forever.

The general ward of the Mental Health Centre reminded me of the cages I had seen as a child in the Thiruvananthapuram Museum and Zoo Complex. In the men's ward, I saw 30-40 patients stuffed in a tight enclosure with each one mentally living in his own world. Through the iron grills, I talked to one of the inmates who narrated his personal story. He was a Non Resident Indian (NRI) businessman who had returned from Dubai two days back. Immediately after landing at the airport he had developed some mental disturbances and his relatives drove him down straight to the hospital. The idea that your mental health is so fickle was scary. For instance, when we relocate to a new residential area don't we enquire about the best schools and hospitals in the vicinity? But we never ask if there is a good mental health facility nearby. We take it for granted that our mental faculties would remain absolutely perfect come what may. The story of the inmate startled me and I stood there appalled. I asked the hospital superintendent about the patient's description and his prognosis. He replied, "What he said is true. The only correction that I would like to make is that his landing and getting admitted to the hospital- everything took place around 15 years ago."

There were many others whose illness was cured but had nowhere to go. Many of them were abandoned by their relatives. I then walked into the building with the solitary cells that housed the 'violent' patients. It was a sight that I can never forget in my life. I saw each inmate squatting on the floor laced along with their own excreta and food waste. One of them had murdered another inmate- an extreme case of schizophrenia. The last solitary cell shattered me completely. I saw an old frail man whose backbone and shoulder bones were pronounced, crouched in a corner of the room. He was carefully and patiently digging into the toilet closet and devouring his own excreta. His unkempt beard dripped of feces mixed with his oozing saliva. He turned his naked body around towards us and spoke something in chaste English. My eyes were burning and I felt as if somebody had clenched and squeezed my tummy. I had hit the extreme limits of my tolerance levels and I hastened my steps away from the solitary cells.

Quickly recollecting my senses, I asked the hospital superintendent to give me the details of the urgent requirements in the hospital facility. It could be beds, clothes, pillows, buckets and mugs, essential furniture etc. He gave me a copy of the earlier letter submitted to one of my predecessors, along with a fresh letter. Things worth a few lakhs only. As I drove back from the hospital to my residence, I understood what he said without saying - many letters had been written and many requests had been made by the hospital authorities and the District Collectors, in vain. It was just my juvenile enthusiasm and emotional overflow that made me think that I was the first one trying to solve this and that I could fix it immediately.

The problem was that the mental hospital and its inmates were not a priority for anyone. They had no leaders, no unions, and no relatives who could voice their demands on their behalf and most importantly they did not have voting rights. They were outcasts in the democratic scheme of things. I reached home, took a bath, and had dinner, but my mind was elsewhere, thoroughly disturbed. I kept looking at the list given by the hospital superintendent and felt ashamed that as the administrative head of the district, I was powerless to put an end to such a basic problem with immediate effect. The feeling of helplessness was overwhelming. Necessity is the mother of invention, they say. And frustration was the midwife in this case.

On 16th of March 2015, I posted the list[22] given by the doctor on my official Facebook page and requested the public to help me sort out this issue[23]. With a total of 22 items, the list included wheelchairs, cots, air beds, nail cutters, scissors, and water purifiers. I did not want money but only the materials that the hospital required immediately. I wanted them to be delivered in kind. We had very few followers on the official page at that time. But within a week the hospital got all the items worth about ₹10 lakhs and more than what we had put out in that list. Kindness and help were overflowing from all parts of the world. This was an eye opener for me and we decided to take the effort to another level. For sure, the patients did not have their family standing by them to fight for their basic right to dignity. While the doctors were pinning their hopes on government funds, we discovered a new world of faceless well-wishers, who were not only addressing the immediate needs, but willing to sponsor the hospital's makeover itself.

Though Kuthiravattam

Mental Health Centre is a name synonymous with mental health care for more than a century, it was yet to be updated on care and treatment using modern psychiatry techniques and equipment. It was not just the ambience of the place that was sober, but the whole element of compassion was missing from every square inch of the building that was deemed to be an abode of care. More than 800 odd people lived in dimly lit and humid rooms in a near dilapidated building with minimal facilities. It was the unbelievable dedication of some of the doctors, nurses and support staff that kept the institution going. There were issues related to quality of life along with treatment and rehabilitation shortcomings. Electroconvulsive Therapy (ECT) machines are one of the basic equipment in a mental health centre. No one would believe that this hospital hadn't had one for 15 years. We finally procured an ECT machine through sponsorship. After getting the machine in July 2015, the hospital superintendent, Dr. Rajendran ran from pillar to post for close to 30 months to get an anaesthetist on duty so that he could safely put the machine into operation. Bureaucracy can be very depressing at times. A few months after I moved out of Kozhikode, the ECT machine became operational from 28 November, 2017 Dr. Saritha, the then District Medical Officer (DMO) played the key role in making this happen.

In retrospect, this is how I reflect - a mentally unstable inmate living as if only two days have passed since he reached the hospital, and a committed doctor who spent more than two years of his life trying to get an operator for a basic hospital accessory. And we curse all the living organisms around us when we are delayed by two minutes to our favourite movie theatre. I say, to hell with Karma, life's a bitch!

During one of the initial hospital visits, I was shocked to learn that the food menu in the hospital was fixed in 1979 and was predominantly wheat-gruel. Someone who is in perfect mental health may also get deranged if confined in such conditions and given nothing but wheat-gruel to eat. What was surprising was that since 1979 nobody had thought about changing the menu. The reason why wheat-gruel, a totally alien food in Kerala, was prescribed is also unknown. Perhaps there was a shortage of rice in those times. I really do not know, but something was surely in short supply in this democratic world.

FOOD for THE SOUL

There are only two sets of people at the mercy of the state, who do not have the right to decide on their food. One is a prisoner and the other a confined mental patient. Recently, when a prominent film star was arrested and put in jail, the media was flush with details about how he was coping in the prison. His food menu and its time-table were widely published by all newspapers which caused domestic unrest in many families in Kerala. The food that they ate at home paled in comparison to the rich and nutritious varieties served to the film star and other prisoners. Of course, the food quality in jails has improved with time with better understanding of the concept of human rights. But how come the food in the mental hospital never improved? Unlike mental patients, criminals in the jail have relatives, friends, politicians, sponsors and many others to help them. They even have a phone-a-friend scheme run by corrupt jailers! Contrast that with a mentally ill patient who is unable to even articulate his own needs.

On 14th December 2015, we held a meeting within the kitchen premises of the hospital to redo the menu scientifically with the help of nutritionists[24].Since sufficient government funding was not forthcoming, sponsors were again engaged for buying the raw material for preparing better, tastier and more nutritious food. Of course we did not have sufficient number of cooks! It was unreasonable to expect just two men to prepare breakfast, lunch and dinner with the limited facilities and ensure the food was tasty as well. Word went out for help again and before we knew, Chef Vijayan Pillai of Paragon Hotel came around to suggest tips and work with the nutritionists to better the menu. We had so many institutions and organisations supporting us in this collective endeavour to improve the quality and quantity of food that it would be unfair to name only a few. College students and volunteer groups were roped in and a time-table was set for helping the kitchen staff. We called them the Chapathi Group. Even today this WhatsApp group is active and they keep posting live pictures of their kitchen adventures in the hospital. More than the shape of the Chapathi made by these boys and girls, it was the intention that mattered. Regular voluntary groups for various activities like farming, entertainment, speciality health care etc. were organized using social media and WhatsApp groups. A crafts shop to sell the products made by the inmates named Soul of Kozhikode[25] was inaugurated by the then Health Minister, KK Shailaja on 15th August 2016 near the front gate of the hospital. Even though the craft and expertise may have had some flaws and limitations, we did not compromise on the price. Our logic was that the products should be priced more to account for the extra effort and pain put

in by the inmates to make them. We surely did good business!

The name Soul of Kozhikode is a parody of "Soul of Kerala" which only avid Malayalam movie buffs would understand[26]. One of the most fulfilling designs we did was the logo of the shop. The logo had seven horses representing seven of the nine initial inmates of the hospital. (Our hunch was that two out of nine, as always, were not mentally ill!) These horses formed a circle - Kuthira Vattam - and one of them had wings, waiting to fly out of the vicious circle.

Each of the painful small little interventions that happened in the mental health centre had a story to tell. And we did it silently without any fanfare. After we overhauled the food menu of the hospital, different nutritious delicacies were introduced in place of the boring, tasteless wheat-gruel. Puttu, Idli, Dosa, Idiyappam, Appam, Porotta, Chapathi - slowly, each one of these made its way into the dark humid building inside the tall walls of the hospital compound[27]. Innumerable sponsors and volunteers took pains to coordinate and facilitate without any financial support from the government. What we took for granted was a luxury for the inmates of the facility. The Bakery Owners' Association sponsored a daily truckload of milk and the black tea served in the hospital got transformed into something they would look forward to. This might sound silly to most of us.

One day, soon after finishing up my 'milk-rich' breakfast tea, I got a call from Dr. Rajendran. His voice was choked. He was on his morning rounds when one of the old inmates in the women's ward tugged at his hands and asked, "Doctor Sir, when do we get to eat Puttu and Kadala next?" An utterly common breakfast dish in Kerala was for her something precious to be waited for. It was these small instances of redeeming hope that made our lives exciting and the efforts worth pursuing despite all odds.

With sustained civil society intervention, better individual care, involvement of more specialist volunteers and whole-hearted support from all stakeholders involved in rehabilitation work, the number of inmates in the Mental Health Centre was brought down from over 800 to around 550. This was stated in a single sentence but the task was rather prolonged, meticulously carried out and tiring. The police, magistracy, doctors, nursing staff and revenue staff along with numerous volunteers contributed to this victory. Hundreds of people toiled behind the scenes for this silent revolution within the four walls of the mental health centre to occur. Activities like painting, music, farming, handicrafts and dance were introduced in the hospital[28]. All of us who were part of the team went through such transformational experiences that each one of us evolved into better human beings at the end of the day. If not for anything else, just providing food in the hospital made our souls a lot richer.

HANAN the ANGEL

We are all busy. The biggest obstacle to rehabilitating the cured inmates of any mental health centre is that nobody has the time to talk to them. Kuthiravattam was no exception. With over 800 inmates, it was impossible for the limited number of staff to engage meaningfully with the patients, give them appropriate medical treatment or understand them accurately. The services of a trained psychiatric social worker become crucial in empathising with the patients and gently probing their details. For 800 inmates we had just two psychiatric social workers, of which only one was then working at the hospital. The staff strength of the hospital was fixed long back at a time when there were far fewer patients. And the proposal for appointing more doctors, nurses and other supporting staff had been pending for ages in the Secretariat. Mission impossible. Again, we decided to look outside the box for a solution.

A Facebook post was put out for the attention of post graduates of social work to volunteer and spend time with the inmates to help understand and rehabilitate them. We received a massive response to this request and the work started in all sincerity. We also enlisted the help of Central Reserve Police Force (CRPF) Jawans to translate and help communicate with those inmates who were hailing from other states. The cases started getting solved one after the other. Ms. Hanan, a student from the Tata Institute of Social Sciences (TISS), Mumbai, had the honour of cracking the first case.

An old Tamilian lady had been an inmate since 2003. Nobody knew how she reached the hospital and it looked like a typical case of abandonment by relatives in a train. Hanan talked to this lady for a couple of hours and understood that she was a native of Tenkasi. Her husband's family was into the wholesale flower business. When we enquired with the District Collector there, only two such families fit the description. Members of one of the families immediately took a taxi and rushed overnight to Kozhikode.

The next day, I was present in the mental hospital to participate in a function when this family reunion happened[29]. I was fortunate to witness how much that family had missed her. In front of me was an old but dignified gentleman whose swollen eyes looked extremely fatigued. Her two sons and husband had thought that the lady had died. Her sons had grown up in her absence and one of them had got married as well. The truth was that she wasn't an abandoned mental patient, but a loving and beloved wife and mother who had got lost in a crowd. They never imagined that they would ever again get to see her. The happy tears and loud emotional outbursts in Tamil charged the atmosphere as if we were all in an electric field. I told Hanan, "You have done the job of a lifetime. Even if you don't do anything further in your life and career, it is OK; you have done more than enough by reuniting this mother with her sons."

This was the first among many such happy, unhappy and sometimes peculiar reunions that followed. For me, the weirdest reunion was when a mentally unstable person came to take home his younger brother who had been cured. Slowly and steadily the weekly adalats started showing an impact. From over 800 inmates when we started, the number came down below the bed strength of 474 for the first time in the history of the mental health centre. It was a big day for us. Most evenings when I went home after work, I used to drop into the Government Children's Home on the way. I distinctly remember that evening, the cutest and youngest child in the children's home and my dear pet, Diya asking me what made me so happy that day. Of course, I didn't know what or how to tell her.

A master-plan and Detailed Project Report (DPR) for renovation of the entire hospital complex with a budget of around ₹500 crores was prepared by top architects and international consultants. The team visited and studied the best hospitals in the world and had pro-bono advice from German and Australian experts. The report itself was worth more than ₹50 lakhs, but we got it done through goodwill and sponsorships. Dr. Idris of Thanal, Mr. Ahmed of the Malabar Gold group and Architect Tony have to be thanked for in this endeavour. For raising the ₹500 crores, we touched base with major trusts and philanthropists who agreed to fund it if the government would set up a dedicated Trust for the purpose. Accordingly, a proposal was submitted to the government. The government order approving the proposal and establishing the Trust came out a week before I was transferred from Kozhikode in 2017. This Trust was to build and transform the mental health centre into one at par with some of the best similar facilities in the world.

With such a strong civil society movement happening, the government also chipped in funds. For the first time in the history of the mental health centre, a capital head allocation of ₹100 crores was made in the State budget of 2016-2017[30].

In 2015, when we stepped into the mental health centre, we had two options. One was to write to the government, wait for budgetary decisions and go through an elaborate procurement process. The second option was to circumvent and short-circuit the whole process, believing that the shock would eventually awaken the system that was in slumber. We had to act swiftly because every day, every minute and every second mattered. Human beings were living there miserably and these small changes could incrementally improve their quality of life, bringing rays of hope to those lives. A minute earlier, the better. We took the second option and that made all the difference.

THE RULES of the GAME

Considerable effort went into designing the Compassionate Kozhikode project. Various rounds of brainstorming sessions were held with all those who seemed to have something to offer. The people who were volunteering in the core group also kept changing. Still, a core group survived. However, the stark differences in nature and philosophy behind the project did not sit right with everyone. Philanthropy and charity had become modes of self-aggrandisement and publicity, to the extent that a project without those elements seemed to be very unappealing to some. So you had the usual suspects, the famous faces of Kozhikode civil society gradually retreating backstage while a whole new group of volunteers emerged from all walks of life.

While going through the process of setting up an institution, entirely based on voluntarism, we learnt a lot of things. There were many who joined Compassionate Kozhikode with ulterior motives and agendas; opportunity to get close to the Collector, gain access to officials, build credibility, get networked and bask in the publicity were some of the intentions. A lot of these people were harmless while a lot were not. The ground rules that we set at the very beginning after rigorous debates and deliberations ensured we would never lose sight of the North Star.

The rules were:

(1) Don't seek publicity (no photography)

(2) Don't collect money (no cash or cheque contributions)

(3) Don't apply for any individual awards or recognitions

Politicians and people who look for social standing through such activities got easily disillusioned with the first rule of no publicity. Since we did not collect cash, there was no money to be siphoned off or any benefit to be made through procurement. Not applying for any award also meant that activities would be very low-key. Without sound, light and smoke, it was very difficult for the traditional socialites of Kozhikode to sustain themselves in this project. Naturally, they dropped out, much to our delight. There were others with business interests, who stuck on to the project hoping that once I got transferred, they could take over the organisation and dilute the rules under the new dispensation.

In hindsight, I feel it was a smart move on my part not to register and institutionalise Compassionate Kozhikode as a Society or Trust like the many other organisations chaired by the Collector. I remember one of those evenings where we rationalised a lot on this. While many of our team members wanted to formalise Compassionate Kozhikode as a Society, I argued that having a matrix organisation with no hierarchy was far cooler. The District Collector should not chair or head the organisation but could be one among the volunteers. Leadership was to be situational and knowledge-based depending on the subject being dealt with. My take was not to have an "organisation" called Compassionate Kozhikode to maintain it for times to come, but to ensure that "compassion" survives and permeates into society as a result of our activities forever. It really didn't matter whether Compassionate Kozhikode as an institution or a group survived or not. But so long as it existed, it should not get corrupted nor should its core values get diluted. As the administrators who ran Compassionate Kozhikode, our role was to function as matchmakers. We would connect the dots and encourage the dots to get connected regardless of whether Compassionate Kozhikode as a project existed or not[31]. Lofty, idealistic and utopian!

An interactive website www.compassionatekozhikode.in was launched[32] on 3rd October 2015. It was the virtual expression of the philosophy that we stood on. It sought to interlink the request for help to those who were compassionate enough to contribute. We could procure the much-required materials for the various care homes and get volunteers to render service and sponsors to fund the educational scholarships. This was a kind of an "aggregator model" where you collect things slowly and steadily than the usual "crowd-sourcing model". As the District Collector, I was always destined to collect things! And I would call the website a virtual "Collectorate" where we would collect the goods and services.

The value of having a good team is best understood when you accidentally deviate from the rule and one of your team members reminds you. After the website was inaugurated, a prominent cine actor decided to make the first donation in kind to one of the institutions enlisted. As usual, a press release and Facebook post were to follow the event. A draft was quickly approved and as I travelled back home, my PA Nijeesh rang me up and voiced a doubt that had not crossed my mind. His point was simple - our declared policy was that 'charity is discreet' and we would not provide photo opportunity or publicity to anyone who is making contributions. Why should the film actor and the inaugural function be an exception? I immediately recalled the press release and removed all reference to the contribution that she had made. Nijeesh had saved us from folly in the nick of time!

Even though we resisted publicity for our actions, we also did realise that the ability of the project to mobilise volunteers was key to our success. This proved to be a Catch-22 situation. Without publicity how does one mobilise resources and people? So, we started using the official Facebook page as a platform where we would give periodic progress reports of the activities and also use it as a mobilisation tool. The language and tenor of the communication was clearly defined and it underplayed the role of the administration and the District Collector while profusely praising the people of Kozhikode for their support.

One of the most memorable and unbelievable responses to our Facebook call for action was the cleaning of the Pisharikavu Temple pond at Vadakara. There is an annual fund allocation for drought mitigation activities, primarily intended to rejuvenate water bodies in summer. However, the funds could only be used to buy refreshments like tea and snacks and not for the substantial act of cleaning up the pond. In short, we cannot engage paid labourers but can buy refreshments for the volunteers. Needless to say, every year the village officers and tahsildars would submit vouchers of food items and claim money, but no pond was seen cleaned up ever. On the eve of the Republic Day of 2016, we put out a Facebook post titled - "Kulam koriyaal biriyani vaangi tharaam". It means that a biriyani is being offered for cleaning up the pond. A subtle and colloquial wordplay in it was the usage of 'kulam koriyal'. It implied digging up or finishing off something - somewhat destructive in connotation - which would immediately attract the attention of any Malayali. Why would the Collector want to be destructive? On 26th January, after the Republic Day parade, we drove down to Pisharikavu Temple pond to see close to one thousand volunteers ready to take the plunge. Under two hours, we transformed the dirty weeded pond of 14 acres into a clean water body. And we had a biriyani feast in the end. That was the official launch of the campaign in the district and the project covered more than 70 big ponds and many other water bodies that year. I learnt later that this impacted the water table positively the next year. The reason for the success of the project was the fun in the campaign. We chose the right words and tonality, we tickled the youth's imagination, and best of all, we didn't have to make a distress call for any special budget allocation.

Incidentally, the entire Compassionate Kozhikode project ran on zero budget with volunteers and contributors from across the globe. Starting from the website design by GIT and Papaya Media to the back end operations, everything was donated in kind. We had an elaborate field network of student-volunteers and an amorphous gathering of well-wishers running into lakhs who would spring up at the call of a single Facebook post. Within the first year of operations, the Compassionate Kozhikode platform delivered goods and services valued at over ₹2.5 crores. I would value it much higher considering the quality of work and the intangible passion that came along with it. If biriyani set the flavour of things to come, the most discussed and popular project under Compassionate Kozhikode was Operation Sulaimani[33].

Hunger GAMES

Before I get into the story of Operation Sulaimani, my first tryst with hunger and food as an administrator needs to be explained. It was also my first attempt to find a solution outside the existing rules and laid-out schema. After completion of training at Lal Bahadur Shastri National Academy of Administration (LBSNAA)[34], Mussoorie, I got my first independent posting as Sub Collector of Mananthavady in Wayanad district in 2009. The Sub Collector held additional charge of the Managing Director of Priyadarshini Tea Estate. Priyadarshini was a tribal resettlement tea estate established as a co-operative society in the 1980s, employing over 300 families of the Paniya tribe.

One of the first things that I noticed was that people were falling sick rampantly and most of them suffered from malnutrition. It was food that was at the core of the problem. I realized that the workers were toiling at the plantation, from morning till evening, without getting adequate food to eat. Matters were made worse by alcoholism and tobacco abuse. I discussed the issue with a few doctors and social workers as the problem was acute amongst the children of the labourers. There were a few tuberculosis cases as well. Quite scary, all in all.

It was evident that a solution had to be immediate. I wanted to make nutritious food available to the workers. But there was no budget for it, nor could the workers pay for it. Meals had to be provided free of cost considering the sensitive nature of the social problem and their social habits. I didn't want to open a can of worms either.

Luckily, my 'eureka' moment hit me when I came across the idea of connecting tribal well-being with tourism.

Wayanad is a charming hill station on the Western Ghats where there was a huge demand for accommodation facilities for tourists. There was a bungalow on the Priyadarshini estate, which was built for its Managing Director. But neither myself nor my predecessor had ever occupied the bungalow since they had a separate Sub Collector's residence in town. Essentially, the bungalow was unused. "Why not convert this building into a tourist resort?" was the simple idea the pristine fogs brought to me in one of the fine mornings of that December when I noticed the nearby resorts were running to full capacity in the season. I was getting calls from many to help them find accommodation using the 'influence' of the Sub

Collector. One thing was clear - the number of available rooms in Wayanad was far below the market demand.

Once I had Babu Rajendran, Secretary of the Priyadarshini Estate - a.k.a my Man Friday - buy my idea, we decided to make Priyadarshini into a tea plantation resort, christening the Bungalow into Wayanad Tea County[35]. The bungalow had just four rooms, but the building and the 400 acre tea estate carried their own unmatched charm. The team readied the bungalow and the estate to host tourists. I clicked a few photographs of the estate that were enlarged and used to decorate the rooms. A few tribal youngsters were trained to become trekking guides. Some were even sent far down the hills to learn to become chefs. A trekking route was mapped out and an enchanting viewpoint identified. We called the viewpoint Vishwas, as a symbol of belief and hope for the people.

Connecting tourism to tribal welfare was not an easy task. We did the impossible by linking it with daily food which everyone could easily relate to. Slowly, tourists started coming in and Wayanad Tea County became a much sought-after resort[36] [37]. The workers did not have to worry about hunger anymore. Their faces gleamed and their sense of relief was palpable. I was the happiest man around.

The nutrition levels improved and the healthcare expenditure made by the estate diminished dramatically. To top it, we achieved record production. What food can do, probably nothing else can.

After tidying up malnutrition, we could move on to housing, education and livelihood. But when I was transferred from Wayanad, an old tribal woman labourer asked me about only one thing, "Will they stop our food if you leave?" Thankfully no, Priyadarshini continues to provide free meals for its more than 300 workers and families even in 2021.

Operation SULAIMANI

Years later, in 2015, I was chairing the Hospital Development Society (HDS) meeting of the Medical College of Kozhikode, one of the largest medical colleges in Asia. The discussion went on to the provision of food to the poor patients and their bystanders. The principal of the medical college described how things stood.

There were a lot of volunteers and NGOs who were providing free lunch. Those who wanted food would stand in a queue, would be photographed by the donors, and often be made a spectacle under the scorching sun. Those who were hungry had no privacy nor was respect shown to them. There were many who preferred to go hungry rather than compromise their dignity. Especially women and children. The mismatch between demand and supply often resulted in huge wastage of food. The unhealthy competition between different cooked food donors on the road next to the Medical College Hospital was a vulgar sight, because there were so many in the city who were going hungry at the same time. Also, to complicate matters, there was a 'hunger-free' project funded by the government, spending one crore on establishing a modern kitchen and another one crore on the operating contractor. Yet the project did not take off because of litigation in the tendering process. It was after this meeting that I started thinking about finding a solution to this problem.

I had read about the "Food on the Wall" concept which was popular in many restaurants in Europe. I liked this concept very much because the dignity of the beneficiary was not at all compromised. A customer pays for his food and also could pay forward, for the next customer. So, a hungry person who comes next could either order from the menu or take an already ordered food which would be displayed as a sticker on the wall of the restaurant. The problem in straightaway adopting this model was that in India a person who might be aware of this and may contribute could be frequenting a high-end restaurant or a fancy fast-food joint, but the hungry ones may not even dare to step into such places. Demand could come more in say, an Udupi restaurant. To solve this, we needed to virtually pool the contributions into a centralised bank account. The blueprint was laid.

The scheme ensures that no one in Kozhikode is denied food on account of an empty or even a lost wallet. It upholds the 'right to food with dignity' whereby the hungry can have food at various restaurants using food coupons distributed through various outlets in the city, like village offices, taluk offices, Press Club, and outlets at bus stands and railway stations. As a policy, no questions are asked while issuing coupons. The coupons are reimbursed at the end of the month upon production by the hoteliers from a central financial pool built and maintained by micro-level donations from the public. A donation box is kept at most restaurants for the public to contribute. Any loss of revenue incurred by participating restaurants is hence absorbed through the system where they match the coupons collected by each restaurant and distribution centre. It is essentially an adaptation of the Food on the Wall concept, popular in the west. This is NOT a poverty alleviation programme but a hunger alleviation programme. Understanding this difference is very important.

The most crucial moment in this project was getting the Kerala Hotel and Restaurant Association (KHRA) on-board. I had to sell the idea to them and make them implement it with our support. Suhail Ikka of Rahmath Hotel was the Secretary of the Association. He is a gem of a person with a golden heart. Convincing him was not difficult. But I needed to get the other office bearers also to fully support this. Like every other association they had their internal politics that had to be taken into account. So, once the blueprint for the project was ready we invited their executive committee to meet the District Collector. While they waited outside the chamber, my 'spy' and PA, Nijeesh, observed them keenly. The smart boy he is, he quickly gauged the mood of the party and came in to brief me.

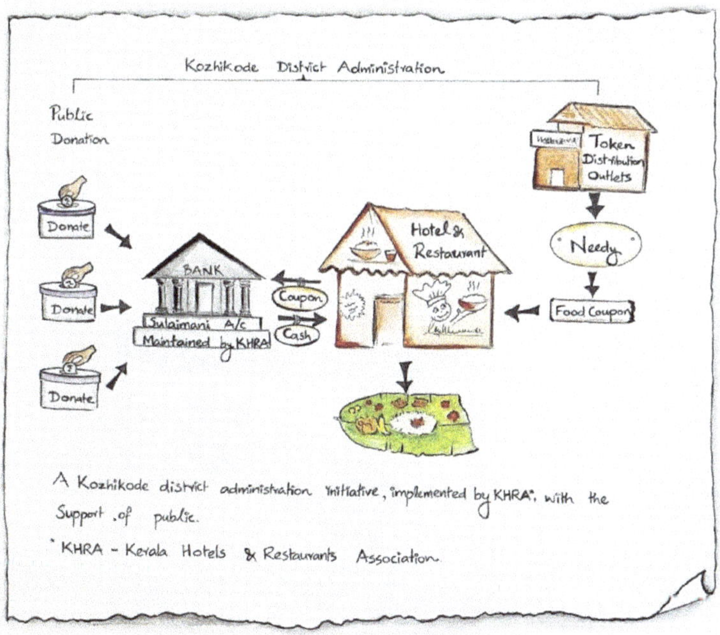

The news was bad. Suhail Ikka was a loner and the majority of the executive committee members were opposed to the idea. They had come to convey a big "NO". Nijeesh wished me all the best and sent the KHRA delegation inside. What followed in the next one hour would determine whether this project would take off or not. I took a deep breath and decided to go in for psychological warfare. So despite knowing that they were against the project, I welcomed them by thanking each of the executive committee members for the big positive step they had decided to take. "No" was not an answer I was willing to end that meeting with.

The members of the executive committee were not amateurs either. They very diplomatically presented one concern after another with the rider that if that concern was taken care of, they could agree to the project. These concerns were genuine as well. Such as, what to do if a drunkard tries to get a coupon? Or what if a shabbily dressed, unhygienic beggar comes with the coupon? Having done sufficient homework, all the doubting Thomases could be silenced swiftly. There were ready answers and even a pre-prepared FAQ to satisfy them. The coupon is meant only to replace money and nothing more - this simple understanding helped us tackle most scenarios.

At the end of almost one hour, the team seemed to be pretty convinced about the project. It greatly helped that Suhail Ikka also was batting for us from the other side. The final question from them was - what will happen if we don't get sufficient collection in the boxes to reimburse the expenses incurred for feeding the hungry? With "due respect" to the tall claims of the Collector, one of the executive committee members gently reminded that people may not always feel like donating and therefore after the initial hype there could be shortfalls and the scheme could prove to be suicidal to the hotel owners.

One of them, who was most vocal in opposing the project, said that had it not been for this issue they would have happily collaborated with the District

Administration. At least one or two lakh rupees should be provided to the association to safeguard it from the risk of shortfall in collection. I laughed as if this was the silliest of all concerns. "Is that the final concern? Well, I have ₹50 lakhs government funding with me. You think that would be enough? The moment you have a shortfall, let me know." The deal was successfully closed.

Nijeesh who was watching the proceedings from behind came up to me after they left. He was thrilled that the government had decided to support our project with ₹50 lakhs. I killed his thrill by revealing that I had lied through my teeth - I had no money.

ROLLING it out with MOHABBAT

They say that the power of imagination is great. Quite true because the power of the imaginary ₹50 lakhs kick-started the project. I was always confident that the people of Kozhikode would never allow any shortfall in collections to happen once the project rolled out. Something more interesting happened once the project kicked off. Soon after the launch, the most vociferous supporters and advocates for the project were the very same individuals who argued tooth and nail against it in my chamber that day. That, I believe, is the magic of compassion.

Having clinched the deal with the restaurant owners, I decided to make the formal announcement, as usual, on the official Facebook page. I was searching for an appropriate picture to go along with the announcement. I used to make extensive use of movie dialogues and imagery to convey messages to the public. My Google search ended with the image of the famous actor Thilakan on Kozhikode beach-side holding a glass of Sulaimani [38][39] from the movie, Ustad Hotel.

Sulaimani is a blend of black tea and lemon usually consumed after a heavy meal. It is a sign of contentment and a full tummy. The words spoken by the grandfather to the grandson in that particular scene are also significant. He says that for the drink to have that special taste one should add a tinge of Mohabbat or love. Love is the secret ingredient that magically transforms any dish.

Prior to being posted as the District Collector, I was working in the home department. There I was part of the team that named and branded initiatives like Operation Kubera. The police hangover perhaps made me name this initiative Operation Sulaimani - an effort to make everyone feel contented.

I believe that most people are genuinely generous and compassionate. They are only waiting for an occasion to express such emotions in action. Within a week of the launch of Operation Sulaimani, an industrialist from Dubai offered us ₹1.25 crores for the project. With all humility, we refused to accept it because the project was to be funded by the community and not by a rich NRI (Non-Resident Indian). Dignity is paramount. The kind of money that is required is often over-projected. The incremental expense that a restaurant incurs in providing one additional free meal is not that high. We had arrived at special rates with all the participating restaurants. The

₹50 lakhs that I had claimed to have with me would have been sufficient to kick-start the project all over Kerala!

Often people have asked me, why should food be given free of cost in the first place? For after all, there are no free lunches in this world. Somebody is footing the cost and it has to be accounted for. These are all valid arguments but if you have ever experienced hunger and understood it, you would know the answer as well. While I was delivering a lecture in IIM Ahmedabad, a student openly asked me, "By providing free food, aren't you teaching the public to be lazy? Why would they ever go to work?" I told her a true story.

As a student, I used to cut down my expenses in order to save money to have fun with my friends. I needed petrol for my bike and money for movie tickets. I was hesitant to ask my parents for a hike in my pocket money. The only thing I could cut down, to save my pocket money, was the expense for food. So I would choose to have food at the cheapest outlets. I remember sharing the table with beggars all around me at Kalasipalyam bus stand where lunch and dinner were served at two rupees. And even when I went hungry nobody offered me free food. Now, as an IAS officer, I get invited to lunch and dinner almost on a daily basis. Indeed nowadays I have to take an effort to avoid them! Remember, I was never offered food when I was genuinely hungry and helpless. While I was posted in Delhi, I remember months going by without me having to spend even one rupee on my food as there were enough luncheons and dinners hosted by dignitaries and ambassadors. But nobody turned around and pointed a finger at me saying that I was becoming lazy because of this free food.

My point is simple. Linking food and hunger with work is fundamentally flawed. Food is a basic human need and hunger ought to be satiated as a natural right. Employment or work should be for higher needs. Food is for survival. To make someone work desperately to earn a morsel of food is in my opinion, exploitation. It is only those countries where the basic requirements of life are met, that people dream of higher goals and targets in life. Imagine how many Einsteins would be languishing in our villages, not dreaming of scientific discoveries but merely wondering anxiously where their next meal was coming from, if at all. My understanding is that connecting hunger and free food with laziness is essentially the result of a mindset rooted in class bias.

All of us create our own universe around us, and our view of life is totally dependent on our own personal experiences. Biases are bound to develop. The challenge before us is to view experiences from another person's perspective, to feel the pain of a stranger, to discern the hunger and appreciate the needs of another human being. If we are able to do that, perhaps we would transcend the physical barriers that delineate individual human minds, breaking down the narrow illusory walls that render us into silly egoistic human fragments of the larger ocean called humanity. We don't need to attain Moksha to feel that, do we?

WORLD Food With Dignity DAY

Our experiences while implementing Operation Sulaimani were quite an eye-opener. Hunger was often hidden, and discovered in unexpected quarters. The self-respect and dignity that a human being desires to maintain is too subtle to be understood without being part of an initiative of this depth.

Beneficiaries of the project are people who cannot afford to buy a meal for whatever reason. This can be a destitute person without any money, a student who lost her lunch box or a traveller who finds that he does not have enough money in his wallet to buy a decent meal. While implementing this project, we as a team learned not to judge people by their looks or attire. We discovered hunger in big homes and rich households. We discovered charity and goodness of mind in the poorest shacks. Some of the incidents were very touching and made us realise how fortunate all of us were.

Apart from the village offices and designated outlets, the Sulaimani coupons were distributed from the Collectorate as well. Once, a young woman approached my office for a coupon. My PA, Nijeesh looked at her and found her to be perfectly healthy and capable of earning a livelihood. She was well-dressed as well. She looked very embarrassed to even ask for or take the coupon. Anyway, as a rule we were not supposed to ask questions if someone turns up for the food coupon, the logic being that his or her hunger was the only criterion that entitles him or her to the coupon. And hunger is something that only that particular person can feel. We didn't want to make the project into yet another typical government project, where you are required to get two gazetted officers to certify your hunger! So she got her coupon without any questions. It was only after handing over the coupon that he observed that her right hand was paralysed. He felt guilty that he had judged her for a moment. A few minutes after she left, the woman came back and very reluctantly requested for one more coupon. Apparently, her father was completely paralysed and bedridden for months now. The second coupon was meant for him. After she left, Nijeesh came into my room and narrated this with his eyes all welled up. If it had not been for the wide table standing between us, and my laziness to get up from my chair, I would have hugged him on the spot. Sometimes wide tables can save you from scandals!

The reality was that people were still reluctant to trust the system and boldly avail of the coupons. We wanted to reach out to that segment of the population who do not read newspapers, watch TV or access Facebook. The poorest of the poor, who are not sure whether they would even be welcomed into a restaurant. We needed the word of mouth to reach those segments and embolden them to make use of this food coupon if they felt the need. To popularise this concept we decided to print the coupons with three-day validity in all newspapers. These coupons could be cut out and produced in the place of cash at the designated restaurants. It was up to the people who bought and read the newspapers to do this. They had the opportunity to find the hungry and the deserving and educate them on this social security net provided by the District Administration. This was a fairly adventurous decision with thousands of coupons getting printed on all newspapers. Though KHRA members were a bit worried that thousands would make a beeline for food, I comforted them with the reserve of ₹50 lakhs still lying with me! Nothing to worry.

We decided to print and distribute these coupons on 13th November 2015, the "World Food with Dignity Day". Not many had heard about this important international day. We could not blame them because this day had just been cooked up just three days back during our usual conspiracy meeting of Compassionate Kozhikode in the Collector's residence! What devilish fun we had when we saw that not a single person cared to verify if there was indeed such a day. Around one thousand people were catered to on this imaginary day and thousands became aware of the scheme. Again, it demonstrated the power of imagination!

Coming back to interesting incidents, one was reported by the village officer of Kottooli. There was this extremely old lady who would every now and then come and request a coupon. There were standing instructions given to all village officers to monitor repeat-

beneficiaries. The idea was to find out whether there was any fundamental problem in their families that could be sorted out by the intervention of the State. It could be provision of some pension, getting them rationed, helping them to apply for some financial assistance, financial support for differently abled etc. So, the village officer made a few enquiries and came to know that our old lady was living by herself in a small house. She did not have any relatives. Even at this age, she worked as a housemaid in a few houses in the vicinity. The village officer reported this and took permission to continue giving her the coupons. The twist in the story came after that. Considering her advanced age and her difficulty in coming all the way to the village office to collect the coupons every other day, the village officer offered to hand over a bundle of post-dated coupons to her. And for that kind suggestion, the village officer got blasted! The woman asserted that she was not a beggar and that she was perfectly capable of earning her living with dignity. Her interest in coupons was limited to fulfilling the desire to have tasty food once in a while when she got fed up with her rice gruel which was the only dish the granny could prepare by herself at her home!

Initially we started off with more than 25 Sulaimani distribution centres in 14 zones of Kozhikode district. The coupons were initially honoured in more than 100 popular restaurants in the district, that included the best and most famed restaurants in Kozhikode. Till date, more than 1,25,000 free meals have been served through this scheme.

Unlike many other government or NGO driven projects, Operation Sulaimani is a silent movement. We do not make a hue and cry, nor do we publicise the initiative. So, I have had people asking me whether this project is still running or whether it has been wound up! There are others who try to gauge the success of the project with the number of coupons distributed without realising that this is a community driven project that provides a social security net to those in need. It is not a project designed to run at full throttle at all times[40]. In fact, I would love to hear that Operation Sulaimanis are not needed anymore in this country.

The concept is similar to Mahatma Gandhi National Rural Employment Guarantee Scheme (MGNREGS), where the state steps in to provide employment when the economy is unable to give gainful employment to an individual. Nowadays we have awards and citations being given to districts that do the maximum number of MGNREGS work. One might even construe it as rewarding and celebrating those districts that have managed to stagnate the economy to such levels of unemployment that a maximum number of people are forced to take refuge in MGNREGS! More people depending on food coupons would mean that there is something fundamentally wrong with the livelihood patterns in the district. And hence as a District Collector I would like to see the dependence on food coupons come down progressively. The real success of Operation Sulaimani, in our judgement, is that we haven't allowed photography of a single beneficiary anywhere till date. The identity of not even one person who benefited from the scheme has been revealed anywhere. Now, that is some food with dignity[41].

Savari GIRI GIRI

This is the travel counterpart of Operation Sulaimani. It is branded using a popular dialogue of superstar Mohanlal and it seeks to fulfil a long cherished vision of helping students to travel with dignity. In Kerala, students have a special bus tariff that is about 1/7 of the actual tariff. It is a normal scene across Kerala how students going to schools and colleges stand in long queues, mostly ignored and harassed by private bus operators. They are not allowed inside the bus before 'adult' tickets are sold out. They are often mistreated and shouted at. Many of them can't even reach their school on time as they 'miss their bus' and those who do reach school have to spend the rest of the day with the nasty taste of the humiliation that they suffered on the bus. It's in this context that Savari GiriGiri was launched[42][43], to bring dignity to all passengers by scientifically studying the reasons behind such behaviour on the part of bus operators.

As per rules, school and college goers get concessions in buses. As most of the bus services are operated by private players, they see the students only as 'numbers' that incur losses to them. From their perspective, any student getting on the bus is a missed opportunity to have accommodated an adult on full fare. While fixing the bus tariffs, the government does consider the fact that the concession given to the students is to be made good from the regular fare. The regular rates for adults are therefore fixed after factoring this in. However, it is a fact that all routes do not have the same number of educational institutions. The disproportionate number of students who board different buses make it unfair on some bus owners while a few others benefit, again disproportionately. Usually, the first bus that travels on a particular route is tempted to 'push over' the students to the next bus as part of their strategy to reduce their loss. The next bus operator does the same. At some point a bus surely has to take these students and that particular bus absorbs maximum "loss". So we invited the Bus Operators Associations and trade unions to discuss the possibilities of how the system as a whole can absorb the perceived losses instead of a select few operators having to incur all the loss[44].

The project seeks to allow the students to travel like a VIP in the bus as the 'opportunity cost' is taken care of through Savari GiriGiri. Smart cards that allow them to travel hassle-free across the district were distributed to the kids. These travel cards could be topped up in advance, minimising cash transactions.

It was agreed that with the help of smart cards, the bus owners association will have an understanding of the number of students who have travelled with them and the potential loss is absorbed by the association which is further divided amongst individual bus operators. In other words, the "perceived loss" is equally shared by equally sharing the "perceived profit" if these students had not travelled in that bus. Bus Operators also now have the option to keep donation boxes through which they can raise funds from the public on bus routes with more educational institutions, hence making up for the 'absorbed losses' as well. A win-win situation we believe that brings in a feel-good to all stakeholders. We even got on board a banking partner, willing to freely sponsor the ticketing machines.

However, it was another story that the staff and trade unions of the workers who ply the buses were not in favour of such a reform. Most of the buses were renegade Frankensteins controlled by the workers themselves and there were widespread anomalies in the daily collection. Digitisation and direct bank collection would ensure that the bus owners get accurate figures. This was not something that the unions wanted. Some of the bus owners were also not happy to have a transparent accounting system. This meant that we had to adopt a carrot-and-stick policy with a considerable amount of patience and perseverance. They didn't have any legal compulsion that made such an arrangement mandatory. A state-level legal provision is necessary. That a day will come when this would be understood and adopted across the state is of no doubt - our children deserve to go to school with a positive mindset, and their dignity intact.

Handicapped ADMINISTRATORS

Most people think that IAS officers are miracle workers. There are many occasions when administrators find themselves helpless and unable to deliver even the statutory obligations placed on them. No matter how honestly and diligently we perceive things, circumstances might be adverse. Not to mention, resource allocation and staffing may not always be timely. There are also times when more powerful entities within the system are interested in thwarting your best efforts.

Barrier-free-Kozhikode was a project aimed at providing a level playing-field for growth to one and all[45]. The transformation of the district into a barrier-free place, especially for women, children, differently-abled and socially deprived sections of society was the primary objective.

It included making public offices, public sector institutions and public spaces differently-abled friendly. For this, not only government owned buildings, but private malls and shops were also approached to make them friendly to the differently-abled. As a demonstration, the beach was first made into a friendly space with ramps. Public funds, Corporate Social Responsibility (CSR) funds and volunteer power were used for these activities.

A detailed proposal with estimates was submitted to the government to equip all the government buildings with ramps and lifts and make them compliant with the provisions of People with Disabilities Act. It is a tragedy that the District Collector's office room itself is on the first floor with only a staircase as the closest access. Often, I would come down to the ground floor to meet many petitioners who could not come upstairs. Sadly, even as I pen this, the detailed proposal prepared by the Public Works Department (PWD) hasn't still come through. We as a society continue to shamelessly violate the provisions of the People with Disabilities Act[46].

This problem is similar to the one the mental health centre faces. The affected parties do not form a powerful enough lobby or vote-bank capable of influencing fund allocations. This is severely pronounced in the case of children with disabilities. So, it is up to officials to push for such reforms, since this may not be the political executives' biggest concerns. But if we have insensitive officials at pivotal decision-making points, the problem is only aggravated.

In June, during the back-to-school season, it came to our attention that there are far too many students in Kozhikode who can't go to schools, colleges or pursue higher studies due to financial problems. The government schemes and support systems are either not agile or inclusive enough to cover them all; a concept difficult to comprehend, unless you are at the receiving end. There are things in governance which look hunky-dory on paper but in practice are quite the opposite. Many of us are oblivious to the fact that despite education being declared as free, there are allied expenditures involved which a student cannot avoid. In the event of a family tragedy, chronic disease or financial breakdown, the family tends to compromise on the education of their children. Scholarships go a long way in alleviating their pain and difficulty, and ensuring them a measure of dignity.

A number of parents who approached the District Collector for some financial support opened up regarding their children's educational issues, a topic that touched me due to personal reasons. I became disturbed thinking that I was unable to effectively solve this problem. Being a patient listener and consoling the parents alone would not do. I had to find a solution. By then the response for Compassionate Kozhikode was overwhelming, and the old-age home, children's home and rehabilitation centres were receiving sufficient support from the public. Though I wanted to support the educational requirements of common citizens in the district, I did not want to go for any fund-raising or accept cash under any circumstances. I was very determined that the students' self-respect is not compromised simply because their studies are being funded externally. In the end, we designed an elaborate solution in collaboration with the banks.

The District Administration would play the role of a facilitator to match the requirements of needy students with those who would like to fund their studies. In match-making, the donor contributes in such a way that the privacy and dignity of parties at both ends are respected and maintained. The donor is contributing to a system and not to an individual. Banks are used here to play the role of the linking-intermediary.

One of my most fulfilling memories of Kozhikode is that during my entire tenure, no child nor parent came to my chamber and returned empty-handed; no child's education was compromised for want of financial support. Not a single student got caught in an education loan trap.

Applications were accepted from deserving students and families, and linked to the compassionate hearts who would register on our website[47]. Around 250 scholarships were facilitated in the first year and an average of 700-800 scholarships were given in subsequent years. Initially it funded only school education, but we went on to award scholarships to graduate students and genuine cases of professional education also. The idea was not to create preconceived standard packages of scholarships, but to award customised scholarships that would solve the problem that children faced - they would range from a few thousand rupees to even lakhs. Many of these students have become an integral part of our 'compassionate' family, giving back much more to the society.

There is nothing like being able to facilitate education. It magically transforms the child and family right in front of your eyes. The feeling of self-fulfilment from being a part of the reason is beyond words. Feigning helplessness and cribbing about lack of resources is only a sign of laziness and lack of imagination. Administrators are never handicapped. The only handicap is what you choose to believe.

Healthy DOSE

A District Collector meets a minimum of 100-250 petitioners every day. I had scheduled this routine from around 11:30 to lunchtime. Petitioners approaching the District Collector would be poor and hapless people who had no political contacts, with nobody to patronise or help them. They had emotionally heavy stories to narrate and one would be emotionally drained by lunchtime. I recollect none coming to give me any happy news except one - an old widow whose 15 year old land tax issue was resolved had come back to thank me. But that was certified as a rarity by my staff. Maybe it happens once in 15 years!

The petitioners had grievances for everything under the sun. But the most compelling cases were those of sudden ill-health, death or misfortune. Accidents and illness befall all human beings, irrespective of their social or economic status, turning lives upside-down, inside-out in a matter of days.

My father was employed with the Indian Space Research Organisation (ISRO) and they had a unique Contributory Health Services Scheme (CHSS). I remember how seamless and easy it was for us as a family to avail of health care with a simple health card. The best hospitals would honour it and give cashless treatment which was later settled by the ISRO. How convenient would it be if everyone on earth got such an amenity! If wishes were horses, the Compassionate Kozhikode team would be running the Kentucky Derby.

The biggest administrative wishes get translated into reality if the public is motivated and convinced. The sustained Pulse Polio campaign run by the Government of India is a classic example. During the polio vaccination drive in 2016, we were faced with a lot of negative propaganda from certain extremist naturopathy groups and certain regressive groups in the Muslim community. Rumours were being spread that the polio vaccine would render the male children sterile. Or that the vaccine has some dangerous side-effect. The poor, the devout and the illiterate were easy victims of such rumours. We had a situation at hand and had to set an example if the public were to trust us.

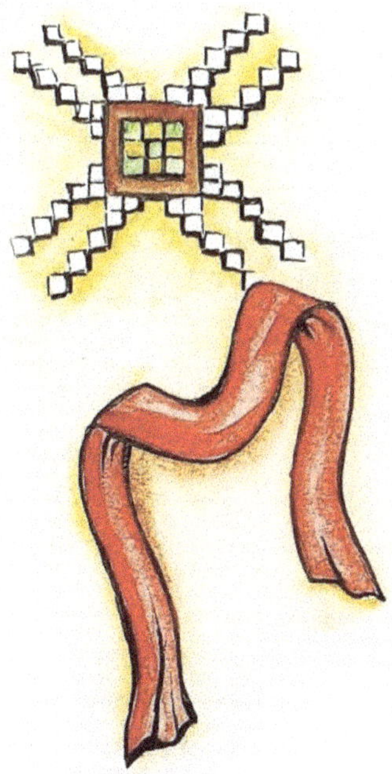

It is basic administrative psychology that we have to get directly involved with certain tasks to instil confidence and motivate the public. Both online and offline. The district-level inauguration of the vaccination drive was held at the famed Juma Masjid in Nadapuram where the much revered Menakkoth Ahmed Khasi administered the first drop of polio vaccine to my son Amrithavarshan who was hardly five years old. The community leaders took my wife, my son and me into the historic Masjid and showed us around. It was the first time that my wife was visiting a mosque. The Khasi gifted us a Veerali Pattu - a ceremonial silken cloth with intricate motifs - as a token of love. The image of the District Collector's son receiving the polio vaccine right inside the mosque from the Khasi sent across a powerful message to the locality and community. We easily won that round of battle against the rumour mongers. We realised that the trust and confidence of the public could be channelised for bigger goals in the health sector.

And so, enter the next project! Sampoorna[48] was designed and detailed by our interns who had joined under the District Collector's Internship Program (DCIP). They were guided by Prof. Saji Gopinath and Dr. Suresh Kumar. It was aimed at enabling equitable access to quality treatment in times of expected or unexpected illness. Sampoorna was a cashless hospitalisation scheme supported by universal insurance for all residents of Kozhikode, irrespective of their financial status. There were nine health beneficiary schemes in vogue at that time. We attempted to explore the existing options in insurance coverage and health schemes and then top it up with innovative insurance schemes. Sampoorna would reach out to Below Poverty Line (BPL) segments who wouldn't need to pay any premium and to Above Poverty Line (APL) segments who would pay a comparatively lower premium than the market rates. We also arranged philanthropic sponsors who would help fund any viability gap.

Detailed discussions were held with nationalised insurance companies and hospitals within Kozhikode. It was ready for launch and since it involved collection of premium from the public, the proposal was submitted to the government for approval.

The government decided to take up the idea for implementation at the state level, meaning we dropped it at the district level as state-wide coverage meant even lesser premium. Integration of the various health

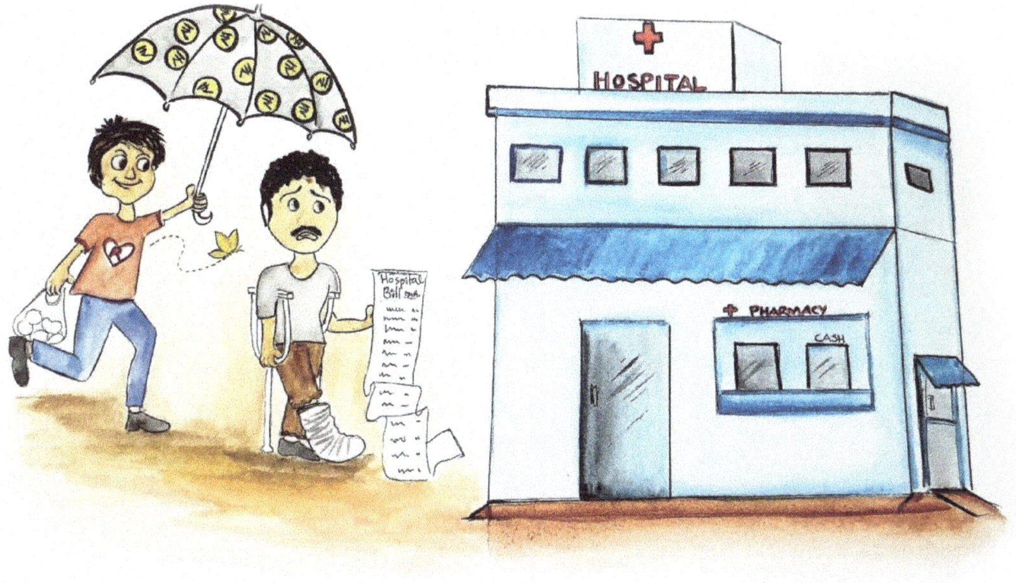

beneficiary schemes was announced in the revised State Budget of 2016[49]. Meanwhile, the central government declared a universal health insurance scheme named Ayushman Bharat[50] in 2018 which made the Sampoorna project redundant.

Now I will tell you something which I am sure many of you would have never known - getting access to a hospital is not enough to ensure that you get treatment. I discovered this in the mental health care centre, a realization that was more shocking to me than the old food menu. There were various critical medical procedures, often involving surgery, prescribed for some of the mental patients but which had not yet been done. These patients included those with heart and kidney problems and those suffering from liver damage. During their routine medical check-up, the doctors of the Kozhikode Medical College hospital would repeatedly recommend them for surgery. They had to be taken from the Mental Health Centre to be admitted in the Medical College Hospital. But the shifting never happened for the simple reason that they did not have relatives or caretakers as bystanders to the patient. It was not exactly the surgery, but the post-surgical care in the ward that required the presence of a relative or a bystander. Most of these cases required hospitalisation for at least a month. It is essential to have a bystander when critical surgeries are performed and a mental hospital that is already short on staffing naturally preferred to postpone these surgeries.

This was a shocking revelation to me because I could never imagine an essential health intervention being postponed or avoided simply because there was no bystander for the ones being treated.

As always, the compassionate hearts of Kozhikode found a solution to this challenge too. We put out a Facebook call requesting compassionate volunteers to become bystanders, nay, relatives for these patients while the operation was done in the medical college hospital. The response was overwhelming and thus started the painful process of finishing all the surgeries that had been pending[51]. Unlike the regular patients, our patients would have their 'relatives' changing every other day. The same patient had 'relatives' from different age groups, different religions, castes and gender. A timetable was set and for each patient, more than 30 bystanders would come by turn. For coordinating the 'relatives', WhatsApp groups were formed for each case. After each patient was discharged from the hospital post-surgery, we would hold a get-together of all the 'relatives' in the mental hospital. It was this casual gathering with tea and snacks with the District Collector that we had to offer in return for their selfless, compassionate act.

It is not as if everything went smooth. There were those who publicly volunteered by commenting on the Facebook page but then backed out when contacted by our team. One fellow had even booked his tickets for Dubai for the next day but didn't miss the chance to publicly volunteer on Facebook to become a 'relative', in an attempt to simply show-off how much he "cared"! But there were even worse cases where the signees agreed to report on a particular day but then just switched off their mobiles and disappeared when the time came to take over the baton, jeopardizing the situation of the person who pulled a night-duty before them! During the 'relatives' gathering over tea at the mental hospital, some of them opined that these absconders should be named and shamed. They are frauds after all. One of our most passionate volunteers, Sabith, was also advocating this line of thought. For some unknown reason, the philosopher inside me woke up and I told him an old story. There was a traveller who took a difficult and less travelled path through the thickest forests, and somewhere in the deepest woods he happened to see an injured bleeding man gasping for breath. The traveller got down from his horse and went up to him. Immediately, the 'injured' man pounced upon the traveller and beat him black and blue. He was a fraud. Brandishing a knife, he took hold of all valuables from the traveller. The rogue then jumped on to the horse, leaving the traveller badly bruised on the ground. Just when he was about to gallop away, the traveller made a strange request, "Please do take everything from me and have a good day. But when you reach the next town do not tell anyone what you have done to me. Otherwise people will stop helping each other when they are in distress on these lonely roads that are less taken." Without hesitation, I told Sabith, "Ours is a road that is less travelled and we are lonely travellers taking risky decisions. If we start spreading stories of deceit and distrust, how will we motivate those around us to trust in the goodness of humans?"

It is like the innumerable stories of goodness being propagated about the autorickshaw drivers of Kozhikode. Having lived for quite long in Kozhikode, I have known the good and bad side of these autorickshaw drivers - they are no saints. But the general perception we collectively try to portray is that the autorickshaw-drivers of Kozhikode are exceptionally good-natured, reliable and kind. This creates peer pressure and a thought within them to subscribe to a certain level of etiquette. This psychology works wonderfully well. That is why you will find a healthy dose of goodness being served on the Compassionate Kozhikode platform. Creation of mythical goodness that sounds believable ultimately leads to real goodness. Or in management jargon, fake it till you make it!

LEGENDS of KOZHIKODE

To create a society that is held together by bonds of compassion, we needed to create a positive attitude and an abundant supply of goodness for it to feed on; we needed to propagate stories of goodness and kindness of the people of Kozhikode. Unless we supply enough goodness to drown out the negativity around us, the plan would not work. We needed to create and buttress an urban myth that it is not only the autorickshaw drivers but the whole of Kozhikode that is good, reliable, honest and compassionate. Consciously, every communication on the official social media handle and every public talk centred around the large-heartedness of the people of Kozhikode.

Interestingly, by now many of our volunteers, donors and contributors were from other districts and states. Colleges and students from Thrissur, Thiruvananthapuram, Kochi, Palakkad, Kannur, Bangalore, Chennai, Pune, Delhi and Ahmedabad were collaborating as earnestly as anyone else locally. And while interacting with the volunteers I would always acknowledge their effort and say that people are the same everywhere and we just need to invoke the compassion within them in order to ignite the change. But in public, we consciously kept giving credit to the people of Kozhikode for everything. Our project area was geographically limited and we wanted to test out the power of such positive feedback on the limited population. To strengthen this mental feedback, we decided to compile and publicise stories of kindness and compassion within Kozhikode. As we sat one evening to short-list such stories, I forgot my mass-psychology theory classes and I really started believing that the people of Kozhikode were indeed the embodiment of compassion!

During Onam we met a lawyer who was spending his time with his extended family at the local children's home. It wasn't the first time for his family. We came to know that for the last sixteen years they have been doing this in silence, without any publicity. They raise funds, they spend quality time, not just once in a year, but as often as it was possible.

We also came to know about a retired high profile Indian Railways Officer who used to stand an hour on SM Street in Kozhikode to raise funds (He collected only one rupee per person!) for bed-ridden patients. What was amazing about him was that he raised awareness about community based palliative care by talking to more than a lakh of people in two years. He did it without hype. He's no longer with us, but his impact is still felt.

There are many people around us who do things unique, compassionate, innovative and different without ever getting noted or wanting to get noticed. These are people who go about doing extraordinary things without even realising the impact they are creating. Under this initiative we tried to make the public aware of such interesting personalities. You could find parallels with the recently popular "Humans of New York" or "Humans of Mumbai" series.

Many interesting and compassionate people worth emulating came into our fold while executing Yo Appooppa[52], a project to improve and extend the quality of life among the elderly, principally those living alone. We tried building a vibrant community of young volunteers, who would be specifically trained on strategies to address the social and psychological needs of the elderly[53]. The Institute of Palliative Medicine under Dr. Anwar was actively involved in this project. The project also sought to connect the inmates of the old-age home and the children's home, both run by the social justice department.

An institution which was not run by the government but by the sisters - Home of Love[54] - was one of the favourite places that I frequented in the city. The dedication and absolutely pure love and compassion of the sisters in taking care of the poor and the destitute are nothing but godly. The 'Thanal' charitable society and the many institutions they ran under the passionate leadership of Dr. Idris was another model to be emulated by the government institutions. Similarly, the Prasanthi School[55] for the differently abled kids was run by Prof. Ramakrishnan Palat using his entire life's earnings. It is connected to these institutions that I have met some of the most interesting people in my life. At the Home of Love, there was a businessman who would dedicate every Sunday to bathe, clean and provide haircuts to the inmates. At the same institution, there was an inmate who would always address me as her long lost brother who had finally come to take her home. And this happened every time I visited there! The sisters who took care of the terminally ill joked, fought and argued with them as if they were kids. There was no trace of mechanical rendition of duty, but pure overflow of love and compassion. There was a teenager who bought and supplied comic books every month for the kids at the Prasanthi School. This boy belonged to the local fishermen community and made his limited earnings from the daily catch. Prof. Palat who had taught him would lovingly discourage him and ask whether he had enough money for all this. "Sir, today I have enough money", was his standard answer. Some people always seem to have enough to spare.

At Prasanthi I met a highly accomplished teacher who would take great care of the differently abled kids. She herself was a parent of an autistic child. Hailing from a very conservative Muslim family, she had no job or means of livelihood of her own when she got married to a businessman in Dubai. After she delivered the autistic child, her husband refused to take her with him to Dubai unless she abandoned the child. She decided instead to abandon that wonderful husband. Now she lives with her son and is a trained teacher capable of bringing solace to hundreds of similar parents at Prasanthi.

It has been four years since I left Kozhikode and even last month I received a phone call from a granny in the old-age home just because she felt like talking to me. She had read something in the newspaper and wanted to share an idea. I get occasional Facebook or Instagram messages from kids who have graduated out of the children's home. They don't want anything in particular from me but they always have something to offer or suggest, just to be able to do something good. Such genuine people are the true 'Legends of Kozhikode'.

ROADS less TAKEN

Autorickshaws and buses are the most important modes of public transport in Kerala. Improving the efficiency of these would have a strong impact on society. The initiative that we took with autorickshaws is nothing extraordinary and not even worthy of being called an

'idea' today. Nowadays, you have plenty of taxi-hailing apps in all major cities. But in 2015 the idea of aggregation and geolocation wasn't so well understood, at least in Kozhikode. Hey Auto[56] was a simple android-based vehicle aggregator model. The name, of course, was taken from a super-hit movie starring Mohanlal, released in 1990. Incidentally, most of that movie was filmed in Kozhikode and Mohanlal played the role of an auto driver.

Autos and Monsoon rains have much in common. When you don't particularly want or need them, both shower down on you; but when you await expectantly, you won't get a single auto nor a drop of rain water. Dozens of auto drivers waste their time waiting for a trip; scores of people curse their failure to catch an auto. Hey Auto is a programme which sought to connect both parties using the common gadget, the smart phone. Smartphone penetration in Kozhikode is one of the highest in India.

A user-friendly free mobile app was designed to ensure that one can always access an auto parked anywhere near a waiting customer[57]. Enlisted autos can be accessed easily, and this reduces queuing for both parties. The app provides a facility to rate the auto service as well. Peer review ensures better services, and travelling with a registered auto driver enhances security for travellers.

Despite creating a free app and making it available to the auto drivers through their unions, the idea never really took off to achieve its fullest potential. The District Administration did not force the app on the drivers, but sought to empower them and make them willingly adopt this. However, the threshold number that is required to make such an innovation work was never achieved[58]. The union leaders were not really impressed with, or fully convinced of the need for such an app. Nor did they trust my alarmist assessment of aggregator-based taxis taking their business away. They were right in the sense that the time for the idea wasn't quite ripe. And perhaps I was a bit impatient as I had other pressing priorities to permit me to devote more time for this. Having given them the option, I decided to move on. Move on to buses, that is.

Imagine you are arriving in a new city, depending on public transport but not able to decipher exactly what is written on the route display board. You talk to people, you check with those standing next to you and by the time you find out which bus to board, the bus has left the stop. This is annoying especially if you can't read the language in which it is written. I recollect one of my childhood visits to Chennai, where the bus numbers were all that we had to remember while exploring the city. Later I found this to be very useful in Bangalore as well where the Kannada script reminded me of Jilebi.

Kozhikode launched a unique numbering system[59] which ensured that each route running through the city would have a dedicated number starting with "K" representing Kozhikode. This is not a new idea, but the process adopted for ideation and implementation was collaborative and co-creative. The faculty from Kannur University did a meticulous job studying the bus routes and the various permutations and combinations. After submitting their report before the Regional Transport Authority (RTA) which is chaired by the District Collector, we cleared it and allocated a token amount for its execution.

The new bus numbering display is designed in such a way that the red coloured circle and numbers are visible even from a distance. A numbering system like that makes travelling easy not only for the locals, but also for the increasing number of migrant populations who have made Kozhikode their home as well as many domestic travellers who visit or pass through Kozhikode. We have world-class institutions like the IIM and the National Institute of Technology (NIT) in the district, bringing in students from all parts of the country. The first phase had 136 city routes numbered with the second phase covering buses originating from New Bus Stand, Palayam Bus Stand and KSRTC bus stands. Once all the city routing was finalised, a mobile app called UNSBR was made available for the public with details of bus numbers and routes. The purpose of bus-numbering is closely linked to the idea of making the district friendly to the differently abled.

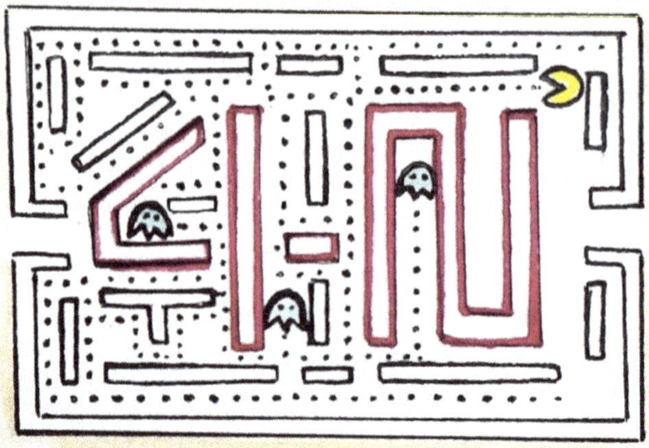

One day, an NRI based in the United Kingdom came to meet me regarding a project proposal that his technology company had submitted. His company specialised in radar and drone based surveying / mapping of roads and allied utilities like underground cables and drains. The technology helped urban developers to plan roads and bridges without digging out the whole place. We also discussed how the roads could be maintained well. It was his idea that I picked for the next project.

The adage says a stitch in time saves nine. But we don't get a pothole filled until it is quite a mess. The reason being that there are administrative procedures involved and every repair work has to be a separately tendered out. Finding and managing funds to allot through multiple agencies involved, that too within a particular time frame, is not easy.

Most of the city roads are not tendered out inclusive of maintenance or guarantee. Laying of the road is a distinct work and maintenance becomes another separately tendered work, as and when damage occurs to the road. If the telecom or sewage or water authorities decide to dig up the road for their operational needs, they make a deposit to the Public Works department / Corporation / Municipality for the re-laying expenses, which goes into the treasury. The subsequent repair has to be sanctioned as a separate work and funds have to be allotted from the treasury afresh. Whether sufficient funds have been allotted under that head for the same year is the next question. To sum it up, repairing a damaged road in this country is second to rocket science!

Project 4N ('Namukk Nammude Nirath Nannaakkam' - we can repair our roads)[60] - is a drive to involve the public to help identify roads that are in disarray well in time, and get the District Administration to play the role of a facilitator in finding sponsors and well-wishers to take up minor repairs of potholes. We figured out that advertisement revenue from hoardings displayed on the repair machinery which get wide public exposure during the repair work could be a source of steady revenue. Residents' associations, merchant guilds etc. came forward in support. The idea is to cut through the red-tape and get things done with civil society participation. None of the roads in the district are owned by the District Administration (they are owned by the local bodies or the public works department) and therefore we could only demonstrate the solution and encourage the real stakeholders to take it ahead.

The first phase was a trial period of two weeks before the onset of monsoon to assess the cost and processes involved[61][62]. We could find sponsors for the trial run and the project after successful demonstration[63] was handed over to the City Corporation. It is another matter that the Corporation authorities, who were never happy with the idea, didn't run it for even a day.

Another basic idea that we need to appreciate is that not all paths and roads are always intended for vehicles. As an IAS trainee at LBSNAA, I had seen the beautiful Mall Road where traffic was prohibited and the entire space was earmarked for pedestrian movement. The evenings were especially splendid with a large number of tourists and locals enjoying the evening stroll along the Mall Street, indulging in window-shopping and shopping proper. I wanted the similarly historic and famed SM Street in Kozhikode to adopt this model.

The history of SM Street, locally known as Mittai Theruvu, dates back to the time when the then ruler Samuthiri invited Gujarati sweet makers to set up their shops just outside the palace walls. 'Sweet Meat' Street derives its name from the thick cubes of luscious Halwa that reminded the Europeans of meat but found it surprisingly sweet too! It is reputedly the busiest street in Kozhikode.

I had with me a tourism department-funded project on beautifying the SM Street. The project components approved by the tourism department included nothing but painting of the shop fronts and trying to maintain a uniform thematic look. The project was a nonstarter because these shops were all owned by private individuals who had no interest in modifying the looks and were even apprehensive of the government making such interventions. But my concerns were deeper, related to the repeated fire outbreaks in the congested street. So, we recast the entire project with safety as the top priority. All the overhead electric lines were to be converted into underground cabling. Fire hydrants were to be provided at key points because when fire broke out, it was difficult to get the bulky fire engines into the narrow street. Both these interventions would automatically make the street aesthetically serene. We only needed to do the road surfacing with rustic stone tiles and co-opt the merchants into maintaining a uniform look. It was very difficult to convince the tourism department to divert their funds towards safety. One official was particularly fixated on the earlier proposal and refused to budge. Nobody was even willing to trust my words that prohibiting traffic and encouraging walking will only improve the business prospects of the shopkeepers. Their problem was that they had not seen the Mall Road and my problem was that I had seen it!

Despite stiff opposition from the tourism department and procedural delays from the electricity board, things finally did move[64]. As expected, I moved out of Kozhikode before it was completed and inaugurated[65]. On the day of inauguration, the TV channels carried live visuals of the then tourism official who had objected tooth and nail to the proposal, proudly exhibiting the renovation of SM Street as his baby. Now, that is what we call street-smartness!

TERE MERE beach MEIN

Kozhikode Beach is a major attraction for locals and tourists alike. Situated close to the city centre, the beach is a popular hang-out area, especially during evenings, weekends and holidays. Even though the beach extends for over 3 km, most people frequent the 1 km stretch situated between two crumbling piers that extend into the sea.

The huge crowds coming to the beach and the lack of proper waste collection and disposal mechanism made Kozhikode beach one of the dirtiest beaches in Kerala. For every city beach, the feeling of ownership felt by the local population is what helps it to remain beautiful. Unfortunately, Kozhikode beach is frequented not only by the people of Kozhikode but tourists and day-visitors from adjacent districts also. Local awareness campaigns therefore had a limited effect. It remained dirty.

On 2nd of October 2015, we had a routine cleaning drive on the beach. We had put out a call for action on Facebook the day before[66] and the response was massive. We had so many volunteers that the cleaning was finished in less than two hours. Since we had leftover time, we did a mass consultative meeting on the beach premises on how to maintain its cleanliness in a sustainable manner instead of making it a one-off event. Pretty much on the spot, we assigned the task of preparing a detailed project to the volunteers of IIM Kozhikode[67][68].

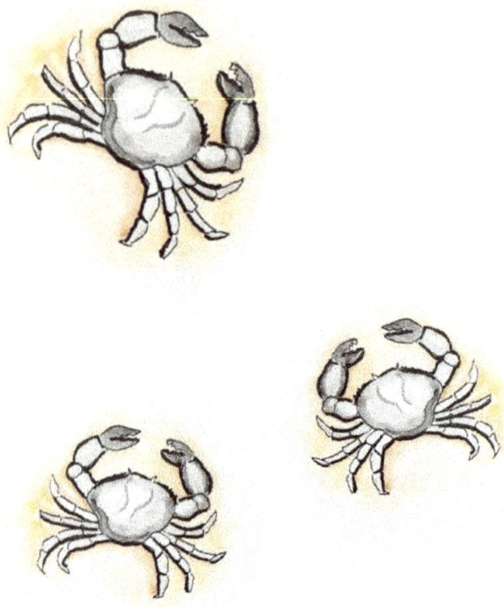

We moved ahead[69] by identifying six business groups as partners who would take up the responsibility to maintain the Kozhikode beach and defray the cost that it involved. Partners were identified on the basis of their willingness and their proposed plan for the different beach segments. The uniqueness of the project was that it was done mostly from CSR funding or even the marketing budget of the partners as a good-will gesture without any claim to overt advertisement or commercial benefits. To get six sponsors on-board, without a reciprocating advertisement agreement, was nothing short of a coup.

All the six business houses together pooled in to keep the beach clean by engaging a professional agency. But within the zones allotted to each one they could add further value and they hit upon unique themes for implementation. Once the sponsors were in, it was all smooth sailing from thereon out.

Sophisticated beach cleaning equipment was procured by the professional cleaning agency and they started night-cleaning of the beach for the first time in Kozhikode. We went for a morning jog along the beach on the day after the first night-cleaning took place. Not only was the beach spic and span, but the discovery of

paved tiles that had been concealed under dirt and filth for ages made a beautiful statement. I still remember the perplexed looks on the faces of the usual morning-walkers who thought someone had freshly paved those stretches overnight!

This project required continuous engagement with the partners and encouraging them to go on to the next step of setting up their value added services for the public. The project was widely appreciated and even adapted for implementation in other parts of India. Although some sponsors were enthusiastic about setting up public facilities like an open gymnasium and an open library on the beach, unfortunately we weren't able to move beyond the cleaning phase. Personally, I would not say that it was due to my transfer at that juncture, but perhaps other pressing priorities were there for my successors or maybe better sustainable solutions are being thought of as we speak. Sometime in the future, it would be lovely to see the fully developed six zones that would enhance the experience of the visitors.

HOW TO DESIGN an Udayip SCHEME

Lord Letitglow says that a good administrator is not someone who does things, but someone who gets things done. As an ardent student of Lord Letitglow, I was always on the lookout for high quality subordinates to whom I could delegate duties and make my job easy! To manage and conduct community-based projects we needed quality volunteers at the 'top' to work closely with the District Administration. And since I had no funds at my disposal, we hit upon a semi-fraudulent idea. A "prestigious" unpaid internship program was planned in collaboration with IIM Kozhikode[70]. We named it the District Collector's Internship Program (DCIP) and gave wide online publicity, besides writing directly to the major educational institutions all over India. While designing the logo of the internship program, we tried to give it an ancient look, as if this had been an ongoing programme since the times of the English East India Company!

The first phase of internship saw more than 700 applications from all over India out of which only 30 were selected after a rigorous selection process. In the first batch, full completion certificates were earned only by 4 interns. To put it briefly, the internship, though unpaid, was extremely tough.

The opportunity to work closely with the District Collector and the prospect of a duly signed certificate were dangled as genuine, organic carrots. This internship program was an 'end to end' journey in itself. An intern started his journey from identification of the problem, designing and testing a solution, rolling it out and overseeing the closure of the project.

When launched in 2015, it was the first internship of its kind in India[71], which is now being replicated in many other districts of Kerala and other states. The DCIP was an attempt to bring in and usefully engage those from the public who wanted to make a difference instead of letting them be satisfied merely with criticism of how a government system works[72]. This gave an opportunity for interns from educational institutes, NGOs and the corporate world to work in support of the District Administration and under its leadership. We partnered with IIM Kozhikode to institutionalize the internship[73][74] and give it an academic framework. There was two-day induction training within the IIM campus, followed by exposure visits to the care homes within the district. The interns were then divided into sub-groups and put under the charge of professional mentors from varied fields ranging from medicine to social entrepreneurship.

The unpaid internship was not for those who expected spoon-feeding, but only for those who could perform as part of a team or blaze their own trail when the situation demanded, thoroughly embracing the value of compassion from day one. The programme ranged from two months to a year and focussed solely on actual results and not on attendance. The interns worked directly on the projects that were ongoing and helped launch many more initiatives that kept coming up from the District Administration.

Most people outside the government think that the government is absolutely unintelligent and that those outside have more informative, efficient, and brilliant solutions for all the problems out there. Sometimes the government is indeed dumb; but whenever we have had occasions for interaction, I have found the private sector easily beating us in stupidity. It is the 'one in a million' successful examples of one or two private companies that are projected against the entire government administration. If you put the whole of private business entities against the entirety of the government, I don't even have to spell out what the result would be.

The experience of managing this young crowd was priceless. Some of them were extraordinary and they quickly grasped the practical tricks of being effective in governance, while some faltered. We could also see how impatient and ineffective some of the hyperactive interns were when assigned with serious and meaningful tasks. It is easy to find fault but difficult to find solutions, and even more difficult to get them executed. As an intern, one was expected to take the avatar of 'government' and transform himself or herself into a solution provider rather than a problem maker or fault finder. The transition from an 'activist' to a 'doer' is an arduous effort.

Some of our brilliant interns after successfully finishing the programme went on to play meaningful roles in various capacities around the world. The interns from Institute of Rural Management Anand (IRMA) led by Shubham Garg were crucial in setting up the Compassionate Kozhikode website and workflow.

These interns formed the nucleus of our youth power. The second rung was formed by the hundreds of students in palliative care. And finally came the hundreds and sometimes thousands of youth volunteers in the field who could be mobilised with a simple Facebook post. Channelizing the initial turnout of these volunteers into our stream of thought and philosophy was crucial. We did not want a mob, but a group that was enthused by the right intentions and motives. For that we designed the first immersion program, Manichithrathoonu.

Manichithrathoonu aimed at painting the walls and pillars in public spaces in the city and beautifying spots that were once places of litter, spit and unruly posters. The walls surrounding the Palayam bus stand and pillars in Mavoor Road were painted in the initial phase and the team systematically covered the rest of the city on all Sundays and holidays. The themes varied from flowers to the abstract, and iconic personalities of Kerala.

Manichithrathoonu means 'beautifully painted pillars'. It vaguely parodied a popular movie by the name 'Manichitrathaazhu'. This was one of the most successful and visible projects undertaken under the District Administration with even visiting foreign tourists willingly being part of the interesting activity.

Not many know that paint has an expiry date. When its expiry date is due, it has to be sent back to the factory from the retail shops. Hardware shops who stock large quantities of paint would not mind sparing a few tins, especially those cans which are nearing their expiry date. All it requires is a gentle request from the District Collector's office. Like all the other projects, Manichithrathoonu too ran on zero budget.

Painting the walls was an excellent group activity to immerse new volunteers who joined team Compassionate Kozhikode. Young boys and girls together created colourful magic on the boring, dirty walls of the city. The

transformation was unbelievable. Anyone who dared to paste posters on these paintings were publicly shamed on social media and even legally proceeded against. As a compromise, the offenders would simply remove the posters and sponsor the paint or snacks for the next painting jamboree! One of my major duties on holidays and Sundays was to join our 'painters', enjoy being 'hands-on' or have a chit-chat with them over tea and snacks.

The internship programme turned out to be an unexpectedly beautiful experiment that infused youthful energy in the Collectorate. The innocence and exuberance that they brought in helped us push the boundaries and think of the unthinkable. Innovation and novel thinking decline as age progresses and it is crucial to be surrounded by young and creative minds. When creativity dries up, you end up merely following precedents. Many have asked me why DCIP turned out to be bureaucratic or superficial when it was 'imitated' in other districts.

"They can't seize our monsoons, can they?" That was the remark of the Samuthiri[75] of Kozhikode when told that his tiny kingdom's pepper shipments had been seized mid-sea by the Portuguese who ruled Central Kerala in the 16th and 17th centuries. No other district could seize a strong academic partner like IIM Kozhikode.

Good Samaritan - THE NANMA MARAM

Compassionate Kozhikode had been initially focusing on marginalized communities and the public institutions set up for them. Except for the scholarships, we were not taking up private or individual causes as such. In Good Samaritan, the idea was to match individuals in need of urgent help with willing compassionate individuals in the community. The most common requirement was financial assistance for medical emergencies. A new link was added to the website to facilitate this[76][77]. Needless to repeat, help has to be offered gracefully and accepted with dignity. And as usual we would not be touching money. We took meticulous care to verify requests for help before posting. We also facilitated verification of all parties whenever required.

In the present day scenario of so many Nanma Marams[78] in Kerala collecting money in the name of helping others for medical treatment and in view of the resultant controversies, the model we designed for Good Samaritan might be useful study material. To do good to people in need, we don't need to collect and hoard money or play 'God'. To facilitate and help join the dots is more important. The more money you handle, the more your focus shifts from the work at hand to accounting and administration. One reason why Compassionate Kozhikode continued to maintain its focus on 'compassionate acts' was because we did not let our attention deviate to managing, executing or financing these projects. We would only diagnose the issue and connect the dots, joining the compassionate hearts with compassionate deeds.

Similarly, Project Oppathinoppam[79] was initiated to help challenged children, giving priority to those with neurological disorders[80]. It aimed at guiding parents of the challenged children through various government schemes and making the paperwork easy, avoiding red tape. There are many central and state government schemes which provide support to the differently-abled and their parents. There are government orders that permit special concessions for such applicants without subjecting them to elaborate, time-consuming procedure. However, most parents are unaware of those.

An Oppathinoppam help desk was set up just adjacent to the Collector's chamber to facilitate quick administrative decisions[81]. In case of any confusion, the volunteers could just walk into the chamber and get things cleared. This positioning was very important to let the message of prioritisation pass on to all other offices in the district.

An Oppathinoppam volunteer would act as a single channel disseminating information and help coordinate the paperwork to get things done. The volunteers got adequate training on various projects and insurance schemes. Akshaya Centres were also in the loop to provide better and timely services to the beneficiaries.

Time is a very relative concept - the time that we 'perceive' and the time that these parents and guardians 'experience' are entirely different. These parents have very little time to waste standing in a queue and we need to appreciate that the 'value' of their time is more than that of ours. While we tried to speed up things on the government side, we also made plans for value-added services like 'privilege cards' for such parents so that they would be given preferred customer service in private shops and establishments.

Implementation of the National Trust Act, 1999[82] was also done in tandem with this. This Act placed the legal responsibility of taking care of a differently-abled person with the District Administration. Appointing their legal guardian and permitting transactions in which the disabled person had an interest were decided by a committee headed by the District Collector. The committee included experts and officials. We were to collectively function as the brain for the affected person and decide what was in the best interests of that person.

We used to conduct unannounced home visits without revealing our identities to ascertain the condition of the children and also to know how their guardians were taking care of them. On one such Sunday, we reached an isolated and gloomy looking middle-class home where a 45 year old guy's guardianship was to be determined. He was not only mentally challenged but was speechless and bedridden with multiple medical complications. We saw him lying crippled on a wet bed on the floor. His mentally unstable younger brother was in half sedation because of his violent behaviour. He was sitting brooding and sulking in the kitchen. But what shocked us completely was when we came to know that their bedraggled widowed mother was a mental patient too. It was their distant relative who took care of their wealth and properties. He occasionally visited them and provided something for their living. As we watched those three souls silently, my eyes fell on a parched old black & white photograph hung on the wall. I saw a rather prosperous mother of two young boys standing next to a handsome man in suit. The boys looked adorable and the family looked extremely happy and blessed. How excited they must have been when they went to the studio to take that picture! My eyes meandered from their cute faces to the crippled, hapless man on the wet bed.

Truth was indeed stranger than fiction on each occasion. The people and lives that we encountered while implementing the mundane National Trust Act conditioned us to think a hundred times before we open our mouth in arrogance or take our good fortunes for granted.

Everything is so very fickle. The state level coordinator for implementation of the National Trust Act, Venu Nair and the Sub Judge, RL Baiju made each of these committee sittings meaningful. The guardians with their differently-abled wards would travel from various parts of the district to attend the statutory hearings. We held marathon sittings to finish the backlog that had been there for years. Hundreds of guardians were appointed and crores of rupees were recovered to protect the interests of the differently-abled. I remember a single case of fraudulent transaction amounting to nearly ₹50 lakhs that we got cancelled through the sub registrar. After every sitting of the National Trust, we would all collectively heave a sigh of relief. Each time was an emotionally draining experience. After getting to know these things so closely, it was very frustrating to interact with people who are ignorant of, or, what is worse, insensitive to their plight.

On one of those designated hearing days, I had 33 differently-abled persons and their guardians waiting outside my chamber where the committee sitting happened. Even though we used to give time slots, most of them would arrive in the morning anyway. It was very difficult to manage some of the affected children and anyone could see the parents struggling with their unwell wards. The sight was heart-wrenching. The preceding night, I had received a fax from the Chief Secretary's office that a last-minute video conference had been scheduled in the morning with all District Collectors. However, it directly clashed with the timing of the National Trust hearing.

I started off the hearing and requested the other members to manage it after a while so that I could take a break and attend the state level video conference. Although I joined the conference about 10 minutes late, I had to still wait for more than 40 minutes before my turn came to speak. I heard from other officers that the Chief Secretary had not been happy at all with my absence in the beginning and he had made his displeasure known before I joined the call.

Trying to sound like a disciplined junior officer, and also because I respected him a lot for the principles he preached, I mailed him after the meeting, explaining my delay. I didn't want him to misunderstand me as being arrogant or non-punctual. The next time I met the Chief Secretary in person, he told me sternly, "You should know who the Chief Secretary is. He is the head of bureaucracy in the state and the cadre-controlling authority who writes your confidential records. No matter what meeting you have, a good officer knows to prioritise and cancel all that when the boss calls him. Don't think that the public and Facebook will save you." That was one more officer shifted to the broken idols corner.

Positions of power and authority are evanescent. Even our health and mental faculties are fickle. The more you get involved in humanitarian projects and the more you get to know how disproportionately you have been blessed with fortune, the more grounded you become. Oppathinoppam would be the most intangible and underrated, and yet most valuable project under Compassionate Kozhikode[85]. Something more valuable than all my career confidential records written by all the Chief Secretaries put together. Something very close to my heart.

GENDER and BEYOND

On a hartal day, our volunteers cleaned the deserted Kozhikode city bus stand in response to the call for action given out the previous night on Facebook. There was a particular spot near the bus bay , where the commuters would publicly urinate, despite a decent toilet being available in the bus stand complex. After the clean-up, on the 9th of April 2015, we announced a Tri-mutri competition on Facebook, inviting crowd-sourced photographs of people who dared to urinate publicly again in that spot. Mutr is the root word meaning urination and the word-play was obviously mischievous. Those who submit the pictures would be rewarded. Interestingly, there were a few comments on Facebook justifying the public urination, suggesting that the toilet may not have been easily accessible or maintained well. But isn't it surprising that only the male commuters felt this urgent requirement of emptying the bladder at that particular spot? Despite the fact that women face the real problem of lesser toilet facilities while traveling, we don't find them doing anything similar. This started off an online debate on the need for more public toilets for women.

The good news was that we did not get a single entry for the Tri-mutri competition and the spot remained clean happily ever after. The widely reported news that the public had been incentivised to report any violation, prevented the act itself[83]. This was a major lesson learnt.

Adopting a similar strategy, we launched Embrace the Night, a surveillance and security scheme to ensure public safety at night, specifically for women and children. It involved decentralized vigilance wherein every trained citizen with a mobile phone in a public place is a potential surveillance agent to thwart any untoward incident. It also called upon civil society involvement and encouraged more women to make their public presence felt in the night.

We found public participatory surveillance to be very effective and easily implementable with minimum cost implications. With proper training, the hundreds of smartphones in the hands of the citizens could function far more effectively than a thousand CCTV cameras, which are anyways notorious not to function when the time and need arises! Obviously, "community surveillance" doesn't mean that citizens have the right to take law into their own hands or become illegal-vigilantes, but to only observe, record and report. The deterrent effect is undeniable.

Easier said than done though. It is clear that the very presence of more women out in public places at night is the best way to instil confidence and encourage more to come out, and ensure safety for all. A bit of a chicken and egg dilemma in the initial stages, from an administration point of view. The essence of this idea was later adopted at least partially when the Kerala state government announced a 'token' one night walk by women, a couple of years later[84]. A threshold number is definitely required to make this perceptible change felt at night. This would in a way apply pressure on the government to stay alert, improve security, provide adequate precautions and safeguards as a default part of the public safety system .

Perhaps, a symbolic starting point would be deploying more policewomen on duty at night. But the moot question is how many women police officers have you seen doing a night patrol in this country? If they cite security and safety concerns to ask for in-house station duty at night and let their male counterparts go for patrolling, how can we expect ordinary women to come out boldly at night? I'm sure that it is the male officers who decide in their 'best interest' preventing them from discharging their duty. The typical Aangala[85] or Bhayya syndrome.

Even after a woman becomes a trained police officer, people have a mental block in accepting her as a capable individual to safeguard the citizens. That is why they feel that she is the one to be protected from society and criminals at night, whereas she is the one who is capable of protecting us!

The more you retreat and surrender to the forces that challenge women's safety, the more you succumb to them. It is like giving up an area or a road for lawlessness and retreating to a safe zone. It is the same rationale used to justify the closing of the women's hostels by six in the evening while the men's hostels don't have shut-down time. By posting trained women security personnel in front of ATMs or deploying more police women on the streets at night, the message that goes out to society would be loud and clear. The State will have to take every effort to ensure not only the safety of these security guards but women in general. Imagine how reassuring it would be for a lone traveling woman that there would be hundreds of armed, trained and equipped women at night, wo-manning the city.

The trouble is that we have preconceived notions of gender roles and we continue to pander to those. We are unable to imagine a night watch-woman in front of a shop or an ATM. We always want a watchman. I've discussed this with a few friends and some believe that this is a dangerous job for women. If you apply the same logic, one of the most dangerous professions is that of a medical nurse. If you think of it, the working conditions are actually vulnerable- working late hours, being surrounded by strangers, having to work in close physical contact with men who are unpredictable, handling medicolegal and drunken cases at night - you name it, every challenge is thrown at them. But what saves them is the substantial number of women in the profession. The presence and visibility of women in large numbers is paramount in every sector. More so in law enforcement. Women security personnel and police officers could be given intensive training, and they could be armed and empowered to use their weapons, like in most western countries. Of course, it would be foolish to deploy untrained women one fine night to keep watch over ATMs and the streets without any preparation. But nothing stops us from equipping them and getting this implemented.

In 2014, while I was working in the Home Department in Kerala, we moved a file to modify the uniform of policewomen, adopting global standards[86]. Until then they were not allowed to wear shirts and pants because apparently women 'liked' sarees. If at all they were to wear a shirt, they were not allowed to tuck-in. They wore a belt over their shirt and walked around like a Kathakali showing off a frock-like part of the shirt dangling to the knees. The men heading the police association enlightened me on "what women want" and advised me not to tinker with such sensitive things as women's uniforms. The feedback that I got from the female members was however different - they wanted to look and feel like smart police officers than a vanitha police. We convinced the Home Minister to take a decision giving an option for women either wear a saree or the normal police uniform that their male colleagues wore. In 2021, if you look around, you will see all women police officers in proper uniforms instead of the brown sarees that once prevailed. Who are we to judge the preferences of women or for that matter, anyone's!

The root cause is the gender bias that gets ingrained in our minds since childhood.

Gender sensitization among school children within their daily environment can generate clear understanding, mutual respect and healthier interactions among genders which they would carry further into the larger social space. Parasparam[87] was a gender sensitization program that organically evolved under the umbrella of Compassionate Kozhikode. It was primarily meant for school children. In a social environment that has serious inequities based on gender, there is a requirement for a balanced perspective on gender and the issues surrounding it.

We selected two schools for piloting the project and convinced them to allow the parents and children to sign up for an entirely voluntary evening-module immediately after the classes got over. One of the schools selected was an up-market, high-end, privately owned school with a very good reputation while the other one was a government school with serious reputation problems when it came to child delinquency and crime. Through experiential modules the students were made aware of bias, perceptions, sources of influence and factual understanding. Influences through home, school, social and media environments were thoroughly explored. Both the schools responded beautifully to the project.

Compassionate Kozhikode always had a lot of girl-power. We further partnered with Maara, a media and arts collective based in Bangalore to design course modules, and to monitor, evaluate and facilitate training. Anjali Menon, the well-known filmmaker was actively involved in designing and rolling out this project from the very beginning. She spent hours with our team discussing and formulating the strategy and came to all the schools where we were implementing it. Her narration and interaction with the kids helped break a lot of stereotypes.

There are a hundred

misconceptions fed into the fresh minds of kids by the society. Boys are expected to play with toy cars while the girls are assigned dolls. Boys are told not to cry while the girls are expected to keep their voices low and not laugh aloud. The subtle idea that women are objects rather than individuals creep into the minds of the boys. Unless they develop a healthy relationship with the opposite gender early on in their lives, this wrong mentality poses a serious problem as they become adults and start spending their time more closely with women from different walks of life. Many anomalies start manifesting as crimes and often it reaches a point of no return. All gender related misconceptions ideally have to be diagnosed and treated from childhood itself.

If there is an anomaly in the behaviour of men towards women, the treatment should not be meted out to women, but to men. But we find that whenever we discuss women's safety, the solution rolled out is teaching self-defence and martial arts to girls! Of course that is very important in the immediate scenario where women have to be equipped to handle the real dangers in society. But we should also focus on molding gentlemen out of the boys. Even women's rights organisations and some activists seem to have completely lost it when it comes to finding solutions. Making a hue and cry or seeking publicity by making bold or shocking confrontational statements alone, without working towards meaningful solutions are only self-serving and sporadic with no genuine long-term impact.

Speaking of gender, we also need to think beyond the binaries. On 12th August 2016, while addressing a gathering of LGBTQI (lesbian, gay, bisexual, transgender, queer or questioning, intersex) community in Kozhikode[88], I saw one of the delegates breakdown on stage and speak about the harassment faced from an auto driver and a policeman while traveling to that very venue! Once the programme ended, we drove back to the office and an order was issued that night itself, setting up a district level grievance redressal committee for the LGBTQI community, the first of its kind[89]. The committee chaired by the District Collector had the Sub Collector as the nodal officer. The committee that shall accept complaints from members of the LGBTQI community, was to have two representatives of the community, the city police commissioner, sub-judge from district legal services authority, the district medical officer, and the district social justice officer.

We need to realise that the most pertinent solutions come from empathy, compassion and understanding of each other as human beings. Antagonising people and recurrent expressions of aggression keep feeding the problems further. After the end of the pilot project of Parasparam, we were all thrilled to see the impact it had on the young girls and boys. The parents who were initially sceptical about the programme were only too happy seeing the results. I was also relieved because in India, even the words gender-sensitisation and sex-education are seen as dirty and dangerous. We had done the great Indian escape act of running such a programme with no controversy or adverse press! Phew!

Our CHILDREN

Not all children are born lucky.

It is heartbreaking when a child is removed from the family, only because the family cannot 'afford' to take care of them. It is even more disturbing when the children are mentally and physically abused at their homes. Then there are children whose parents are no longer alive. To make it worse, many children like that end up in the children's homes, where they may not be cared for enough and end up facing harassment at the hands of other inmates or even caretakers.

Kozhikode, like most districts, has a system to take care of the destitute, the old, the differently-abled and other marginalised people. Vellimadukunnu has a large campus where many of these institutions are established. Unfortunately, these institutions aren't designed to be run by professionals or those who understand the needs of their wards. The staff in an old-age home are not trained in geriatric care. The warden in a children's home is clueless about pedagogy or children's psychology. The caretaker in an Asha Bhavan doesn't know enough about rehabilitation of people who had undergone psychiatric treatment. The list goes on. All these jobs are transferable too, which means that even if someone manages to gain experience by working in one institution, is bound to get transferred to another facility making the exposure gained ineffective due to the transition. In short, no one knows in depth the job he or she is supposed to do.

Compassionate Kozhikode attempted working with children's homes, Asha Bhavan, institutes for differently-abled, old age homes, women's shelters etc., with a goal to understand the difficulties the caretakers as well as the inmates face. Playing the role of a facilitator yet another time, the District Administration matched the requests with the donors and supporters. We also pursued steps to get the buildings renovated using government funds. The old age home, after-care home and the girls' home run by the government were renovated at a cost of ₹4.55 crores and an additional ₹3 crores were spent on the children's home. The fact that Dr. MK Muneer, Minister for Social Justice hailed from Kozhikode itself helped in this case. I was happy that the renovated homes were inaugurated exactly on the first anniversary of my joining the district[90].

Later, boys and girls living in the Children's home were introduced to Kalaripayattu, Yoga and theatre workshops, thanks to the kind hearts of Kozhikode. It goes without saying that these activities not only enhanced the well-being of the children, but also upped their morale and confidence.

We pushed the proverbial envelope even more and introduced another novel concept to the people of Kozhikode. We asked, "Why don't we take these children out for a movie, treat them to a dinner or show them around the city, as if they were our own family members?" However odd an idea it may seem to many, our audience certainly didn't think so. It was as if they were waiting for an opportunity to show their love. As planned, the kids were taken out for simple treats and get-togethers with pre-vetted families and even individuals. We ensured the whole process was done without ever scratching the dignity of these children. One of the most memorable moments was when we took out the girls from the children's home for a joint shopping experience with the kids from Sadhbhavana School. We paired the kids in a way that each child from the children's home was guided by a slightly senior girl from the Sadhbhavana School. For the first time in their life, our kids experienced a shopping mall and they picked their favourite dresses and toys with abandon.

None of these experiments were a walk in the park. It was literally a daily fight with various officials who did not want to take any responsibility for the new ideas we proposed. Everyone had notions of the kids going astray, injured or missing with no one willing to show accountability. Their sole motive was to ensure their own 'safety' and avoid any sort of 'extra work', even if it meant keeping the children in captivity resembling the cages in a zoo. Sheeba Mumtaz, the then District Child Welfare Officer would vouch for the challenges.

Most of the new generation kids fortunate to have good parents, relatives, friends, resources and facilities do not realise how fortunate they are. Isn't it strange that they stay glued to electronic screens for hours, missing out experiencing the true fortunes and small joys that they are actually blessed with! Only if they opened their doors and stepped out instead of swiping yet another window!

During the break after the annual school exams, we wanted to give a treat to the kids of the boys' home. At one of the late night brainstorming sessions, a suggestion came up to arrange a 'drum circle' by the beach. A drum circle is essentially a gathering of the public with whatever percussion instrument they could lay their hands on - water bottles, sticks, bells, drums or pretty much anything that could make a sound. Before getting out of the office at around 9:30pm, I put out a call on the official Facebook page, requesting the public to turn out in large numbers to the beach the next evening for entertaining our children from the boy's home[91].

The next sunset at the beach was magnificent. The parting sun saw thousands of people holding all sorts of noise-making apparatus in their hands. There were two professional bands who drove down from Bangalore and Thrissur just to entertain our special kids. A few celebrities and music composers joined us on the podium to lead the performance. There were many other musicians who had voluntarily turned up. I brought my son and daughter too. The Mayor of Kozhikode, AK Premajam was on the scene. Each one on that beach was performing to impress the kids from the children's home. With gratitude in return, their faces gleamed with joy and the light breeze from the sea made it heavenly. It was indeed one of the loveliest evenings ever on that beach. The fun, music and frolic went on till around nine in the night. As we wound up, I left for home with my tired son and sleepy daughter. Midway, I got a phone call.

"One of the boys has gone missing from the beach."

The PRODIGAL BOY

A kid from the children's home gone missing after a highly visible public programme was ideal for the channels to carry as flash news. I had known this kid for long by now. It was his routine to scoot from the children's home and go around for a few days before he turned up at either his distant relative's house or back at the children's home. The superintendent of the boys' home was extremely relaxed as he was quite used to his routine. But I wasn't.

I was worried about the safety of the kid. What if someone kidnapped him and we never got to see him? What if this was not one of those usual escapades that he made? My wife had always been advising me not to take up risky adventures like these and she was proven right for once. I was also worried that his irresponsible behaviour would further scare the officials from permitting anything innovative. All the initiatives that gave freedom and exposure to the outer world would come to a grinding halt.

An NGO in Kozhikode used to collect money in the name of children's homes and make a living out of it. They would conduct some namesake programmes or put their label on government initiatives and market it as theirs using photographs. There were many people who wanted to celebrate their birthdays or anniversaries by spreading joy to the less fortunate amongst us. Such people would pay this NGO to conduct programmes or entertainment events in the children's home. Their business became so lucrative that they expanded to other districts also - an ingenious conversion of charity into business. With the help of the District Legal Services Authority (DLSA) we had unknowingly hurt their business interests. With Compassionate Kozhikode insisting on no cash transfer and no photography besides enabling people to directly participate in these institutions, the business of this NGO plummeted. The proprietor of that business was an ex-journalist with extensive media and political connections. He tried his best to utilise this unfortunate incident to personally attack me and the project. But to his utter disappointment, the missing boy turned up as usual after his brief moonlighting.

Though we were all relieved, as a measure of abundant caution, the more proactive and 'risky' innovations shifted to the girls' home from then on. That prodigal boy later became aware of the damage that he unknowingly caused. He is now a sensible college student and my Instagram friend!

These kids are just like the ones we have at our homes. When our kids throw tantrums and cry for clothes and toys we ensure that they get it. Have you ever wondered who buys these for the kids in an orphanage? How does the 'government' procure and give clothes to the inmates? Tendering process leading to purchase of the cheapest cloth and converting them to similarly stitched dresses from the lowest bidder is not what you would gift your child for Onam or new year. It is here where Compassionate Kozhikode sought to fill in the blanks.

However, there are some intangible things that these kids always miss out on. Not being able to see a functional family in itself is a huge psychological disadvantage. Foster care as a concept is not as popular as adoption in Kerala or in India. We pushed aggressively for foster care, inviting parents to take home our kids from the children's home for their vacation[92]. The idea was to expose our kids to regular family life and give them an opportunity to understand how the family functions. The response was overwhelming. The credentials of the applicant parents were checked through a special branch team and their antecedents were verified.

At the formal event of handing over the kids to their foster parents, all their concerns were discussed threadbare and proper counselling was provided. If the kids and the foster parents develop positive bonds, avenues could be explored to formalise the relationship further. We had a detailed Q&A session as well. One of the parents had a query, "What if we get so emotionally attached to the child that we don't feel like giving back the child after the vacation?" Another lady asked, "We all know that this is not a permanent solution for the kids. After this vacation won't they feel more sadness when they come back? Why make them more sad?" To be honest, I liked both these questions. Answering their questions, I went back to my childhood days, when I used to go to my grandparents' place during the vacations. Every time the vacations were over, I would cry and resist coming back. That sadness was however not an excuse for me not to go for vacations with my grandparents! I wanted our kids in the children's home to experience those small joys and sadness as well. After all, that is life. In fact, I would consider the project successful if I could see the parents and the kids in tears when they parted at the end of the vacation.

About two months later when the parents brought back the kids to the children's home, the smiles made it clear that the project indeed worked - an icing of tears was the irrefutable proof.

"Real Estate" to the "REAL" ESTATE

During my initial days in Kozhikode, I had an unusual visitor. It was a middle-aged lady who insisted on seeing me ahead of the usual visitor's time. She had a genuine request to make. She had a son who was very active and normal till the age of five. Suddenly the child started losing his faculties of speech, vision and mobility. Within a few months, he was totally paralysed. The mother had been taking care of the child ever since. The son was now aged 21, but continued to be a 'child', totally dependent on her.

The woman's whole life had been spent on taking care of her son, as nobody else would do that. Naturally, she had to let go of her career and other normal things in life to be able to attend to her son all the time. The fact is, parents of such children spend their life devoting every minute to their unfortunate offspring. It's also a fact that it is the mother who takes the burden, most of the time. My lady visitor had a simple, straightforward request to make on behalf of many other mothers like her. She said there were two dozen mothers in the Karaparamba area of Kozhikode alone, who were going through such a turmoil. All that they wanted was a basic day-care centre where they could leave the child safely for at least a couple of hours, so that they could have a few moments of their own life for themselves. I was dumbfounded. The request was so moving that I immediately had to agree to sort it out in a month. And as a newbie, I assumed it would be an easy task.

Exactly one month later, two other ladies from the gang of Karaparamba came to check up on the progress made on the promise that I had made. Caught off guard, I was embarrassed that we had made no headway whatsoever. But after they had left my chamber, I discovered a solution lying right there on my table.

Nayanar Balika Sadanam. If you recollect, I had read about this place in the newspapers on the day I took charge at Kozhikode. By now I knew about Sadanam better. This historic building replete with memories of Gandhiji was lying dilapidated in the centre of the city, completely abandoned but illegally wanted by many. The fight between the trustees, real estate investors and land mafia was intense. A really bad situation. VR Nayanar, freedom-fighter and philanthropist who had established the Balika Sadanam in 1942 for the orphaned girls in the aftermath of cholera would have turned in his grave. There were a dozen cases in various courts concerning this prime property and finally, the matter had come to my office for a decision. This problematic file was the solution lying on my table.

After taking the trustees into confidence and after getting permission from the Courts, Nayanar Balika Sadanam was renovated and converted into a day-care centre for differently-abled children who had become 'adults' and whose parents were growing old[93]. This was made possible entirely through civil society support. A reputed charitable entity, the UL Foundation, was roped in to run the day to day affairs with voluntary support. A vegetable farm was done up on the campus and a pond was also dug. The passion with which our volunteers and Abhilash of UL Foundation put their heart and soul into this project showed quick results.

A salient feature of the property was that it once housed a portion of Mahatma Gandhi's ashes which was brought here by freedom fighter K Kelappan, as it was an unfulfilled wish of the Father of the Nation to visit the Sadanam. It would have been a disgrace if that became a mere piece of real estate. Converting the property for something that would be in tune with the principles of Gandhiji and the philanthropic intentions of Mr. Nayanar was not only a rewarding experience but perhaps the best way to keep off the land mafia. Abundant with the memories of Mahatma, the historic building got poetic justice when the weakest of the weak and the most vulnerable found solace in that compound[94]. On the 2nd of October that year, the new day- care centre became operational.

In the next phase, teachers for crafts, book making etc. from the nearby Iringal Craft Village[95] were assigned to teach the 'kids'. The handicrafts that came out as a result of the programme were marketed through the Craft Village and the kids began to earn a decent income. The day-care centre has since then evolved into a premier vocational training centre. As of today, 86 of the rehabilitated and trained kids have got employment in various commercial establishments[96]. Usually, training and rehabilitation institutions have to employ trainees on their own as nobody offers them a job out of will. But in our case, these talented and trained youngsters were taken on by private institutions where our teachers would make weekly visits[97] , to ensure everything was going smoothly afterwards or offer support if needed. Every year after the Sadanam was established, I find that it has grown steadily and reached new heights. I'm forever indebted to those three women who forced a lazy District Collector to think outside the box.

Pushpavalli, Smitha and Thangamani made this project happen out of thin air.

Compassionate INDIA

The initiatives mentioned so far are only a few selected experiments from the more than hundred odd bizarre ideas that were tried out over a span of two years in the district of Kozhikode. There were more adventurous and riskier ideas that got tested out - a few successfully and many unsuccessfully - but the ones discussed here supplement a fair insight into the method in the madness and help us understand the dynamics of participatory decision-making, collaborative implementation, its success or failure, sustainability, or the lack of it, and the real challenges in the field. And how I as a person went through it all.

After moving from Kozhikode, I had been discussing and exploring on expanding this plain and replicable idea of Compassionate Kozhikode to Kerala and eventually the whole of India. That may sound overly ambitious, utopian and even quixotic. But I believe that we could easily make a nation-wide platform of Compassionate India, where the needy are matched to those who are willing to help, without compromising their dignity. This could be a powerful platform which can magically transform India - because we Indians have enough, it's just that we need to help each other and share our resources. Even a simple and single idea of "collaborative scholarship" can transform the Indian education sector drastically. The aged and the destitute, the orphaned, the differently-abled, the mentally challenged, and the economically weak - can all get 'diagnosed' for their requirements by volunteer forces. And the web platform would enable donors all over the world to contribute for these needs in the most transparent and dignified manner.

During the 2018 Kerala floods, our team scaled up the Kozhikode system to give 25,000 scholarships in the flood-affected district of Alappuzha[98]. We called ourselves Team Compassionate Keralam.

If it can be done successfully in Kozhikode district with a motley crowd of volunteers and the limited credibility of the office of the District Collector led by an unknown guy as the Collector, I'm convinced we can do it across India in a way that makes more sense and is logistically more efficient. It could be led by more credible individuals and institutions. It could transform India to an unbelievable extent. It is a promise we could make to every fellow Indian that all his or her genuine basic needs would be taken care of, compassionately. We could have thousands of volunteers getting involved in millions of compassionate acts. Helping one another and getting transformed in the process. It could be a collective explosion of compassionate bombs planted all over India and beyond, spreading empathy and love.

On a personal note, I'm happy to state that I've managed to orchestrate a few dear friends and volunteers who are passionate about life and compassionate about human beings to devise a dynamic roll-out plan that could reach even the remotest of villages of India; aiming to tender to the last Indian, just like a mother selflessly looking after all her children. It may or may not happen ultimately. But we will definitely keep trying silently and we have more compassionate people joining force with us every day.

We are now used to attempting a hundred things and succeeding in a few. This is perfectly OK. At the same time, the realization that the journey is in the right direction, however slow it may be, is profoundly more enlightening than the arrival party at the destination. It is indeed the journey, not the destination, that enriches each one of us and makes us evolve as human beings. Making haste to reach the target isn't always smart. If you think about it, the journey of human life too is exciting only so long as you are able to experience it; only so long as it lasts. The destination is a full stop - death. Indian Railways quite philosophically says that, a journey is more comfortable with lesser luggage. So is it with life. We get so obsessed with our baggage that we fail to experience the little pleasures and nuances of the journey and before we know, the destination may arrive. Therefore, for all of us, this short journey called life is in every sense, a once in a 'lifetime' opportunity to experience and explore all it offers.

Being focused on the North Star and keeping the journey in the right direction without bothering about the destination or the luggage or the commentators gives you mental peace and spiritual contentment. I wish to believe that this elevated sense of being is what Sri

Aurobindo envisages as the supra-mental transformation of a human into a superman. I strongly trust that compassion is the magic key to that transformation.

Not everyone understands the simple fact that you are helping yourself when you become part of compassionate programmes to help others. It is not charity. Neither is it philanthropy. Compassion is one of the most beautiful and powerful of emotions. People are generally scared to show compassion for various reasons, one of which is that they don't want their vulnerability exposed. I speak of turning the tables and discovering unbelievable strength in this vulnerability within you. To move from fear to fearlessness. To experience infinite moral power that equips you to handle any adversity. To ground you to reality that makes you invincible. To make you a superhuman, or better still, make you a real human being. Compassionate Kozhikode to Compassionate India, speaks of unleashing something within yourself that transforms you beyond imagination. Remember, when you express an act of compassion it drastically changes someone's life.

And that life is yours.

REFERENCES

1. 'Jalanidhi' - Kerala Rural Water Supply and Sanitation Agency (https://www.jalanidhi.kerala.gov.in)

2. 'Bujji' - Short for 'Budhijeevi' in Malayalam, or intellectual

3. 'Enthuvaadei ithu?' - Colloquial Malayalam version of 'What is this man?'

4. 'Wakke' - Colloquial Malayalam version of 'ok', much popular in southern Kerala.

5. 'Django njan pettu' - Malayalam for "I am trapped"

6. 'Bureaucrazy Gets Crazier: IAS Unmasked' by M. K. Law

7. Compassionate Kozhikode (www.compassionatekozhikode.in)

8. 'Thallu' - Colloquial Malayalam version of bragging / self-praising

9. 'Mortal remains of Mahatma Gandhi, has been preserved in the city at the Nayanar Balika Sadanam, an orphanage started by one of the unsung heroes of Indian freedom struggle Varikkara Rairu Nayanar' - Deccan Chronicle, 23 Feb 2015 (https://www.deccanchronicle.com/150223/nation-current-affairs/article/gandhiji%E2%80%99s-ashes-rest-orphanage-kozhikode)

10. Institute of Palliative Medicine Kozhikode (www.instituteofpalliativemedicine.org)

11. 'Kozhikode No.1 in Commercial Tax Collection'- Collector Kozhikode Facebook account: 12 Apr 2015 (https://www.facebook.com/CollectorKKD/photos/a.1588800208023420/1613125392257568/?type=3)

12. Government Mental Hospital Kozhikode (gmhckkd.com)

13. Kozhikode Collector Connect mobile App and Facebook page launched (https://www.facebook.com/CollectorKKD/photos/a.1588800208023420/1589366237966817/?type=3)

14. 'Maapu' - Malayalam for apology

14a. https://youtu.be/EbPIkNHag_0

14b. https://www.thehindu.com/news/cities/kozhikode/Facebook-hosts-a-%E2%80%98map%E2%80%99-war/article14468198.ece

15. 'Happy to inform you that the free WiFi project is progressing well. The first few hubs should be functional in a week or so' - Collector Kozhikode :17 Apr 2015 (https://www.facebook.com/CollectorKKD/photos/a.1589925731244201/1615149365388504/?type=3)

16. When the District collector of Kozhikode in Kerala, Prasanth N, saw the pitiable conditions of his local mental health centre he decided to take action - Facebook official page: 4th July 2016 (https://m.facebook.com/facebookappIndia/videos/1043216139048640/?refsrc=http%3A%2F%2Fwww.google.com%2F&_rdr)

17. 'Compassionate Kozhikode in FB: In a first, Facebook has featured a three-minute video on Compassionate Kozhikode, an initiative of District Collector N. Prasanth, aimed at bringing together people interested in philanthropy.' - The Hindu, 6th July 2016 (https://www.thehindu.com/news/cities/kozhikode/Compassionate-Kozhikode-on-FB/article14472690.ece)

18. 'Collector Bro's 'Compassionate Kozhikode' initiative wins over Facebook' - India today: 5 Jul 2016 (https://www.indiatoday.in/india/story/kozhikode-collectors-social-iniitiative-gets-noticed-by-facebook-327517-2016-07-05)

19. https://www.facebook.com/CMOKerala

20. 'How a Kerala Collector became a Facebook hit' - The Hindu: 9th May 2016 (https://www.thehindu.com/news/national/kerala/How-a-Kerala-Collector-became-a-Facebook-hit/article14310266.ece)

21. Later replaced by Mental Healthcare Act, 2017

22. 'Government Mental Health Centre Urgent requirements list' - Collector Kozhikode Facebook page: 16 Mar 2015 (https://www.facebook.com/CollectorKKD/photos/a.1589925731244201/1600403090196465/?type=3)

23. 'How a Kerala Collector reached out to public for help and got an amazing response'- TheNewsMinute: 19 Mar 2015 (https://www.thenewsminute.com/article/how-kerala-collector-reached-out-public-help-and-got-amazing-response-17159)

24. 'It has been suggested that if some of the consumables get delivered as contributions from people willing to help, the menu can be improved now itself. ' - Collector Kozhikode Facebook post : 18 Dec 2015 (https://www.facebook.com/CollectorKKD/photos/a.1588800208023420/1697899680446805/?type=3)

25. 'Soul of Kozhikode, the charity shop to sell products made by inmates of Government Mental Health Centre , Kozhikode was inaugurated this morning' - Collector Kozhikode Facebook post: 7 Jul 2016 (https://www.facebook.com/CollectorKKD/photos/a.1588800208023420/1773631699540269/)

26. Soul of Kerala - scene from a Malayalam movie Kalippattam (https://youtu.be/oqyUwrp8qkQ)

27. 'A lot of small changes are now happening at GMHC. Volunteers start helping in the kitchen today'- Collector Kozhikode Facebook post: 28 Dec 2015 (https://www.facebook.com/CollectorKKD/photos/a.1588800208023420/1701513200085453/)

28. 'Kerala: Mental hospital farming idea yields organic vegetables' - Deccan Chronicle: 9 Feb 2017 (https://www.deccanchronicle.com/nation/in-other-

news/090217/kerala-mental-hospital-farming-idea-yields-organic-vegetables.html)

29. 'Reunion with family after five years! Great job our volunteer-professional team at Government Mental Health Centre!' - Collector Kozhikode Facebook post: 9 Apr 2016 (https://www.facebook.com/CollectorKKD/photos/a.1588800208023420/1739950362908403/)

30. 'Government of Kerala has earmarked one billion rupees for renovation and development of Government Mental Health Centre, Kuthiravattom, Kozhikode. ' - Collector Kozhikode Facebook post: 8 Jul 2016

31. 'Prasanth Nair and the Compassionate Kozhikode project'- Business Line On Campus: 4 May 2020 (https://bloncampus.thehindubusinessline.com/case-studies/prasanth-nair-and-the-compassionate-kozhikode-project/article31504155.ece)

32. Compassionate Kozhikode Website launch - Collector Kozhikode Facebook :3 Oct 2015 (https://www.facebook.com/CollectorKKD/photos/a.1588800208023420/1677438209159619/)

33. 'Operation Sulaimani - Compassionate Kozhikode initiative' (http://compassionatekozhikode.in/initiatives-details/27)

34. https://www.lbsnaa.gov.in

35. 'Tea County, a resort with a mission' - The New Indian Express: 2 Dec 2010 (https://www.newindianexpress.com/states/kerala/2010/dec/02/tea-county-a-resort-with-a-mission-207451.html)

36. 'How a Thoughtful IAS Officer Used Tourism to Combat Hunger and Malnutrition in a Tribal Community' - The Better India:12 Sep 2016 (https://www.thebetterindia.com/66124/ias-officer-prasanth-nair-priyadarshini-tea-estate-tourism-hunger-malnutrition-tribal-people-wayanad/)

37. 'A state government run tea estate-Priyadarshini Tea Estate, in Wayanad has registered record production by introducing free noon meal for its workers' - The Indian Express: 15 Mar 2015 (https://indianexpress.com/article/news-archive/web/kerala-tea-estate-turns-a-new-leaf-with-midday-meal-scheme/)

38. 'Operation Sulaimani - By second week of May we are planning to launch the initiative that ensures that the hungry gets to eat with dignity.'- Collector Kozhikode Facebook post: 23 Apr 2015 (https://www.facebook.com/CollectorKKD/photos/a.1588800208023420/1618125618424212/)

39. 'Operation Sulaimani: A District Collector's Mind Blowing Initiative to Feed the Hungry in Kozhikode'-The Better India: 24 Apr 2016 (https://www.thebetterindia.com/52436/citizens-kozhikode-feed-the-hungry-operation-sulaimani/)

40. 'Operation Sulaimani' in play to abolish poverty from Kerala district: Everything you should know about the initiative'-India Today: 13 May 2016 (https://www.indiatoday.in/education-today/gk-current-affairs/story/operation-sulaimani-322703-2016-05-13)

41. Feeding The Needy "Operation Sulaimani", the concept to get a food coupon that can be exchanged for free meals at designated hotels in the city. - The logical Indian:22 Aug 2015 (https://thelogicalindian.com/news/feeding-the-needy-operation-sulaimani)

42. 'Savarigirigiri, the travel with dignity program for students, is getting launched.' - Collector Kozhikode Facebook Post:28 Feb 2015 (https://www.facebook.com/CollectorKKD/photos/a.1588800208023420/1721948091375297/)

43. 'Bus Operators Associations and Trade Unions are invited to meet Collector to discuss the possibilities of how the system can absorb the perceived losses' - Collector Kozhikode Facebook post: 31 Aug 2015 (https://www.facebook.com/CollectorKKD/photos/a.1588800208023420/1668172306752876/)

44. 'Savari- giri-giri the new safety mantra for student bus travellers'- India Glitz: 12 Aug 2016 (https://www.indiaglitz.com/savari-giri-giri-the-new-safety-mantra-for-student-bus-travelers-malayalam-news-165047)

45. 'Kozhikode to be first barrier free district '- Deccan Chronicle: 1 Dec 2015 (https://www.deccanchronicle.com/151201/nation-current-affairs/article/kozhikode-be-first-barrier-free-district)

46. 'Kozhikode yet not 'barrier-free' - Deccan Chronicle: 2 Sep 2016 (https://www.deccanchronicle.com/nation/in-other-news/020916/kozhikode-yet-not-barrier-free.html)

47. Scholarship Requirements-Compassionate Kozhikode (http://compassionatekozhikode.in/scholarship-list)

48. Sampoorna -Inclusive Health Care initiated by Compassionate Kozhikode (http://compassionatekozhikode.in/initiatives-details/21)

49. 'New health insurance scheme soon'-The Hindu: 16 June 2018 (https://www.thehindu.com/news/national/kerala/new-health-insurance-scheme-soon/article24181610.ece)

50. 'Central government declared a universal health insurance scheme named "Ayushman Bharat"' (https://pmjay.gov.in/)

51. A patient from Trichur got operated in Kozhikode Medical College hospital The surgery was made possible by a large group of young people who decided to be the 'family' for this man who did not have a bystander' (https://www.facebook.com/CollectorKKD/photos/a.1588800208023420/1708595789377194/)

52. 'Yo Appooppa': Initiative by Compassionate Kozhikode

53. 'Yo Appooppa is an attempt to improve and extend the quality of living among the elderly, principally of those living alone.' - Collector Kozhikode Facebook: 31 Oct 2015 (https://www.facebook.com/CollectorKKD/photos/a.1588800208023420/1684761301760643/)

54. Home of Love -Institution run by the sisters (http://homeofloveclt.com/)

55. Prasanthi school for Children with Special needs (https://www.facebook.com/prasanthicalicut/)

56. 'Hey Auto'- Initiate by Compassionate Kozhikode (http://compassionatekozhikode.in/initiatives-details/31)

57. 'Hey Auto mobile app will be released on ONAM'- Collector Kozhikode Facebook post: 14 Aug 2015 (https://www.facebook.com/CollectorKKD/photos/a.1588800208023420/1662783843958389/?type=3)

58. 'Hey Auto Progress Report ' - Collector Kozhikode Facebook post: 2 Jan 2016 (https://www.facebook.com/CollectorKKD/photos/a.1588800208023420/1703183026585137/)

59. 'Unique Numbering System for Bus Routes' Initiative by compassionate Kozhikode (http://compassionatekozhikode.in/initiatives-details/24)

60. 'Project 4N-Maintenance by through Public Participation' - Initiative by Compassionate Kozhikode (http://compassionatekozhikode.in/initiatives-details/29)

61. Project 4N- 'We can do this! - Collector Kozhikode Facebook post:16 Jul 2015 (https://www.facebook.com/CollectorKKD/photos/a.1588800208023420/1652323118337795/)

62. 'Successfully completed Project 4N trial run'- collector Kozhikode Facebook post: 4 Aug 2015 (https://www.facebook.com/CollectorKKD/posts/1659223707647736)

63. '4N project to fill potholes starts in Kozhikode'- Times of India (https://timesofindia.indiatimes.com/city/kozhikode/4N-project-to-fill-potholes-starts-in-Kozhikode/articleshow/48106840.cms)

64. 'S.M. Street beautification work begins'-The Hindu:5 May 2017 (https://www.thehindu.com/news/cities/kozhikode/sm-street-beautification-work-begins/article18393740.ece)

65. 'Renovated SM Street Inauguration by Chief Minister on 23rd Dec 2017' - Collector Kozhikode Facebook post: 22 Dec 2017 (https://www.facebook.com/CollectorKKD/posts/2026167794286657)

66. 'Let's clean the Kozhikode beach on Gandhi Jayanti day' - Collector Kozhikode Facebook post:29 Sep 2015 (https://www.facebook.com/CollectorKKD/photos/a.1588800208023420/1676501075919999)

67. There Mere Beach Mein' Project progress report - Collector Kozhikode Facebook post: 30 Dec 2015 (https://www.facebook.com/CollectorKKD/photos/a.1588800208023420/1702308766672563/?type=3)

68. 'There Mere Beach Me-Indian Institute of Management has come up with a master plan for a sustainable program'- Collector Kozhikode:3 Nov 2015 (https://www.facebook.com/CollectorKKD/posts/1685555918347848)

69. 'Tere Mere Beach Mein' - Beach beautification initiative by compassionate Kozhikode (http://compassionatekozhikode.in/initiatives-details/34)

70. 'Udayip': Mischievous or fake in Malayalam

71. 'District Collector`s Internship Program' - Initiative by Compassionate Kozhikode (http://compassionatekozhikode.in/initiatives-details/30)

72. 'Collector's Internship Programme' - The Hindu : 2 Jul 2015 (https://www.thehindu.com/news/cities/kozhikode/collectors-internship-programme/article7377055.ece)

73. "The first batch of District Collector's Internship Programme start their journey on 2nd July at IIM-K campus' - Collector Kozhikode Facebook post :1 Jul 2015 (https://www.facebook.com/CollectorKKD/photos/a.1588800208023420/1646810158889091/)

74. 'Collector's Internship Programme: Training for First Batch Starts' (https://iimk.ac.in/websiteadmin/inmedia/upload/187.jpg)

75. 'Samuthiri' (https://en.m.wikipedia.org/wiki/Zamorin_of_Calicut)

76. We are now initiating a new project named "Good Samaritan' to support individuals / families in severe distress.'- Collector Kozhikode Facebook post: 1 Oct 2016 (https://www.facebook.com/CollectorKKD/photos/a.1588800208023420/1810124459224326/)

77. 'Good Samaritan': Initiative by compassionate Kozhikode (http://www.compassionatekozhikode.in/samaritan-list)

78. 'Nanmamaram': In Malayalam literally meaning a 'tree of virtue' referring to a proverbial good Samaritan who is too good to be true.

79. 'Oppathinoppam': Literally means 'on an equal footing' or 'at par' in Malayalam.

80. ''Oppathinoppam' project was initiated to help challenged children, giving priority to those with neurological disorders' - Collector Kozhikode: 14 Oct 2016 (https://www.facebook.com/CollectorKKD/photos/a.1588800208023420/1816543461915759/)

81. 'Help desk setup for people with disabilities'- Times Of India:17 Oct 2016

(https://timesofindia.indiatimes.com/city/kozhikode/Help-desk-setup-for-people-with-disabilties/articleshow/54890928.cms)

82. National Trust Act- 1999 (https://thenationaltrust.gov.in/upload/uploadfiles/files/National%20Trust%20Act%20-%20Englsih.pdf)

83. 'Kozhikode Collector's 'wall' teems with answers'- The Hindu: 11 Apr 2015 (https://www.thehindu.com/news/cities/kozhikode/kozhikode-collectors-wall-teems-with-answers/article7091576.ece)

84. 'Kerala Govt Announces night walk to reclaim public spaces for Women''- News Click: 28 Dec 2019 (https://www.newsclick.in/kerala-govt-announces-night-walk-reclaim-public-spaces-women)

85. 'Aangala': Malayalam for Brother

86. 'To tuck in or not, women cops are confused' - Deccan Chronicle: 28 Nov 2014 (https://www.deccanchronicle.com/141128/nation-current-affairs/article/tuck-or-not-women-cops-are-confused)

87. To reduce crime against women, let's teach school children to question gender bias, says Anjali Menon - Times of India:29 Mar 2017 (https://timesofindia.indiatimes.com/entertainment/malayalam/movies/news/to-reduce-crime-against-women-lets-teach-school-children-to-question-gender-bias-says-anjali-menon/articleshow/57872614.cms)

88. 'LGBT Rainbows pep up Kozhikode' - Deccan Chronicle: 13 Aug 2016 (https://www.deccanchronicle.com/nation/in-other-news/130816/lgbt-rainbows-pep-up-kozhikode.html)

89. 'Kozhikode takes the lead in addressing LGBT issues'- TimesOfIndia: 20 Sep 2016 (https://www.thehindu.com/news/cities/kozhikode/more-amenities-at-social-justice-complex/article8270115.ece)

90. 'More amenities at Social Justice Complex'- The Hindu:23 Feb 2016

(https://www.thehindu.com/news/cities/kozhikode/more-amenities-at-social-justice-complex/article8270115.ece)

91. 'Drum Circle - Let's celebrate the vacation. Come and join with Boy's Home kids on Kozhikode beach ' - collector Kozhikode Facebook post : 12 Sep 2015 (https://www.facebook.com/CollectorKKD/photos/a.1588800208023420/1671652426404864/)

92. 'We are looking for families in Kozhikode willing to invite some of the homeless children from our Childrens' Homes as guests to spend the vacation with them.'- Collector Kozhikode: 5 Mar 2016 (https://www.facebook.com/CollectorKKD/photos/a.1588800208023420/1723918334511606/)

93. 'A Day Care Center for Differently Abled Adolescents and Adults is getting ready at Nayanar Balika Sadanam building in Kozhikode.'-Collector Kozhikode Facebook post: 15 Oct 2015 (https://www.facebook.com/CollectorKKD/photos/a.1588800208023420/1681004252136348/)

94. 'District Collector visits Nayanar Balika Sadanam' - The Hindu:12 Apr 2015 (https://www.thehindu.com/news/cities/kozhikode/district-collector-visits-nayanar-balika-sadanam/article7094790.ece)

95. 'Sargaalaya': Kerala Arts And Crafts Village Iringal (https://www.sargaalaya.in/)

96. 'UL Foundation Empowers 70 Intellectually-Challenged Adults'- UL Times:3 Sep 2019 (https://ultimes.ults.in/ul-foundation-empowers-70-intellectually-challenged-adults)

97. 'Five from Nayanar Sadanam get Placement in A Week'- UL Times:10 Jan 2020 (https://ultimes.ults.in/five-from-nayanar-sadanam-get-placement-in-a-week)

98. https://www.ndtv.com/education/kerala-floods-2018-compassionate-keralam-announces-project-to-give-scholarships-for-25-000-flood-aff-1911842

HASHTAGS

#Kerala
#keralam
#CollectorKozhikode
#CollectorKKD
#Collectorbro
#Collector
#stategovernment
#IAS
#legendsofkozhikode
#CleanBeach
#CivilService
#UPSC
#compassionate
#Compassionatekeralam
#compassionateindia
#india
#socialservice
#SocialJustice
#HumansOfIndia
#Justice
#Love
#affection
#operationsulaimani
#Manichithrathoonu
#Keralaflood2018

IN CLOSING

Now that you have managed to reach this page, I would love to know what you think. Of the book and the ideas. If even a single word in this book inspired you in any way I would be relieved that my effort did not go in vain. I would still be a happy man if your infinitely agile brain got some random spark reading this book. My apologies beforehand if I unintentionally hurt anyone during my self-centric narrative. Thousands of compassionate human-beings have contributed in making the efforts mentioned in this book a reality. Not being able to name each of them is the biggest drawback of this book.

Having been used to the instant reactions and feedback on social media, I would love to know what each one of you think about the book. I promise to read every single line you write in return.

prasanthnair.ias@gmail.com

www.ingramcontent.com/pod-product-compliance
Ingram Content Group UK Ltd.
Pitfield, Milton Keynes, MK11 3LW, UK
UKHW061539190726
13845UKWH00031B/1115

9 789354 570889